Theory and Method in Religious Studies

Theory and Method in Religious Studies

Contemporary Approaches to the Study of Religion

edited by
Frank Whaling

Mouton de Gruyter
Berlin · New York 1995

BL
41
.T47
1995

Mouton de Gruyter (formerly Mouton, The Hague)
is a Division of Walter de Gruyter & Co., Berlin

♾ Printed on acid-free paper which falls within the guidelines of the ANSI to ensure
permanence and durability.

This paperback edition contains selected articles from the original clothbound editions of
contemporary approaches to the study of religion, volume I: the humanities and volume II: the social sciences,
edited by Frank Whaling (Religion and Reason 27)

Library of Congress Cataloging-in-Publication Data

Theory and method in religious studies : contemporary approaches
to the study of religion / edited by Frank Whaling.
    p.   cm.
Includes bibliographical references and index.
ISBN 3-11-014254-6 (pbk. : alk. paper)
    1. Religion – Study and teaching – Methodology. 2. Religion –
Study and teaching – History – 20th century. I. Whaling, Frank,
1934–   .
BL41T47   1995   95-34214
                                                CIP

Die Deutsche Bibliothek – CIP-Einheitsaufnahme

Theory and method in religious studies : contemporary
approaches to the study of religion / ed. by Frank Whaling. –
Berlin ; New York : Mouton de Gruyter, 1995
   ISBN 3-11-014254-6
NE: Whaling, Frank [Hrsg.]

Printing: Werner Hildebrand, Berlin
Binding: Dieter Mikolai, Berlin
Printed in Germany

Contents

1. Introduction
   Frank Whaling   1

2. Historical and Phenomenological Approaches
   Ursula King 41

3. The Scientific Study of Religion in its Plurality
   Ninian Smart 177

4. The Study of Religion in a Global Context
   Frank Whaling 191

5. Psychological Approaches
   David Wulff 253

6. Sociological Approaches
   Günter Kehrer and Bert Hardin 321

7. Cultural Anthropological Approaches
   Jarich Oosten 351

8. Cultural Anthropology and the Many Functions of
   Religion
   Wouter E. A. van Beek 385

Index of Names of Scholars 399

General Index 407

Introduction

FRANK WHALING

1. Introductory Preface

In 1984/85 *Contemporary Approaches to the Study of Religion: The Humanities* and *Contemporary Approaches to the Study of Religion: The Social Sciences* were published in hardback. The combined price of the two books was high but they were well-received, and eventually they sold out. Demand for them continued, and the decision has been made to publish the main chapters from both books in a one-volume paperback edition. It is this edition that you have before you now.

In selecting which chapters to include in this work, balance, length and merit have been taken into account. For example my own original chapter on 'Comparative Approaches to the Study of Religion' in the *Humanities* volume was reviewed as being a creative piece of work, but its length of 132 pages made it too long for this shortened edition. In the nature of things it also included material that was sometimes alluded to elsewhere but treated it from another angle. Thus, while chapters such as this one have been left out for reasons of space, the overall balance of the original two volumes has been maintained. Moreover, the separation between the Humanities and the Social Sciences no longer applies in the combined work, and approaches taken from the two areas are brought together in a single paperback. Treatment is given to the psychological, sociological, social and cultural anthropological, and historical and phenomenological approaches to the study of religion; there are also chapters on the scientific study of religion in its plurality, and the study of religion in a global context. An overall consideration is therefore afforded to the main approaches and themes that are of weight in the general study of religion.

This work was seen, and is still seen, as a sequel to Jacques Waardenburg's *Classical Approaches to the Study of Religion* (1973). Indeed his book is also being brought out later this year in a paperback edition. There is a sense in which his book traces the early and classical period in the study of religion up to World War II. There is a sense also in which we are coming to another watershed at the end of this millennium. The fifty years from World War II until now can be seen as a second period in the study of religion. By the year 2000 a third era will be dawning. As we read and ponder this page now we look forward to the twenty-first century and what it will bring.

Later in this introduction I will consider reflectively some of the currents that are developing out of the chapters that are already part of this book and which anticipate future developments. However, the epoch dating from the Second World War to the end of the century is a discrete period covered in principle within the covers of this work. And we anticipate that in its cheaper and more accessible form this book will have an important part to play not only in summarising and analysing what has gone before but also in paving the way for what is to come. When supplemented by Jacques Waardenburg's *Classical Approaches to the Study of Religion* it will give an overview of the development of theories, approaches and methods within the modern study of religion.

2. The Difference between the Classical and Contemporary Periods in the Study of Religion: The General Background

What then are the contrasts between the classical and contemporary approaches to the study of religion? These can conveniently be divided into two sections: the general cultural background within which religion is studied, and the particular approaches to the study of religion arising out of the general cultural background. World War II was a watershed in both respects. What happened before it culturally and in the study of religion received a jolt as a result of the trauma of World War II. Although there are continuities bestraddling the pre- and post-Second World War situations, the contrasts are more marked. They are such as to make 1945 a significant symbolic date. What then were the main factors in the aftermath of World War II that affected in a new way the background in which the study of religion and the living of religion moved and had its being?

(a) The first main factor was the disappearance of a number of European empires. The passing of colonies and suzerainties of various kinds was a symbol of the passing of western political dominance. A by-product was that Christian missionaries, who had been helped by the fact of empire, were less able to go abroad and engage in proselytisation. Leadership and mission passed into the hands of local Christians in Africa, India, China, and so on. The centre of gravity of world Christianity began to move inexhorably from the West to the non-western parts of the world church. This had consequences for the study of religion. Alongside this the coming to independence of former imperial territories often signalled a renaissance in the religious traditions of those areas. Since 1945, due to a number of factors, including the gaining of independence by various Muslim countries and the economic influence of OPEC as well as more obviously religious causes, there has been a striking renewal of self-confidence within the world of Islam that is of major importance for the study and living of religion. The same is true of the renewal of the Hindu tradition in India, the revival of the Buddhist tradition in South-East Asia, the efflorescence of Japanese religious traditions and their study after the fall of the Shinto state in 1945, and the emergence of a national and educational homeland for the Jews after the setting up of the state of Israel in 1948.

(b) A second factor was the rapid spread of Marxism after World War II out of the USSR into China, Cuba, Asian countries such as North Korea, Vietnam, Laos and Cambodia, and into areas of Africa and Europe. What had been a Russian preserve seemed to become a universal possibility in spite of differences between Russia and China, and Russia and Eastern Europe. Marxist studies of religions grew, and the notion of Marxism, or Maoism in China, as 'secular religions' also emerged. The recent apparent decline of Marxism has further consequences for the study of religion and of atheism by scholars of religion and by Marxists.

(c) A third factor was the rise of new nation states in the aftermath of empire. They were motivated by varied factors, one of which was nationalism. Without experience of nationalism which had arisen as a European phenomenon, the new nations had to cope with the pressures of independence in the light of their own culture. Nationalism and religion often intermingled, or nationalism and Marxism often intermingled, in the working out of independent nationhood. Religious traditions were often important in promoting, sustaining, or even challenging the nation states that evolved. Nationalism itself, like Marxism, often developed functionally as a kind of 'secular religion' with its own civil religion or capacity for evoking faith. Recently events in places like Bosnia, Rwanda and Chechnya have revealed the latent power of ethnic nationalism—or rather ethnic 'groupism'. Basic questions were raised for the study of religion: what is the relationship between religion and society, between religion and nationalism; in what sense should the study of religion include the study of 'secular religions' such as Marxism and nationalism; is civil religion a meaningful concept, and if so in what way?

(d) A fourth factor was the application of models of economic development and modernisation in most countries whereby services such as education, medicine, social welfare, and economic affairs came more under the aegis of the state, whether the state system was Marxist, capitalist, or mixed. According to some secularisation theorists, this moving of control of religiously run matters into the hands of the state presaged the decline of religion. This hinges however on whether religion is defined institutionally or functionally. Moreover it is to equate modernisation with a certain form of western secularisation. Other states and cultures can modernise in their own way without acquiescence in a rigid western model. Nevertheless there is little doubt that the process of modernisation, however defined, has influenced religion itself and the study of religion. The Shah of

Iran's mistake was to modernise in too western a fashion. Nations and cultures are coming to terms with the modern world in their own way. With the end of the Cold War and the seeming superiority of the capitalist economic world-view, nations and religious traditions are having to decide whether and in what way they wish to pursue the capitalist path. Professor Huntington of Harvard has recently suggested that the next substantial opponent of the West may be the Islamic world, partly because of its opposition to the materialistic side of western capitalism. This theory begs a number of questions but it is clear that the relationship between religion and economic development and modernisation is an important matter in the study of religion.

(e) A fifth factor is the ongoing debate between the proponents of science and of religion. At the pragmatic level the natural and allied sciences developed rapidly in the post-war world due in part to the stimulus to scientific invention given by World War II. The development of nuclear power, the human achievement in reaching the moon, the technological revolution, the computer revolution and the revolution in genetics are symbols of the roaring success of modern science as an instrument in changing the world. The self-confidence of modern science in view of its pragmatic success, and its positivist and empirical assumptions that scientific knowledge is proven knowledge of the world as it is, seemed to have given scientific thought and achievement the edge over religious thought and achievement. However, since about 1975 there has been a growing awareness of the problems engendered by science through the escalation of nuclear weapons, the growth of world population, the ecological crisis, and growing extremes of wealth and poverty. Philosophers of science have questioned the simplistic scientism of former days; there has been the soul-searching agonising among eminent scientists of the calibre of Einstein, Heisenberg, Bohr and Polanyi; and there has been a dawning sense, enhanced by the failure of secular scientific regimes to stamp out religion, that science has no answer to the basic religious questions of meaning, awe, purpose, transcendence, value, love and inwardness.

Discussions about the relationship between science and religion, such as whether they are complementary or opposed, have spilled over into the study of religion. Is it a 'science', and if so what sort of a science is it? At one extreme scholars such as Huston Smith (1992) would argue that we have moved into a post-modern situation wherein scientific objectivity in the sense that what the western world has taken for granted is now at an end. It is therefore futile for the study of religion to follow canons of scientific objectivity that science itself is questioning. In any case scientific truth, such as it is, operates at an inherently more superficial level than the truth of metaphysical religious spirituality. At the other extreme scholars such as Segal and Wiebe would argue that there is no irreducibly religious factor which justifies the study of religion as religion and they would wish to reduce the study of religion to a facet of the social sciences or to a series of area studies. In other words, for them religious studies is not a science; it is not a discipline in its own right with its own subject matter and its own methods.

We will come back to these matters. However it is clear that the engagement between science and religion is an important backdrop to a consideration of the study of religion. Is science in some sense a 'secular religion'; is religion a 'science'; how do they relate; and how do the study of religion and the study of science fit together in the totality of knowledge?

(f) A sixth factor operating in the post-war situation is the acceleration of the process of industrialisation. In many parts of the world there has been a shift of the population from villages into towns or cities. Mao's China was a partial exception to this but in general there has been the rapid growth of cities to cater for the demands of industry. As people have moved into cities they have been faced with a change of work, a change of environment, a change of life-style, and in effect a change of world-view. For some this has been liberating. For others it was not, and the capacity to undergo a new experience and to live through it creatively was sometimes provided by a religious tradition or a new religious movement. For some primal societies the experience has been very traumatic indeed. Increasingly, scholars of religion, and especially social scientists, have become interested in the social and religious implications of rapid change. The impulse so to become involved has arisen from the experience inherent in our modern world of industrialisation and sudden change.

(g) A seventh factor was the accelerating domination of nature by human beings that has come to light in the last 20 years. This has immediate consequences for primal peoples in places such as Central Africa and the Amazon. We are coming to realise that the long-term consequences of global warming, pollution, the using up of finite energy resources, the puncturing of the ozone layer, the growth of world population, the rise of deserts, the diminution of jungles, and the disappearance of natural species will have an effect upon all human life as well as on the environment. A rapidly increasing interest in the ecology of religion is to be welcomed and anticipated.

(h) An eighth factor was the increasing movement of people and information around the world. Not only did persons move from villages to cities in their own land, they also moved to different lands. Sometimes this movement was enforced as had been the case with Jews in Nazi Germany or Poland (where the pre-war population of four million is down to a few thousand today). Elsewhere the Dalai Lama's flight from Tibet took the Tibetan Buddhist tradition into other lands, the migrations of Ugandan and other African Asians brought Hindus, Muslims and Sikhs to the West, the Vietnam War led to migrations from South-East Asia especially into the West, and the Palestinian exodus has had increasing repercussions for Muslims, Jews and others in the Middle East and beyond.

Voluntary migration has also been important. Religious movements have accompanied the movement of various groups of people from the Indian sub-continent so that, for example, there are nearly two million Muslims in Great Britain, which makes them the second-largest religious group in the land. In addition to the movement of various branches of religious traditions to other lands by migration there has also been the steady conversion of others, including westerners, to those religions. There has also been the spread of new religious movements into different parts of the world. The result is that most religions are now world religions in the sense that there are small numbers of believers in various parts of the world. And much more is known about different religious traditions by people around the world.

All this movement and religious inter-change is exacerbated by the tremendous growth in airline travel, television, computer services, international communications and the possibility of almost immediate travel to or informing oneself about virtually any group or tradition on the face of the earth.

The impact of the growing movement of people and information around the globe is considerable for both the practice and study of religion.

(i) A ninth factor was the rise of new cultural/religious blocks around the world. We assume that within these religious blocks nationalism and secular world-views were present in differing degrees. One such block remained the modern West which was however not as dominant as it had been before World War II. It included North America and Europe and had offshoots in Australasia. In spite of the demise of Christendom, and the minority presence of other religions in it, this block remained largely Christian, white and democratic. Although some state churches still remain, the growing tendency, despite the work of movements such as the Moral Majority, is towards effective separation of church and state.

A second, now much depleted, block was the Marxist one with its former heartlands in the USSR and Eastern Europe. Remaining only in places such as China, Cuba, and North Korea, the Marxist tradition exercised state control over religion but was unable to subdue it.

A third block centred upon Islam. Its original heartlands in North Africa and the Middle East remained crucial and it had offshoots out to Malaysia and Indonesia and beyond. Despite tensions between Shī'ite Islam centred upon Iran and Islam in Sunni areas, and between liberal and more fundamentalist strains of Islam, this period has seen a remarkable renewal of confidence within the Islamic world, which has led Huntington to suggest that it has replaced Marxism as a threat to the West.

A fourth block centred upon the Hindu tradition in India. Although India became a secular state in 1948, although offshoots of the Hindu tradition have sprung up in new areas of the world, and although the Hindu caste system is now outside the civil law of India, the heart of that tradition remains in India and has its own ethos.

A fifth area of importance (perhaps too minute to be called a block) is Israel as the homeland of contemporary Judaism. Although Jews reside in other parts of the world, notably in the United States, the new nation of Israel represents the emotional heartland of the Jews and of the Jewish tradition.

A sixth block centres upon the Buddhist heartlands of South-East Asia. Although the Buddhist tradition has undergone traumatic experiences in the Marxist area in and around China, in the exciting religious melange of the new Japan and South Korea, and in the Theravada nations of Burma, Sri Lanka and Thailand, it remains an important influence in the area whether it has political power or not.

A seventh potential block is the Far Eastern Confucian complex covering China, Japan and the 'four dragons' of Taiwan, Hong Kong, Singapore and South Korea. Although diverging politically they are moving along a similar economic journey and they share culturally the three ways of the Taoist, Mahāyāna Buddhist and Confucian traditions. The rise of contemporary New Confucianism is especially significant, centred as it is upon the work of thinkers such as Wei-Ming Tu who has been asked to advise countries such as Singapore on Confucian educational values and who brings a faith perspective to bear in his Confucian thought.

A final and more amorphous block covers a swathe of societies in the southern hemisphere, including Black Africa, Latin America and the Pacific peoples of Polynesia and Melanesia. They have a background in primal religion but have assimilated some of their primal religious expressions into independent churches and other Christian forms.

Such a picture contrasts strikingly with the picture at the beginning of the century when the classical approaches to the study of religion were emerging. Europe had still been the fulcrum of world civilisation: a Christian continent, the purveyor of empire and mission, ruled by monarchs and class values, and intellectually supreme. During this century Christian Europe has fomented two world wars, its empires and missions have diminished or gone, its monarchs and class values have been transformed or replaced, the notion of Christendom has gone for ever, and the very concept of Europe—as it has split into East and West and then ended the split—is under intense debate. Needless to say, the new and developing situation has deeply influenced the study of religion since World War II.

(j) A tenth factor is the emergence since 1970 of a sense of living in a global world. This sense arose partly as a result of the cumulative effect of the nine factors mentioned above. There have been changes in the human condition since the dawn of human history but in the post-World War II period there has developed a rising curve of ever-increasing change that has swept us into a new global situation. The fact of change is a constant in human affairs. It is the breadth, depth, variety and all-encompassing nature of contemporary change that makes our age so different and that has made us aware as never before that we are living in a new global age.

Since the original Club of Rome study of 1972 the global threat and opportunity has been analysed at three levels. The first level, alluded to in *The Limits of Growth* (1974), was that of potential ecological crisis wherein the fate of the earth would be linked to the fate of the people living on the earth. At the humane and social level there was the increasing poverty gap between rich and poor nations, the rapid growth of world population, anxiety about whether food could always be provided for this increasing population, concern about racial and sexual discrimination, political tension between East and West, and economic tension between North and South. At the moral and spiritual level there was a concern for the future development of space and the sea which belong in principle to the human race, a concern about the global use of electronics and genetics which affect everyone, a sense that the perennial search for meaning and wholeness was the spiritual birthright of humankind, and a sense that there needed to be peace among the religions in order for global peace to be made possible. In short, there was a sense in which the nations, peoples and religions of the world were in it together in a way that had never been true before; there was a need for global dialogue in which religions would have an important part to play; and although the global threat was real, so were the global resources at the natural, human and spiritual levels.

The conceptual and practical consequences of globalism for the study of religion have been working themselves out for the last 20 years, alongside the seemingly opposite thrusts in the direction of regional religious blocks and local ethnic nationalisms.

It is clear from analysing the above ten factors in their cumulative effect that we live in a different world from that of pre-1945. The study of religion since 1945 has changed in radical ways and stands in contrast with the study of religion before 1945. We turn now to investigate how it has changed in the post-World War II period and what its contemporary themes are. We could only do that after looking at the wider changes in culture and religion which form the background for the changing story of the study of religion.

3. The Difference between the Classical and Contemporary Periods in the Study of Religion: The Detail

(a) Waardenburg, in his *Classical Approaches to the Study of Religion*, gives a succint account of the development of the study of religion from the time of Max Muller to about 1945, and then he includes an anthology of extracts on theory and method from the work of over 40 scholars who were pioneers in the field of the study of religion. It was possible to describe the classical period in this way because specialisation and diversification were less rampant than they are today, scholarly disciplines and academic knowledge generally were less developed, and the world itself was a less complex place. Today, as we shall see, there is an extraordinary ramification within the study of religion, a vast growth of academic knowledge of all kinds, a springing up of new seeds within the field, and a complexification and globalisation of the context within which religion is studied that made easy generalisations, reliance upon a select anthology, and a one-person treatment difficult if not impossible. This book, therefore, is not an anthology and it is not by one person. It is the work of a team who aim to summarise, insofar as they can in the covers of one work, the contemporary approaches to the study of religion. This summary is not a compilation of select passages of key authors (the bibliographies contain well over a thousand entries); it does not attempt to impose a particular viewpoint (the authors were born in different countries and work in different universities in three different continents): it is a narrative of the main developments and discussions since World War II in the fields of history and phenomenology of religion, sociology of religion, psychology of religion, the scientific study of religion in its plurality, and the study of religion in a global context.

However, although an account is given of a vast body of material gathered from varied parts of this complex area of study—a more ambitious account than has been attempted before—an endeavour is also made to give an overview of the whole field. Indeed it was hoped that it would be possible so to summarise the mass of developments since 1945 that an integral and acceptable way forward would be opened up for the whole study of religion. Such a grandiose aim has not been fully realised. Nevertheless, in the course of this work, a number of suggestions are made as to how, on the basis of past research and present directions, future programmes may proceed. And at the end of this Introduction I hope to present an implicit way forward arising out of what is mentioned in this work.

Before we focus more fully on the differences between the contemporary period and the classical period dealt with by Waardenburg, there are three brief points that need to be made. Firstly there is *some* continuity between this volume and that of Waardenburg. There are no rigid breaks in the web of history and even a dramatic date such as 1945 must be to some extent arbitrary. Nevertheless periodisations, however arbitrary, are useful, and in the case of this book the basic cut-off point is 1945 and the limits set by Waardenburg's work.

Our second point is that, like Waardenburg, we do not aim to cover all aspects of the study of religion. Our purpose is not to summarise the *content* of the various religious traditions of the world. This is done with reasonable accuracy by bibliographical reference volumes such as Charles Adams' *A Reader's Guide to the Great Religions* (1977) and Mircea Eliade's *Encyclopaedia of Religion* (1987) as well as specialised encyclopaedic volumes in different disciplines and fields of study. In this book there will be some reference to content, for method and content never can (or should) be fully separated, but our main concern is for methods and theory rather than for content per se. We will deal with contemporary approaches to the study of religion rather than with the contemporary content of the study of religion which is generally taken as read.

Our third point is that, insofar as this work is written in English, the references and quotations from books in other languages are mostly given in English, and reference to the original works is made elsewhere, usually in the bibliographies at the end of the chapters. This does not detract from the international coverage. As we have stated before, this book is written by an authentically international team and our only regret is that it has not been possible to include a non-western member in the team.

(b) *Increasing Diversification in Contemporary Approaches.* Before 1945 the study of religion was mainly concentrated around a relatively small number of scholars in the great universities of Europe. Only a few posts were available and a coterie of scholars was working in the field. The scene was dominated by the history of religions and comparative religion. Studies were focussed on texts, on the religions of classical antiquity, and on what were then called 'primitive religions'. European philosophical and theological assumptions underlay a good deal of work in the study of religion. It operated within a particular culture looking beyond its geographical and spiritual boundaries in a somewhat condescending way.

Today things are vastly different. At the Mexico Congress of the International Association for the History of Religions that will meet in the summer of 1995 around 5000 people will come together from many parts of the world and from many religious traditions (or from none). The history of religions, comparative religion, textual studies, the religions of classical antiquity, primal religions, and the philosophy and theology of religion will form a small part of their enquiry. As well as general sections the congress will include more specialised sections on a plethora of topics ranging from women in religion to Mithraism, from the major religions to new religious movements, from religion in Africa to religion in other geographical areas, and from the phenomenology of religion to the psychology of religion. It will mirror the complexity within the study of religion at this juncture.

For we live at a time of increasing diversification. Not only has the mass of accumulated religious data multiplied, so has the variety of methodological reflection upon those data. It is not merely the case that the number of methodological approaches with a serious interest in religious data has increased, there has also been an intensification of discussion about religion in *each* approach. Growing specialisation within each approach has resulted in a growing ramification of discussions about religion and, in addition to this, new 'seeds' have sprung up ranging from the ecology of religion to the academic dialogue of religions. The pity of it is that some of this discussion is virtually unknown. The temptation is for scholars of one nationality or language group to know only each other's work, or for scholars of one discipline to be acquainted solely with the research in their own area. This book is an attempt to gather together and to put into some sort of order the diverse discussions about method and theory since 1945. At the same time it is an attempt to overcome the fragmentation that is inevitably occurring in the field.

Within each chapter certain basic questions are addressed, either implicitly or explicitly, to focus the discussion. In each approach the basic method is described, and questions are raised as to what the method is attempting to do in the study of religion, whether it is complementary to other methods, and whether it is centred inside or outside the basic study of religion. The basic position implied within the approach concerned is also investigated: Is it one of neutrality or are truth claims implied? And if so, are those truth claims related to a particular discipline, to religion in general, or to a particular religion? The question of definition is also raised: What definition, if any, is implied in the approach concerned? A further area of interest relates to the scope and nature of the data used in a particular approach: are they first or second hand; do they arise out of primal religion, historical religions, or the major religions; are they concentrated upon the study of one religion and if so which one? The main part of each section focusses upon a description and discussion of the major trends within the area concerned. Attention is also given to future prospects for the approach concerned.

Clearly the above concerns—method, standpoint, definition, nature of the data, and future prospects—are interrelated. We will deal with some of the implications later in the Introduction. We are content at the moment with pointing out the complex nature of the discussion of theory and method within each of the above-mentioned approaches, and with outlining the criteria whereby we have sought to bring order to each section and integration to the whole.

It is our hope that scholars with particular interests in history and phenomenology of religion, anthropology of religion, sociology of religion, psychology of religion, the scientific study of religion in its plurality, and the global context of the study of religion will, after they have read the chapter on their own area, read the other chapters so that they can obtain an overview of the wider discussion. Although our work is significant in that it brings together and orders a vast amount of material within each approach, its more important function is to summarise the general field of method and theory in the study of religion in a way that has never been so fully attempted before. There is an urgent need for scholars of religion to supplement their areas of specialisation to gain a total view of the field as a whole, and a major aim of this book is to contribute to this end.

(c) *Greater Research Involvement of Social and Humane Sciences.* Another major difference between the classical and contemporary approaches to the study of religion is the increasingly complex relationship between the humane and social sciences and this sphere of research. Durkheim, Weber, Freud, Jung, and James may have departed from the scene, but it is possible to submit that, in the contemporary situation, any theory or method of investigation in any of the humane or social sciences is or may be applied to the study of specific sets of religious data.

In the overall planning of this volume, a balance has been struck between the chapters related to the social sciences that concentrate upon the methodological findings of particular disciplines, and the chapters related more implicitly to the humanities where the treatment is geared as much to themes as to disciplines. It is our hope that this way of dealing with the material illustrates the sheer variety of contemporary approaches, the complexity of treatment within and between different approaches, and a balance between the minutiae of detail and wider connecting themes.

(d) *Importance of Improved Communications for the Study of Religion.* Another factor that played a minor role in the period of classical approaches but is more important in contemporary studies is the fact of quicker communication. A new prophet arising in Africa, a new religious movement arising in some part of the West, a new indigenous expression of religion in the developing world can now be investigated on the spot by anthropologists, psychologists, sociologists, or historians taking a plane out of Kennedy or Heathrow or going by train or car to the area concerned. The present-day scholar has access not only to books written by travellers or scholars but also to tape-recordings, films and so on, which record in sight and sound the formerly barely accessible data of various religious groups ranging from nomads to peasants to syncretistic sects. The rapid development of the technical and other devices of the communications media has made religious data available in a way undreamt of by scholars before World War II. It is causing the flavour of the study of religion to change.

These communication issues have a subtle influence upon three questions referred to in this volume. In the first place there is a discernible shift of attention in the study of religion away from an obvious involvement in the history of past religions to a greater interest in present developments. Thus the focus of all the chapters in this book, although not neglectful of the past, is geared more obviously to present religious developments than would have been the case before 1945. Secondly, the social scientific approaches, for example the chapter by David Wulff, bring out the increasing use of quantificatory data in religious research. The balanced presentation of Wulff and his colleagues masks the extent to which statistics and quantificatory data are becoming dominant in some of the social scientific investigations of religion. This leads us to our third point. Insofar as the silicon chip is already affecting scholarship, and computers have become part of the apparatus for research, there is the need for reflection upon the consequences of this trend for the study of religion. What kind of data can computers store? According to what criteria should the ordering of these data be organised? Is computer information exhaustive of, or complementary to, other kinds of information?

(e) *Implications of the Western Nature of much Religious Research.* A further factor that is assuming more importance within the contemporary study of religion in contrast with the situation that pertained at the time of the classical approaches is an increasing concern for the implications of the fact of the western nature of much past research. This book traces in detail the contributions of scholars of different western nationalities to different approaches—and this in itself is salutary because past surveys have tended to proceed along national lines—and yet the wider question that is emerging is whether the study of religion has not been too dominated by western categories. Although the balance is partly redressed by the highlighting of the work of Mbiti, Radhakrishnan, Coomaraswamy, Buber, S. H. Nasr, Wing-tsit Chan, and D. T. Suzuki, the point still remains.

What is the significance of the fact that religions outside the West have been studied in a western way and, to a lesser extent, that religions outside

Christianity have been studied in a Christian-centred way? To what extent has this pre-1945 attitude of often unconscious superiority been superseded in the contemporary situation? To what extent have western scholars of religion subsumed the whole spiritual creation of humankind under one interpretation of religion and then absolutised it? To what degree, in spite of the concern for *epochē* and *Einfühlung* fostered by the phenomenological approach, do western scholars feel that it is *they* who must research and interpret the religion of others for others? Can and should scholars from other cultures study western religions in the West; can and should western and non-western scholars study western and non-western texts together; can and should western anthropologists interpolate the views of the persons in primal tribes into their academic investigations?

It is clear that scholars from independent countries take a deep interest in their own religious and cultural traditions. This may well lead to a rediscovery in terms of their own culture of their own religious heritage, and also to scholarly selections and evaluations which can be explained by reference to the present-day spiritual, psychological and social needs of the traditions concerned. One has only to analyse the work of a phalanx of African scholars from John Mbiti to Kwame Bediako to realise the truth of this. An approach by western scholars based upon dialogue, co-operation, and willingness to learn would apear to be more in order than dialectical tension in defence of western methodologies. It is perhaps no accident that one of the most persuasive exponents of the academic dialogical method, Raimundo Panikkar, was born of an Indian Hindu father and a Spanish Christian mother. Or, as Wilfred Cantwell Smith puts it, 'the truth of all of us is part of the truth of each of us' (Smith 1981: 79).

(f) *Greater Involvement of Secular Religions and Inter-religious Dialogue.* Related to the last point, a further factor differentiating the contemporary from the classical period is a greater awareness of the involvement of what may loosely be called secular religions and inter-faith dialogue in the contemporary study of religion. Firstly, there have been forthcoming more Marxist studies of religion in relation to ethnographic studies, studies of Africa and Asia, the theory of scientific socialism and dialectical materialism, discussions of institutionalised religion, and searchings for the roots of religion in terms of social conflict, escape, or projection. It will be interesting to see what happens to Marxist studies of religion in the new dispensation that appears to be arising, wherein, as the Chinese would put it, the Mandate of Heaven seems to be slipping away from institutional Marxism. Will this lead to a renewal of theoretical Marxism as seems to be the case with the New Confucian tradition after its institutional demise in China?

Secondly, there has arisen an amount of research into and discussion about the role of secular religions in the study of religion. These include Marxism, secular humanism, nationalism, and also civil religion. Smart's researches (1981) into the 'religious' force and role of nationalism, and Bellah's researches (1975) into the force and role of civil religion have been important landmarks in this area of study. From a functional point-of-view secular religions have the functional power to evoke faith. In practice they usually lie alongside more formal religions as partners, as opponents, or as enthusiastic helpmates.

Thirdly, there has been the rise of inter-faith dialogue and understanding, especially between Christianity and other religious traditions. This dialogue has had an impact upon the interpretation of present-day religious expressions, and in the light of it encounters of religious attitude and systems are seen to be basically peaceful and constructive. In very reent times the centenary in 1993 of the 1893 Chicago World Parliament of Religions has given a stimulus to inter-faith dialogue and to academic discussion concerning its role in the study of religion. In practical terms the discussions about the feasibility of setting up an ongoing parliament of world religions involves a number of scholars of religion from different religious traditions as well as religious leaders.

In some quarters the term 'ideology' has been loosely used about both Marxism and the secular religions and about inter-faith dialogue, on the grounds that neither the secular religions nor inter-faith dialogue are impartial, albeit from opposite directions. The word 'ideology', with its emotive overtones, does not perhaps convey the correct resonance to do justice to the contribution that is being made by Marxism and inter-faith dialogue. This is especially the case as the notion is arising in other quarters that western positivistic science can also operate as an 'ideology', and this leads us back to some of the points made in our last section.

However, the question remains as to whether the study of religion is destined to become an arena for competing 'ideologies', whether there is a bedrock and sub-stratum of data and theories to which so-called 'ideologies' can contribute and which they can amend constructively without producing a cacophony, or whether the study of religion itself has an ideology-critical function. This range of issues is addressed in the chapters by Ninian Smart and Frank Whaling.

(g) *Truth-claims, Phenomenology and Theology.* Our next contrast relates to the status of truth claims, phenomenology, and theology in regard to the study of religion, and this debate, of course, goes back to the earlier part of the century although it has intensified since 1945.

In the first place it is pointed out in various places that 'truth claims' are not necessarily confined to phenomenology and theology and that much depends upon what we mean by 'truth-claims'—are they methodological or ontological, general or specific, 'first-order' or 'second-order'? It is clear that greater specificity as to the different levels and motivations of truth is required. After all, any respectable discipline, method or approach would hardly disclaim all concern for 'truth' of some kind. Different chapters allude to this matter in their own way.

Secondly, much discussion in the post-World War II period has centred upon the role of phenomenology of religion. Part of the reason for the growing interest in phenomenology of religion in the earlier post-war period that followed on from the work of Kristensen and van der Leeuw was the feeling that the component of 'religion' had been under-emphasised in earlier times. Theology, by its implied value-judgements, had undervalued the religions of others. By means of its concepts of *epochē*, putting one's convictions into brackets in order to understand another person or tradition, and *Einfühlung*, empathising with the other positively by 'walking in his or her moccasins for a couple of miles' it was possible for phenomenology to avoid theological value-judgements and in some way to allow believers to see the universe through another's eyes.

As far as other disciplines were concerned, such as oriental literatures and languages, history, sociology, psychology and anthropology, the question that was raised by the phenomenologists of religion was twofold. Were these other disciplines, when they studied religion, primarily interested in the study of religion or in the study of their own discipline? And the second question was whether these other disciplines were able to

compare religions? The implied answer was no, and so the phenomenologists of religion attempted to compare religious phenomena typologically
through their principle of eidetic vision; they attempted to give a greater
integration to the study of religion; and they emphasised that 'religion'
was at the heart of the study of religion.

In recent times a sharp attack has been made upon the whole raison
d'être of phenomenology of religion by Segal (1989) and Wiebe (1985,
1990). They call it religionism and argue that religionists are committed
to the defence of religion, that they uphold the truth of religion against
the natural sciences and philosophy, that they defend the religiosity of
religion against the social scientists, and that they safeguard the irreducible
religious analysis of the origin, function and meaning of religion. Segal
and Wiebe argue that scholars such as Eliade and Wilfred Cantwell Smith
take with absolute seriousness the believer's viewpoint, and that they also
take seriously the believer's focus of faith (as Smart [1973: 62] calls it), the
holy (as Otto [1917] puts it), the sacred (as Eliade [1959] puts it). This, it
is argued, leads them into theology rather than phenomenology of religion. In short, it is further argued, the need for phenomenology of religion is no longer present because there is no irreducible religious factor
that justifies the study of religion as religion in separation from theology
or the social sciences. It can therefore be collapsed into theology on the
one hand and the social sciences on the other hand. In effect this is a
form of reductionism. It is not on a par with the classical reductionist
theories of Durkheim, Freud and Marx but its effect is the same—to
reduce religion to something else.

Although classical phenomenology of religion has undergone modification since 1945 in ways described in this book, its basic intuitions concerning the need for suspension of judgement, empathy, and non-judgmental
comparisons remain sound. Segal and Wiebe misrepresent the intention
of phenomenologists of religion, which is not to get inside the conscious
view of believers in a literal sense but to understand them in such a way
as not to give offence. Moreover, Smart's focus of faith, Eliade's sacred
and Smith's transcendent are not portrayed as ontological or essential
realities. The phenomenologist is concerned to understand the believer
and his faith and retains suspension of judgement in relation to the object
of the believer's faith. Moreover, the phenomenologist agrees that the

believer's conscious belief is only part of the sum total of his religiousness, not the whole of it. Furthermore, methodological arguments relating basically to western and Christian matters cannot apply in a universal sense even if they had worked in a western sense. Finally, phenomenology is ultimately a co-operative and dialogical method rather than a dialectical one, as Segal and Wiebe would want to make it. Nevertheless we can be grateful to them for enabling phenomenology of religion to advance in response to the sharpness of their insights.

In the third place the perennial question remains of the relationship between the study of religion and theology. The contributors to this book are in agreement that theology as traditionally conceived is separate from the study of religion in the sense that, although it provides data for such study, its categories do not and cannot dominate it. They also agree that institutional considerations have tended to accentuate the differences between the two educational domains. They agree too that insofar as theology operates from within particular religious traditions and focusses upon the *nature* of transcendent reality, its concerns are different from those of the study of religion.

At certain places in this volume some unease is expressed at the confrontational attitudes sometimes implied between monolithic views of theology and the study of religion. There are various views of what theology basically is and of what the study of religion basically is, and the need is for flexibility and complementariness rather than confrontation.

Unease is also expressed occasionally at the implied assumption that theology is to be equated with Christian theology. The other religious traditions have their own theology (or Buddhology or Rāmology).

More far-reaching is the contemporary search for a global theology of religion. Essayed in the work of scholars such as Hans Kung, Wilfred Cantwell Smith, John Hick, Raimundo Panikkar and others it attempts to seek for universal theological categories that arise out of and are applicable to all the religious traditions of the world. The starting point for such a global theology of religion is not the theology of any particular tradition but the global situation itself. By working back from the global crisis and opportunity to the theological categories that can speak to global needs, there is the chance to transcend normal theological differences hermeneutically for the sake of the human race on planet earth under transcendence.

There is a sense in which a global theology of religion may well develop into a separate discipline which is relevant to the study of religion and to particular theologies from its detached viewpoint. Durwood Foster's quest for what he calls an ultimology would fit into this endeavour (Storey and Storey 1994: 155–163), as would Masao Abe's notion of a positionless position 'in which the diversity and unity of world religions can be fully and dynamically realised' (Storey and Storey 1994: 164).

(h) *Definitions of Religion.* In the course of this book countless definitions of religion are mentioned or assumed, and to summarise them here would be unnecessarily to lengthen this introduction. Perhaps one of the reasons why western philosophy of religion has found it difficult to grapple with the study of religion is because that study has not been amenable to agreement on any one definition of religion. Conversely one of the probable reasons why the study of religion has not become even more important than it is lies in the fact that it has not been content to settle upon an agreed set of given data which would constitute it as a rigid discipline wherein a particular definition would be universally applicable. Thus the question of definitions is necessarily part of our wider discussion of methods and theories.

Our volume does not solve the question of definition although it does pose it, and it does open up the various definitional alternatives in a more comprehensive way than is usually the case.

However there is another sense in which this book performs a restricted and yet equally valuable task in the sphere of definitions. Attention is paid in various places to the need for a more exact definition of terms that are important in the study of religion. Thus, more sophisticated views on terms such as myth, history, phenomenology, science, hermeneutics, understanding, and interpretation are given throughout the work. Clarification of terms and concepts within these more limited areas is important.

(i) *Scope and Nature of the Data.* Another difference between the classical period of the study of religion and the contemporary situation lies in the contrast between the scope and nature of the data considered worthy of study. In the classical period there was relatively greater stress put upon the data of primal religion, archaic religion, the religions of antiquity, and the classical forms of the major living religions. Anthropologists such as Tylor and Frazer, sociologists such as Durkheim, and psychologists such as Freud theorised on the basis of the data of primal religion. When they ventured into comment upon the major religions, the likelihood was that their data would be taken from their own Judaeo-Christian tradition.

At the present time, the situation is different. Not only has there been an explosion of knowledge in regard to *all* the religious traditions of the earth, the greatest relative accumulation of data has encompassed the major living religions. There are a number of reasons why this is so and we will look at them briefly now.

(ia) One reason is the relatively less important position of anthropology in the contemporary study of religion. During the classical period, the data of the primal religions provided the jumping-off point for some of the early formative theories of religion. With the exception of the work of Lévi-Strauss, anthropology is now less significant in theory-formation.

(ib) Another reason lies in the change of emphasis within sociology of religion. Durkheim's famous definition of religion (1976: 62)

A religion is a unified system of beliefs and practices relative to sacred things, that is to say, things set apart and forbidden—beliefs and practices which unite into one single moral community called a church, all those who adhere to them

was erected, in the main, on the basis of research into primal religion with its more static flavour. Present-day sociology of religion has a greater interest in contemporary religion and change.

(ic) A third reason lies in the rediscovery of religious traditions in a number of recently independent nations. As we saw earlier, the focus of religious attention and study inevitably falls upon the major religious traditions that are the basis of religious life in those nations.

(id) Another reason lies in the increasing western interest in major non-western religions. Non-academic factors have fostered this growth of interest: the immigration of Buddhists, Hindus, Muslims and Sikhs into the West; the steady trickle of converts to eastern religions; the effects in the USA of political events in Korea and Vietnam; the aftermath of empire in Britain; the spread of eastern sects into the West; and the growing importance of Islam. The effect of the above developments has been to focus more attention upon the major religions in their contemporary as well as classical forms.

(ie) A further reason lies in the fact that the pre-1945 situation of more static and stabilised systems is no longer with us and religious change is the order of the day. New religions are multiplying in Japan, numerous Indigenous African Churches are springing up constantly, and new sects are sprouting in different parts of the West. The general effect of the obvious presence of religious change around the world is to create a greater interest in the contemporary religious scene and in the major living religions.

(if) A sixth reason lies in the concern for the present state of western religion and culture among scholars of religion in both East and West. Whether that concern be for the seeming weakness of Christianity in the West, for rampant materialism in the West, for the help that eastern religions may be able to give to the West, or for the possible dangers that eastern cultures face from the West, the inclination once again is to focus upon the present context and the major religions. The past for its own sake is no longer an end in itself.

(ig) A final reason lies in the growing interest since World War II in religious education in schools, especially in Britain and the United States and increasingly in Europe. The American constitution had banned the teaching of denominational or dogmatic religion in state schools, but this ban did not apply to the non-evaluative teaching of world religions or descriptive teaching about Christianity. Since 1945 such teaching has advanced in American schools. In Britain the pre-1945 stress upon Christian education as a nurturing or even proselytising process has been replaced by a greater emphasis upon teaching world religions and a less theological emphasis upon the teaching of Christianity. Inevitably attention focussed upon the teaching of the living world religions rather than archaic or primal religion, and this development interacted with the study and teaching of religion in higher education to reinforce the emphasis upon the major living religions.

4. Possible Future Direction

So far we have looked at the contrast between the classical and contemporary approaches to the study of religion. There is much more that could be said but it is time to press on and try to erect, on the basis of our work, possible future directions for the study of religion.

(a) *What Religious Data are Involved in the Study of Religion?* We saw above how contemporary interest in the study of religion centres mainly upon the contemporary major living religions. In fact this is only a three-quarter truth, even in western academia. Continental European scholars are more likely to make greater use of the data of the religions of antiquity, the classical forms of the major religions, and (to a lesser extent) primal religions, whereas Anglo-Saxon scholars are more likely to make use of the data of the major living religions in their contemporary as well as classical form. The reasons for this are partly academic, but there are non-academic causes too: the lack on most of the continent of an imperial background, the smaller presence of immigrants, the lesser presence of eastern sects, a lesser facility in the English language, a weaker concern for new forms of religious education, a greater predilection for Christian inward-looking-ness, and relatively less contact with religious change.

However, as we have seen, the contemporary religious scene in regard to both study and practice is far wider than the confines of Europe. And in principle the study of religion has to do with the study of all religious traditions. No religions are excluded from the study of religion whether they be ancient or modern, living or dead, primal or major. And let us be clear that there is a connection between the kind of religious data that a scholar studies and the theories and methods that the scholar is likely to develop as a result of wrestling with *those* religious data. For example, had Wilfred Cantwell Smith not begun his career in Islamic Studies, had Eliade not gone to India or used the data of primal religions, and had Dumézil not immersed himself in Indo-European Studies, it is likely that their theoretical approach to the study of religion would have taken a different course. Data and theory are interlinked. What then are the different kinds of religious data involved in the study of religion? What are the different varieties of world religions?

(i) Firstly, there are the living religious traditions of the world. Five of them can be classed as major: the Buddhist, Christian, Hindu, Jewish and Muslim traditions, and a case can be made for designating the Baha'is as a major tradition. The first five certainly have an impressive history, a

worldwide presence and a complex nature and this compounds the problems involved in trying to understand and study them.

(ii) Other religious traditions are active and alive on the face of the earth
today, but it is disputable whether they can be classed as major. They
include what we might call the minor living traditions: the Confucians,
the Jains, the Parsis, the Sikhs, and the Taoists. Although less 'major' than
the first group, they are unique and significant in their own right.

(iii) A third facet of the present-day religious scene is the presence of
various new religious movements of one sort or another. There are many
of them and they range from the Jehovah's Witnesses, Mormons, Seventh
Day Adventists, Spiritualists, and Swedenborgians to the Cargo Cults of
Melanesia, the New Religions of Japan, the Rastafarians and the Unification Church. It is estimated that in the United States alone there are
something over 900 new Christian religious movements, and around 600
new religious movements with no roots in Christianity.

(iv) A fourth factor on the world scene can be summed up under the
heading of primal religion. There are thousands of primal tribes and therefore thousands of primal religions scattered over the surface of the planet.
They lacked writing (at any rate until recently), and they generally lack
scriptures and historical documents. The hallmarks of their religious life
tend to be sacred stories in the form of myths together with the rituals
and symbols that are handed down from one generation to another.

(v) In the fifth place there are religious traditions that are no longer alive
on the face of the earth. At one time humans had access to transcendence
through the medium of these archaic religions but they are present no
more: they are dead. Examples are Palaeolithic and Neolithic religion,
Egyptian and Mesopotamian religion, Greek and Roman religion, Gnostic
and Manichaean religion, and the Aztecs, Incas and Mayas of the Americas.

(vi) A final group are the secular religions which function as 'religions'
from one point-of-view and are secular alternatives to religion from another point-of-view. They include Marxism, Humanism and Nationalism.
Whether they can be called 'religions' is a moot point. Nevertheless they
operate as what Tillich called quasi-religions and they have the functional
force of religions.

Such is the vastness and complexity of the field of world religions. All of them in principle have an equal right to be studied even though, in the nature of things, some will be studied more than others. In practice different methodological approaches tend to concentrate upon certain kinds of religious traditions; for example anthropologists often study primal religions, sociologists are more likely to study new religious movements, philologists may be drawn to literate dead religions, pre-historians of religion may be interested in non-literate dead religions, social scientists may study secular religions, and historians of religion may home in on the major or minor living religions.

(b) *Global History of Religion as a Bedrock of the Study of Religion.* The history of religion has always been a key element in the study of religion and it has recently become possible to establish a global framework for the history of religion. Upon this framework of pegs the history of religion can be hung.

There are methodological problems associated with creating this global history of religion. It presupposes the western historical-critical method but yet relies upon the interpretation of pre-historical artefacts; it is difficult to insert primal religions into global history because of their lack of historical documents; it is necessary to establish the relationship between 'secular' history and 'religious' history; it is not easy to divide the global history of religion into recognisable stages; it is essential to avoid evolutionary or other 'judgmental' presuppositions; it is not easy to conceptualise how different caches of historical records can be fed into a global history of religion, and last but not least the history keeps on changing either through the discovery of new historical records or through the reinterpretation of old ones. For example, the dates of Zarathustra have recently been recalculated by scholars such as Mary Boyce, and the same has happened to the dates of the Buddha in the work of scholars such as Richard Gombrich.

We are now in a position to lay out a framework for a global history of religion into which new historical discoveries and reinterpretations can be inserted. Although this works better with historical religions than with pre-historic and primal ones it does provide a good groundwork for the general study of religion.

(i) The first stage, that of Palaeolithic religion, is shrouded in the mists of pre-history. Palaeolithic humans were hunter-gatherers. From half-a-million years ago, with Peking Man, there is evidence of the ritual treatment of skulls; there is evidence of burial from about 75,000 B C E; and from about 30,000 B C E onwards there is the evidence of cave paintings that illustrated Palaeolithic religiousness. It is easy to read too much into the evidence of Palaeolithic skulls, artefacts and caves but that far-off age brought a breakthrough to 'humanity' and evidence of an early religiousness in human beings.

(ii) The second age, starting about 10,000 B C E, was the Neolithic, which gave to human beings a close relationship to the earth and the start of dominance over it by the creative invention of agriculture, animal husbandry, spinning, weaving and pottery. The sacred was seen to be active in nature as well as in human beings in a rhythmic and cyclical way. There was felt to be an inter-linking between human beings, the earth that they tended, and the transcendent powers (including female) that were held to reside in both. Their religious consciousness remained this-worldly; it was experienced in groups, and their myths, rituals and symbols held persons, nature and the transcendent together in a linking bond.

(iii) The next stage saw the rise of town civilisations about 3,500 B C E in Mesopotamia and then in Egypt with diffusion into the Indus Valley, and a spontaneous generation of towns in China. The invention of the plough, sea travel, irrigation, metallurgy, and above all writing enabled town-dwellers to develop interests and specialisations outside agriculture. Contacts were opened up with other areas by sea or land so that trade and ideas could expand. Religious specialisms also came into being in the form of separate priesthoods, temples, festivals and theologies; sacred kings such as the Pharoahs made sure that religion remained linked to life. Although humans, the earth and transcendent forces stayed interconnected, there were premonitions of the later distancing of town civilisations from nature, and existential questions to do with meaning, suffering and life after death began to surface.

(iv) The next major stage (there were other minor ones) emerged in the Axial Age around the sixth century B C E. Great religious leaders and thinkers arose independently in four areas of the world: Greece, the Middle East, India and China. The Ionian philosophers in Greece, the

Hebrew prophets and the out-workings of Zarathustra's genius in the Middle East, the emergence of the Buddha, the Mahavira and the Hindu Upanishads in India, and the presence of Confucius and the premonitions of Taoism in China heralded a great religious and cultural breakthrough. With the hindsight of history we can see from that time the emergence of four great civilisations moulded by religious factors, and they were to co-exist for two thousand years on a roughly equal, parallel and separate basis. They were: Europe stemming from Greece and eventually becoming Christendom; India stemming from Hindu roots but using Buddhist, Christian, Jain, Jewish, Muslim and Parsi sources to build a multi-religious grandeur; China using its three ways, the Confucian, Taoist and Buddhist, to form the glory of Chinese civilisation; and the Middle East, which after a time of decline recovered its former élan through the rise and spread of Islam. None of these civilisations or religions was dominant over the others and they remained roughly in balance. They were civilisations that were affected and formed by religious forces.

Although these four religious civilisations were different, common factors can be detected that began to distance them from developments elsewhere in the world, for example in primal areas. There was a strong sense that one's present worldly life was not paramount by contrast with the pull of another world in heaven, *mokṣa*, or *nirvāṇa*; a sense of the inwardness of the real self and true faith as seen in various monastic systems; a sense that reason, analysis and intellectual synthesis could be important in religion; a sense that through mission religions could grow and conceivably become universal; a sense that religious communities, rituals, ethics, social involvement, scriptures, concepts, aesthetics, and spirituality were integral parts of religion and of culture; and a sense of the importance of transcendence and its mediating focus, whether it be God in Christ, Allah through the Koran, Yahweh through the Torah, Brahman through a Hindu personal deity or the Ātman, or Nirvāṇa through the Buddha or the Dharma.

(v) The next main stage in global religious history began in the sixteenth century C E when religious and other matters were dominated by the rise of the West. Europe broke out of its medieval captivity through seapower and later through technological power so that it came to supremacy over the other civilisations with which it had formerly been equal. It also uncovered new worlds such as the Americas, Southern Africa and Australasia inhabited by primal religious peoples. This period brought together a time of great strength in the European West with a time of relative weakness in India, the Middle East and China. The vibrant West became dominant.

The religious tradition of the West, Christianity, also spread into different parts of the world. The newly discovered continents of South America, North America, Southern Africa, and Australasia were settled by Europeans and became Christian continents. Christian missionaries went into most parts of the world, partly on the coat-tails of the empires that came into being, and churches, albeit sometimes small ones, were set up in many areas in the world.

The West not only took its religion (albeit in many denominational forms), it also importantly took its scientific and industrial revolutions into the wider world. At one level this brought medical facilities, material progress, city life, railways, factories and expanded trade. At another level it also introduced among intellectual élites elsewhere the scientific secular worldview and towards the end of this period, which lasted until 1945, it brought an awareness of nationalism and also the Marxist version of the secular viewpoint. Through western science and technology the world began to come together and it seemed to become smaller.

Again comparisons are difficult but certain general points can be made. Primal religions began to undergo dislocation in various parts of the world; laymen and vernacular devotion became more significant in the major religions; the relevance of religion for bettering life in this world received more attention; other religions and cultures were impressed by and to some extent reacted against the West's cultivation of progress; human domination over nature began to increase apace; and a greater knowledge of other religions came into being both at the level of scholarship and at the level of believers, although full-blown dialogue was not yet in view.

The sixth stage in the global history of religion is the one we are living in now. We covered its main facets earlier and so will not repeat them now. This sketch of the outline of a global history of religion has been all too brief. It has merit in itself by providing a framework into which historians of religion can insert their stories, or make their changes, or interpolate their interpretations.

It also has two other merits. In the first place it opens up many fruitful avenues of historical comparison. To mention but four out of numerous possibilities, around 1250 C E there was a convergence of philosophical/ theological intellectual syntheses in many parts of the world through Maimonides in the Jewish world, Aquinas and Bonaventura in the Christian world, Chu Hsi in the neo-Confucian Chinese world, Rāmānuja in the Tamil/Vedanta Hindu world, and (somewhat earlier) Al-Ghazālī in the Muslim world. Most of these remarkable and architectonic systematic syntheses of faith were done in isolation from each other yet at roughly the same time in different parts of the world. The Axial Age itself is an even better example of an age when great things were happening independently in varied parts of the globe.

Another example of historical comparison can be seen in the sixteenth century C E. There was a simultaneous emergence of devotional vernacular religion in scattered areas of the world. The Protestant Reformation arose in Europe using Luther's German or Cranmer's English or other vernaculars as its medium of expression; in India Guru Nānak's devotionalism through the medium of Punjabi heralded the rise of the Sikh tradition; in India also Tulsī Dās wrote his great paeon to Rāma in Hindi, not in Sanskrit, and Caitanya went into devotional ecstasies in Bengali; in Persia there emerged the new Shī'ite devotionalism using Persian; and, in Buddhist South East Asia, Pure Land devotionalism had already stressed the role of laymen and used local vernaculars in praise of Amida Buddha.

A final example relates to our present age. As religious traditions have responded to change it is possible to trace comparatively four different responses that have been made. The first is to retreat into one's shell and to pretend that change is not happening; the second is the fundamentalist option which works for the creative or sometimes non-creative restoration of tradition; the third is the way of evolutionary reform which seeks to enable religions to adapt to the changes around them; and the fourth is the way of radical reform which demands a radical reinterpretation of tradition in order to do justice to the crisis that is held to have arisen. Studies of all these developments in individual traditions are in progress, especially in relation to the various fundamentalist movements in different religions. More interesting is to take a comparative overview of the responses to change across religions, and this kind of scholarship is beginning to happen.

A second merit of a global history of religion is that it highlights periods when there have been radical effects of one or more religions on other traditions. Religious traditions have deeply affected each other either for better or for worse and inter-borrowing between religions, whether at a conscious or unconscious level, has been rife. Examples of inter-borrowing can be found widely, for example the interchange between Hindus, Buddhists and Jains in the sixth century C E; the interplay between Jews, Mysteries, Greek religion and thought and Christianity at the time of Christian origins; the interplay between Mani, the Zoroastrians and others in fourth century C E Persia; the interplay between the San Chiao, the three ways of China (Confucian, Taoist and Buddhist) at various times in Chinese history; the events surrounding the emergence of the Sikhs as a separate tradition in sixteenth century C E India; and the influence of the West and Christianity upon the modern Hindu reformers.

(c) *The Role of Phenomenology of Religion.* Phenomenology of religion has four important roles in the study of religion as a non-theological and non-reductionist enterprise.

(i) In the first place its categories of *epochē* (putting one's convictions into brackets and suspending judgment in order to understand) and *Einfühlung* (empathy with the position of others) are helpful in the general study of religion. They avoid the interpolation of value judgments which get in the way of a real understanding of the position of others, and they open up the possibility of seeing the world through the eyes of other people. As such they remain important general principles behind the whole enterprise of the study of religion.

(ii) Secondly, the phenomenological aim to take the position of believers seriously in order to avoid misrepresenting them is another important principle. Verifying with others that our representation of them accords roughly with how they see themselves is an important verification principle. It depends on what kind of other does the verifying—presumably a rigid fundamentalist verification would not suffice! Nor is conscious verification by believers the only criterion of understanding. There are unconscious and structural factors at work as well. Nevertheless an empathetic awareness of the position of others by checking our understanding with their own self-apprehension is important not only for our critical understanding of their being in the world but also for our own critical self-awareness of our own.

(iii) Thirdly, the phenomenological attempt to give greater integration to the study of religion by maintaining that 'religion' is at the heart of this study rather than the methodological canons of another discipline retains its significance as a principle. As such, phenomenology remains a co-ordinating endeavour within the study of religion rather than a methodological approach based upon the canons of history, theology, sociology, psychology, or any other discipline with its controlling roots outside religion. This does not mean that other approaches are not important. Nor does it make phenomenology into a kind of religion in itself. It is part of a wider enterprise—but an important part.

(iv) Fourthly, the phenomenological stress upon comparison remains deeply relevant. The particular method of comparison opened up by the principle of eidetic vision, basically that of phenomenological typology, is only one of the possible ways of comparing religions. Historical comparison that was mentioned earlier which takes historical contexts seriously in a way that phenomenology does not, and the method of comparison in depth between two religions whereby it becomes clear that typologies do not always work (for example Christ is in some ways more comparable with the Koran as the Islamic Word of God than with Muhammad) are of equal significance (albeit Christ can still be compared with Muhammad). Nevertheless the phenomenological emphasis upon the deep significance of comparison as a category remains important even though phenomenological typology is only one among many methods that can be used.

(d) *Complementarity of Methods and Approaches.* We have seen how a whole set of disciplines and approaches in interplay make up the study of religion. It incorporates a field of studies rather than being a narrow enterprise. No methods are excluded whether they centre upon religion or not, whether they belong to the social sciences or the humanities, whether their approach is inductive or hermeneutic, whether they focus upon data or persons. The only exception applies to the type of method that centres upon one religion and explicitly applies its categories to others (as with some kinds of theology and even philosophy) and the type of method that seeks to absolutise itself into a metaphysic thereby exceeding its methodological brief by attempting to reduce religion to itself.

This book implies the need for a complementarity of approaches. Although each chapter focusses upon a particular approach and in this respect advances its claims, this does not imply that other approaches are inappropriate or that any one approach should unduly dominate the others. However, despite the variety of materials, issues, theories and angles thereby introduced into the study of religion, the stance of complementarity does not obviate the need for overall integration in the field. As we have seen, that need for integration is partly supplied by the combined roles of history and phenomenology. To this can be added the role of anthropology of religion which provides a bedrock of data on primal religion arising out of empirical studies.

In what way, then, are the different approaches to the study of religion complementary? In large part because they operate a division of labour, and we can see this by means of two examples.

(i) It is clear that the study of religion is different from natural science insofar as it deals with data that involve persons rather than data that centre upon objects in nature. The study of data involving persons relates the study of religion to various disciplines in the arts and social sciences. It can be seen in terms of the religion of groups of persons (sociology and anthropology of religion), the religion of individuals (psychology of religion), the faith and intentionality of persons (phenomenology and hermeneutics of religion), the myths and texts of persons (the study of myths and texts), and so on. This involvement of religious data with persons, their social groupings, their individual religious experiences, their unconscious moulding by heredity and environment, their history, means that the study of religion has to do with human beings and that it needs complementary approaches to be dealt with in its wholeness.

(ii) Since 1945 various models of religion have been evolved to try and afford a framework of understanding whereby religions can be seen as organisms containing different elements or dimensions. Two contributors to this volume have produced models that are fairly similar, and these models point to the need for a complementary set of approaches to do justice to the study of religions as organisms. Ninian Smart's model stresses six dimensions of religion: doctrines, myths, ethics, rituals, social institutions, and religious experience. Frank Whaling's model stresses eight elements of religion: religious communities, rituals, ethics, social and political involvement of religions in wider society, scripture/myth, concepts, aesthetics, and spirituality. Doctrines and concepts imply some input from, but not control by, philosophy and theology; religious communities and social involvement come mainly under the umbrella of sociology; scripture involves the work of textual experts; religious experience and spirituality include the expertise of psychologists of religion; myth is studied partly by anthropology, as are rituals; ethics involves a range of skills; aesthetics invites the skills of iconography and fine art. These divisions of labour are not watertight but they are clearly relevant. The study of religion is, in the nature of things, a collaborative entreprise involving a complementarity of skills.

(e) *New Developments in the Study of Religion.* Many new developments in the study of religion are brought out in this volume. In closing this introduction let me briefly mention seven new developments that appear to be of more than passing importance.

(i) The role of aesthetics in religion is now receiving more attention. For most of history and for most people aesthetics in the form of painting, mosaics, music, sculpture, calligraphy and wider literature has been more relevant and compelling than studying doctrines or even reading scripture. Giotto's frescoes of Jesus at Padua and of St. Francis at Assisi, Buddha images illustrating through the five main *mudras* his compassion and significance, Indian classical dance, Muslim calligraphy, and many other aesthetic representations, not to mention the shape and intentionality of churches, mosques, temples, synagogues, pagodas and gurdwaras have given to ordinary people a visual theology that was vivid and real. The study of the aesthetic side of religion, both in separate traditions and in comparative studies, is growing apace. It is likely to continue to grow.

(ii) Another element in the above models, namely spirituality and religious experience, is receiving more attention and study. This is partly due to a rise of interest in spirituality in the mainstream religions, in new religious movements, and in the western New Age phenomenon. However, academic and publishing attention is being given to the whole area of spirituality as well as experiential interest. This is emerging not only in the work of psychologists of religion but also in major textual series. For example

the Classics of Western Spirituality published by the Paulist Press beginning in 1978 has brought out nearly 70 volumes of spirituality classics
from not only the Christian tradition (although mainly so) but also from
the Jewish, Muslim, and American Indian traditions. Another series, World
Spirituality: An Encyclopaedic History of the Religious Quest, published
by Crossroad, New York, beginning in 1985 and planned in 25 volumes,
is nearing completion. A series on the Classics of Eastern Spirituality is
also planned as an update of Max Muller's Sacred Books of the East.

(iii) We have mentioned earlier the rise of interest in a global theology or
religion which overlaps the traditional boundaries of theology and the
study of religion. Its concern is to conceptualise universal theological categories that transcend the particularities of particular theologies in order
to deal with theology as such rather than the theology of a particular
religion. Its view of transcendence is wide and open and not basically
ontological or essentialist. Its concern is to speak religiously on global
issues beginning from the concerns of the global situation rather than
from the concerns of particular theologies. It is important in itself; it may
well be becoming a new discipline; and it may herald a new relationship
between theology and the study of religion based upon complementariness rather than suspicion.

(iv) A fourth nascent development is the growing interest of the study of
religion in global issues and what might be called global scholarship. Passages in this book glance briefly at the relationship between the study of
religion and wider scholarship, and at the relationship between the study
of religion and our emerging global world. One of the main tasks of the
study of religion is to study world religions which are global in setting,
and it bestraddles a number of disciplines and interests that have as their
areas of concern the study of global matters involving nature, human
beings, and transcendence. The days when the study of religion was suspected from the side of faith and neglected from the side of reason are
passing or past. That the study of religion should play a creative role in
contemporary general scholarship is increasingly seen to be important not
only for the study of religion but also for the world of learning and the
world in general.

(v) The study of religion is also becoming more involved in political
matters. This is partly because religion itself is having a wider impact in
the world in either the negative sense of Waco and Jonestown, or religious

conflicts in Sri Lanka, the Punjab, the Middle East, Northern Ireland, the Sudan, and Bosnia—or in the positive sense of making eirenical contributions to local and global matters in various parts of the world.

Samuel Huntington's quixotic comments about Islam being the new analogue for the USSR in the Cold War as an adversary, and some of the remarks on religion in Paul Kennedy's otherwise intelligent *Preparing for the Twenty-first Century* (1993), illustrate the interest taken in religion by political commentators, and the need for insightful advice to be given by scholars of religion to political leaders at all levels. Good books on religion are increasingly being read by political leaders and advisors, and the study of religion has an important part to play in local and global political affairs. Simple matters such as the setting up of significant museums of religion in places as disparate as Glasgow, Marburg and Moscow are straws in the wind. It is very likely that the input of the study of religion into politics and political thinking will grow in the near future.

(vi) A sixth matter of growing interest to the study of religion concerns the role of women and gender in religion. Ursula King has formed a Women's Group at the international meetings of the main International Association for the History of Religions, and her books such as *Women and Spirituality: Voices of Protest and Promise* (1989) are part of a growing input into this field. Interest in this topic can only increase.

(vii) A final matter picks up the theme of emancipation within a different context. In this book the role of religion in processes of liberation from oppression is mentioned in connection with studies of religious movements that have a prophetic, puritanical, messianic, or reform element within them. Religion is seen not as an obstacle to social development but as a spur to social regeneration. More studies of religious liberation movements can be expected.

5. Conclusion

We hope that readers will find this book to be a worthy companion to Jacques Waardenburg's *Classical Approaches to the Study of Religion*, and that it will be widely read and commented upon. May the constructive comment that will inevitably be forthcoming when people wrestle with matters of such immense scope serve creatively to advance the cause of the study of religion. Our purpose has been so to summarise the contemporary approaches to the study of religion that momentum may be given to such an advance at an inter-disciplinary, inter-cultural and inter-personal level.

Select Bibliography

Adams, Charles J. (ed.) (1977), *A Reader's Guide to the Great Religions.* New York: Free Press.

Bellah, R. N. (1975), *The Broken Covenant: American Civil Religion in a Time of Trial.* New York: Seabury.

Boyce, Mary (1987), *Zoroastrians: Their Beliefs and Religious Practices.* London: Routledge.

Cousins, Ewert (General ed.) (1978–), *The Classics of Western Spirituality,* 70 volumes. New York: Paulist Press.

—(General ed.) (1985–), *World Spirituality: An Encyclopaedic History of the Religious Quest,* 25 volumes. New York: Crossroad.

Dumézil, G. (1958), *L'idéologie tripartie des Indo-Européens.* Paris: Presses Universitaires de France.

Durkheim, Émile (1976), *The Elementary Forms of the Religious Life.* London: Allen and Unwin.

Eliade, Mircea (1959), *The Sacred and the Profane: The Nature of Religion.* New York: Harcourt Brace.

—(Chief ed.) (1987), *The Encyclopaedia of Religion,* 16 volumes. New York: Macmillan.

Gombrich, Richard (1988), *Theravāda Buddhism.* London: Routledge.

Hick, John (1973), *God and the Universe of Faiths.* London: Macmillan.

Huntington, Samuel (1992), 'The Clash of Civilisations,' *Foreign affairs,* 72(3): 22–49.

Kennedy, Paul (1993), *Preparing for the twenty-first Century.* London: Harper Collins.

King, Ursula (1989), *Women and Spirituality: Voices of Protest and Promise.* London: Macmillan.

Kristensen, Brede (1960), *The Meaning of Religion* (translated by John Carman). The Hague: Nijhoff.

Kung, Hans and Kuschel, K.-J. (1993), *A Global Ethic.* London: SCM Press.

Limits to Growth; A Report on the Club of Rome's Project on the Predicament of Mankind (1974). London and Sydney: Pan Books.

Otto, R. (1917), *Das Heilige.* Munich: Breslau.

Panikkar, Raimundo (1979), *Myth, Faith and Hermeneutics.* New York: Paulist Press.

Segal, R. (1989), *Religion and the Social Sciences: Essays on the Confrontation.* Atlanta: Scholars Press.

Smart, Ninian (1969), *The Phenomenon of Religion*. New York: Seabury.

—(1973), *The Religious Experience of Mankind*. New York: Scribner.

—(1981), *Beyond Ideology*. London: Collins.

Smith, Huston (1992), *Essays on World Religion* (edited by M. D. Bryant). New York: Paragon House.

Smith, Wilfred Cantwell (1964), *The Meaning and End of Religion*. New York: New American Library, Mentor.

—(1981), *Towards a World Theology*. Philadelphia: Westminster.

Storey, C. and Storey, J. (eds.) (1994), *Visions of an Inter-faith Future*. Oxford: International Inter-Faith Centre.

Tillich, Paul (1965), *Ultimate Concern*, London SCM Press.

van der Leeuw, G. (1938), *Religion in Manifestation and Essence: A Study in Phenomenology* (translated by J. E. Turner). London: Allen and Unwin.

Waardenburg, Jacques (1973), *Classical Approaches to the Study of Religion*, 2 volumes. The Hague: Mouton.

—(1978), *Reflections on the Study of Religion*, The Hague: Mouton.

Whaling, Frank (ed.) (1984), *The World's Religious Traditions: Current Perspectives in Religious Studies*. Edinburgh: T & T Clark.

—(1986), *Christian Theology and World Religions: A Global Approach*. Basingstoke: Marshall Pickering.

—(1987), *Religion in Today's World*. Edinburgh: T & T Clark.

Wiebe, Donald (1985), 'A Positive Episteme for the Study of Religion,' *Scottish Journal of Religious Studies* 6(1): 78–95.

—(1990), 'Disciplinary Axioms, Boundary Conditions and the Academic Study of Religion: Comments on Pals and Dawson,' *Religion* 20: 17–29.

Historical and Phenomenological Approaches to the Study of Religion

Some major developments and issues under debate since 1950

URSULA KING

If one examines the major developments in the history and phenomenology of religion over the last thirty years, there can be no doubt that there has been a considerable growth of activities. This is apparent from the number of publications, the frequency of conferences and the range of issues under debate. A lively discussion by an increasing number of scholars around the world is taking place as to the very nature of the subject. The year 1950 does not mark a completely new beginning but it provides a convenient watershed for a survey of recent developments. The middle of the twentieth century saw the emergence of a new era when in the wake of the Second World War a post-colonial world was born. It saw the birth of numerous new nations as well as the growth of a new kind of internationalism, not to mention the many new problems linked to quickly expanding populations and an equally quickly shrinking globe, developments which were not without significance for the study of religion.

1950 is also the year when the International Association for the History of Religions (IAHR) was formed, soon to be followed by the foundation of new national sections, the establishment of new journals as well as the renaming of old ones, the launching of new bibliographical ventures and the concern for greater international cooperation. Another reason for starting at this date is the fact that the major developments in the study of religion have been described up to 1950 by Jacques Waardenburg in his *Classical Approaches to the Study of Religion* (1973: 2 vols.; see especially 'View of a Hundred Years' Study of Religion,' I, 1–73). A general survey for the years following that period has not been undertaken so far although several excellent studies exist which analyse specific developments and arguments in greater detail than is possible here. Articles apart, the most up-to-date survey in book form is found in the concluding chapter of Eric Sharpe, *Comparative Religion. A History* (1975: 267–93, 'Twenty Years of International Debate, 1950–1970').

When Professor C. J. Bleeker, in his capacity as general secretary of the IAHR, addressed the XIIth International Congress at Stockholm in 1970, he explicitly stated that 'It would be a great source of satisfaction if we could get to know the results the history of religions has reached in the past twenty years, in which direction the study is moving, and whether there has been progress in the discipline. Unfortunately, we have no systematic surveys of the whole field of research.' It would be a challenging task indeed for a group of scholars to collaborate in such a venture for, as Bleeker went on to say, 'the type of scholar who is capable of surveying the total field of the history of religions, or at least great parts of it, seems to be slowly dying out. This is why it is impossible at present to satisfy the desire which we all feel to know what has happened in this branch of scholarship during the past twenty years' (Bleeker 1975b: 27).

However, it is perhaps less the case that such a type of scholar is dying out than the fact that the material available for surveying has become so voluminous that it is impossible for any single individual to provide a comprehensive summary on his or her own. The study of religion, as presently conceived and pursued by many scholars around the world, is much wider than 'the total field of the history of religions' of which Bleeker spoke. It represents an increasingly international and multi-disciplinary as well as an interdisciplinary field of studies and research. It would be presumptuous for any one scholar to claim that such rich and varied developments could be adequately surveyed in any other way than by close international collaboration and the intensive team-work of specialists in the various disciplines which have a bearing on the study of religion. The present article is offered as a modest attempt to survey recent literature within the given constraints of space and time, and to ask how far current publications implicitly demonstrate or explicitly contribute to the major issues in the methodological debate of the contemporary history and phenomenology of religion.

There has been much discussion over recent years as to what constitutes the proper subject area and the specific method(s) of the history and phenomenology of religion and whether these two approaches to the study of religion are separate, interrelated or even identical or, on the contrary, opposed to and exclusive of each other. This debate has gained enormous momentum, especially over the last ten years or so, as is evident from a large number of publications and also from several conferences which have expressed an explicitly methodological concern. Although the size of the debate is considerable, the area of common agreement is perhaps less large than one might hope for. There is a growing trend towards greater methodological self-awareness and closer analysis of the presuppositions of one's research among many scholars today, yet much further clarification is still needed in this area.

What is available to anyone surveying the scholarly harvest in the history and phenomenology of religion during the last thirty years? In other words, what research results have been produced in the form of books, articles and conference proceedings? What are the major concerns of the scholars of religion belonging to the present generation and where is the discipline going in the future? Important too, what are the organisational developments which have affected the production of scholarly works, facilitated intellectual exchange and stimulated the debate on methods?

Given these questions, the approach adopted here will of necessity be synoptic; it may occasionally involve critical comparisons and will attempt an analysis of some of the conceptual tools currently used in the history and phenomenology of religion. It must be emphatically stated that this chapter can neither reflect all the discussions and developments which have taken place around the world nor can it provide a complete bibliography of relevant publications in all major languages. The emphasis lies primarily on the analysis of the recent practice and discussion of methods found in the history and phenomenology of religion. The aim is not to give a survey of developments country by country (for this see *Religion*, Special Issue, August 1975) nor to discuss publications in this field in a strictly chronological order. The need for this is adequately filled by such indispensable bibliographical reference works as the *International Bibliography of the History of Religions*, published by the IAHR from 1954–80, now replaced by *Science of Religion—Abstracts and Index of Recent Articles* (before 1980: *Science of Religion Bulletin*) published by the Free University of Amsterdam, the quarterly issues of the *Bulletin Signalétique: Sciences Religieuses*, published by the Centre National de Recherche Scientifique in Paris and the *Religious Studies Review*, published by the Canadian Council on the study of Religion. In fact, the most recent publications will be drawn on rather more frequently as they are less well known than earlier studies; they possess the additional advantage of incorporating discussions about preceding works.

The present survey will mainly, but not exclusively, focus on a third-level analysis of the data provided by research in the history and phenomenology of religion over recent years. At the first level, many specialised studies and monographs exist which cannot be directly taken into account here. At the second level, various reference works have been produced which bring together and, in certain cases, integrate a host of individual data into an overall framework. These works often, but not always, include analytical reflections and discussions of the methods underlying such attempts at integration. At the third level, an analysis of the materials and methods found in such reference works and in many other sources can be undertaken in order to map out the common core of the history and phenomenology of religion and to explore their fluid boundaries. It should be clear by now that this survey will mainly be concerned with works which have attempted an integration of subject-matter or have made a significant contribution to the current debate about methods in the two fields under review here. In actual practice this means that most examples will be taken from post-1960 publications for it is only after that date that the methodological debate came in a new way fully into its own.

To counter any possible criticism at the outset, it must be mentioned that only a limited range of arguments can be examined here. Thus, this chapter is far from exhaustive nor can it be as truly international as it should be. I am painfully aware of the diverse constraints working against a fully international conception of the science of religion as a scholarly discipline. Although international in scope and intention, the study of religion is not always approached from such a wide and integral perspective in the works of all scholars. There is the obvious built-in defect that individual scholars only have access to limited data, not merely because of their chosen field of specialisation but even more because some major modern languages are not easily accessible. Few can follow the latest developments in the study of religion around the world. For western scholars this is particularly true with regard to eastern languages, especially Japanese and Chinese, and also with regard to recent developments in the study of religion in Eastern European countries and the USSR. Out of necessity rather than choice the present survey refers largely to western publications. To some readers, especially eastern ones, it may thus appear unduly western-centred, a shortcoming for which I apologise although I know that it is to a large extent unavoidable at present.

Even if one examines major publications in western languages, one cannot help but notice a certain duplication of work undertaken by different scholars working in different languages, often unknown to each other. In spite of growing collaboration, there is still a lack of close communication and, as a result, a lack of urgently needed clarification about the objects and methods of the discipline. A repetition of similar arguments occurs in this debate of many schools and voices; in fact, sometimes there seems to reign more of a cacophony than harmony. If we can pick out some of the main melodies, interpret the reigning leitmotifs and possibly discover a new note here and there which may stimulate further reflections on the part of the reader, then the present survey will have been amply worthwhile.

1. What are the historical and phenomenological approaches?

Towards the end of his important address on *Religionswissenschaft*, given at the inaugural meeting of the American Society for the Study of Religion in 1959, Erwin R. Goodenough pleaded that at 'the present stage of the Science of Religion, we would do well to ask small questions until we have established a methodology we can all approve and use' (Goodenough 1959: 94). But more than twenty years later have we come any nearer to this aim of a generally approved methodology? Over the last decade or so the cry for methodological clarification has repeatedly been raised; the number of papers, monographs, and conferences devoted to methodology has grown fast, previously developed methods have been criticised and found wanting, several new methods and theories about the study of religion have been proposed. There can be no doubt that a vigorous, if not always sufficiently rigorous debate about methodology has come into existence; at the same time many works are still being published which include little or no theoretical reflection at all. There is much need for a clarification of the terminology in use and for a critical examination of the objects and methods specific to the study of religion. Scholars with enough imaginative grasp and vision to reflect on the future have clearly perceived that the most urgent requirements for a further creative development of the subject are a well formulated research programme and bolder theory formation.

However, the plea for greater methodological awareness does not in itself answer the question whether the classification, analysis, and interpretation of religious data on as comprehensive a scale as possible represents basically one single discipline, a wide field of related but different studies, or whether it is a science, a craft, or possibly even an art, only to be mastered by a few extraordinarily endowed and creative scholars. All these possibilities have been suggested and one may venture the opinion that these differences of approach in handling data from the complex and multidimensional reality that is religion allow for creative tension which reflects the healthy state and vitality of the discipline, if indeed this is the right word. For although large areas of agreement have been reached in the way scholars understand and practise their research, a general lack of consent exists as to what the study of religion is or ought to be called. The fluidity of terms given to this subject in the English-speaking world alone is baffling. Intellectual fashions of the day have repeatedly affected common usage. There are a great many names in circulation but none has become so universally accepted as to be definite. The debate about what the subject ought to be called has oscillated a great deal over the years; it is closely interwined with the *Methodenstreit* in general, i.e., the arguments about respective methods and their problems are closely interrelated with what is perceived to be the nature of the subject (see the excellent survey article by R. Pummer 1972). Thus, the problem of definition is a matter of central concern, for the name given to a subject both reflects and in turn affects the choice of suitable objects and methods of study.

The multidisciplinary thrust and new directions taken by the study of religion in the last two decades or so has been institutionally recognized by the founding or renaming of university departments devoted to religious studies (sometimes called 'department of religion,' especially in North America). However, this term can be both a help and a hindrance as its adoption does not by itself settle the methodological debate or clarify the boundaries of the subject area. It is certain that many different orientations, not all consistent with each other, have found umbrage under this new term. However, the conception of religious studies definitely expresses a new development which does not represent a sudden, sharp break with the past but is to some extent continuous with what went on earlier in the study of religion. Yet it is also a new attempt to go beyond the mere collection, description, and empirical analysis of religious data and seek an interpretation within a wider theoretical framework which allows a more systematic perspective. This effort to develop an integral approach and a more comprehensive theory of interpretation for the study of religion may be the hallmark of what could eventually prove to be the most stimulating and promising aspect of the contemporary methodological debate.

Before the developments of recent years can be fully reviewed, an initial mapping of the territory will be of help. Anyone eager to discover the route taken by the subject in recent years can easily be confused by the abundance of contradictory signposting and the many different roads which have been taken. Which are the ones pointing in the right direction for the study of religion not to end in a future cul-de-sac?

The contemporary study of religion covers a wide range of interests and methods which often complement each other. A special difficulty of the methodological debate is the question whether all methods are equally important, whether some are more indispensable than others, and whether any particular method is so crucial that it lays the foundation for all others. The present chapter concentrates on the historical and phenomenological approaches which, if not understood in the narrowest sense, raise many difficult issues about meaning and interpretation. History and phenomenology are here discussed together because theoretical debates about their nature and method are often closely related. To enter the debate at its simplest level, an attempt will be made to state briefly what is meant by the 'historical' and 'phenomenological' approach when protagonists argue about the respective appropriateness of these methods for the study of religion.

Both the historical-descriptive presentation as well as the systematic analysis and classification of religious data belong to the history of the study of religion. Both approaches are an integral part of the nineteenth century inheritance of the subject and both have found further refinement in subsequent theory and practice. If anything, the historical approach is easier to define; it has been better established and longer practised. It has also produced more works of scholarship. What is precisely understood by the historical approach is frequently related to the wider discussions about the nature of history as an academic discipline. The protagonists of a strictly historical approach emphasize the use of historical-critical methods, a rigorous practice of philology and other subsidiary disciplines necessary for the study of history, and insist on factual-descriptive expositions, not infrequently accompanied by a minimum of interpretation as to the meaning of the data presented.

It is necessary to stress again and again that the plurality of religions in the present world and the variety of cultures moulded by different religious traditions cannot be adequately understood without a thoroughly historical study of the origin, growth, and development of particular religions, affected by the ongoing dynamic of continuity and change. At an earlier stage, the sharp emphasis on the knowledge of historical facts arose perhaps from the need to counteract the general ignorance of non-western religious and cultural traditions in the West. It was not only the concern for historical truth but also the need to free the study of religion from the dominance of *a priori* theological and philosophical speculation which required a strong insistence on the use of the historical method.

The historical-philological method has yielded a rich harvest for the study of religion. But it would perhaps not be incorrect to say that, in certain overworked areas at least, it has also led to a surfeit of data suffering from a lack of integration. In some cases it has had the unfortunate result of an isolationist position whereby individual scholars, through their overspecialisation in one specific aspect or period of a particular religion, have been unable to relate their knowledge to wider questions and concerns, whether those of the study of religion or of the intellectual life and scholarship of their time.

But history itself is open to a wide range of interpretations and cannot be practised without a concern for systematic reflection and theory, a point proved by the existence of very different philosophies of history. (The American serial publication *History and Theory* regularly examines different theoretical orientations affecting the study of history; see especially Beiheft 8, 1968 'On Method in the History of Religions,' edited by J.S. Helfer.) History may be understood in a very narrow or much wider sense. There exists what might be called the descriptive and the interpretative use of history. Each approach has its own adherents and means of expression. For example, the French journal *Revue de l'Histoire des Religions* (founded in 1880) still carries a programmatic statement today saying that 'the review is purely historical; it excludes any work of a polemical or dogmatic character' (back cover; my translation). Many French scholars have favoured this strictly historical approach, perhaps best exemplified in the work of the *École Pratique des Hautes Etudes* (Paris) but it has well-known protagonists among other European scholars too, particularly in Scandinavia. At the other end of the spectrum lies the American journal *History of Religions* (founded 1961 and subtitled 'An International Journal for Comparative Historical Studies;' edited by M. Eliade, J. Kitagawa, and J. Smith) which since its inception 'has been instrumental in providing materials and creating a methodology for the study of world religions' (publicity brochure). However, on closer inspection one discovers that apart from Eliade's own important statements and a few other articles on methodology, most contributions deal primarily with historical-factual data.

Another important aspect of the history of religions as practised today is the question of which period of history is most emphasized in the work of particular scholars. Is the research primarily concerned with the religions of the past or with the living religions of the present? However, such a distinction between extinct and living religions may be unjustifiable, as has been argued, because it implies wrong assumptions about historical discontinuities. But while it is legitimate to give due prominence to the formative period of a religious tradition or to the exemplary height of its development, one wonders why in many works this is accompanied by a neglect for the present, too often only considered in terms of loss and decline. Is there a marked preference for classical rather than modern materials among historians of religions in the strict sense so as to bypass the problem of meaning which grows more urgent and difficult the nearer one gets to the present? But is religion even in the far-away past not too often seen primarily in terms of ideas and institutions in isolation from the concrete context of a particular society? All these questions have been asked and, depending on the answers given, particular orientations result in the study of religion, as will be seen later. At present it is enough to be aware of their existence and realize that when the term 'history of religions' is used to describe a methodological stance, the emphasis may well lie on the factual-descriptive approach which, however, begs further questions of a theoretical and essentially philosophical kind about the nature of factual data and their explanation.

In contrast to the history of religions approach in the narrow sense some scholars understand 'history' to mean an enquiry of such magnitude that it embraces most phenomenological studies whilst others regard the phenomenological approach as clearly distinct from the historical one. Phenomenology is then primarily understood as a systematic and comparative classification of all religious phenomena whatever they are. Undertaken at its widest, this must also include the historical development of these phenomena and this leads, from a different angle, back to the question of the relative importance and relationship of history and phenomenology. Several sides have been taken in this debate which goes back to an earlier part of this century. It is a debate beset with many philosophical thorns, few of which have been removed so far (see Sharpe 1975: 220–50; the Dutch contribution to phenomenology is discussed in Waardenburg 1972).

In contrast to the historical approach which is always diachronic, the phenomenological approach presents data in a synchronic, classificatory manner, frequently irrespective of any historical sequence. Thus, in the view of many, it appears to be too ahistorical if not to say anachronistic at times. The term 'phenomenology of religion' was first used by Chantepie de la Saussaye (in his *Lehrbuch der Religionsgeschichte*, 1887) prior to the development of Husserl's philosophy of phenomenology. It described the attempt to investigate the essence and meaning of religious phenomena and to group phenomena in a typological manner independent from space and time. The early phenomenology of religion was thus a discipline of classification used by many different scholars. However, this early empirical phenomenology is distinct from the classical phenomenology of religion developed in the first half of the twentieth century and perhaps best known through the work of the Dutch scholar, Gerardus van der Leeuw (especially his *Religion in Essence and Manifestation: a Study in Phenomenology*, trl. 1938, 1st ed. 1933). The specific methodological principles characteristic of this classical phenomenology were initially dependent on Husserl's influence but it must be emphasized that the subsequent developments of the phenomenology of religion remained unconnected with philosophical phenomenologies or the more recent discussions about phenomenology in the social sciences.

At its simplest, phenomenology seeks to understand the phenomenon of religion or, rather, specific phenomena of religion. The phenomenological method is summed up by the use of two distinct principles, derived from Husserl, namely the *epoché* and the eidetic vision. The *epoché* is often described as 'bracketing', that is to say, a suspension of judgment on the part of the investigator as to the truth, value, and in some cases also the existence of the phenomenon. The eidetic vision aims to grasp the essence of phenomena by means of empathy and intuition. Whereas the use of the *epoché* is pursued to achieve detachment and some kind of pure objectivity, the intuitive grasp of the essentials of phenomena in their wholeness clearly introduces a large measure of subjectivity. Thus, phenomenological methodology is characterized from the outset by an inherent tension, if not to say contradiction, of its underlying principles.

Phenomenological discussions have been influenced by developments in biblical interpretation or hermeneutics and the philosophical explorations of German *Verstehensphilosophie*. Large claims have been made on behalf of the phenomenology of religion; the most significant of these was that the phenomenological approach 'provided a path to the understanding (*Verstehen*) of religion, and to a grasp of its essence (*Wesen*), by means of an as far as possible value-free examination of its manifestations (*Erscheinungen*)' (Sharpe 1975: 220).

Traditional phenomenology has been largely practised by Dutch and German scholars of an earlier generation whose work has come in for much criticism recently. In spite of the investigation of numerous religious phenomena, little theoretical advance seems to have been made and much phenomenological work lacks methodological rigour and precision. The field is characterized by an extreme fragmentation so that one can discern almost as many different phenomenologies as there are phenomenologists. More frequently than not the term 'phenomenology of religion' appears to refer to a general approach rather than a specific method. This approach emphasizes the need to distance oneself from speculative and normative *a priori* categories in the study of religious phenomena; it also pleads for an overall orientation where the scholar investigates what the believer believes himself rather than what others believe about him.

Through the use of *epoché* and the search for objectivity, phenomenology may seem to share the aims of descriptive science but on closer examination it appears, as Oxtoby has pointed out, that '*Epoché* and eidetic vision are neither critical nor objective in the commonly understood sense of critical objectivity. Just as *epoché* suspends criticism, eidetic vision suspends objectivity. There is nothing outside one's intuitive grasp of a pattern which validates that pattern ... phenomenological expositions of religion are in fact very personal appreciations of it, akin more to certain forms of literary and aesthetic criticism than to the natural or even the social sciences' (Oxtoby 1968: 597). In the opinion of many scholars phenomenology represents an extremely subjective approach in strong contrast to the objective approach of the history of religions. Furthermore, much phenomenological work depends on specific theological assumptions, derived in particular from liberal Protestant theology. The apologetic and theological presuppositions of several phenomenologists have been pointed out; Van der Leeuw in particular considered himself always primarily as a theologian (see 'Gerardus van der Leeuw as a Theologian and Phenomenologist', in Waardenburg 1978a: 187–248). Much phenomenology may thus be considered as theological propaedeutics.

The methodological presuppositions of phenomenology imply several philosophical assumptions regarding the essence of religion and the nature of religious experience, too easily assumed to be the same in all people and places. Another practical difficulty arises from the vast multiplicity of religious phenomena. No phenomenologist can ever deal with all phenomena and the particular ones chosen for investigation are often dealt with in isolation from the wider context necessary for their explanation. Moreover, the very choice of phenomena to be studied must rest on criteria other than those supplied by the phenomena themselves.

Although the phenomenology of religion seems to have reached few answers and little clarity, it has raised important questions many of which are still with us today. One wonders how far the emphasis on 'bracketing' in the search for objectivity has not led to a 'bracketing out' of some of the most central and decisive questions of religious existence, namely those of ultimate truth and value, of the focus of the transcendent, and the place of its revelation to man. This also raises the further difficulty of what difference there may be between investigating a historical 'fact' about religion(s) and understanding a religious 'phenomenon'. Does one need to distinguish between 'understanding a religion' and 'understanding a faith other than one's own' and if so, wherein lies the difference between these two approaches? Furthermore, why is the 'history of religions' usually expressed in the plural whereas the 'phenomenology of religion' is always referred to in the singular?

These and similar issues point to the difficulties of interpretation in the study of religion. It is true that historical and systematic considerations have from the earliest days of the discipline been combined with reflections about the understanding and interpretation of religion. But it is only recently that a more concerted and systematic effort has been developed to create a unified, adequate method and a comprehensive hermeneutic for the study of religion. This has included a new look at phenomenology and a critical reconsideration of its nature and method (see especially the important plea for methodological awareness made by Waardenburg (1978a), and the discussion in Honko (1979: 141–220)). It has also been argued that the term 'phenomenology of religion' is so ambiguous as to be misleading and consequently should be abandoned in order to avoid any association with philosophical phenomenologies. Instead, it might be replaced either by the term 'systematic *Religionswissenschaft*' or 'the comparative study of religion.' To many scholars this is unacceptable, however, as the latter term appears to be too closely associated with an earlier, less methodologically aware understanding of 'comparative religion.'

The search for clearer concepts, definitions, and methods is still going on. There seems to exist a built-in dialectical relationship between the historical and systematic aspects of the study of religion since its beginning. Whether this inherent tension will ever be resolved and transcended by a more comprehensive and integral approach is at present much debated. The historical and phenomenological approaches are generally understood to be non-normative, that is to say, to describe and examine facts, whether historically or systematically, without judging them from a particular theological or philosophical standpoint. Whether this is at all possible or can only be practised on a limited range of data and questions, has come in for much discussion recently. However, only the future can show whether currently proposed methodologies will prove to be of more lasting value than those of previous generations.

The phenomenological approach, in spite of serious shortcomings, has much to commend it as it is closely connected with the attempt to develop a hermeneutic appropriate to the study of religion as an integral part of human knowledge and experience. At any one period, the study of religion is always closely related to and dependent upon the general understanding of religion dominant at that time and related to the wider intellectual and cultural developments of society. During the nineteenth century, scholars were fascinated by the question of the origin and evolution of religion, now largely abandoned, whereas twentieth century studies have been dominated by questions about the nature and essence of religion and, more recently, its meaning and function in society.

Many of the issues mentioned so far have found both protagonists and antagonists among contemporary religion scholars. The most characteristic feature of the methodological debate since World War II is not an either/or position—*either* the historical *or* the phenomenological approach—but a critical reexamination of the classical approaches to the study of religion and the attempt to develop a more differentiated and comprehensive methodology than before. Besides the critical evaluation of the legacy of an earlier *Religionswissenschaft* and 'comparative religion' this includes a strong concern for definitional issues, the attempt to refute any kind of reductionism in the understanding and explanation of religion, however closely connected to other branches of knowledge and their methods, and an increasing appreciation of the wider cultural role of the study of religion.

Waardenburg's indispensable survey of the *Classical Approaches to the Study of Religion* (1973a) already emphasized the fact that the study of religion is less one particular discipline than a field of studies with a strongly interdisciplinary character. In his view it is this rather than a specific object or method which distinguishes it most from other disciplines. Many specialists belonging to a wide range of disciplines and working with different methods and theoretical assumptions contribute to our understanding of the complex and multidimensional phenomenon of religion. Whether this multiplicity can ever be theoretically accounted for by one comprehensive theory is at present very much open to debate.

Not all scholars will see the important methodological issues in the same way as they are presented here. But whatever their methodological stance, even when it is primarily one against the consideration of methods, their arguments form part of the wider developments which have taken place since the 1950s. To understand particular aspects and arguments of the current methodological discussion it is necessary to see them within a much wider regional and international context. Before specific arguments about the history and phenomenology of religion are examined in detail, it is imperative to give first an outline of the growth of the debate at the international level. This will be done by considering the main areas of the contemporary scholarly network in the study of religion, by describing the organisational innovations which have greatly facilitated and strengthened research in this field, and by looking at important reference works and handbooks which have been published in the history and phenomenology of religion over recent years.

2. Growth of the international debate

2.1 Geographical distribution of the participants in the debate

It is important to stress the growing international and intercultural character of the study of religion today. From its early beginnings in Western Europe more than a century ago, the systematic study of the religious heritage of mankind has now grown into a worldwide pursuit which links together scholars from many different nations. The major emphasis and approach to the study of religion may vary widely but, in one form or another, the subject is represented among the teaching and research interests of numerous contemporary universities and colleges. In some of the newly founded nations, and sometimes in the older ones too, the study of religion is also not unrelated to a renewed search for origins and spiritual roots. Different motivations and divergent cultural and scholarly traditions help to explain the wide range of attitudes taken towards what are considered to be the objects and most appropriate methods of the study of religion.

To locate the participants in the contemporary debate, it may be helpful to give a brief overview regarding the major geographical distribution of the subject. Waardenburg (1978b) has distinguished three main geographical areas in the contemporary study of religion, namely the developing countries of the third world, the socialist countries of marxist inspiration, and western countries (North America and Europe, with four further subdivisions according to language areas and different cultural traditions in Europe). But in spite of these linguistic and cultural subdivisions, Waardenburg's main categories seem to be less related to geographical areas than to current political alliances. It is very difficult indeed to delineate neat geographical boundaries for the study of religion. It may be more accurate to speak of overlapping circles with fluid boundaries and a shifting centre of gravity.

Looked at from a different point of view, one might distinguish five major areas with different cultural, religious, and scholarly traditions, representing different clusters of interest and related to wider historical and political developments: (1) The historical roots of the subject developed in continental Europe and several west European countries possess major centres for the study of religion. There is a strong historical tradition in Holland, Britain, France, Germany, Italy, and Sweden whereas the development of the phenomenology of religion is particularly closely associated with Holland and Germany. (2) More recently, North America has become an important centre for the study of religion (with numerous university departments and college courses in the USA and Canada), bringing with it a marked methodological shift in the understanding of what the subject is and ought to be about. There exists a considerable disagreement over method between scholars from the USA and certain European countries, in Scandinavia and Italy for example. By and large, the North American developments have been characterized by a search for a more integral approach to the study of religion as can be seen from the continuing debate about an appropriate hermeneutic or theory of interpretation, especially as initiated by the so-called 'Chicago school'. Profound methodological differences notwithstanding, the European and North American centres have so far generated most activity and been the major contributors in the debate about methodology. (3) However, over the last two decades or so, participants from other areas have entered the methodological debate and made important contributions. They range from the Middle East (Israel) to South East Asia (India and Thailand) and the Far East (Japan, Korea, Australia). Eastern developments in the study of religion have been influenced by earlier work done in Europe and even more the USA, but these influences have been blended with strong indigenous traditions, especially in India and Japan. Unfortunately, far too little is generally known about these important eastern developments. (4) An even heavier curtain of ignorance divides the West from the socialist countries of East Germany, Poland and the USSR—in all of which the study of religion is pursued in one form or another. East Germany has a longstanding tradition in the study of *Religionswissenschaft*, particularly at the University of Leipzig which has perhaps remained more closely in contact with western developments than any other university in a socialist country and maintains a high standard of historical-critical scholarship. Lively methodological discussions are taking place in Poland but the emphasis is very much on a rigorously defined scientific approach, based on a narrowly understood objectivity close to verging on 'scientism'. Both in Poland and the USSR the sociology of religion is an important discipline. Soviet scholars, particularly members of the philosophical and oriental sections of the Academy of Sciences, are also carrying out considerable research in the history of religions but few of their publications find their way to the West. It is impossible to discuss the manysided aspects of the study of religion in the USSR here. Comparatively little information is directly accessible to the western student but a survey of developments is now available in the recently published study by J. Thrower, *Marxist-Leninist Scientific Atheism and the Study of Religion and Atheism in the USSR* (1983). (5) Another important area of development in the study of religion is represented by the African subcontinent. Research work and teaching in different subjects is carried out in West, East, Central and Southern Africa with a great increase of activities in recent years, to be distinguished from research on African religions which has been going on much longer. A possibly further area to be considered is South America but little information regarding research developments in the study of religion seems to be available.

In fact, the general lack of information on worldwide developments represents a serious lacuna in current scholarship if one seeks a well-informed assessment of the scholarly network and scope of the study of religion which would adequately show its intellectual and cultural importance for the modern world. Specialised studies on specific countries apart, the best and most easily accessible international survey currently available is the one undertaken by the British journal *Religion* (August 1975) although it is by no means comprehensive. Articles of various length and depth deal with the study of religion in continental Europe, Scandinavia, and Great Britain; with North America; with South Asia, Japan, Australia and New Zealand; with developments in different African countries; and briefly, with the academic study of religion in Israel. Unfortunately, the issue contains no information on any of the socialist countries. It is not only regrettable that scholarly interests and orientations are so closely dependent on political and linguistic divisions but it is also abundantly clear that the future viability of the subject will depend on much closer international collaboration and a more comprehensive and rigorous methodology. However, these necessary developments will not be brought about if over-specialised scholars maintain a cultural ghetto mentality and remain unable to relate their particular researches to wider concerns. Although much remains to be done to develop a more adequate international network of scholarship, it is true to say that the realization of a truly global framework is closely interrelated with the development of the *International Association for the History of Religions* (IAHR) during the last three decades. This is not the place to review in full the history of the IAHR and its discussions, examined in considerable detail in Eric Sharpe's *Comparative Religion* (1975: 267–93; see also the monograph by Bleeker (1975a)). However, contrary to Sharpe, it would seem that the developments connected with the IAHR provide more than merely 'a convenient focus' (Sharpe 1975: 268) for recent methodological discussions. The initiative of the IAHR in developing an organizational structure for promoting conferences and publications has been of central importance in the development of the methodological debate over recent years, especially as the IAHR has organised two conferences explicitly devoted to methodology, and brief reference must be made to some of its activities insofar as they have affected the methodological debate since World War II.

2.2. *The growth and development of the IAHR*

The development of the IAHR, founded in 1950 by primarily European scholars at Amsterdam, represents an innovation without being a completely new beginning, for its organisation is built on earlier foundations laid during the first half of the twentieth century. The IAHR continued the custom of holding international congresses in the study of religion, first begun in Paris in 1900. Six congresses had been organised when the seventh was convened in 1950 at Amsterdam. It was during this congress that 'The International Association for the Study of the History of Religions' (IASHR) was formed, with its name subsequently being shortened to the 'International Association for the History of Religions' (IAHR, Rome 1955). The continuity with the earlier congresses has been consciously maintained and recognized by the fact that the first IAHR congress is number VII in the series. However, the earlier congresses (I–VI) had always been prepared by an ad hoc committee with no permanent organisation during the intervening years. It is only since the foundation of the IAHR in 1950 that there has been a continuing international body with its own journal (*Numen* 1954–), an international secretariat, and a continuous flow of publications (*Supplements* to *Numen*, and most important, the *International Bibliography of the History of Religions* 1954–80, now replaced by *Science of Religion Abstracts and Index of Recent Articles* (1980–).

Between 1950–80, eight international congresses have been held; in addition, five regional conferences were organised between 1964–79. Detailed information about these can be found in the published *Proceedings* of each congress (up to 1980), the reports in *Numen*, and the survey up to 1970 in Sharpe (1975). As the information about the congresses held so far is not easily accessible in one place, all relevant data have been gathered in a diagram (see Table 1) which readers may find helpful for reference. Without wishing to repeat discussions found in Sharpe, some of the most significant developments which have a bearing on our investigation may be mentioned here.

Milestones in the development of a fuller methodological awareness, accompanied by the realization that many different perspectives exist side by side in the study of religion, are represented by the IAHR

Table 1. CONGRESSES

INTERNATIONAL ASSOCIATION FOR THE HISTORY OF RELIGIONS (IAHR—1950–80)

Six international congresses in the history of religions preceded the IAHR:
I Paris (1900), II Basel (1904), III Oxford (1908), IV Leiden (1912), V Lund (1929), and VI Brussels (1935)

	Date	Place	President	Secretary	Published Proceedings
VII	1950	AMSTERDAM	Van der Leeuw (Holland)	Bleeker (Holland)	Amsterdam 1951
VIII	1955	ROME	Pettazzoni (Italy)	Bleeker	Leiden 1959
IX	1958	TOKYO	Pettazzoni (Italy)	Bleeker	Tokyo 1960
X	1960	MARBURG	Widengren (Sweden)	Bleeker	Marburg 1961
XI	1965	CLAREMONT	Widengren (Sweden)	Bleeker	Leiden 1968
XII	1970	STOCKHOLM	Simon (France)	Brandon (England) d. 1971 Sharpe (England) 1971–75	Leiden 1975
XIII	1975	LANCASTER	Simon (France)	Werblowsky (Israel)	Leicester 1980 (contains details of all congress proceedings since 1900; see pp. 180–1.)
XIV	1980	WINNIPEG	Simon (France) Schimmel (Germany/USA) newly elected	Werblowsky (Israel)	Waterloo 1983

Table 1. *(cont.)*

Regional IAHR study conferences:

Date	Place	Theme	Publication
1964	STRASBOURG	Initiation	C.J. Bleeker ed., *Initiation*, Leiden 1965
1966	MESSINA	Gnosticism	U. Bianchi ed., *Le Origini dello Gnosticismo*, Leiden 1970
1968	JERUSALEM	Redemption	R.J.Z. Werblowsky and C.J. Bleeker eds., *Types of Redemption*, Leiden 1970
1973	TURKU	Methodology	L. Honko ed. *Science of Religion, Studies in Methodology*, The Hague 1979
1979	WARSAW	Methodology	unpublished so far

congresses in Tokyo (1958), Marburg (1960), and Claremont (1965). The international methodological discussion was taken further at the regional conferences in Turku (Finland) (1973) and Warsaw (1979).

During the first two decades of the IAHR, the centre of activities in the study of religion was found in Holland, Sweden and, to some extent, Italy. The first two congresses (Amsterdam 1950, Rome 1955) continued to reflect the historical and philological research interests of earlier generations. Thus, there was little explicit reference to methodological issues. There were also few eastern delegates present at the early congresses. The first congress outside Europe, and so far the only one held in the East, was organised in Tokyo (1958) and for several reasons it is of particular importance. It brought with it a greater awareness of the East-West components in the study of religion although the IAHR counted among its official eastern members only Japan and Israel at that time. However, from Tokyo onwards the IAHR developed into a more fully international body and the methodological debate soon came into its own. Whilst western scholars became painfully aware of their ignorance regarding the development of research in the East, a considerable gulf appeared between eastern and western interpretations of the essence and manifestation of religion (see Sharpe 1975: 271).

Werblowsky (1958), in his report on the Tokyo Congress (see *Numen* 5) writes: 'the emancipation of the study of religions from "religious studies" (whether theology or religious philosophies) is not yet fully recognised by many students of the subject. Particularly in the East this development . . . has not yet greatly progressed.' Werblowsky points out that this danger has been recognized by the IAHR through the conscious choice of 'history of religions' in its name. Even though the latter is meant to include many other disciplines, it indicates a resolve to adhere to strictly historical and scientific standards, whereas a broader designation might easily encourage less strict, unscientific criteria.

The Tokyo Congress also included an East-West Symposium, sponsored by UNESCO on 'Religion and Thought in the Orient and Occident: A Century of Cultural Exchange'. Its major subjects of discussion were: (1) the characteristics of oriental and occidental culture; (2) the influence of the West on the East; (3) the common concern: the problems of an emerging world civilization. At the conclusion of the

Tokyo Congress it was recommended that the IAHR should give greater emphasis to the study and research of eastern religions and their relations to the West. It should also stimulate scholarly and popular publications in the field of the history of religions since these will promote mutual understanding between East and West. For this purpose, a series of specific recommendations were submitted to UNESCO, pointing out the important cultural function of the scientific study of the history of religions in its different branches in fostering a better appreciation of eastern and western cultural values (for the full text see *Numen* 5, 1958: 238–40). Since the Tokyo Congress, the East-West relationship and participation are an indispensable aspect of the IAHR but the suggestions made then to hold a further East-West symposium and international congress in the East have so far not been realized (a congress planned to be held in India in 1963 unfortunately could not be organized for various reasons).

The next congress at Marburg, in 1960, was in many ways 'a watershed, for the simple reason that there methodological discussion established itself for the first time as an integral part of IAHR procedure' (Sharpe 1975: 277). It was realized that the different methodological positions do not divide neatly along East-West lines. In the West, too, the intuitive method found its supporters and there was a growing pressure on scholars to make a contribution to the reconstruction of cultural and religious life. Professor Bleeker (1960), the secretary general of the IAHR at that time, outlined what he considered to be 'The Future Task of the History of Religions.' Although international understanding may be a by-product of the scholar's work, it can never be his primary aim. Discussions revolved around the scientific and scholarly orientation of the study of religion and the term 'phenomenology of religion' appeared to be especially confusing to some. R.J. Zwi Werblowsky circulated a statement regarding 'the basic minimum presuppositions' of the scholarly studies aimed at by the IAHR which found support from many well-known scholars present at Marburg. It emphasized that there was no question of an 'East versus West' situation in terms of the criteria and standards brought to bear on the study of religion: 'The history of religions is a branch of the humanities, not of theology and still less of international politics; it is simply there, to be discussed as dispassionately as possible on the principle of truth for its own sake' (in Sharpe 1975: 278; see also the ardent plea made subsequently by Werblowsky (1960) to protect the IAHR from dilettantes, theologians and idealists).

However, the tension over different methods had by no means been resolved. It came even more to the fore at the Claremont Congress (1965), the first international congress held in North America. Sharpe thinks that at Claremont 'the ideal of disinterested, objective scholarship *for its own sake*, while not abandoned, had been relegated to a position of only relative importance' (Sharpe 1975: 284). This shift in the overall orientation was not unrelated to the different perspectives of study which had been developed by both Mircea Eliade and Wilfred Cantwell-Smith. The latter in particular shows a much greater openness to the 'religious approach' championed by several eastern scholars. In Brandon's assessment, made from the traditional perspective of historical scholarship nurtured by the academic traditions of Europe, there existed a tension between the European concern with the history of religions and the American disposition to concentrate on the existing situation. He termed the latter, quite wrongly, the 'sociological approach' in contrast to the critically historical one. Although he noted that the emphasis of the Claremont Congress was on 'the present and future significance of religion in human culture' (quoted in Sharpe 1975: 285), he thought it unlikely that the European tradition of scholarship would succumb to the new American approach which stressed a dialogical disposition.

In the years to come, European scholarship tended, on the whole, to be dominated by the purely historical approach. Thus, the understanding and practice of the history of religions in America and Europe seemed to drift apart. However, this tendency was to some extent overcome through developments at the Stockholm Congress (1970) which 'marked both an end and a beginning. What had ended was perhaps the period in which scholars had locked themselves into a rigid methodological "either-or" and had failed to recognise the essentially complementary character of alternative approaches. What had begun we cannot yet know: we can only hope, and work' (in Sharpe 1975: 290f.; see also the address given by C.J. Bleeker (1975b) at Stockholm on 'Looking Backward and Forward').

The methodological discussion has fully come into its own during the seventies, as is evident from the many specialised publications in this field as well as the numerous journal articles devoted to discussing alternative approaches to the study of religion. The IAHR Congress at Lancaster (1975) included a separate section on methodology (chaired by Professor N. Smart). The Winnipeg Congress, in 1980, the second international congress to be held in North America, also comprised among its twenty different sections one on 'methodology and hermeneutics' (chaired by Professor W.G. Oxtoby).

The need to clarify methodological questions was recognised by holding a regional study conference entirely devoted to the 'Methodology of the Science of Religion' at Turku in Finland (1973). While the initiative came from the IAHR, the main responsibility for organising the conference was undertaken by the Finnish Society for the Study of Comparative Religion (founded in 1963, with its annual publication of *Temenos*) which enlisted the support of UNESCO and other organisations. In the words of the organisers, the aim was 'to review central problems within the methodology of the science of religion, and to attempt by means of active discussion to evelute the strength of old and new methodological trends, and their directions of development' (*Temenos* 8, 1972: 5). The need for such a conference was more explicitly discussed in *Numen* 19 (1972: 241):

The methodology of the science of religion was unanimously regarded as a timely and relevant theme. Recent developments in the field have been characterized by acute criticisms of traditional approaches and the impact of increasing inter-disciplinary exchange. Certain new modes of thought have revealed new vistas for comparative religion. The classic topics of debate have become somewhat uninspiring for the younger generation of scholars. Looking around they have noticed the increase of empirical field-work, the trend towards operationalization of scientific terms and the possibilities of confronting problems at various levels of abstraction. Regardless of one's theoretical allegiance there certainly exists a need for a more general evaluation of the present methodological situation. . . .

The conference explored different methodological approaches under three main themes: (1) oral and written documentation of religious tradition; (2) the future of the phenomenology of religion; (3) religion as expressive culture (for a report see *Temenos* 9, 1973: 15–24; the papers and discussions of this important conference are now available in print (Honko 1979)).

The second methodological conference of the IAHR was held in Warsaw in 1979, at the joint invitation of the Polish Society for the Science of Religions (founded in 1958 and affiliated to the IAHR in 1970 with its own journal *Euhemer*—The Science of Religions Review, published since 1957) and the Institute for Philosophy and Sociology of the Polish Academy of Sciences. Papers and discussions were again grouped around three themes: (1) methodological problems in the history of religions; (2) religions in the process of social development; (3) religion in relation to secular culture. So far, no published proceedings are available yet but, to judge by the opinions of participants, no new perspectives seem to have emerged. Although participation was lower than at Turku (39 as compared to 49 participants), the special importance of this conference lies in the fact that it represents the first official gathering of history of religions scholars in a socialist country.

At the Rome Congress (1955) twelve different member groups were listed (including already the 'Japanese Association for the Science of Religion'). At present, the IAHR consists of about 20 member associations based on individual countries. These include one association in Africa (Nigeria), one in Latin America (Mexico) and three in Asia (Japan, India, and Israel). In addition to the national member groups, international scholarly organisations have become affiliated to the IAHR as, for example, the International Old Testament Society, the International Association for Buddhist Studies, and the Society for Mithraic Studies. Nationally based associations for the study of religion become officially affiliated at international congresses. Several national associations have been formed in recent years, such as the New Zealand Association for the Study of Religions (1979), the Swiss Association for the Study of Religion (1978), and The Australian Association for the Study of Religions (founded in 1976 with its first national congress held in Adelaide; see V.C. Hayes (1977)). There are a number of other countries where the study of religion at university level is growing but where no national associations have been formed so far. Departments of religious studies can be found, among others, at universities and colleges in South Africa, Sri Lanka, and Thailand (especially at Mahidol University, Bangkok). Among the delegates of the Winnipeg Congress (1980) there were, for the first time, several participants from the People's Republic of China. The Australian, Belgian, Nigerian, and Swiss associations were newly affiliated to the IAHR and it was decided to hold the next IAHR Congress in 1985 in Sydney (see R.J.Z. Werblowsky's report on the Winnipeg Congress in *Numen* 27, 1980: 292–4).

Besides the information on the study of religion in different countries contained in the 1975 survey of *Religion*, the founding of national associations and their development can be followed through regular reports in *Numen*. The most obvious source for further information about particular developments are the journals published by national associations; see, for example, L. Honko's 'The Finnish Society for the Study of Comparative Religion in 1963–1973' in *Temenos* 9, 1973: 5–14. The development of the Canadian Society for the Study of Religion, (founded in 1965 and affiliated to the IAHR in 1970), is described by E. Combs in 'Learned and learning: CSSR/SCER, 1965–1975' and published in *Sciences Religieuses/Studies in Religion* 6, 1976–77: 357–63, the new journal launched by Canadian scholars in 1971. The recent developments of the British Association for the History of Religions (founded in 1954 and affiliated in 1955), can best be followed in its quarterly Bulletin, unfortunately only available in cyclostyled form. The activities of the Polish Society for the Science of Religions (founded in Warsaw in 1957 and affiliated to the IAHR in 1970), are briefly described by W. Tyloch in *Euhemer* 3 (113), 1979: 3–8. For a detailed study of the historical development of Polish studies on religion, see P.O. Szolc (Scholz) 'Religionswissenschaft in Polen' (1971: 45–80); A. Kee, 'The Study of Religion in Poland' (1980: 61–7); and M. Pomian-Srzednicki, *The Politics and Sociology of Secularization in Poland*, (1982). A great deal more could have been written about the development of national associations but I shall now proceed to a discussion of some major publica-

tions which illustrate the complex threads of the contemporary debate
regarding the study of religion.

2.3 Recent reference works and handbooks

Over recent years, a number of important handbooks and reference
works have been produced in both the history and phenomenology of
religion. In looking at some representative titles one may ask whether
the authors are at all method-conscious in the presentation of their data
and if so, what methods they advocate for the study of religion. If, on the
contrary, they remain methodologically inarticulate and unaware, what
methods do they implicitly practise?

It has been maintained that, due to the different orientations of the
subject, a comprehensive work on the history of religions, by its very
nature, requires several authors whereas a book on the phenomenology
of religion must be written by one author in order to bring across a
unitary conception of the phenomena under review. If one surveys the
publications since 1950, it is apparent that a greater number of books has
been devoted to the historical study of the major religions, both ancient
and modern, than to specialised works in the phenomenology of religion. Excellent reference works in the history of religions exist in
several European languages, especially German, French and English,
not to forget Dutch, Scandinavian, Italian, and Russian publications.
The West European works in this field have been critically analysed by
Kurt Rudolph (1973; 1979) and I shall only selectively refer to the most
important books.

Since the sixties, several new handbooks have been produced which
have gained high praise from critics, notably the German series *Die
Religionen der Menschheit* (1961–, edited by C.M. Schröder), the French
publication *Histoire des Religions* (1970–6, edited by H. Puech), and the
two volumes edited by C.J. Bleeker and G. Widengren, *Historia
Religionum. Handbook for the History of Religions* (1969–71). Each is different in conception and structure and each serves a different purpose.
Ideally, the handbooks in the three languages should be consulted
together as they complement each other and, if read critically, they

provide a good opportunity for a fruitful cross-fertilization of ideas. Published closely together in time, they will remain standard reference works for years to come.

Die Religionen der Menschheit (RM) is an ambitious and monumental project. Originally planned to have thirty-seven volumes, it will probably now have forty-two of which twenty-two had been published in Germany by 1979, with additional translations into French and English. Each title is the work of one or several specialists in the history of religions and the series represents without doubt the best collection of handbooks dealing with the history of particular religions giving an overall view of their development. It comes rather as a surprise, however, to discover that the books do not include any discussion of the purpose and plan of the series nor do they consider methodological issues. The historical approach used in the series is nowhere discussed nor is there a general preface introducing the entire series. Without introduction or explanation the series begins with a first volume on phenomenology by Friedrich Heiler (1961); one of the last volumes planned is a *Geschichte der Religionswissenschaft*. As this work is still outstanding, it is uncertain whether this history will be confined to strictly historical-descriptive data or include an analysis of different methodological approaches underlying the practice of *Religionswissenschaft*. If one views the series as a whole, there is no attempt at integration and an impression of particularity, if not to say fragmentation, cannot be avoided. No general framework has been provided, no systematic or comparative questions have been asked, no methodological issues have been raised, even though the project is not without its own classificatory schema.

The French series *Histoire des religions* is also a collective, but nevertheless much briefer work comprising three volumes which have been judged the best single reference work in the history of religions available at present. Here, the treatment of particular religions is also classified according to historical and geographical criteria but, in contrast to the German series, this work begins with a thorough methodological discussion by Angelo Brelich (1970: 3–59) dealing with the presuppositions and problems of the history of religions. Considered to be one of the best introductions to the entire field, its arguments will be examined later. The series concludes with an article on the history of the history of religions as a discipline (III, 1279–1328). As this covers only an outline of the major developments and remains rather brief, the forthcoming volume of *RM* on this subject will certainly fill a need (for a recent review of *Histoire des Religions* and other publications, see R.J.Z. Werblowsky (1979: 250–5)).

The individual contributions to *Histoire des Religions* remain unconnected, however, in spite of the excellent introduction. Each article stands on its own so that the reader is still confronted with 'unconnected monographs', a difficulty which the editors of the English series, *Historia Religionum*, sought to overcome by inviting all contributors to follow the same basic outline in presenting their subject. Each author was asked to submit a 'short description of the essence of religion', 'historical development', 'conception of the deity', 'worship (cult, ethics, myth or doctrine)', 'conception of man (creation, nature, destiny: path of salvation, personal and general eschatology)', 'religions of the past: subsequent influence; religions of the present: present religious situation', 'short history of the study of the religion', 'selected bibliography' (Preface, I: VII). This scheme, with suitable adaptations where necessary, is first applied to the religions of the past (vol. I), and then to the religions of the present (vol. II). As is evident from the outline, historical and phenomenological approaches are here interwoven with the aim to present 'an organic unity' in marked contrast to other handbooks of the history of religions where one 'never gets a survey of the history of religions presented as a unity and thus revealing not only the individual peculiarities of the religions of the world, but also, and more particularly, the similarities in their structure, the formal parallels in their development and their most hidden interrelation and interdependence.' The two editors, Bleeker and Widengren, present their handbook as 'a description of the religions of the world in such a manner that their ideological parallelism is made manifest' and they hope that their new venture 'will stimulate further the systematic study of the history of religions' (I: VII, and VIII). The conception of the editors, only briefly stated in the succinct preface, is fully expressed in Bleeker's 'Epilegomena' (II: 642–51) from which a particular phenomenological stance becomes fully apparent.

Not all contributors were able to conform to the original outline with the same satisfactory results. The shortcomings of the handbook have been pointed out by several critics (see Rudolph 1973a; Waardenburg 1975a; Penner 1976). Although it may be too strong a criticism to say that *Historia Religionum* 'is not a history in the proper sense of the word' (Waardenburg 1975a: 28), its presentation certainly raises the question of how far the framework, developed for comparative purposes, is such a straightjacket as to distort historical data. If the editors wanted a survey of the history of religions which would at the same time present the unity of religion and reveal its structure, this goal has not been achieved. In the opinion of one reviewer, it is not only the contributors who do not agree on this issue, but not even the editors express clearly what constitutes the essence and structure of religion.

Other recently published handbooks in the history of religions are either revised editions or reprints of earlier works. This is true of the well reviewed and detailed Italian series *Storia delle religioni* by P. Tacchi Venturi (originally published in 2 vols., 1934), now available in revised form in five volumes (edited by G. Castellani, Turin 1970 f.), but perhaps hard to find outside its country of origin. Its substantial introduction on 'La storia delle religioni' by Ugo Bianchi (I: 1–171) discusses at length the object, method and problems of the history of religions up to the present day. A fuller account of the contents of the five volumes is found in Rudolph 1973a: 411–2. Bianchi's introduction is now available in English translation as *The History of Religions* (1975)—see especially Part I 'Object and Methodology of the History of Religions' which also contains a brief section on 'The organization of studies concerning the history of religions,' and Part IV 'Modern Problems of Methodology and Interpretation' which, among others, includes a discussion of Otto, Pettazzoni, and Eliade, and of 'The "history of religions" and "comparative religion" in the USA'.

The German translation of the Scandinavian work by J.P. Asmussen and J. Laessoe, *Handbuch der Religionsgeschichte* (translated and edited by C. Colpe, 1971–2), although published recently, contains primarily older material. It is based on a revised work by J. Pedersen (1948) which in turn relied on a much earlier study by E. Lehmann (1924). The German editor has followed the arrangement of the original Danish edition (Copenhagen 1968). Much of the material seems old-fashioned which, given its age, is perhaps not surprising. There is little systematic reflection on the ordering of the material; in fact, much emphasis is laid on earlier ethnographic and archaeological evidence. The distribution of the articles leaves the reader with the impression that the history of religions, far from being an international discipline working within a global perspective, is a western branch of scholarship heavily over-shadowed by its own history, steeped in a fascination with the origins of western civilization, the ancient Near East, and a traditional classicist and orientalist interest of a particular kind (compare 66 pp. on Sumerian religion, 56 pp. on gnosticism and mystery religions, 28 pages on Mandeism with 49 pp. on the whole of Hinduism and a mere 21 pp. on Tibetan 'lamaism'!). The most valuable addition is the new section, supplied by the German editor, on 'Synkretismus, Renaissance, Säkula-risation and Neubildung von Religionen in der Gegenwart' (vol. 3).

In marked contrast to *Historia Religionum*, the three volumes of *Handbuch der Religionsgeschichte* lack a unitary conception. Instead of an overall framework they present a 'mixture of geographical, cultural-historical and chronological points of view' (Rudolph 1973a: 411). Other reviewers have been more outspoken. Reacting to both the content and mode of presentation, N.Q. King has written that much of the handbook

is the work of European brahmins pontificating about the religion of other people. There is too little use of books by Indians and other Asians who can speak of their religion from inside. The texts and artefacts are not allowed to speak for themselves. There is little hint that the writers are aware of the modern academic ferment in this subject outside Europe and America .... In most of the articles there is a tendency to treat History of Religion as a strictly scientific, objective, cut-and-dried self-contained discipline and to neglect the interweaving of attention to music, art, devotion, ritual, hagiography and first-hand impression with the sequence of major historical happenings (*Scottish Journal of Theology* 26, 1973: 378).

King's criticism might be applied to other publications. Only highly motivated students will find the necessary determination and patience to plough through the dull and arid pages of certain books in the history of religions. By and large it is true to say that the field is not noted for an original and imaginative presentation of its materials. Here, too, the issue of methodology is paramount. To advance the subject beyond the narrow circles of erudite *literati* it will be necessary to develop a greater self-critical awareness, promote theoretical reflections and work on a refinement of methods adequate to the study of religions.

It may not be out of place here to refer to a recent British publication addressed to mature students. In 1977, the Open University produced a variety of study materials for programmed learning. Integrated with a network of radio and television programmes, especially made for the course, the fourteen textbooks produced by a team of scholars introduce the student to the historical development of the major religions of the past and present as well as to some central theoretical perspectives. As with *Historia Religionum*, the contributors were given a particular outline beforehand which was to be used in the presentation of their material. But here the chosen framework was expressed in the form of three questions relating to the human religious search asking 'from what? by what? and to what?'. It is interesting to see that again not every one of the twenty or so contributors was willing to conform to the imposition of such a structure. The books have called for scholarly criticism pointing out the 'quasi-religious' character of these questions which in certain cases can lead to a distortion of historical data (see 'Man's Religious Quest. A review of Open University materials,' *Religion* 9, 1979: 116–39). Yet in spite of certain obvious shortcomings, this course on the history of religions in the wider sense represents a highly original venture. Through the efforts of teamwork, the results of the study of religions over the last hundred years are made available to a large public far beyond the traditional limits of the university world. The potential consequences of such a step of introducing historical and systematic thinking about the religious traditions of mankind within a comparative and scholarly context to society at large cannot be fully assessed at present but should not be underestimated. It is important to know that the methodological reflections include, among others, materials drawn from the phenomenology and sociology of religion. The textbooks also comprise a short history of the study of religion and introduce some of the major issues of the current scholarly debate, although admittedly rather brief and incomplete (see especially the book units 1–3 *Seekers and Scholars*, and units 31–32 *Quest and Questioning*, Milton Keynes 1977).

Besides the handbooks comprising several volumes, shorter one-volume works are also available as introductions to the history of religions. *Religions of Mankind. Today and Yesterday* (edited by H. Ringgren and A.V. Ström, 1967) claims to summarize modern research and emphasises that religions are expressions of faith and life rather than mere objects for curiosity and study. However, careful examination reveals again that this is a rearranged text of an earlier Swedish work (3rd ed., 1964). Besides the systematic discussion of religious phenomena in the introduction, the main sections follow a primarily ethnological, historical, or geographical orientation with no overall conclusion.

By contrast, T.O. Ling's *History of Religion East and West* (1968), widely used as a textbook for students, implies a thematic approach and unitary conception throughout. Each chapter treats individual religious traditions in a parallel manner. This helps to outline major developments and allows for comparisons but it leads to a certain amount of discontinuity within the religious traditions themselves. Also curious is the use of the singular 'History of Religion' in the title which may create the idea of a false unity imposed from without on the diversity of the data. Although someone might produce a more definitive work in the future, there are at present few books available in the history of religions which make as stimulating reading as this one. Such an introduction can motivate many a student to take the challenge of the subject seriously by proceeding to more demanding and specialised works.

The German work by E. Dammann *Grundriss der Religionsgeschichte* (1972, 2nd ed. 1978) has mainly been written for theology students. It is characterized by a distinct emphasis on living religions and new religious movements of today. By contrast, S.A. Tokarev's *Die Religion in der Geschichte der Völker* (1968) is based on Marxist philosophy, underlining the evolutionary development of religion in history. The book is a translation of an earlier work by one of the leading Soviet historians of religion, now available in a new two-volume edition in Russian *Religiya v istorii narodov mira* (Moscow 1976). Another Russian work on the history of religions is by I.A. Kryvelev, *Istoriya religii* (1975).

These examples of currently available surveys must suffice to give an idea of the growth of publications in different languages over recent years (for more detailed bibliographical information consult the *International Bibliography of the History of Religions*; see also the excellent survey of works published since 1968 by Waardenburg (1975a) and the review article by Rudolph (1979); a survey of Italian publications is found in Culianu (1981) who mentions no less than 101 books in the history of religions published in Italy since 1975).

There can be no doubt that more and more historical materials relating to the study of religion have become accessible to a greater number of readers. The results of specialised research have been incorporated into widely available handbooks and surveys, especially if one thinks of large reference works such as *Religion in Geschichte und Gegenwart* (7 vols., Tübingen 1957–65), not to mention many still very valuable older publications and the newly established journals in the history of religions. It has been noted, however, that there is a marked current trend away from purely historical-descriptive works towards a more systematic treatment of religious data, involving a greater acknowledgment of the need for methodological and theoretical reflections. Waardenburg's survey (1975a) expresses this by distinguishing recent works in the 'history of religions in the proper sense' from those publications which deal with 'the study of religion in a wider sense' or with 'method and theory in the study of religion,' and it is only to the two latter categories that he assigns the term *Religionswissenschaft*. Ninian Smart in his book, *The Phenomenon of Religion* (1973a), proposes a different distinction of studies, namely: (1) histories of religions; (2) historical-dialectical studies (with (1) and (2) further subdivided into holistic, divisional, aspectual, and itemized histories); (3) phenomenological and structural studies (with further subdivisions); (4) dialectical-phenomenological studies (where sociology, anthropology, psychology and philosophy of religion are included; see Smart 1973a: 45–8).

Works in the phenomenology of religion are an integral part of the systematic reflection of *Religionswissenschaft*. However, there is a greater tendency on the whole to incorporate certain phenomenological perspectives rather than to produce specific works wholly devoted to the phenomenology of religion. Yet several such works have appeared in recent years. The most substantial and widely acclaimed is G. Widengren's revised *Religionsphänomenologie* (1969), based on earlier

Swedish editions (1945, 1953). This is all the more surprising if one considers that Widengren has been called 'one of the most powerful advocates of the "purely historical" approach to the study of religion' (Sharpe 1975: 243). It appears that for Widengren the phenomenology of religion is the systematic counterpart of the history of religions; the synthesis of the former is based on the historical analysis of the latter so that no phenomenologist can ever work without the historical method. Some scholars are of the opinion that this publication combines in an ideal manner the philological-historical method with a systematic presentation of the data. In fact, Bleeker ranks the work so highly that he thinks no one in his generation possesses either the imagination or the energy to create something new after Widengren's *Religionsphänomenologie*—the book represents a milestone in the history of the discipline (C.J. Bleeker 1971c). This appreciation is shared by Rudolph (1971a) who considers the work a pioneering attempt to reclaim the name of phenomenology for the integration of historical researches and systematic reflections within a truly comparative framework of *Religionswissenschaft*.

One of the most recent, but much more modest, publications in the phenomenology of religion is Günter Lanczkowski's *Einführung in die Religionsphänomenologie* (1978a). Primarily written for students, it includes a discussion of many earlier reference works and provides a succinct and helpful survey of the field. Unfortunately, the author seems to be little aware of the complexities of recent methodological discussions at the international level. No attempt is made at a comprehensive presentation of phenomenology; one is left with the impression that the work depends far too much on earlier German publications without taking into account recent works in the English language.

Friedrich Heiler's *Erscheinungsformen und Wesen der Religion* (1961) is a copiously documented work, based on an earlier German publication (1949). Its introduction discusses the concept of religion, presents a brief history of the systematic study of religion and develops a model of the phenomenological method which has been strongly criticized for its theological presuppositions (Sharpe 1975: 244 f.). In Heiler's analysis of religious phenomena historical and phenomenological approaches are closely intertwined. He is also one of the few who considers the personal attitude of the researcher as an important factor in the selection and presentation of data. However, his stance is too narrowly normative here, influenced by a particular understanding of faith which uses the phenomenological method as a substitute proof for the existence of God and is too dependent on Otto's idea of the Holy. Kurt Rudolph describes Heiler's work as 'eine theologische Religionswissenschaft und eine religionsgeschichtliche Theologie' whilst admitting that the volume provides a mine of information about historical data (see his 'Die Problematik der Religionswissenschaft als akademisches Lehrfach' 1967). Meanwhile, C.J. Bleeker judged Heiler's book as 'ein sehr verdienstliches Werk ... in dem aber die neueren Ansichten über die Methode und Struktur der Phänomenologie nicht verarbeitet sind' (*Numen* 14, 1967: 162).

The phenomenological work of another German scholar has now become widely available, particularly in India, through its recent translation into English. Gustav Mensching's *Structures and Patterns of Religion* (translated by H.F. Klimkeit and V. Srinivasa Sarma, 1976) presents a general typology of religions and of particular religious phenomena. Its systematic framework is provided by a specific approach to 'comparing and understanding' and 'the unity of religions.' Far fewer historical data are cited in support of the main arguments than is the case in Heiler's work. The overall perspective of the book reflects many of the earlier concerns of Otto and van der Leeuw and much of the secondary literature is out of date.

Much more theoretically aware in the discussion of method and the analysis of comparative historical data is the handbook *Phenomenology of Religion* (1973) by Mariasusai Dhavamony. It stresses the empirical character of 'historical phenomenology,' understood as the combined use of the historical and phenomenological method. The author considers the elucidation of the essence of religious phenomena as the legitimate aim of phenomenology, to be achieved on strictly empirical and not on philosophical or theological grounds (1973: 3–27). This approach is then illustrated by a comparative discussion of wide-ranging religious phenomena, concluding with a part on the 'scope of religion and salvation.' To some, the orientation of the book may still appear to be too dependent on theological perspectives but on the whole the main themes of the study of religion are introduced in a systematic and critical manner. Written for students and the general reader, this work deserves to be more widely known, for its clarity of structure and style provide a helpful introduction to the contemporary study of religion. It also includes a more up-to-date bibliography than some better known works in this field.

Earlier works in the period under discussion include W. Brede Kristensen's *The Meaning of Religion* (translated by J.B. Carman, 1960), representing post-humously published lectures given before 1953 (for a discussion of Kristensen's work see Sharpe 1975: 227–9; other Scandinavian and German publications on phenomenology are also considered in pp. 242–6). Two well established and still widely used earlier works which present a systematic classification of religious phenomena, each set in a very different framework, are Joachim Wach's *The Comparative Study of Religions* (1958)—see the critical review by R.J.Z. Werblowsky (1959)—and Mircea Eliade's *Patterns in Comparative Religion* (1958). The latter is a translation of Eliade's earlier French work *Traité d'Histoire des Religions* (1949) with a different introduction. The thematic presentation of certain religious phenomena, largely drawn from archaic and exotic thought-forms and compared at the level of symbolism with little reference to their wider historical and social context, is here considered as 'history of religions,' as the original title of the work clearly states. The work is even described as a 'science of religions' (see preface to the French edition) although Eliade's methodological stance is very different from what this term has come to mean in more recent debates.

If one compares the titles of recent publications, it is evident that fewer handbooks have been produced in phenomenology than in the history of religions. Perhaps more books and articles exist discussing the phenomenological method from a theoretical point of view than fully developed phenomenologies where this method has been consistently applied. In general it is true to say that the historical handbooks contain too little methodological self-reflection whereas phenomenological works, due to their systematic orientation, usually include a discussion regarding the specific objects and methods of studying religious phenomena. This often implies the consideration of how far it is legitimate to separate the phenomenological from the historical perspective or vice versa. But most phenomenologies are not rigorous enough in the examination of their underlying assumptions and remain bound by a preconceived framework.

Over recent years, the absence of a common body of theory in the contemporary study of religion has been repeatedly pointed out and new avenues to remedy this situation have been explored. Given the use of very different and even disparate methods in the study of religion, the subject of methodology has come into its own, implying the examination of existing methods and the development of new ones, producing a whole body of metatheory for *Religionswissenschaft*. I shall list some of the most important books published over the last decade or so, giving an idea of the wide range of questions raised in the study and interpretation of religion today. However, the substantive issues discussed in these works will only be examined in the next section on the methodological debate.

The best orientation about current theoretical developments can be gained by studying the works which continue to appear in the series *Religion and Reason* (RR), begun in 1971 and explicitly devoted to 'method and theory in the study and interpretation of religion' (edited by J. Waardenburg). The series comprises almost thirty titles so far, including the recently published papers of the IAHR methodology conference held in 1973 at Turku in Finland (*Science of Religion. Studies in Methodology*, 1979). Another recent title is J. Waardenburg's *Reflections on the Study of Religion* (1978a), bringing together many of his earlier papers which reconsider the nature of the phenomenology of religion and its relationship to the history of religions. The work provides a valuable description, assessment, and critique of the so-called 'classical phenomenology of religion' and pleads for phenomenological research in a new style. Other titles of particular interest to the methodological debate are G. Schmid's *Principles of Integral Science of Religion* (1979) and D. Allen's *Structure and Creativity in Religion. Hermeneutics in Mircea Eliade's Phenomenology and New Directions* (1978); J.E. Barnhardt, *The Study of Religion and Its Meaning. New Explorations in Light of Karl Popper and Emile Durkheim* (1977); T.P. van Baaren and H.J.W Drijvers, editors, *Religion, Culture and Methodology*. Papers of the Groningen Working-group for the Study of Fundamental Problems and Methods of Science of Religion (1973); M. Pye and R. Morgan, editors, *The Cardinal Meaning*, Essays in Comparative Hermeneutics (1973) and R.D. Baird, *Category Formation and the History of Religions* (1971). For a critical review of the early volumes of *RR* see Rudolph (1979).

Questions of methodology were also at the centre of an earlier study conference organised by the Italian section of the IAHR on 'Problems and Methods of the History of Religions, 1959–69,' held in Rome. The conference proceedings were published as a Supplement to *Numen*, edited by U. Bianchi, C.J. Bleeker, A. Bausani as *Problems and Methods of the History of Religions* (1972) (see the review by N.G. Holm (1972)). Several important papers deal with the place of phenomenology and the problem of definition in religion.

In reviewing a work by Mensching, H. Biezais has said that it may be difficult to speak of a German *Religionswissenschaft* truly independent from theology (*Temenos* 8, 1972: 160 f.). This may be true of the older generation (Biezais refers to the last forty years), but there can be little doubt that there are many signs indicating a search for greater methodological clarification and a striving for the independence of the discipline. Wide-ranging methodological concerns are reflected in several collective works. The conference proceedings of the *Deutsche Vereinigung for Religionsgeschichte* (the German section of the IAHR) are entitled *Der Religionswandel unserer Zeit im Spiegel der Religionswissenschaft* and are edited by G. Stephenson (1976). The last section of this volume is explicitly devoted to *methodologische Versuche*. The volume of articles on *Selbstverständnis und Wesen der Religionswissenschaft* edited by G. Lanczkowski (1974) is a useful compilation of material found in different journals and includes German translations of methodological discussions previously published in *Numen* and IAHR (conference proceedings). Another collective work on *Theologie und Religionswissenschaft*, edited by U. Mann (1973), is more oriented towards theology as the title indicates. A more specialised survey of methodology is found in the article by C.H. Ratschow, 'Methodik der Religionswissenschaft' in *Enzyklopädie der geisteswissenschaftlichen Arbeitsmethoden* (1973: 347–400). However, it only lists publications up to 1966 and has met with detailed criticisms regarding its presuppositions (see Stephenson 1975: 201–8).

Important questions as to the way in which the study of religion may be considered scientific are raised in N. Smart's book, *The Science of Religion and the Sociology of Knowledge. Some Methodological Questions* (1973b). Another work which analyses in great detail the objects and methods of the science of religion is the study by M. Meslin, *Pour une science des religions* (1973). It is characterized by a humanistic emphasis and includes a history of the study of religion as well as an analysis of contemporary approaches to the phenomenon of religion. By contrast, the collective work, *Introduction aus sciences humaines des religions* (edited by H. Desroche and J. Séguy, 1970) possesses a stronger orientation towards the social sciences. It provides informative surveys on different methods in the study of religion and the section on phenomenology is considered to be a basic contribution to this field (see Isambert 1975: 217–40).

Few books on methodology will have gone through as many editions as the essays edited by Mircea Eliade and Joseph Kitagawa, *The History of Religions, Essays in Methodology* (1959–1973). This collective work must not be confused with the subsequent publication, also edited by Joseph Kitagawa together with M. Eliade and C. Long, *The History of Religions, Essays on the Problem of Understanding* (1967). Besides older material (i.e., J. Wach's 'The Meaning and Task of the History of Religions,' originally written in 1935), the latter includes several articles attempting a particular hermeneutics of comparative religious data. This hermeneutical concern is at the centre of Eliade's own work, best represented in his collection of articles, *The Quest. History and Meaning in Religion* (1969). These three volumes have exercised considerable influence by stimulating much argument and critical debate and they continue to be often cited. However, they primarily belong to the middle of the period under review here, namely the 1960s, representing a fluid, transitional stage towards the growth of greater methodological awareness and critical theory which have come into their own since the 1970s. The best summary statement in article form about current methodological concerns is J. Waardenburg's 'Religionswissenschaft New Style. Some Thoughts and Afterthoughts' (see especially part IV, 'Methodological and Theoretical Issues' (1978b: 189–220)). It outlines the major developments since the 1960s and emphasizes the growing need for fundamental research with regard to problems of method and theory.

Another very helpful survey which takes the reader up to the early 1970s is R. Pummer's 'Recent Publications on the Methodology of the Science of Religion' (1975). Here the publications are grouped under specific themes such as the problem of defining religion, the category of understanding, the meaning of explanation in the science of religion, the role of comparison, and the multimethodic nature of the study of religion, all of which are discussed in considerable detail. A recent, more descriptive literature survey is G. Lanczkowski's 'Literaturbericht zur Religionswissenschaft' (1978b: 285–320) which is unfortunately not up-to-date, however.

The most recent publications indicate very clearly that the study of religion, as currently conceived, is undergoing a great deal of change involving much critical self-examination and a search for clearer self-definition. As with all change, this implies both continuity and discontinuity with what went on beforehand and may well lead to a 'new style' *Religionswissenschaft*. In Waardenburg's opinion such a 'new style' study of religion rests 'not only on the discovery of new facts previously unknown, but also on a further refinement of the way in which facts can be ascertained and interpreted. Investigations of method and theory are highly relevant for the assumptions and the existence of the study of religion itself as a distinct field of scholarly research' (1978b: 189).

New surveys and handbooks in the history and phenomenology of
religion continue to appear. One can note a marked increase in publications primarily devoted to discussing theoretical questions and I shall
now analyse in some detail the major issues prominent in the methodological debates of the last thirty years.

3. The methodological debate since world war II

The contemporary methodological debate possesses an important
historical dimension often unduly neglected. The ongoing discussions
about the most appropriate methods for the study of religion often relate
to earlier work in this field or continue to rely on unexamined assumptions of previous generations. The majority of present-day scholars
would probably concede the multi- or poly-methodic nature of the study
of religion and the potential vastness of its objects in both time and
space. Such a general statement can easily be agreed upon but it does not
solve specific difficulties when it comes to detailed methods and procedures. At present, the methodological debate consists of numerous
interwoven themes and overlapping areas, often difficult to disentangle.
However, some dominant themes can definitely be noted although there
is no orderly progression of argument nor a general consensus about
methods which has emerged since the end of World War II.

For analytical purposes, four major issues may be distinguished in the
current methodological debate, namely: (1) the debate about the history
of religions; (2) the debate about the phenomenology of religion; (3) the
debate about hermeneutics; (4) the debate about the science of religion.
These four themes have been singled out for their dominance in recent
discussions, the volume of which has greatly increased since the early

1970s. These topics constitute neither four distinct and completely separate enquiries nor must they be viewed as following each other in chronological succession. On the contrary, they are best considered as four interrelated areas of the ongoing methodological debate about the study of religion today. Although specific arguments pertaining to these four themes are often interwoven in practice, they are here distinguished and treated under separate headings so as to gain clarification about the characteristic thrust of each. I shall now look at each area in turn by examining some representative arguments and contributions produced over recent years.

3.1 The debate about the history of religions

The term 'history of religions' is still widely used today to describe a wide range of non-theological approaches to the study of religion. But there has been much debate as to the precise meaning of 'history' in this context. Is it simply intended to be a mere fact-finding exercise, solely concerned with the analysis of descriptive data, the study of original sources, particularly ancient religious texts requiring philological expertise or does it, on the contrary, require a wider theoretical framework which makes use of comparative data and systematic classifications, leading to typologies and generalisations?

Both positions are held and in terms of the actual works of scholarship produced, as distinct from methodological reflections about them, Waardenburg (1975a) has conveniently divided the field into 'history of religions in the proper sense' (dealing with 'general studies', 'religions of the past', 'religions existing at present' and 'comparative studies') and 'the study of religion in a wider sense' which he equates with *Religionswissenschaft*, a term also applied to works on 'method and theory in the study of religion.' Several other scholars have little room for the history of religions in the narrow sense; they simply equate the term with its wider meaning and understand it as the direct equivalent of *allgemeine Religionswissenschaft* (Goodenough 1959, Kitagawa 1968, Streng 1968, Baird 1971). This immediately raises questions about other systematic approaches to the study of religion, particularly about phenomenology.

Mircea Eliade has characterized this tension among the students of *Religionswissenschaft* as follows:

The different historical and historicist schools have reacted strongly against the phenomenologists' claim that they can grasp the *essence* and the *structure* of religious phenomena. For the historicists, religion is exclusively a historical fact without any transhistorical meaning or value, and to seek for 'essences' is tantamount to falling back into the old Platonic error. (The historicists have, of course, neglected Husserl). This tension between phenomenologists and historicists corresponds in some measure to the irreducibility of two different philosophical temperaments. For this reason, it is difficult to suppose that one day the tension will completely disappear. Besides, the tension is creative; by virtue of this tension *Religionswissenschaft* escapes dogmatism and stagnation. ('The History of Religions in Retrospect: 1912–1962', *The Journal of Bible and Religion* 31, 1963: 98–109; a revised version is found in *The Quest*, chp. 2).

One of the most lucid and conceptually clear statements about the object and methods of the history of religions in a strict sense is found in Angelo Brelich's 'Prolégomènes à une Histoire des Religions' (in Puech vol. I, 1970: 1–59); in Puech's opinion this comes close to a '*storicismo assoluto*' (*ibid.:* XIX). Brelich does what few authors do, namely, he presents a conceptual elucidation of both terms of the conjunction 'history of religions.'

By first asking 'What is religion'?, he highlights some inherent difficulties in the cross-cultural use of this historically and culturally conditioned concept. For him, a historian can neither accept the objective existence of the sacred as pre-given nor postulate a religious dimension as innate to man, as is usually done in the phenomenology of religion. The permanent dilemma of historical enquiries consists in the fact that history does not know 'religion' in the singular but knows only a plurality of religions, and yet it requires a unitary concept of 'religion' to look at religions in the plural. One may also point out that the modern study of religion is in addition based on unitary concepts of 'history' and 'humankind' without which a universal 'history of religions' within a global framework could hardly be conceived.

Brelich rightly emphasizes, however, that our unitary concept 're-ligion' is a societal and cultural one, having been defined at a special epoch and in a specific milieu. Thus, 'religion' has no eternal meaning but is a historic product of our own culture, subject to changes throughout history. Although it is true to say that all historically known civilizations include certain manifestations which may be termed 'religious,' only post-classical western languages possess a separate word for 'religion.' Our concept 'religion' applies to a whole set of phenomena which separate 'religious' from other cultural manifestations. Other civilizations do not have this separating concept. If insufficient attention is paid to these contextual differences, similarities may be seen in phenomena which strictly speaking are not comparable. Many false generalizations in works on the history of religions are due to this lack of conceptual differentiation (this point has been more fully developed by W. Cohn (1969)).

In terms of procedure Brelich pleads for an initially empirical investigation of what is included under the term 'religion,' followed by a critical sifting of the data in order to obtain a functional definition of religion which can serve further scientific investigation. In fact, he admits that religion can never be exactly defined but, rather, its field can only be circumscribed. He also emphasizes that religion must always be discussed with reference to a particular 'human group' and 'society,' for empirically there exists no individual religion but only the religion of groups to which individuals belong. Even religious founders are no exception here as they always somehow relate to a surrounding religious milieu, even when refuting it.

After clarifying the concept 'religion,' Brelich goes on to ask 'What is the history of religions?.' He sees the autonomy of this discipline as given by its object and methods. Its autonomous object consists in religious as distinct from other cultural manifestations of human groups. Its most distinctive method is the use of comparisons, founded on the unity of human history rather than on a so-called common 'human nature' or a uniform 'evolution.' However, this raises the difficulty of how far one can conceive a unity of human history independently from a certain unity of human nature and development. For Brelich, only the consistent use of the comparative method can elucidate the data of the history of religions and account for the originality of each religion. Others might consider this systematic task to be part of the phenomenology of religion but in Brelich's understanding the latter suffers from the defect that it considers concrete religious phenomena on a merely horizontal level, treating them as 'variables' of the presumably same fundamental phenomenon. However, this leads back to historical questions about the origin and development of these phenomena in a wider historical and social context and the need to distinguish clearly between the qualitative differences found in diverse expressions of one and the same phenomenon.

Brelich also states the need for close collaboration among different scholars specialising in particular aspects or periods of the history of religions. No scholar can produce a work like Frazer's *Golden Bough* singlehandedly anymore. Any history of different religions must of necessity be based on teamwork. But in spite of the diversity of the data, the unity of the history of religions as a discipline is warranted by the existence of a common language, a common problematic and a common methodology—except of course that Brelich's narrowly circumscribed methodology will not find general approval. His exposition presents the history of religions in the narrow sense of *Religionsgeschichte*, to some extent opposed to the science of religion or *Religionswissenschaft*, equated with the search for the essence of religion. The emphasis lies entirely on the *faits religieux*, on the priority of history from which phenomenology can alone receive its facts. Henri Puech has summed up Brelich's methodological stance by saying (1970: Vol. I: IX): '*Etudier les faits religieux en eux-mêmes et pour eux-mêmes indépendemment de tout préjugé, de tout jugement de valeur, au même titre et sur le même plan que n'importe quelle autre catégorie de faits accessibles à l'expérience et à l'observation humaine.*'

Jean Bottero (1970: esp. 108–24), too, pays close attention to the use of a strictly historical method in the study of religions. Significantly, he refers to 'histories of religions' rather than to 'history of religions' for there can only be a multiplicity of histories dealing with specific religious systems through which alone the 'phenomenon of religion' finds expression. Epistemologically, one can refer to the 'history of religions' in the singular in terms of one coherent discipline of knowledge whose methodology is that of '*histoire tout court*'. If Brelich primarily emphasizes the social dimension of religion, Bottero's starting-point is quite the opposite by giving priority to the individual religious experience or feeling ('*le sentiment religieux*,' '*un phénomène essentiellement individuel*') which leads to social expression. In many ways Bottero seems to share Otto's

approach to the numinous yet in the study of religious systems, often co-
extensive with social and cultural systems, he wishes to remain strictly
scientific and leave all generalizations to philosophers. Thus, the question about the appropriate method of the history of religions is identical
with the question about the nature of the historical method. Here,
Bottero clearly distinguishes between 'history-as-knowledge' ('*histoire-
connaissance*') and 'history-as-becoming' ('*histoire-devenir*'). The former is
at great distance from the latter and even at its best can only achieve a
fragmentary knowledge of the past. Thus, there is always a place for
conjectures and hypotheses in the development of historical knowledge.
Bottero places equal emphasis on the need for archaeology and philology in the study of religious systems, together with the appropriate
attention to the wider historical, geographical, and social context.
However, after a detailed discussion of the methods of analysis, criticism, and synthesis, he states in an almost complete *volte-face* that a true
historian of religions

'*doit se laisser mener par une compréhension totale de son objet d'études, et, par conséquent, vu la
constitution de ce dernier, par une profonde communion à la religiosité qui en est l'élément premier
et essentiel, communion que peut seule lui assurer une expérience personnelle du sentiment religieux*'
(1970: 122).

One wonders whether this is an afterthought, or is it the return of
phenomenological presuppositions otherwise not admissible? For
Bottero remains emphatic in denying that there ever could be one single
'history of religion' as a quintessence of the diverse histories of religious
systems. Such a goal, although conceivable, would be unrealistic in face
of the insurmountable difficulties of the objective limits of historical
knowledge. Religion as such does not exist except in and through
diverse religions with their countless concrete expressions. Thus, history in general and the history of religions in particular is as limited or
limitless as the ongoing development of human knowledge. That
Bottero has a very clear idea of what the term 'history' implies is also
evident from his outspoken criticism of Eliade: '*Par exemple, le titre
d'Histoire des religions que M. Eliade a donné à son traité connu* [1949] *me paraît
pour le moins un abus de langage*' (1970: 126, n.15). But one might well ask
whether the idea of human knowledge itself does not structurally re-

quire the conception of unity which both encompasses and transcends the fragmentary multiplicity of its constituent parts.

Many arguments in the methodological debate focus around two questions: what is meant by 'history' in the history of religions? and, what is the historical method in the study of religion? If the ideal of objective scholarship is to achieve a historical and analytical understanding of religion as a human phenomenon, is it enough to apply the methods of philology, archaeology, ethnology, and anthropology? The stringent demands for objectivity and scholarly precision are of prime importance but will they not ultimately leave us with fragmentary results or even a destructive analysis, if not in some way complemented by synthesis? The attempt to seek the latter is perhaps often misunderstood as a flight into pure subjectivity, too easily seen as abandoning the necessary detachment and objective criteria required for research.

The Swedish scholar, Geo Widengren, one of the best known champions of a strictly historical approach, regards the phenomenology of religion as the systematic counterpart of the history of religions (see his work *Religionsphänomenologie* (1969) and also the preface to *Historia Religionum*)). In his presidential address to the IAHR Congress at Stockholm (1970) he reaffirmed the predominantly historical character of the study of religion ever since the beginning of the discipline. Although recognizing the importance of the growth of phenomenology, he expressed his misgivings about its 'overwhelming domination,' seeing it as

a characteristic trait of our time, which as we all know is extremely anti-historical—in marked contrast to the preceding century and the period up to the First World War. Since then there has been an ever growing hostility against all historical research and against every historical interpretation of facts, except for those having to do with "modern" times (the term "modern" being in general very vaguely defined) (1975: 20).

In his plea for a renaissance of historical studies, Widengren bypasses the *real* difficulty, acutely felt by other scholars using the historical method, namely the problem of what is the nature of historical interpretation. There never exists a 'pure' religious datum; to make historical 'facts' available always involves the formulation of historical meaning, implying evaluative criteria of some kind, not deducible from the facts themselves. Not every historical moment or 'fact' is necessarily of equivalent value. To arrive at historical understanding and discern a pattern of development, the historian must interpret his 'facts' within a much wider context and it is well known that no two historians interpret the same facts in the same way.

In reflecting on the problems of historical methodology in the study of religions, Frederick Streng has written:

In order to deal significantly with religious data, then, as *religious* it is a false procedure to interpret the phenomenon of religion simply in terms of that which is not religious. On the basis of this assumption, I would say that one cannot even begin to write a history of religions that is based on a positivistic presupposition. The fact that the historian deals with human phenomena rather than simply physical phenomena requires him to use interpretive techniques that permit the humanness—and in terms of religious history, the religious character—to be expressed.

Because the "facts" of the historian are different from the empirically provable evidence of the physical scientist, the assertions made by the historian are capable only of degrees of probability. The historian's facts are the products of human existence; his aim is to understand people through these products rather than to dissect "objective events". (1968: 160 f.)

Streng is one of those who strongly advocates the use of both historical and phenomenological methods in the history of religions, equated again with *allgemeine Religionswissenschaft*. For him, this also includes the self-consciously raised question about the meaning of religious phenomena and the nature of understanding, bringing him close to modern hermeneutical concerns to be considered later.

It is generally true to say that the understanding of the history of religions in the narrow sense is largely, though not exclusively, found among European scholars. A much wider interpretation is given to the history of religions in North America with, at its extreme, Eliade's use of this term which often implies an ahistorical, if not to say antihistorical, perspective. To some extent, however, this opposition between a narrow and a wide sense of the term is misleading. The IAHR, for example, has always represented a wide variety of different scholarly methods and disciplines even though the term 'history' has been retained in its name. Thus, the very existence of the IAHR embodies the wider understanding of 'history' as a discipline. This was explicitly

stated by its former general secretary, C.J. Bleeker (1960, reprinted in
1961), chiefly known as an ardent phenomenologist, when he addressed
the Congress at Marburg, in 1960, on 'The future task of the history of
religions.'

He reviewed the methodological debate up to that time and attempted
to clarify the underlying principles of the history of religions and the
phenomenology of religion. In his formulation of "regulative ideas" for
the conduct of the history of religions Bleeker combined theoretical
with practical concerns. He asked scholars a) to investigate more closely
the question what is religion? in order b) to gain a clear picture of the
different types of religion and c) to assess the value of religion for the
present and the future. More historically oriented and methodologically
aware scholars would perhaps not agree with Bleeker's statement 'that
the study of the history of religions should give its contribution to the
clarification of present religious questions' nor would they accept his
'regulative ideas' formulated to 'stimulate the practical application of the
results of purely scientific research' (Bleeker 1961: 238). Sharpe (1975:
277) describes Bleeker's address as 'the first methodological pronounce-
ment of its kind at a congress'; this is historically incorrect and seems
surprising, coming from such a strongly historically oriented scholar.
The 1908 Congress at Oxford already included a section on the 'method
and scope of the history of religions' with, among others, papers on
'Les sciences auxiliaires de l'histoire comparée des religions' (Goblet
d'Alviella), 'Das Verhältnis von Religionsgeschischte und Religionspsychologie' (Titius), 'The Relation of Comparative Religion to the
History of Religions' (Jordan), and 'Comparative Religion and
Sociology' (Hobhouse) (see *Transactions*, Oxford 1908, vol. II). Questions about the appropriate method in the study of religion and about
the nature of the historical method have been raised ever since the first
congress in Paris, 1900; for this reason the French scholar Clavier (1968)
prefers to speak of the 'resurgence' rather than the newness of the
methodological problem.

Ten years after Marburg, at the IAHR Congress in Stockholm, in
1970, Bleeker once again surveyed the major developments in his address on 'Looking Backward and Forward' (1975b: 23–32). Bleeker
expressed the ambiguity of the situation in the following words:

the study is steadily moving in the direction of an increasingly refined specialization. This means a loss in breadth of vision. It can also involve a gain in precision of study procedure. . . . In the meantime a new problem is arising, concerning the ultimate aim of the history of religions. Numerous studies are appearing which stick fast in philological or historical researches, clever and illuminating though these may be. Philology and history are of course indispensable auxiliaries of the history of religions. But they have no higher value than maidservants' (1975b: 27).

One may query whether there must be an overall aim of the history of religions which goes beyond the discovery of historical knowledge and truth and, moreover, whether a clear conception of such an aim is possible before the question of method has been adequately clarified. For Bleeker there exists an overall aim, namely, the perception of the essence of religion:

It is imperative that historians of religions should clearly realize what the ultimate aim of their studies is, viz., insight into the essence and the structure of religion in the manifold forms in which it appears. This is the criterion for the value of their researches. The history of religions is an autonomous discipline. Its very nature prescribes a critical, independent and yet congenial study of the religious phenomena so that their inner religious logic becomes transparent (1975b: 30).

For Bleeker, this is achieved through a particular phenomenology and therefore history as such plays a subservient role. However, Bleeker's practical aim, for which one may have considerable sympathy, goes far beyond the possibilities of scholarly investigation. It is ultimately a religious and spiritual aim, not as unequivocal as he makes out, and open to many further questions when he concludes:

Let us not forget that we are living in a period in which religion and cultural values are compelled to fight for their very existence. The question arises: What will be the future of religion and of our civilization? Science cannot corroborate, nor can it renew a faltering faith and a decaying culture. Nor can the history of religions. But it could make its contribution to the solution of the crisis by presenting a clear picture of the intrinsic value of religion. The history of religions, studied impartially and critically, shows that religion has always been one of the noblest possessions of humanity, and that it has for the most part served to spiritualize culture. This is a truth which might bring new hope to the present generation, a generation which is struggling for more spiritual certainty and for a culture permeated by the ideas of justice and peace (1975b: 32).

Bleeker does not so much investigate the precise nature of the historical method as pronounce ideas of a general kind for conducting research on religion. However worthy his aims, they include causes which for others can only be by-products of their scholarly work. This at least is the view of Kitagawa who sees the primary object of the history of religions as 'the scholarly task of "integral understanding" of the structure and meaning of man's religious history, in elucidation of the fact that in order to be really human in every culture and every phase of history, man has always seen the total aspect of existence in relation to sacral reality' (1968: 201). Kitagawa makes a basic distinction between the study of specific religions and the history of religions as a discipline in a technical sense. By equating the latter so strictly with a 'scholarly enquiry into the nature and structure of the religious experience of the human race and its diverse manifestations in history,' he is open to the objection that his particular view of *Religionswissenschaft* is much closer to hermeneutic phenomenology than it stands for a historical discipline with a consciously formulated method.

Contrary to the view of Bleeker and others, the search for a precision of method does not necessarily include a loss of vision. It all depends what is subsumed under the idea of 'vision,' for a refinement of method can lead to a more differentiated and enriched result. The analysis undertaken by Robert Baird in his book *Category Formation and the History of Religions* (1971) has demonstrated that a close examination of basic categories can produce greater clarity and distinction in the orientation of research. For Baird, the history of religions is neither normative nor merely descriptive. It cannot be isolated from other disciplines on whose work it depends but it is not to be equated with or subsumed under them for it possesses its own distinct methodology. His functional definition of history is that 'history is the *descriptive study of the human past* ... historical study cannot be the study of "the Sacred"'. Baird admits that history has numerous uses but 'to *use* historical knowledge is to go *beyond history*' (1971: 32, 33). However, in Baird's understanding religion is ultimate concern, a position in turn dependent on a prior theological standpoint derived from Tillich. Thus, for Baird the history of religions is concerned with both historical *and* religious questions:

The history of religions, then, is systematic in that it asks the religious question at various points in history. The religious question, involving ultimacy, involves a systematic answer. But it is also historical in that the answer is fully rooted in the cultural setting and is related to the shifting of the subordinate and the ultimate at various times and places. The history of religions is further historical in that it makes no attempt to give any more than an accurate description of the religious dimensions of the human past (1971: 36 f.).

Perhaps fewer would query this statement than the definition of the history of religions, also given by Baird, as 'a description of the ultimate concerns of men and communities in the past (including the immediate past which we sometimes mistakenly call the present)' (1971: 35). However, he emphasizes the historical givenness and particularity of these concerns and dissociates himself from Kitagawa by saying that the historical study of religions cannot mean to study historical religions in their wholeness.

Baird affirms the possibility of religio-historical knowledge by which he means 'accurate descriptions about man's religious past' (1971: 37). He also discusses the limits of applicability of the statements an historian of religion makes although 'the descriptive study of the human past can never answer ultimate questions on the normative level, the religious question is probably the most significant *historical* question that one can ask' (1971: 52).

Although Baird closely examines fundamental categories of the history of religions, he is more concerned with defining the object of the discipline, as he understands it, than with a detailed analysis of its method. In fact, his insistence on the descriptive study of the human past begs the further methodological question about the nature of description. There cannot be *pure* description which does not also involve some kind of explanation.

The most vigorous defence and illuminating analysis of a strictly historical-comparative method, already advocated and practised at an earlier stage by Pettazzoni, comes from the Italian scholar Ugo Bianchi (1972, 1975, 1979). Bianchi objects to Baird's definition of religion as 'ultimate concern' by arguing that is is of no use if one is not at the same time prepared to define the categorical quality of what is 'ultimate.' In

Bianchi's view the problem of a definition of religion can only be solved through inductive research which

is not a matter of a selection of facts or aspects operated *a priori*, but rather a matter of penetration. This penetration is realized through the progressive and articulated extension of the historical knowledge of the enquirer, in relation to the different milieus that he is methodically considering.... Only this dialectic between contact with the object and progress in the conceptual determination of it makes it possible to surmount the impasse ... of a definition that is at the same time the presupposition and the aim of research... (1979: 317).

According to Bianchi, the historical-comparative method establishes and compares historical-cultural milieus and complexes and investigates historical processes linked to the categories of genesis and development. For this, the historian of religions has to be in constant contact with the concrete data of religion and religions. Only then will he be able to perceive 'those real "continuities" (which does not exclude oppositions or radical innovations) which provide the basis for a general concept, but of inductive origin, of religion' (1979: 317).

The three essential qualifications of the historical-comparative approach are for him: (1) the concept of a 'historical typology' which allows for the development of types of beliefs, etc., in terms of a series of concrete affinities derived from the study of the historical process rather than being abstract 'ideal types;' (2) the concept of 'analogy' to bring out the comparative similarities and differences between phenomena; and (3) the concept of the 'concrete or historical universal' applied to the vast continuity of religion 'as a family of phenomena that, though various and often irreducibly different, nonetheless do show, if not always a continuity or real connection in a historical succession proved by facts, at least some affinities of character and of function (but not of function only); affinities that should not be less profound than the differences themselves. Of course these affinities too will have to result from the pertinent application of the historical-philological method' (1979: 321).

It is not always easy to see what is concretely meant by statements such as these. One of the main issues seems to be whether the history of religions has a distinct method of its own and therefore represents a distinct discipline or whether the history of religions works with the same methods as other historical disciplines. The Dutch scholars T.P. Van Baaren and H. J.W. Drijvers (1973) object to the view of the history of religions as an autonomous subject but see it instead as one of the branches of the science of religion which does not differ from other subdivisions of the science of history in its method of working (especially see 1973: 35–56 and 57–77). Drijvers has also pointed out that there is no single historical method but only a number of different methods used in accordance with the problem under investigation. Theoretically, he distinguishes four stages of progression in the application of historical methods:

1. Examination of the facts on the basis of the available data;
2. Formulating an explanatory hypothesis;
3. Analysis of the implications of this hypothesis;
4. Checking these implications by means of additional data.

For every interpretation of data a theory is needed; this holds good for the setting up of the problem, for the ordering of the data found, for the formulating of an hypothesis as well as for the whole process of argumentation, so that the function of theory in the science of history and consequently in history of religions is the same as in other sciences, that is to supply questions to the researcher whereby information is turned into data that can be used scientifically (1973: 62).

Many historians show little interest in theory but simply practise some kind of historical positivism in their accumulation and description of historical 'facts.' There is no lack of data and factual information in the history of religions (although much more needs to be collected still), but there is a lack of explanatory theories which can be tested, adjusted and retested. So far, the history of religions, like other human sciences, belongs to what has been described as the 'underveloped' areas of research (Pummer 1972: 121). Whether in history or in the history of religions, isolated facts have little value on their own. To collect the necessary data is often not the most challenging problem but to explain or relate them within a wider context is a more difficult task. This is where the role of theory formation is most important for a theory 'has the heuristic function of making events comprehensible and explicable, and therefore we often need more theories to approximate to reality, and these theories must not be too comprehensive to be workable.... All-embracing theories are only too apt to pass for reality itself, as depicting all that happens in the world in a single consistent theory that explains every fact. Such theories, however inspiring, no longer have any heuristic value; they cannot be made to work' (Drijvers 1973: 63).

There seems to be a large area of agreement about the need for more theory in the study of religion but very little consensus about what this theory should be. The demand for further critical theory formation has been equally stimulated by the absence of theoretical perspectives in much historical work as by the presence of all-inclusive theories found in much phenomenological work. In the quest for a solid, workable methodology there is a discernable development away from subjective value categories and arbitrary deductions towards inductive generalisations which can be backed by evidence. This is a healthy development and much more research in fundamental methodological and theoretical issues is needed. But it is one of the symptomatic dilemmas of the discipline that at present very few scholars are actively engaged in such research into fundamentals. This is a fact deplored by Smart (1978) who wished that 'more historians of religion were bolder in theory' (see also the detailed discussion in Waardenburg, 1978a).

To sum up the many issues raised in the current methodological debate about the history of religions, the following questions seem to recur most frequently: Should the discipline be understood in a narrow sense and be restricted to historical/factual/descriptive matters, or should it be interpreted in the wider sense of *Religionswissenschaft*? Should it include a systematic hermeneutic which might elucidate the meaning of religion and relate past religious history to the contemporary self-understanding of human beings?. Put differently, the history of religions may be considered as part of the wider cultural and intellecutal or, if one prefers, scientific history; alternatively, it may be understood as an autonomous discipline in its own right, with its own method. But this still leaves unanswered a host of further questions such as what is the historical method(s), what is the nature of historical generalisation, what is the place of philology and other subsidiary disciplines in historical studies, and how legitimate is the use of the comparative method? A further problem is posed by the relative emphasis given to the study of the distant and more recent past and the comparative importance assigned to extinct and living religions. Is the main emphasis placed on the origin and full development or possibly the decay of religions, on continuity or change, or on the dynamic of the geographical and cultural transplantation and acculturation of religions? This points to the continuing problem of diversity and unity in the history of religions, the existence of different histories of religions as against the attempt to present one unitary history of religion. There is always the tension between the ideal of objectivity versus the problem of subjectivity involved in the choice of a particular perspective which shapes the interpretation of the basic facts.

Even when the immense historical diversity of religious traditions is acknowledged, there remains the difficult question whether religions are fully theoretically accounted for if they are solely taken as historical phenomena. Their inherent, though diverse, claims to embody trans-historical meanings and values point to a focus or rather a multiplicity of foci which may have to be somehow accounted for by criteria other than those of history. All these questions involve the clarification of fundamental conceptual issues such as how one defines 'history' and 'religion' and, moreover, what such terms as 'meaning,' 'understanding' and 'interpretation' are thought to imply. At a certain level this is closely related to the nature of language and how far it can adequately express or even reflect the fullness of human experience. It is precisely such questions which find fuller elucidation in the discussions about the phenomenology of religion.

3.2 The debate about the phenomenology of religion

The survey undertaken so far shows that it is not easy to draw a sharp distinction between the subject-matter of the history of religions and the phenomenology of religion and fully separate their respective methods, at least not when these terms are understood in their widest sense. Generally speaking, the phenomenological approach has stressed the need for objectivity by insisting on a value-free, detached investigation, as far as possible free from all presuppositions, and it has upheld an ideal of accurate scholarship which is sympathetic towards its data. The aims of phenomenology have been variously expressed as the search for patterns and structures, or for the essence of religion behind its multiple manifestations or as understanding the unique quality of religious phenomena, particularly religious experience, or even of comprehending the role of religion in history and culture. Yet it is hard to see how some of these and similar aims can be combined with a non-normative approach to the study of religion.

The interdependent relationship between historical and phenomenological approaches has formed the substance of many methodological arguments over recent years and created much confusion in turn. At the simplest level, one can distinguish between a descriptive phenomenology, more empirically grounded in the examination of data, and an interpretative phenomenology which seeks to grasp a deeper meaning of religious phenomena; in some works both approaches are fruitfully combined. The search for an adequate theory of interpretation for the cross-cultural and comparative study of religious phenomena has also led to the development of an explicitly hermeneutical phenomenology, particularly in North America. Further distinctions have been drawn more recently between the 'classical' or 'traditional' phenomenology of religion (comprising both the descriptive and interpretative variety) and 'new style' phenomenological research (see especially Waardenburg 1972a, 1972b, and 1978a); the latter might simply be called 'neo-phenomenology.' I shall examine the argument for and against phenomenology in its descriptive, interpretative, and 'new-style' orientation in turn but will consider the debate about hermeneutics in a separate section.

The term 'historical phenomenology', used by several authors (Bianchi 1979: 317; Dhavamony 1973: 8–11, 15–21; Smart 1973a: 40), is perhaps the most appropriate to describe a strongly historically grounded, but systematically and comparatively oriented study of religious phenomena. In emphasizing the empirical basis and non-normative orientation of phenomenology, it comes close to the meaning of earlier designations such as 'comparative religion,' 'the comparative study of religion' or even *allgemeine Religionswissenschaft*. Religious phenomena are here systematically studied in their historical context as well as in their structural connections. In discussing the method of the historical phenomenology of religion, Dhavamony underlines the close and systematic relation between theorising and experience in the development and use of the scientific method:

'Observation and experiment furnish us with evidence for generalisations and hypotheses which are tested (verified or falsified) by making deductions from them and comparing these with the results of further observations and experiments'. However, phenomenology faces the particular problem that its 'field of study consists of religious facts that are subjective: the thoughts, feelings and intentions of people expressed in outward acts. . . . In other words, religious phenomena are objectively ascertainable but subjectively rooted facts' (Dhavamony 1973: 16).

Thus Dhavamony maintains the principle of *epoché* to realize the necessary objectivity in letting the facts speak for themselves. Whilst it belongs to the task of the phenomenologist to explain the meaning of religious phenomena, he cannot consider the grounds on which religious beliefs are held or ask whether religious judgements possess objective validity, for this belongs to the domain of philosophy of religion or theology. The methodological principle of the eidetic vision aims to grasp the meaning and intentionality of religious data which are expressions of an inner religious experience and faith. Dhavamony discusses the complexity of different types of understanding operating at different levels and emphasizes that the understanding of the meaning of religious phenomena is always and solely achieved through the understanding of expressions or what others might call manifestations. Summing up the phenomenological method he writes:

The phenomenological method does not just yield a mere description of the phenomena studied, as is sometimes alleged, nor does it pretend to explain the philosophical essence of the phenomena; for phenomenology is neither merely descriptive nor normative. . . But it does give us the inner meaning of a religious phenomenon as it is lived and experienced by religious men. This inner meaning can be said to constitute the essence of the phenomenon; but then the word essence should be understood correctly; what we mean is the *empirical essence* (emphasis added) that is in question here. Phenomenology of religion is an empirical science, a human science which makes use of the results of other human sciences such as religious psychology, religious sociology and anthropology. Still more, we can even say that phenomenology of religion is closer to the philosophy of religion than any other human sciences which study the religious phenomena, for it studies the religious phenomena in their specific aspect of religiousness (1973: 27).

Geo Widengren, author of the well received handbook *Religions-phänomenologie* (1969), has relatively little room for methodological reflections even when he explicitly writes 'Some Remarks on the Methods of the Phenomenology of Religion' (1968) where he largely reviews the methods of earlier phenomenologists. Widengren considers the phenomenology of religion practised by most modern scholars as a systematic, but non-historical sub-discipline of the history of religions (see his *'La méthode comparative: entre philologie et phénoménologie'*, 1971, which with slight stylistic modifications is also in Bianchi, Bleeker, Bausani, 1972). Widengren subscribes to a general principle formulated by Bleeker:

la phénoménologie prend sur soi d'arranger les faits dans un ordre systématique, pour essayer ensuite d'en saisir la portée et le sens; somme toute, elle cherche à les comprendre en tant que faits religieux, sans les violer en aucune manière en tant que faits historiques (Widengren 1971: 171 f.).

However, Widengren's discussion of the phenomological method still remains at the descriptive level for he in no way analyses the methodological difficulties involved in the 'description' and 'interpretation' of 'facts' or in the elaboration of 'types' and 'structures.'

La méthode phénoménologique, en se basant sur la philologie et la méthode comparative, comprend donc les stades suivants: 1. la description des faits; 2. l'arrangement des faits dans un ordre systématique; 3. l'interprétation des faits pour comprendre la signification; 4. l'essai d'établir un type, une structure, un méchanisme, sans violer en aucune manière les faits historiques mais aussi sans confondre phénoménologie et histoire (Widengren 1971: 172).

He does, however, point out serious shortcomings in the overall approach of some phenomenologists and his valid criticisms in this respect should be given due consideration:

It surely must be something wrong with a methodological approach where the greatest living religions are not asked to give their contributions to the phenomenological researches, but obscure African or Indian tribal beliefs or even modern folk-lore are heavily drawn upon. In this regard Heiler deserves to be praised for having extensively quoted both Christian and Indian illustrative examples. That Islam so little has been utilized for phenomenological research is regrettable. To some extent, however, this is due to the fact that some highly important phenomena such as e.g. myth, sacrifice, and confession of sins, are extremely difficult or even impossible to illustrate from Islam (Widengren 1968: 260).

In spite of the praise for Heiler expressed in this passage, Widengren and Heiler cannot be further apart in their understanding of the phenomenological method. Heiler's handbook on phenomenology (1961) begins with a long section on methodological questions where three different possibilities of finding the essence of religion are discussed (see *'Die phänomenologische Methode'* (1961), also translated in Waardenburg, 1973a: 474–8). First, one can approach the study longitudinally by surveying individual religions from a geographical-historical point of view; second, one can undertake a cross-section by treating several types of religion comparatively; third, one can envisage the study of religion in terms of concentric circles. The latter represents Heiler's own method but includes the earlier perspectives of his mentors Nathan Söderblom and Rudolph Otto. In his own words

this method treats the religion of mankind as a whole, and views the lower and higher forms of religion together. Every single manifestation is traced from its most primitive to its most spiritual form. In concentric circles we penetrate from the outer manifestations to the inner ones, to the experiences, and finally to the intended object (quoted in Waardenburg 1973a: 475).

Heiler has expressed his methodological model through a diagram of three concentric circles which progressively move from the outer to the inner world of religion. At the periphery lies the world of outer manifestations (*sinnliche Erscheinungswelt*), followed by the world of ideas and the rational element (*geistige Vorstellungswelt*), which in turn is followed by the world of psychic experience, the dimension of values and the mystical element in religion (*psychische Erlebniswelt*). At the centre of these three circles is found the object of religion itself, i.e., 'divine reality,' whether revealed or hidden.

Criticisms of Heiler's method are directed to the fact that this model, however inspiring for discussion, is not a universally applicable one but has been constructed on the premises of Christian theology. Furthermore, he emphasizes personal pre-suppositions in the attitude of the researcher which go far beyond what is either necessary or legitimate from a scholarly point of view.

Besides the necessary scientific requirements for the study of religion he speaks of three religious postulates: '*Ehrfurcht vor aller wirklichen Religion*'; '*persönliche religiöse Erfahrung*'; '*Ernstnehmen des religiösen Wahrheitsanspruches*' (Heiler 1961: 17). Heiler's presuppositions are untenable: '*Die phänomenologische Methode dient ... ihm als Gottesbeweis ... Diese wenigen Belege zeign sehr klar, dass Heiler im Grunde genommen eine theologische Religionswissenschaft oder "religionsgeschichtliche Theologie" vertritt, was nicht auschliesst, dass sein Werk eine Fundgrube religions-geschichtlichen Materials ist*' (Rudolph 1967: 36). For a recent discussion of Heiler's work, see C.J. Bleeker (1978).

Heiler's strong insistence on the need for religious experience as part of the scholar's equipment would be shared by few western scholars. It brings Heiler perhaps much closer to certain eastern, particularly Indian scholars, such as Radhakrishnan for example. However, in spite of this insistence Sharpe thinks that Heiler's work 'kept to the phenomenological rules' although indirectly it might imply a great deal about inter-religious *rapprochement* (Sharpe 1975: 279). Heiler's religio-practical motivation is much more explicit in the paper he delivered at the IAHR Congress in Tokyo, in 1958 (see, 'The History of Religion as a Way to Unity of Religions', in Heiler (1960: 7–22), and discussed in Sharpe (1975: 272 f.); see also Heiler's 'The History of Religions as a Preparation for the Cooperation of Religions' (1959: 132–60)).

Most scholars do not ask for special personal qualifications from the researcher practising the phenomenological method beyond those inherently belonging to the subject matter. But it is here that the greatest difficulty arises. Is religion a special area or dimension of human experience demanding a specific method for its understanding and explanation? Moreover, is it necessary for such a method to include some 'extras' over and above what is required in the study of other areas of human experience so as to be fully appropriate to the study of religion?

Different answers can and have been given to these questions by scholars of religion in both East and West. Many difficulties in the debate about the phenomenological method arise from the fact that not enough careful attention has been paid to the nature of method and the way it works in concrete detail. 'Method' is all too often simply understood in terms of wide philosophical generalisations rather than precisely defined in terms of a rule or rules for procedure in specific cases. It is this lack of precision and conceptual distinctions which has bedevilled the debate up to now and taken much force out of the argument for a distinct phenomenological method. To define the historical method is comparatively easy if one restricts it to the factual-descriptive or even the historical-comparative approach. By contrast, to handle the issues raised in phenomenology is much more difficult and calls for a great refinement of method. The fact that many phenomenological works cope only poorly with methodological questions and unjustifiably blur many distinctions is not sufficient evidence that the questions posed are not of vital importance for a systematic understanding of religion.

One of the best known contemporary representatives of traditional phenomenology using wide philosophical generalisations is the Dutch scholar C. Jouco Bleeker, closely influenced by the earlier work of Van der Leeuw. However, Bleeker himself disclaims any philosophical presuppositions as he is emphatic in wanting to keep phenomenology at a distance from all philosophical implications. The nature of his phenomenological work can be seen from the collection of essays *The Sacred Bridge. Researches into the Nature and Structure of Religion* (Bleeker 1963) and from his frequent methodological statements on the history and phenomenology of religion (see Bleeker 1959, 1960, 1969, 1971a, 1971b, 1971c, 1972, 1975b). I shall draw here on one of his latest and clearest statements on 'The Contribution of the Phenomenology of Religion to the Study of the History of Religions,' a paper originally delivered to the regional IAHR Study Conference in Rome in 1969 (in 1972: 35–45).

Bleeker finds it easy to describe the history of religions for in his view there 'can hardly be any difference of opinion about the character of the history of religions. It aims at what its name expresses, i.e., the study of the historical development of the religions of the past and the present, primarily of separate religions or of certain segments thereof. In order to reach a scholarly level, this study should be founded on knowledge of the sources of information, primarily of the texts' (1972: 38). Although phenomenology uses facts from different religions to construct types and structures, it must not be equated with comparative religion which 'may compare religions at the best of its ability.' Bleeker is fully aware that there is still no agreement about the nature and the task of phenomenology but he distinguishes three different types of phenomenology in the post-1940 era: (1) the descriptive school which is content with a systematisation of the religious phenomena; (2) the typological school, which aims at the research of the different types of religion; and (3) the phenomenological school in the specific sense of the word, which makes inquiries into the essence, the sense and the structure of religious phenomena' (1972: 39). Bleeker counts his own work among the latter category wherein scholars have not only reflected on the aim, but also on the method of phenomenology.

This methodology-conscious reflection has in Bleeker's view resulted in a twofold meaning of the word 'phenomenology.' On one hand it is used to designate a specific discipline or independent science of religion; on the other it refers to a particular method of scholarly investigation linked to the use of the *epoché* or suspension of judgement 'in regard to the question of the truth of religious phenomena' and the eidetic vision which is the search for 'the essence and the structure of the religious facts.' Although borrowed from Husserl, these terms are only 'used in the figurative sense' and have no philosophical connections (1972: 40).

In describing the task of the phenomenology of religion, Bleeker has developed further theoretical constructs. He distinguishes three dimensions in religious phenomena which the researcher has to inquire into: (1) the *'theoria'* discloses the religious meaning of the phenomena; (2) the *'logos'* of the phenomena penetrates into the structure of different forms of religious life where four permanent categories may be distinguished (constant forms, irreducible elements, points of crystallization, typical factors); and, (3) the *'entelecheia'* of phenomena is the way in which an essence reveals itself in the dynamics or development visible in the religious life of mankind (see 1972: 42; a more detailed discussion of these concepts is found in Waardenburg 1972a: 183–90).

Bleeker maintains a difference of procedure between the history of religions and phenomenology of religion but thinks that the distinct phenomenological method can also be applied to the history of religions. Together with other Dutch scholars (see Van Baaren 1973: 44; Drijvers 1973: 48) he considers the four traditional branches of the science of religion to be history of religions, phenomenology of religion, psychology of religion, and sociology of religion. These four go hand in hand but there seems to exist a special relationship between the first two whilst the last two may be considered to be subsidiary as they supply

further data to the history and phenomenology of religion. The phenomenological method can be of help to the history of religions in five
respects:

(1) It can impel the history of religions to assess the principles of its study because it has
    evolved a distinct theory about the method how to deal with religious phenomena.
    Historians of religion who mostly work empirically by paying attention to philolo-
    gical, historical or archaeological evidence, are thus led to examine the presup-
    positions of their own work.
(2) It sharpens the eye 'for the specific nature of religion and for its function in cultural
    and social life.' By studying religion within the wider context of non-religious facts,
    the historian is 'in danger of losing sight of the true nature of religion.'
(3) It can help the historian to reach 'the true end of his study: the clarification of the
    meaning of religious phenomena.'
(4) It can give him 'insight into the essence and structure of religious phenomena' and
    help him to develop the scholarly courage and power of imagination characteristic of
    the phenomenologist. However, it is also true 'that the sometimes bold statements of
    the phenomenologist must time and again be tested and corrected by the factual
    knowledge of the historian of religions. So there can raise a fruitful cooperation
    between the two disciplines, in the line of what Pettazzoni had in mind.'
(5) The phenomenology of religion 'can induce the historian of religions to ponder on
    the definition of religion which he uses' (in Van Baaren, 1973: 43–5).

During the discussion following this paper at the Rome Conference,
several of Bleeker's underlying assumptions were called into question,
particularly by Bolgiani who argued that the relationship between
'history and phenomenology', although decisive for both the history and
science of religions, is viewed very differently by historians on one hand
and phenomenologists on the other. Without going into the difficulties
of historical methodology here, one of the most problematic aspects of
phenomenology is the complex concept of 'phenomenon' itself.
Bolgiani quite rightly pointed out that it will not do to practise phenomenology of religion as some empirical system of the classification of
data and typological approximation whilst considering the epistemological problems of phenomenology merely from a layman's point of
view: 'A phenomenology which does not aim to consider a problem of
"essences" is not phenomenology, at least in the specific sense of
modern phenomenology from Husserl onwards.' Whilst, in the view of
historians, the phenomenology of religion appears still too abstract and

conditioned by *a priori* arguments, it runs the additional risk that authentic phenomenologists regard its methodology as primitive (in Van Baaren 1973: 47).

Arguments about the aims and methods of phenomenology also took up much of the debate at the IAHR conference on methodology in Turku, Finland, in 1973. In fact, a third of the programme was devoted to 'the future of the phenomenology of religion' (see Honko 1979: 141–366) and a substantial part of this section was concerned with the evaluation of previous methods pursued in phenomenological research. As Honko has written in his introduction to the published conference *Proceedings*:

'The future of the phenomenology of religion' implies a question both about the past and the future: what is the value of the phenomenological research traditions which have dominated comparative religion for so many decades? Are they still usable, and if so, in what form? Have there arisen new approaches to research which might be attracting increasing attention? (Honko 1979: XIX).

Two new approaches which were especially mentioned were ecology of religion and anthropology of religion; both were discussed under the section on phenomenology. Very different positions were held by the participants of the debate: phenomenology of religion was considered from such diverse points of view as being the basis of the study of religion, or a comparative branch within the science of religion, or being the science of the essence of religion or mainly concerned with religious systems of meaning. For some, phenomenological studies are primarily undertaken from the standpoint of subjectivity whilst others want them to be made more empirical. Phenomenology may be understood to include historical studies or, on the contrary, it may be considered to be based on a metahistorical basis. Bleeker argued that both the name of 'phenomenology' and the traditional shape of the discipline should be maintained. Whilst others consider the history of religions and phenomenology of religion to be two essentially different disciplines, Bleeker sees them as distinct but interrelated sharing the common aim of 'the description and the understanding of religion as a human phenomenon with a deeper dimension' (in Honko 1979: 175).

However, Bleeker's views on the requirements of methodology are naive to the extreme when he affirms that the average historian of religions should abstain from speculations about matters of method but leave these to scholars in philosophy and philosophy of religion. He expressed his firm conviction:

As to methodology, there actually exists only one general rule, i.e. that one should study the religious phenomena both critically, unbiasedly, in a scholarly manner, and at the same time with empathy. Furthermore it depends on the approach to a certain side of the religions in question whether one will use sociological, psychological or anthropological standards (in Honko 1979: 176).

Yet the current methodological difficulties cannot be adequately met by merely maintaining 'that the true evaluation of methods would be to retain only those methods which let religious people themselves testify their faith' (in Honko 1979: 177). One might object that if this were correct, no scholar could ever progress to an understanding of religious phenomena which goes beyond that of the believer. Bleeker's statement, if taken to its logical conclusion, leads to a reductionism of a different sort, namely an essentialist-intuitive one which leaves many aspects and dimensions of the phenomenon of religion out of its purview. His phenomenology is based on the use of the intuitive method and it therefore seems all the more surprising that he concluded his commentary at Turku with the appeal *'retournons à la philologie et à l'histoire'* (in Honko 1979).

Bleeker's phenomenological method was critically evaluated by other scholars present in Turku, particularly by H. Biezais in his paper on 'Typology of Religion and the Phenomenological Method' (in Honko 1979: 143–61) which analyses a wide range of approaches to the phenomenology of religion and different uses of typology. Biezais's critical examination leads to the recognition 'that the phenomenological method is one-sided and, as a result of its philosophical orientation, leads to abstract generalization; it is not capable of grasping and explaining the historically given religious reality' (in Honko 1979: 148). Moreover, the demand for the use of 'historical typology' and a 'historical typology of religion,' particularly as made by Bianchi, does not remedy this situation. The case for the use of typology has not been put convincingly; the relationship between phenomenological and typological method remains confused. To arrive at some clarification in this matter, Biezais offers three alternative interpretations of the concept of types. The first two allow the typological method to be employed within the limits of empirical history of religions and make it radically different from the intuitive phenomenological method:

(1) empirically-based types of the facts studied in the history of religions;
(2) types as abstract, normative principles of a systematization carried out on the basis of the similarity or divergence of the characteristics of the phenomena in question; types operate here as a category of scientific theory (in Honko 1979: 160).

The third interpretation of types is very different from the previous two because the typological and phenomenological methods become identical here:

(3) 'By means of phenomenology, types can establish direct relationships between the object to be understood and the person understanding it, between the spheres of the empirical and the transcendental, and thus they can reveal contextual meaning. In this case, the typological method becomes a special epistemological method of speculative comparative religion' (in Honko 1979: 160).

Whilst Biezais concedes that the use of this latter type must be considered as a specific path in the history of religions, he also concludes that it passes beyond the boundaries of empirical research.

It is impossible to report here in full on all the relevant papers delivered at Turku as well as their substantial discussion (chaired and summarized by Werblowsky; see Honko 1979: 212–20). During the latter, Lauri Honko expressed the view that the past methodology of phenomenology had not been as much attacked during the conference as expected and, in any case, Van der Leeuw's methodology was hardly worth 'evaluating' anymore. With regard to the question of typology he mentioned a further possible distinction between 'core typologies' which try to express the essence of each religion, open to testing against the view of the believers, as Bleeker had suggested, and 'contrastive typologies' involving the comparison of different religions with each other (see Honko 1979: 218).

Although the question about the essence or nature of religion cannot be answered empirically, Juha Pentikäinen suggested several ways in which the phenomenology of religion could be made more empirical, namely, by studying religion from a structural point of view, by pursuing cross-cultural research, which would mean a more statistical approach to comparative religion, by introducing the ecological approach which examines the relationship between religion, environment and habitat, and lastly, by developing a 'regional phenomenology' which means 'that the drawing up of the vocabulary for a religio-phenomenological model must presuppose a general historical, ecological, and sociological analysis within a given, relatively homogeneous cultural area' (in Honko 1979: 217).

No general consensus as to the nature, method, and usefulness of phenomenology emerged at Turku. It is clear that several voices pleaded for more narrowly circumscribed aims and a more empirically grounded approach whereby a theory could be tested in practice. Theories relating to the language, symbols and meaning of religion also formed an important part of the discussion but their examination will be postponed until the next section devoted to the wider issues of hermeneutics.

In his summary of the conference, Lauri Honko stated that 'there were three disciplinary "clusters"—history of religions, phenomenology of religion, and anthropology of religion—which formed a triangle within which the major methodological discussions were carried on.' As to the debate between the phenomenology and history of religions, if any conclusion emerged it was the long familiar one that both are essential to the study of religion and complement each other. But in Honko's judgement, history had the more effective protagonists of the two at Turku:

The phenomenological front was scattered: there were a few unconditional supporters of the old phenomenology à la Van der Leeuw, but in general this approach was labelled as intuitive, metaphysical, or non-empirical, and it found little support. It is significant that none of the newer hermeneutic modes of investigation has, as yet, found acceptance in phenomenology of religion either. It became clear, however, that some people wanted to save phenomenology by creating a balance between positivism and hermeneutics, or rather between an empirical approach to research and an interpretative understanding. It was especially interesting that the reformers and supporters of phenomenology viewed the possibility of an alliance with anthropology of religion favourably, while the strongest defenders of a historical approach went into the attack against anthropology (Honko 1979: XXIII f.).

One of the clearest statements about phenomenology as a predominantly empirically oriented, scientific research method is found in an earlier article by Ake Hultkrantz (1970) of Stockholm. He defines phenomenology as 'the systematic study of the forms of religion, that part of religious research which classifies and systematically investigates religious conceptions, rites and myth-traditions from comparative morphological-typological points of view.' Thus it is in principle identical with the older 'comparative religion' or with *vergleichende Religionsgeschichte* (a view also maintained by Kurt Rudolph of Leipzig). Only if phenomenology is pursued in terms of strict, positive research, can it form durable scientific results. The main characteristics of this kind of phenomenology consist in its search for objectiveness and neutrality in questions of value, and its connection with the problems studied in anthropology (including ethnology) and folklore (see Hultkrantz 1970: 74 f.).

Together with Bleeker and others, Hultkrantz considers the phenomenology of religion as one of the four branches of the empirical science of religion. It constitutes a special field of research which works in close contact with the history of religions. But whereas phenomenology has played a relatively subsidiary role for a long time, it has now taken over the leading position in religious research, a position formerly held by the history of religions in the narrow sense. Hultkrantz lists three major points in describing the general aims of the phenomenology of religion:

(1) It seeks the forms and structures of religions, and finally of religion. But this does not imply a search for ideal types and Platonic essences. The real *essence* of religions cannot be known through studying their *forms* which are bound up with culture-historical, social and ecological presuppositions. The phenomenologist seeks to identify firm components in religious material as well as structures (which may appear as independent phenomena or as relations between phenomena) and functions of phenomena. Thus, the emphasis lies on the study of the *morphology* of religious material rather than on the development of typologies which are only of limited value.

(2) Besides compiling classifications of the contents of religion, the phenomenology of religion also seeks to *understand* religious phenomena. No specific intuitive quality is needed for this but 'just a general perception of the world of religion and of the logic of the religious conception and feeling'. Such understanding operates at two levels: firstly it seeks to understand the place of a religious trait in a certain culture, that is, what it means to those who belong to it; secondly it involves the understanding of the general import of a religious element in a wider connection, its theoretical meaning.

(3) The phenomenology of religion also provides the history of religions with a meaning by holding it together and integrating it. The strictly regionally limited, specialized historical research has led to an atomization of the history of religions so that it runs the risk of disappearing as an independent discipline or of being swallowed up by parallel anthropological or philological researches. The phenomenology of religion offers a way out of this dilemma by providing a common perspective for all historians of religion and in addition it might provide a framework 'for the new research which increasingly takes over the place of the old, philologically orientated history of religion: the study of the present-day religious situation, the religious acculturation, the emergent new forms of religion'. Thus it is only with the help of phenomenology that the history of religions can become a discipline spanning all religions (see Hultkrantz 1970: 77–81).

Hultkrantz also emphasizes that, ideally speaking, the phenomenological perspective is so extensive as to be universal; it potentially encompasses all forms, structures and elements of religion. But there exists no specifically phenomenological method, only a phenomenological perspective which makes use of certain methods also used elsewhere, particularly the comparative method, introduced early into the study of religion but refined recently, especially through the research on culture produced by American anthropologists. Comparing an earlier kind of phenomenology with that practised today in certain Scandinavian countries and also in Italy, Hultkrantz concludes

that the vices of the older research on the phenomenology of religion, hasty conclusions on the basis of material which had been quickly put together and alienated from the context, had to give way to an all-round, careful analysis of the religious material within a limited area where the researcher is a specialist. There is every reason to believe that the methods will become more refined, not least through the cooperation between phenomenologists of religion on the one side and folklorists and social anthropologists on the other (Hultkrantz 1970: 88).

Hultkrantz's view that phenomenology represents a general perspective rather than a specific method or epistemology is also shared by the French scholar Isambert (1970). He doubts the originality of phenomenology as the latter seems to consist mainly of a comparative method which is little specific in its detail, even after the introduction of *epoché* and eidetic vision (a term he considers redundant and would like to see replaced by Husserl's own '*Wesensschau*'). He considers these two principles as mere prolegomena which may open the way towards a science but they do not represent a methodology as such. He writes: '*Le bilan méthodologique de l'époché est en lui-même nul, si ce n'est pour débloquer l'entrée vers une* science' (Isambert 1970: 231).

In Isambert's view, recent phenomenologies are only derivations of the work done by earlier phenomenologists; various alternatives are now emphasized as being most important, whether they are introspection or observation, monistic or pluralistic solutions, or the search for archetypes on one hand or cultural empiricism on the other. One might accept phenomenology as a philosophy consistent in itself but in the eyes of a science concerned with religious 'facts,' phenomenological analysis can only be a transitory phase. If one wants to remain at the level of such a strictly positive science, phenomenology has to be treated as an interpretative hypothesis to be submitted to the necessary psycho-sociological verifications. The most important results of phenomenological developments at present are a certain mental attitude which seeks to uncover the '*signification*' and meaning of phenomena and some guiding concepts such as that of '*manifestation*,' by which Isambert understands the specific form of relationship between subject and object apparent in religious phenomena. Isambert describes as the mental attitude common to all phenomenology: '*celle d'un* respect de la signification, *c'est-à-dire à la fois une intuition qui vise à se dégager de toute croyance, de toute valorisation, de toute théorie et même de tout doute, et le sentiment d'une difficulté à saisir le sens, d'une nécessité de la familiarité, de l'attention prolongée, de l'insuffisance des impressions immédiates*'. The concept of '*manifestation*' designates '*la forme spécifique prise par la relation du sujet et de l'objet dans les phénomènes religieux. L'object religieux, par définition, se voile, c'est-à-dire se montre caché. Et le propre du sujet religieux est de dévoiler tout en voilant ce que le regard cherche, mais dont il ne peut soutenir la vue*' (Isambert 1970: 240).

The criticisms of phenomenology have taken too many forms to be all individually listed here. The contention that there are as many phenomenologies as there are phenomenologists can be further extended to the conclusion that there are also as many criticisms of phenomenology as there are phenomenologies. These criticisms have ranged from phenomenology being too descriptive, without having made any theoretical contribution to the study of religion, to it being merely subjective, apologetic, pseudo-religious or even solipsistic. It has been strongly questioned whether phenomenology has a method of its own and, if so, what this might consist of and in what relationship it stands to any kind of philosophical phenomenology derived from Husserl (see especially the lucid discussion of H.H. Penner (1970)). Many critical voices have come from North America where the development of hermeneutical phenomenology has also gone farthest. The best critical overview of the classical developments of phenomenology in Western Europe, especially in Holland, is found in Waardenburg's work which combines a succinct description of the historical aspects of the discipline with a detailed analysis of its assumptions and aims in the light of contemporary new style phenomenological research on the meaning and underlying intentions of religious phenomena (see Waardenburg 1972a, and especially 1978a: *Reflections on the Study of Religion*, including among others separate sections on 'A Plea for Methodological Awareness' and 'Phenomenology of Religion Reconsidered'; the latter consists of the two important papers 'Phenomenology of Religion: A Scholarly Discipline, a Philosophy, or an Art?' and 'Toward a New Style Phenomenological Research on Religion,' pp. 91–112 and 113–37, respectively).

In Holland alone Waardenburg can distinguish five different ways in which phenomenology of religion has been traditionally understood, namely as:

(1) a classification of religious phenomena from different religious traditions;
(2) the search for basic motifs or ideas in different religious traditions;
(3) a division of religious phenomena within a fundamental structure as such;
(4) the understanding and discernment of religious phenomena according to a fundamental structure of man; and,

(5) the interpretation of man's religious history in terms of a development (direct or broken) in time-sequence.

Notwithstanding the diversity of approaches, the representatives of
the classical phenomenology of religion also share a number of common
characteristics in the practice of their discipline. Besides regarding
religion as a non-reducible, autonomous value-category, they bring
together what are considered to be 'objectively' religious facts from
different times and cultures which are compared within a general encompassing framework. These comparisons and classifications are
thought to be comprehensive and have universal validity. There is also a
search for certain basic structures and forms, and an endeavour is made
to determine the meaning of religious phenomena as such, arrived at by
means of what is held to be an ideal structure or idea of religion or,
alternatively, an experience of or insight into what is thought to be the
essence of religious reality. Thus, classical phenomenology of religion is
not founded on a strictly rational basis or derived from stringent
philosophical reflexion:

It strongly accentuates the religious experience or sensitivity of the student of religion,
and accepts as a part of its methodology an immediate intuition on the part of the scholar.
This intuition should be able to penetrate into what is held to be the irrational side of
religious experience, as the deepest foundation of religion itself (Waardenburg 1978a:
121).

Waardenburg stresses the fundamentally ambivalent position of the
traditional phenomenology of religion; in the last analysis it represents a
particular interpretation *of* rather than research *into* religion. It has in fact
played an ideological role in the study of religion 'through being a kind
of anti-theology or mirror-theology in the service of a given theology'
or as 'a kind of apologetic if not of a particular historical religion, then at
least of an idealized religion or of the fact of religion as such' (1978a:
128). In its resistance to positivistic reductions of religion, classical
phenomenology has reduced religion to a purely religious experience or
to a purely religious idea. This emphasis on ideal contents had made it
incapable of paying sufficient attention to the behavioural and institutional aspects of religion. Among the many important criticisms
which Waardenburg lists, the following deserve special mention: pheno-

menology has been unable to investigate a-religiosity, unbelief or atheism as authentic human possibilities; it is scientifically insufficiently founded, for its generalizations do not apply to concrete facts of specific religions and epistemological foundations; it has not been sufficiently reflective and self-critical as to its methods; it has hardly entered into discussions with other disciplines. Generally speaking, classical phenomenology has led to much intellectual confusion and, through its lack of communication, finished up in a kind of solipsism. The hypotheses which it has developed 'do not really make religious data intelligible and certainly do not explain them' (Waardenburg 1978a: 129).

However, unlike certain other scholars, Waardenburg does not restrict research into religion to empirical fact-finding and rational theory-building but has proposed a 'new style' phenomenological research 'concerned with the study of religious meanings, of human religiosity and of the religious mental universes which man has made throughout history.' A distinctive feature of such research is

that the meaning of the religious facts or phenomena is here not only studied as a meaning which they have as objects in themselves or in their context, but also as a meaning which they have for people, that is to say they are studied on a level of *intentions*. The 'facts' of empirical research are here interpreted as human 'expressions', that is to say as the specific traces of human problems, ideals dreams and aspirations. If there is enough documentary material, we may reconstitute as a hypothetical probability some of the religious intentions which prevailed, or prevail, in a given society at a given time, and of which the religious phenomena that then occurred or occur may be considered to provide evidence. Let us stress the wording 'as a hypothetical probability' since phenomenological statements have to be constantly verified and checked by factual research . . . . . As phenomenological *reflection* has moved over the last fifty years from metaphysics to human existence, so phenomenological *research* is developing from the search for timeless essences to a search for meanings inside time, including those meanings which have a religious quality for the people involved (Waardenburg 1978a: 87).

This is not an entirely new approach but represents a further advance and methodologically self-critical development vis-à-vis earlier, less differentiated phenomenologies. It also shares a number of related concerns with some representatives of hermeneutical phenomenology as well as with recent attempts to develop a more integral science of religion. As Waardenburg says elsewhere, it is a phenomenology 'new style' centred around the investigation of 'subject's meanings' ('the meanings which given expressions and phenomena have for given persons and groups who are concerned or involved with them', 1978a: 40) and their underlying intentions. Although a number of examples are listed to which these new research orientations may be applied ('analysis of images according to their intentions and intentional perspectives,' 'of communication in discussion and role-taking,' 'of religious expressions,' 'of significations,' or the investigation of 'religious representations;' 'religious ideals' and 'ritual action;' see 1978a: 40 f. and 117 f.), one may object that the level of discussion still remains far too abstract; for the methodological argument to be convincing it requires more concrete application to specific case studies. Waardenburg maintains that his theoretical starting points can be made operational in actual research and that by accepting intention as a basic concept or, more hesitantly expressed, by at least assuming the presence of explicit and implicit intentions 'as a scholarly hypothesis of considerable probability' (1978a: 134), further areas can be opened for research which have largely remained outside the vision of classical phenomenology of religion such as, for example, the confrontation between different religions, the dynamic relationship between religion and institutions as well as the process of its institutionalization, the clash of intentions visible in the tensions between 'religion' and the 'world.'

The particular attraction and strength of this research orientation appears to lie in its holistic approach. The emphasis on intentions allows for a particularly fruitful investigation of living religions and new religious movements; it is also able to overcome the strict separation between religion, non-religion or what some have called quasi-religion. But besides the positive task of investigating intentions and meanings, Waardenburg also assigns to phenomenology 'the eminently critical function of analyzing and investigating further the concept of religion wherever it occurs in a discipline.' It can be shown that the classical phenomenologists who understand religion in terms of essence and manifestations, depend just as much on a prior concept of religion in the interpretation of religious data as the empirical scientists who largely observe religion in terms of facts (1978a: 136). By including such analytical-critical research into the meaning of basic concepts under the tasks of the phenomenology of religion, Waardenburg's understanding of the discipline seems to be more akin to that of *systematische Religions-wissenschaft* than to the empirical-descriptive or essentialist-reductionist orientations of phenomenologists elsewhere (German readers may like to know that Waardenburg's article on which I have extensively drawn here, first appeared in German as '*Grundsätzliches zur Religionsphänomeno-logie*' in *Neue Zeitschrift für Systematische Theologie und Religionsphilosophie* 14, (1972b)).

Phenomenology is not merely *vergleichende Religionsgeschichte* here (as for Hultkrantz and Rudolph, for example) but is understood as a systematic and integral approach which creatively combines current critical requirements for methodological precision with some of the most challenging questions in the study of religion by insisting on the need for research into the meaning and intentions of religious pheno-mena. This approach represents a synthesis of some of the best aspects of traditional phenomenologies with some of the newest methodological concerns and may rightly be considered as a neo-phenomenology which holds much promise for future studies.

It is apparent from the above discussion that there is a general dissatisfaction and wide criticism of the intuitive-essentialist approach of earlier phenomenologists. At the same time it is also clear that phenomenology still attracts much attention and, if rightly understood and practised, holds out a number of fruitful possibilities for the study of religion. We have now arrived at a period of critical re-assessment where many of the earlier questions must be asked in a more stringent form and cautious manner but the future of the discipline depends very much on the development of a more widespread methodological awareness and further clarification of the central issues in the study of religion.

Many scholars recognize that the phenomenological approach makes an important and indispensable contribution to the modern study of religion but it is by no means clear whether phenomenology should be considered an independent or subsidiary discipline to the history of religions in the wider sense, and whether there is a specific phenomeno-logical method or merely a general phenomenological perspective in the study of religious phenomena. Many of the important questions about the form and content of religious experience, the nature of theoretical as distinct from existential understanding, the role of interpretation and explanation, the meaning of religious phenomena, and the function of language in the description of religious data are ultimately difficult philosophical issues which have been legitimately raised but not always very satisfactorily answered by earlier phenomenologists. These questions are still very much with us today, and this is perhaps nowhere more apparent than in the ongoing debate about the role of hermeneutics in the study of religion.

3.3. The debate about hermeneutics

The study of religion may be conceived in a primarily historical and phenomenological framework but even then many further questions arise about the meaning and interpretation of religious data which demand special attention. As the foregoing discussion has shown, many crucial issues relating to the understanding of religion have been debated by phenomenologists; important questions have been raised though few satisfactory answers have been found. The same may be said about the general debate on hermeneutics which overlaps to a considerable extent with phenomenological arguments but presents a more conscious attempt to develop an overall comprehensive theory of interpretation for the study of religion. It would not be inaccurate to describe several of these attempts as examples of a 'critical phenomenology' (a term used by C.H. Long 1967: 80). One might also expect that a closer examination of authors and arguments will reveal a similar diversity of positions as has been found elsewhere in the methodological discussion. Thus, there are probably as many different hermeneutics as there are conscious hermeneuticists.

It is difficult to know when the term 'hermeneutics,' originally coined in the area of biblical exegesis, was first applied to the wider study of religion. In biblical exegesis, hermeneutics has been defined as 'the science (or art) by which exegetical procedures are devised' and hermeneutical theory has arisen 'out of the awareness of the ambiguity of a sacred text and the consequent analysis of the act of understanding' (*The Oxford Dictionary of the Christian Church*, 1978: 641). This definition points to several important issues in the study of religion in general, namely, whether its interpretative procedures are a science or an art, what is involved in the act of understanding, and how far hermeneutics can offer the necessary theoretical framework or, on the contrary, might itself be problematic. The further distinction made by some theologians between 'hermeneutics' (as preliminary to exegesis) and 'hermeneutic' (as the wider study of how the message of the Bible may be expressed in the language of different cultures) does not apply to the debate within the history and phenomenology of religion; authors seem to use both terms interchangeably without implying a distinction between 'hermeneutics' and 'hermeneutic.' Similarly, the wider cultural debate about hermeneutics in contemporary literature, philosophy and the social sciences seems to be little reflected in theoretical discussions about the interpretation of religion, occasional references apart.

However, the development of and wrestling with theories of interpretation is of paramount importance in the contemporary study of religion. But there exists a wide divergence of views as to what such an interpretation can and must imply. One may distinguish between two different meanings of hermeneutics which are not always clearly kept apart: (1) in a strict sense, hermeneutics may refer to a theoretical elucidation of the interpretative process which allows for the development of a theory of interpretation closely controlled by the available data and by step-by-step analytical procedures; (2) in a much wider sense, hermeneutics stands for a theory of its own by which, it is claimed, the hidden meaning of religious phenomena can be uncovered or recovered. In the latter form, hermeneutics may become a form of cultural criticism, strongly dependent on particular philosophical and normative stances, however implicit in some cases.

Both usages are applied to the history of religions, particularly in North America, as can be seen from the following two quotations written during the same year:

The history of religions, like other disciplines, is grounded in an hermeneutic situation: that is, in an interpretative framework which establishes the possibilities and limits of critical analysis and creative synthesis . . . the hermeneutic situation, taken in its totality, is the source of assumptions which operate as methodological conventions for the scholar; . . . the hermeneutic situation establishes the problems and provides the heuristic devices which determine the purpose of using a particular method and the manner in which it is used (J.S. Helfer 1968: 1, 2).

When describing 'The Making of a Historian of Religions,' Kitagawa referred to the 'hermeneutical task' as

a dimension that constitutes the unique contribution of the history of religions to other disciplines concerned with religious studies. I refer to the articulation of the nature, structure, and meaning of man's religious experience, an articulation based on historical and systematic inquiry into concrete religious configurations—past and present, primitive and historic, and Eastern and Western. Granted that the hermeneutical task of the history of religions has been greatly influenced and enriched by the contributions of normative and empirical studies of religions, in the final analysis it is only the historian of religions who must carry the awesome burden of articulating what Joachim Wach termed the "integral understanding" of religious phenomena, as required by the discipline of the history of religions. This is probably the most controversial aspect of our discipline in the sense that "integral understanding" involves selectivity of data and a telescoping of the long and complex historical development of man's religions. The lack of data is not at all our problem. Our real problem, to use a phrase of G. van der Leeuw, is that the manner in which the data are "significantly organized" inevitably varies according to the personal sensitivity, religious outlook, and scholarly training of the individual historian of religions (Kitagawa 1968: 200).

This quotation illustrates how a particular understanding of the history of religions may be combined with a hermeneutic perspective and also, how the latter depends in turn on certain questions asked by earlier phenomenologists. It is particularly the so-called Chicago hermeneutical programme, based on the foundations laid by Wach and further enlarged by Eliade, Kitagawa and others, which has considerably widened the meaning of the term 'history of religions.' This overriding hermeneutic concern was outlined in Eliade's programmatic statement 'A New Humanism' with which *History of Religions* began as a new journal, published from Chicago since 1961 (see vol. 1: 1–8; reprinted in Eliade 1969: 1–11), having as one of its aims the explicit attempt 'to improve the hermeneutics of religious data.' In fact, many readers may equate Eliade's well-known plea for a 'creative hermeneutics' with the hermeneutical debate as such but several other participants and themes can be recognized in this important discussion. The following questions seem to recur most frequently:

(1) What is interpretation?
(2) What is understanding?
(3) What is meaning and, in particular, what is the meaning of religious symbols?
(4) What role does faith play in the study of religion?

For the sake of greater clarity these questions can be distinguished at the theoretical level but in actual practice they are often closely interwoven. If their implications are unpacked, they all eventually lead back to the basic problem of how one can validly describe, explain and understand the structural unity and historical diversity of religion and religious experience. Thus the problem of interpretation, together with the conceptual difficulties involved in this process, is fundamental. One may well ask what it means to improve the hermeneutics of religious data, whether it is primarily a 'reading into' rather than a 'drawing out' of meaning so that exegesis is transformed into an illegitimate *eisegesis*.

Eliade's understanding of hermeneutics has given rise to a wide-ranging discussion (see in particular the comprehensive study by D. Allen (1978)) and has frequently been criticized for its antihistorical bias and eclectic use of data drawn from the religions of non-literate peoples (for recent criticisms see the detailed studies by John A. Saliba (1976) and Guilford Dudley III (1977); also see the discussion by N. Smart (1978)). In Mircea Eliade's most recent publication, a three-volume work entitled *A History of Religious Ideas* of which two have so far appeared in English (1979, 1981), the methodological reflections are kept brief but succinctly restate what has been said at greater length elsewhere before:

For the historian of religions, *every* manifestation of the sacred is important: every rite, every myth, every belief or divine figure reflects the experience of the sacred and hence implies the notions of *being*, of *meaning*, and of *truth*.... In short, the "sacred" is an element in the structure of consciousness and not a stage in the history of consciousness. On the most archaic levels of culture, *living, considered as being human*, is in itself a *religious act*, for food-getting, sexual life, and work have a sacramental value. In other words, to be—or, rather, to become—*a man* signifies being "religious" (Preface, 1979: XIII).

Eliade is one of the few modern scholars of religion who has developed a comprehensive theory of man's religiousness set within a framework provided by the notion of universal history on one hand and the consciousness of the unity of the spiritual history of humankind on the other. Thus the hermeneutical enquiry must lead from the data of history to the search for their trans-historical meaning and value (see especially the methodological reflections brought together in Eliade's *The Quest*, 1969). In actual fact this means, however, that Eliade, in his search for meaning, assigns priority to a particular interpretation of the data which overlooks much of their historical context and closely verges on being anti-historical altogether. Thus there can be no question of identifying the history of religions in a wider sense with the hermeneutical interpretation given to it by Eliade and his disciples (see U. King's review article (1981); also F. Whaling's (1979) review).

Eliade's starting-point is the fundamental polarity between the sacred and profane. The sacred regularly manifests itself through 'hierophanies' but Eliade's examination of these manifestations draws rather too exclusively on the archaic and exotic, the spiritual universes of primitive and eastern peoples which, in his view, will open new horizons and avenues of meaning for western civilization, bound by the terror of history and its fall from primordial cosmic unity. In Eliade's view, the modern western world has reached the ultimate stage of desacralization where the sacred has become completely camouflaged through its identification with the profane. The historian of religions has an important cultural function in the contemporary world for through his hermeneutical enquiry he can transmute historical materials into spiritual messages for modern man. So far, hermeneutics is the least developed aspect of the study of religion as scholars have often neglected to study the meaning of religious data. The historical and comparative study of religions embraces all the cultural forms so far known but it must involve more than a quantitative increase in our knowledge of man; it must itself become culturally creative. If this hermeneutical task is not taken seriously, the history of religions would be reduced to a purely historiographical task and disappear as an autonomous discipline.

However, Eliade has frequently affirmed the independence and autonomy of the history of religions which he understands not merely as a historical discipline but equally as 'a *total hermeneutics*, being called to decipher and explicate every kind of encounter of man with the sacred, from prehistory to our day.' He has described the 'spiritual timidity' of many history of religions scholars as both paradoxical and tragic but thinks it not impossible to reestablish the discipline in the central position it merits. The immensity of the task should not be an excuse for delay; the search for more data does not necessarily further understanding. Eliade writes that

no man of science has waited until *all* the facts were assembled before trying to understand the facts already known. Besides, it is necessary to free oneself from the superstition that analysis represents the *true* scientific work and that one ought to propose a synthesis or a generalization only rather late in life. One does not know any example of a science or a humanist discipline whose representatives are devoted exclusively to analysis without attempting to advance a working hypothesis or to draft a generalization. The human mind works in this compartmented manner only at the price of its own creativity (1969: 58, 59).

When Eliade refers to the 'science of religion', he envisages it as such a task of integration, synthesis and creativity; he does not doubt that creative hermeneutics will finally be recognized as 'the royal road of the history of religions:' 'In the end, the creative hermeneutics *changes* man; it is more than instruction, it is also a spiritual technique susceptible of modifying the quality of existence itself. This is true above all for the historico-religious hermeneutics' (1969: 62). Today for the first time history is becoming truly universal and culture is in the process of becoming planetary. In Eliade's understanding, the history of religions 'can contribute to the elaboration of a universal type of culture' (1969: 69); in the end, it envisages 'cultural *creation* and the *modification* of man.' And he continues to say that 'all the methods of liberation of man— economic, political, psychological—are justified by their final goal: to deliver man from his chains or his complexes in order to open him to the world of the spirit and to render him *culturally creative*' (1969: 67).

In the last analysis the history of religions is given here a soteriological function which goes far beyond the limits of its possibilities. Not only must Eliade be criticized for his basically normative thrust but also for his preference of archaic to modern forms of religious life, the place he gives to religious symbolism above all other expressions of religion, and the attendant neglect of complementary theoretical frameworks for the study of religion, particularly those elaborated by the social sciences. However stimulating and insightful many aspects of Eliade's theory are, one cannot but concur with Smart's conclusion that regretfully 'his creative hermeneutic is in the end restricted—the vehicle of a certain worldview, and a means of giving life to much of man's archaic religious symbolism, and yet somehow cut off from the wider explanatory task which religion can and should perform' (Smart 1978: 183).

Eliade's approach illustrates the problematic status of hermeneutics. It raises the question of the nature and objective of interpreting religious data: can something new be created through such interpretation or is the scholar's interpretative task restricted to the examination of historically given materials?

This question of interpretation also figures centrally in the attempt to develop a 'comparative hermeneutics' relating to two or more religious traditions. A more cautious approach to a comparative framework (applied to the interpretation of Buddhism and Christianity) was explored at a symposium held at the University of Lancaster in 1972 (see M. Pye and R. Morgan (1973)). It is claimed that this 'is the first serious expression of comparative hermeneutics as an intellectual enterprise in the study of religion' which may provide the seed for future developments (1973: 196). Discussing 'Comparative Hermeneutics in Religion' (1973: 9–58), Michael Pye defines comparative hermeneutics as an essentially theoretical pursuit by which he understands 'the comparative study of *procedures* and *problems* of interpretation, as these are understood whether faintly or clearly by the representatives of recognisable religious traditions' (1973: 58). So far, however, the seed sown at this symposium does not seem to have borne much fruit, methodologically speaking. The most important problem arising from this collection of essays is perhaps the question of different levels at which interpretations and theories of interpretation may exist. Discussing these matters in his epilogue, Ninian Smart points to the underlying ambiguity of the term 'comparative hermeneutics' which could imply: (a) the comparison of the development of interpretation given by a person of a particular religious tradition; or (b) at a more reflective level, the comparison of ideas about the criteria, evolved in different traditions, as to the method of interpreting the respective materials by the traditions; or (c) it could mean both of these approaches together. At yet another, higher level of abstraction one might arrive at a 'general theory of religious interpretation' possessing 'trans-cultural validity.' But such a general hermeneutical theory is not a theory of the criteria of truth in religion nor is it a prescription for the genuine interpretation of any given tradition or of all. It is helpful to distinguish between these three different levels of interpretation—the basis (given by the believer himself), the tradition-bound theory, and the general theory of interpretation, but Smart also emphasizes that these three cannot always be kept effectively apart. There exists a dialectic tension between the descriptive and normative which ultimately cannot be escaped in the attempt of doing comparative hermeneutics. But the development of such a hermeneutics 'is part of the ongoing debate as to the right ways to study religion' (see Pye and Morgan 1973: 196–99).

The interpretation of religious data is closely interwoven with the problem of understanding which, in Kitagawa's view, is 'the central task of *Religionswissenschaft*' requiring 'a hermeneutical principle which would enable us to harmonize the insights and contributions of both historical and structural inquiries, without at the same time doing injustice to the methodological integrity of either approach' (Kitagawa 1967: 42). But the notion of understanding, so central to much of the phenomenological debate, is often not sufficiently unpacked. How far must theoretical understanding be distinguished from existential understanding, and is it necessary for the former to be grounded in the latter? It cannot be taken for granted that understanding will necessarily lead to the most satisfactory explanation of religious phenomena but this important theoretical distinction between understanding and explanation is frequently overlooked. The emphasis on understanding is often closely linked to the central place assigned to religious experience in the study of religion, for example when it is said that 'The discipline of History of Religions seeks to *understand*, from a description and analysis of all of mankind's religious expression, the *nature of religious experience* and *expression*' (Long 1967: 77; emphasis added). The methodological difficulties involved in the task of understanding religious experience are perhaps nowhere more apparent than in the comparative study of mysticism. Contrary to normative demands, no unitary answer as to the nature of either understanding or religious experience can be found. On the contrary, a critical analysis of the rich mystical materials can lead to a highly differentiated, complex picture pointing to a strong pluralism with regard to the methodological tools and levels of interpretation required for the understanding of religious experience (this is forcefully argued in the symposium edited by S.T. Katz, 1978; see especially the contributions by Steven Katz, Peter Moore and Ninian Smart.)

Many scholars might concur with the statement that the goal of the history of religions is 'to understand' but besides the difficulties inherent in the act of understanding itself, there is the problem of what 'understanding' may mean within the different western and eastern religious traditions, given their distinct semantic, philosophical and religious contexts. In Streng's view the goal of understanding in the study of religion is not

a scientific understanding in the sense of an objectifiable, empirical proof; nor is it the 'understanding' that is an appreciation or assent of the believer. To 'understand' means neither empirical absolute proof nor agreement to an unprovable interpretation of life. Rather (1) it means to enter into the mental and emotional framework of the believer to the extent that the investigator can see *how* this religious meaning is possible for the person. (2) Secondly, it means that the religious concepts, actions, and institutional forms are examined according to their relations to the psychological, social, and physical elements of human existence in a cultural context and historical situation. (3) Thirdly, it means to be aware of how the interpreter's own presupposition about such universal concepts as 'man', 'history', 'religion' contribute to his understanding of a particular phenomenon, and how the study of a particular religious phenomenon contributes to the universal images that he uses. (4) It also means that the investigator seeks to locate and expose the particular meaning of what it means to be religious in the data under scrutiny (Streng 1968: 158 f.).

One of the most detailed discussions of the category of 'understanding' is found in R.D. Baird's book *Category Formation and the History of Religions* (1971; see especially 54–125). Baird draws a distinction between the psychology and logic of understanding and offers a strictly functional definition of 'understanding' religion. It is

any valid knowledge about religion communicable in propositional form. This is not to deny that knowledge *about* religion is not the same as knowledge *of* religion in an existential and experiential sense. Nor does it deny the possibility of the latter. What is denied is that religious experience is a valid goal for the historian of religions as an academician. Academic study and research is admittedly penultimate. But such an admission should assist us in avoiding religious experience as an operative part of the methodology of the historian of religious. . . .

Furthermore, if an 'understanding' of religion is achieved when valid knowledge about religion has been acquired, then it follows that the history of religions is not to be distinguished from other disciplines in its goal of 'understanding'. . . .

There are no strictly religious data. There are human data, of which a variety of questions may be asked. To the extent that the answers to these questions are probable and valid, to that extent understanding has taken place. While certain types of religion may be mystical, *the study* of religion has no reason to be so (Baird 1971: 59).

This is a different approach to understanding than Streng's but the two perspectives are not necessarily incompatible. Baird also distinguishes several levels of understanding which he illustrates through the work of particular thinkers, indicating their method and content of understanding and the limits within which they operate. These levels are: (a) functional understanding (B. Malinowski); (b) phenomenological understanding (M. Eliade); (c) personal understanding (W. Cantwell Smith); normative understanding (H. Kraemer, H. Küng, S. Radhakrishnan). Baird is convinced that the historical and phenomenological questions cannot be asked simultaneously, nor can the historical and normative ones. The phenomenological method always implies an ontology. It is only 'a legitimate level of understanding to the extent to which one is convinced of the reality of the transhistorical structures and archetypes. These cannot be supported by merely citing historically derived data' (1971: 90). Summing up the different levels of understanding he writes:

One has acquired religio-historical understanding when he has offered an accurate description of the pattern of ultimacy for a person or community, or has accurately described the changing historical dimensions of ultimacy. Functional understanding (psychological or social) occurs when one has described the function or functions of a religious rite, belief, or myth. Personal understanding has taken place when one has described the faith of another person or group in such a way that they can affirm the description. Normative understanding has occurred when one has understood the degree of truth contained in the religious expressions under consideration. This requires that one not only has the necessary empirical data at his disposal, but also that his

normative system is true. And, it is difficult to deny ... that phenomenological understanding occurs when the data it uses is accurately reported *and* to the extent that the
ontological system on which it is based is true (1971: 125).

The wrestling with the meaning of understanding has gone a step
further in Georg Schmid's *Principles of Integral Science of Religion* (1979),
where the tasks of description, comprehension and understanding are
seen as complementary aspects of an integrally conceived science of
religion. Its methodological programme will be considered in the next
section but let it be mentioned here that in reviewing the main arguments in relation to the nature of understanding, Schmid provides a
perceptive analysis of the overall thrust and difficulties in the discussion
about understanding religious phenomena (see his sections 'On the
Theory of Understanding in the Science of Religion' and 'Understanding' in 1979: 80–9, 89–96). To Schmid, understanding 'is something like both the crown and the abyss of all efforts to perceive in
the science of religion.' That this cannot be achieved in isolation but is
interdependent on other approaches is clear from the following

Without comprehension, description leads to a hodge-podge of more or less accidentally
similar data. Without understanding, comprehension leads to a setting-in-relation of
religious data without interest in the meaning of the data. Both description without
comprehension and comprehension without understanding, measured by the task of an
integral science of religion, miss the whole and are therefore of little promise. Only
understanding asks about the meaning of religious data—not only about the relations *in*
which religious data stand but also about *the relations* which these data are *according to their
own intention* (1979: 89).

This leads to further questions about intentions, intentionality, and
the role of meaning, all of which are examined by Schmid. These issues
also found attention at the Turku conference which devoted a considerable amount of time particularly to the discussion of the meaning of
religious language and religious symbols (see Honko 1979: 429–83 and
485–545). The debate about the meaning and structure of symbols is a
very lively and fruitful one but short of writing a monograph, if not a
whole book, it would be impossible to analyse the complex and conceptually demanding aspects of the contemporary discussion on sym-

bols. Anthropologists, psychologists, sociologists and philosophers have explored numerous paths in the deciphering of symbols. In the history of religions field in a wider sense the comparative study of religious symbolism has found its best known champion in Eliade but his comprehensive approach has often been criticized as it lacks empirical grounding and the possibility of verification. Eliade completely decontextualizes symbols and interprets their meaning within a pre-given framework independent of time, place and history (for Eliade's methodological approach to symbols see his 'Observations on religious symbolism' in 1965: 189–211; see also the perceptive discussion of the different functions of religious symbolism according to Eliade and the dilemma of the 'functional fallacy' by H.H. Penner, 1968).

At Turku, Kurt Goldammer considered different aspects of symbols as revealing the depth-structure of religious experience and tried to explore a hermeneutic which might give access to this depth-dimension whereas Jacques Waardenburg examined the study of religions as sign-systems (for both these papers see Honko 1979: 498–518 and 441–57 respectively). A full discussion of these issues would have to consider recent developments in semiotics and semiology and look beyond the sign-systems of words to that of images. The important role images play in all religious traditions has been little explored so far and the field of iconography, although given more recognition recently, still provides a largely unexamined area for further theoretical analysis (attention was drawn to this point in some papers delivered at the IAHR congresses at Stockholm and Lancaster; see also the effort of documentation undertaken by the Institute of Religious Iconography at the Dutch university of Groningen and its published series on the 'Iconography of Religions' which aims 'to present major iconographic expressions systematically in a survey concerned with all religions of any importance in the world both of literate and illiterate peoples.' Of great interest is also the documentation and collection of objects in the '*Religionskundliche Sammlung*' in Marburg, originally founded by R. Otto, but considerably extended since then. At the IAHR Marburg congress a project for a further museum in Brussels was announced but I have been unable to obtain more recent information on this; see M. Mehauden '*Un "Musée comparatif des Phénomènes Religieux"*', Marburg *Proceedings*, 1961: 191–3)).

The themes of interpretation, understanding and meaning closely intertwine in Waardenburg's new-style phenomenology where he clearly distinguishes between several approaches to 'subjective meanings' as compared to those seeking 'objective facts' (see Waardenburg, 1978a, especially the two papers on 'Objective facts and subjective meanings in the study of religion' and 'Toward a new style phenomenological research on religion'). Particularly valuable for stating his approach to the problem of meaning is his paper 'Research on Meaning in Religion' (in Van Baaren and Drijvers 1973: 109–36). The emphasis on meaning is by no means new but continues a well-known theme of classical phenomenology although Waardenburg explores new and original ways of treating it. In his view the historian of religion encounters the problem of meaning professionally and is compelled to admit, especially if he works on one of the living world religions, 'that a religious faith comprises a view on life and reality either as something meaningful or as referring to something meaningful' (1973: 109). It is a primary datum of the history of religions 'that within a given culture certain things have a meaning for certain people, and that within a given context such a meaning may have a religious quality for a particular group or person' (1973: 110). Whilst in the classical phenomenology of religion research on meaning largely coincided with a search for objective patterns, Waardenburg wants to analyse the contents of 'subjective meanings' which must be distinguished from the meanings facts may have in themselves or the meanings attributed to phenomena by certain scholarly categories of interpretation. The earlier phenomenological stance to go back to the facts has to be reformulated as the need to go back to the basic intentions. The primary focus of interest should be 'the meaning of given data for given people' (1973: 112) requiring the analysis of the underlying intentions of religious expressions and phenomena.

As Waardenburg himself admits, this approach is most fruitful for the study of living religions where direct religious expressions are available. To develop a hermeneutics of subjective religious meaning leads to an interpretation of religious data in terms of human existence. The phenomenon of religion is approached differently today than it was fifty years ago or earlier. This is not only due to the development of the study of religion as a discipline but it is also related to the fact that the problems of religion and meaning are being reformulated in contemporary culture. In the past, theologians may have used phenomenology to make certain theological and philosophical pronouncements on the level of conviction rather than on that of enquiry and reflection, whereas scholars in the humanities applied the phenomenological suspense of judgement in such a way 'that religious phenomena became in practice objects of literary and historical research without too much attention being paid to their significance for the people who lived with them, or to the evident claims with regard to truth and reality as they are contained in material varying from myths to sacred scriptures' (1973: 115). In exploring the personal dimension of subjective meanings, the role of the other person has to be taken seriously:

what the other means with his expressions, what something means to the other, what place to give him, how to relate to him, etc. Such questions are, indirectly, of fundamental importance for the interpretation of religious expressions and phenomena emanating from 'the other' with regard to whom the student somehow takes a stand. Two extreme attitudes may usefully be recalled here: on one hand the consideration of religious data as objects in themselves, not to be interpreted in terms of any human dimension or reference; and on the other hand the consideration of religious data as testimonies of a religious faith of people with whom one wants to identify oneself. Unfortunately, these attitudes were often connected with the absurd alternative of being either 'against' or 'for' religion in the study of religion itself. (in Van Baaren and Drijvers 1973: 135)

Waardenburg wants to avoid both extremes by studying religion as a self-expression of human existence in different cultures and circumstances of time and place. But objections have been raised to his preference for living religions and his approach in general for he may not have left traditional phenomenology as far behind as he thinks. For example, it may be asked how far his concept of subjective meanings differs from 'the faith of the believers' and whether it is legitimate to assume that the meaning of human existence is only uncovered in religion. Waardenburg's critics object to the strong emphasis he puts on subjective meanings and the ultimate sense of life which, in their view, is not a profitable method for historical comparisons (for these criticisms see Van Baaren and Drijvers, 1973: 166–8).

The meaning of faith and the role of the believer in the study of religion have given rise to much debate, often without the necessary conceptual clarification, however. The most perceptive plea for attention to faith is found in the work of W. Cantwell Smith (1964, 1965, 1977, 1979). Smith argues strongly against the reification and objectivization of religion; instead, he prefers to speak of cumulative religious traditions and of faith. He criticizes the phenomenology of religion for being 'object-oriented in that it has addressed itself to religious phenomena but hardly to the persons who relate themselves to some or other among these and thereby make them religious' (1979: 7). For Smith, as for Waardenburg, it is the meaning of religious data for those who are committed to them which matters most. The study of religion thus becomes the study of religious persons and their faith. Faith is first and foremost to be understood in terms of a personal relationship between subjects (God and man). To be religious is ultimately a personal act but faith also finds objective expression in community, social institutions, art, ritual, words, ideas, etc. To develop personal understanding of another person's faith, one has to enter into dialogue with the person concerned and ensure that one's statements about a particular faith are acceptable to the believer himself (for this dialogical approach see W. Cantwell Smith, 1959; a critical reply to this article is given by Per Kvaerne (1973), followed by an additional discussion from W. Cantwell Smith in *Temenos* 9, 1973: 161–72). The question of religious truth is also a crucial one for Smith but it is primarily a question about persons and not about religions. Truth is expressed and embodied through personal existence rather than found in propositions.

It has been objected that 'faith' is open to similar ambiguities as 'religion' and has been equally reified in the past. It has also been said that personal understanding of the faith of other men, although in principle applicable to all historical periods, is in practice mainly restricted to living persons with whom one can engage in actual dialogue whereas such access is impossible to persons of the past. Although drawing on a wide range of historical and comparative data, Smith's works are often considered to belong to a primarily theological perspective rather than to that of the history and phenomenology of religion. The questions he asks are valid and important for the study of religion, and always challenging, but perhaps they are best understood as providing a foundation for the radical reconstruction of theology on the basis of comparative material. Faith is a comprehensively human and even more than human quality for Smith which he distinguishes from the varieties of historically developed beliefs. Although he approaches faith and belief very differently from Eliade, he is not unlike the latter in seeking a hermeneutic position which creatively combines the religious insights of the past with the new needs of the present. This is clearly stated in the preface to *Faith and Belief* (1979) where Smith describes his work as a partial answer to the following highly important and relatively new question:

what can our present awareness of the world history of religion and comparative culture contribute to our understanding of man; and particularly, of faith. . . . To think clearly and to live faithfully, in the new world in which we begin to find ourselves, means a radical revising of our inherited religious—and also secular—categories. . . . Man is entering a new phase in his and her self-consciousness, planetary pluralist, and historical; and human society, a new phase of global conflict or community. The ideas of our new life together must themselves be new. . . . The new thinking is radically new, yet is based upon, and continuous with, the past: the variegated classical heritage (Smith 1979: viii f.).

(For a more detailed discussion of Smith's approach see Baird 1971: 91–106 and Sharpe 1975: 282–5; for major themes and a bibliography of Smith's work, see W.G. Oxtoby (1976)).

From a different point of view Waardenburg has argued that the concept of 'faith' can be fruitfully used in phenomenological research if it is understood as a scholarly and not a religious concept (see Waardenburg (1978a), 'The Category of Faith in Phenomenological Research', also in IAHR Stockholm *Proceedings* 1975: 305–15). He tries to see the phenomenological approach to faith as quite separate from a normative-religious-theological one. In Waardenburg's view, the scholarly speech about faith is fundamentally different from the believers' speech about it. Research on faith cannot deal with faith as a metaphysical entity in itself but is always concerned with faith in a given culture, among certain people at a particular time and place. One might almost think of Cantwell Smith when Waardenburg writes:

Scholarship which is critical towards others and itself will ... observe that a number of statements and affirmations made by scholars about the faith of other people are, when it comes to the essentials, in fact more revealing for the spiritual qualities of the scholar and the climate of his milieu than for bringing into the open a quality of faith existing "behind" the religious facts (1978a: 82).

Whilst Waardenburg points to the difficulties in perceiving a faith behind given religious expressions and the ambiguous role of any (religious or human) faith held by the researcher or of relating the study of religion to interfaith developments, he is equally emphatic in not wanting to restrict research on religion to empirical fact-finding and rational theory-building. The question of faith has been one of the most intricate problems of the phenomenology of religion since its inception and in a 'new style' phenomenology, concerned with the study of meanings, human religiosity and religious mental universes, faith still has a place as a 'limit-concept' indicating the origin of the religious meanings which are being investigated (see Waardenburg 1978a: 88). This provides a much more comprehensive base for the study of religion for if the meaningfulness of faith and its expressions were primarily restricted to a circle of believers, little advance could be made in the theoretical and practical understanding of religion at the scholarly level. This is forcefully argued by J.E. Barnhart (1977) who has undertaken a detailed analysis of the different levels of 'meaning' in relation to religion. Whilst the self-understanding of the believer is an important factor in the study of religion, it cannot provide the sole or even major basis for the understanding and interpretation of religious phenomena. If one accepted without questioning the meaning attached to religious expressions by believers themselves, this could hardly provide sufficient data for the scientific study of religion.

Many more points could be raised in connection with the hermeneutical debate about the nature of interpretation, understanding, meaning, and faith, and their respective importance for the study of religion. The debate is an ongoing one and its participants and themes well demonstrate the need for a great deal of further reflection and conceptual refinement. Generally speaking, hermeneutical issues pertain perhaps more specifically to the problems raised by the phenomenology of religion than by the history of religions, especially if understood in a narrow sense (further aspects of hermeneutics are considered in the insightful discussion on 'The Hermeneutical Situation Today' in Allen 1978: 69–101). The entire debate about methodology, and about hermeneutics in particular, has enlarged the horizon of the history of religions field to such an extent that in the mid-seventies the history of religions could be described as 'a non-normative and non-theological approach to the study of religion' whilst it was also asserted that this approach 'using comparative and phenomenological methods became especially significant and influential in religious studies among scholars all over the world in' the 1960s' (*Encyclopaedia Britannica* 1975; Micropaedia V: 66). Strictly speaking, this is mistaken as the study of religion as an academic discipline enjoys a history of more than a hundred years. But if one understands the statement as applying to a new hermeneutic orientation within the discipline, as one must, it points to important new developments which are still in the making. Both the history and the phenomenology of religion continue to pose essentially philosophical questions about the understanding, interpretation, and explanation of religious data where the issues are not clear-cut but often debatable. The inherent tension of this situation comes clearly to the fore in the contemporary debate about the possibility of a 'science of religion'.

3.4. The debate about the science of religion

The term 'science of religion' has been in use since the late nineteenth century but only in a general and imprecise sense. Sometimes it has simply been equivalent to 'comparative religion' whilst at other times it has been a direct translation of *Religionswissenschaft*. More recently, the term has also been used to describe a more integral approach to the study of religion which intends to overcome the inherent tension between the history and phenomenology of religion. Pettazzoni and Eliade, for example, speak of 'science of religion' in this sense. For others, the term refers primarily to a specific understanding of the human and social sciences which might appear to be too restrictive for studying the multiple phenomena of religion. It is interesting to note, for example, that at the IAHR Marburg Congress, in 1960, the suggestion was made to change the name of the 'International Association for the History of Religions' to 'International Association for the Science of Religion.' However, this was not accepted and the reasons given clearly underline the limited understanding of 'science of religion' at that time. The report on the discussion states: 'The Secretary General is not in favour of this term as Phenomenology, Sociology and Psychology of Religion only have a rather small number of scholars in the sections. Moreover, "Science of Religion" would include Philosophy of Religion which is not in the field of our Association' (*Proceedings* 1961: 21 f.).

Discussing the different terms applied to the study of religion, Reinhard Pummer could still write in 1972 that 'science(s) of religion(s),' although used for a long time, was not generally accepted as a translation of *Religionswissenschaft* 'since the German term *Wissenschaft* has since Leibniz a much wider meaning than the English or French "science".... It designates every kind of disciplined research ... and not only natural science' (Pummer 1972: 103). After examining the existing theories in the study of religion, he endorsed the conclusion that, like all human sciences, the field of the history of religions belongs to the under-developed areas of research. Intense theoretical reflection on the basic premises of the study of religion is urgently required. 'What is needed are explanatory theories that are tested, adjusted and re-tested and so on, the test material being the data.' Although some scholars may find methodological discussions unattractive and secondary, they are necess-ary for 'hardly anybody will contend that it is better to follow an implicit methodology that has not been reflected on, rather than have a fully elaborate position' (Pummer 1972: 121).

In a subsequent article, however, written after the methodology conference in Turku, in 1973, and following a symposium on 'Methodology and World Religions' at Iowa University in 1974, the same author used the term 'science of religion' in a fully accepted sense without further discussion (see Pummer 1975; for the Iowa proceed-ings see Baird 1975). Pummer's article represents a comprehensive discussion of methodological publications up to 1975, and only a few aspects will be mentioned here. He points out that many methodological discussions turn around issues which have been under consideration for a long time now so that one can perceive an 'ongoing process of rethinking fundamental concepts in the attempt to clarify and refine them in accordance with the changed views in other areas.' There is also evidence of a 'continuous trend towards a more balanced study of religion that will not be as predominantly a study of texts as it traditionally has been. The inclusion of sociological, psychological, psychoanalytic, structural, etc., analyses in reflections on a theory of the science of religion should eventually lead to a more rounded approach, even though the possibilities and problems of interdisciplinary research still await exploration.' A review of the current literature shows 'the spreading of the awareness of the necessity for a comprehensive philosophy of the science of religion.' In reply to those who question the value of a continuous examination of methods, he rightly points out that methodology is not an end in itself. Yet in order to develop the scientific study of religion further now, it is necessary to discover the underlying methodological presuppositions, to delineate the limitations of a given method for a particular type of data, to adapt traditional methods or methods from other disciplines so that improved results may be obtained and last, not least, to attempt totally new approaches to the study of religion (see Pummer 1975: 179 f.).

In recent years, the term 'science of religion' has come to be much more widely used. It has acquired a more specific content relating to the ongoing discussion of what are the precise objects and methods of the study of religion, and it is with these attempts that we are concerned here. It is again indicative that the discussions on methodology at the Turku conference have been published under the title *Science of Religion* (ed. Honko 1979). Other books and articles, too, carry (science of religion' in their title, yet on closer examination it becomes clear that this term is far from unequivocal. Whilst it is true to say that the term 'science of religion' generally indicates a sharper focus on methodological questions in recent works, the expression itself covers a whole spectrum of different meanings, depending in particular on what is understood by 'science.' This wide divergence becomes apparent if we look at some of the recent publications, largely dating from the 1970s.

Two works published in the early 1970s explicitly use 'science of religion' in their title although both lean heavily on phenomenology, albeit in a different way. Michael Meslin's book *Pour une science des religions* (1973) refers to 'science' only in a general sense for he is primarily concerned with a study of the methods of analysis and understanding of *homo religiosus* in close dependence on earlier phenomenological views, especially those of Otto. According to Pummer's criticism, this cannot be considered as science however:

> To define religion as man's response to, or relationship with, the sacred either implies a theological or ontological understanding of the sacred, or, in the absence of such an understanding, requires a definition of it.... Mostly, 'the Sacred' is not defined at all; sometimes it is said that the sacred cannot be defined but only experienced. It is obvious that one thereby leaves the realm of scientific research (Pummer 1975: 164).

By contrast, Ninian Smart's work *The Science of Religion and the Sociology of Knowledge* (1973b) is much more directly concerned with the nature of explanation and the sense in which the study of religion may be considered to be scientific. He draws a clear distinction between doing theology in the sense of articulating a faith, and studying religion where theology itself is part of the *phenomenon* to be understood. Smart admits that although 'an overall strategy of a science of religion is desirable,' it has not yet been fully worked out. He then proceeds to describe the scientific study of religion as 'an enterprise which is aspectual, poly-methodic, pluralistic, and without clear boundaries' (1973b: 4, 8). This open-ended statement is made more explicit in his conclusions regarding the way in which we can speak of the scientific study of religion:

> First of all, it is scientific in the sense that it is not determined by a position within a field—that is, it begins neither from a theological nor from an atheistic standpoint. Second, though it looks for theories, it does not begin by building theories into phenomenological descriptions and it adopts methodological neutralism in its descriptive and evocative tasks. Third, this description and evocation begin in a sense from the participants and attempt to delineate the way the Focus looks from their point of view. Phenomenology thus differs from the physical sciences, because it has to deal with conscious beings who think and feel. Fourth, it is scientific in having an analogy to the experimental method, which is the use of cross-cultural comparisons. Fifth, it makes use of such methods as may be evolved in the disciplines which share in the study of religion, as being aspectual and polymethodic. Sixth, the scientific study of religion incorporates

dynamic and static typologies, which attempt to illuminate and explain religious phenomena, but relates always to the particularities of historical traditions.

It is worth stressing that the scientific study of religion is scientific in a manner
appropriate to its subject-matter; it is not simply bound to statistics and still less to causal
laws of a hard kind. Very rarely can one say in the field of religion that 'whenever X
occurs, then Y occurs', even if we can point to recurrent patterns. But this should not
discourage us from trying to put the study of religion on a scientific and at the same time
human basis (1973b: 158 f.).

In 1976, Penner concluded his retrospective review of the methodological debate with the statement that current publications and
activities 'all indicate that the science of religion is once again building
up new theoretical capital' (Penner 1976: 16). He also argued against the
widely held view that the science of religion is distinctive and non-
reductive. In his opinion, this is based on a misunderstanding of the true
function of 'reduction;' the latter is needed in developing an adequate
explanation for religious phenomena. He agrees with the anthropologist
Spiro in saying that the determinants of religion have to be analysed and
established empirically; by so 'reducing' religion to its various con-
stituents, one does not in any way destroy its essential quality but one
can explain aspects of it. In the scientific study of religion such search for
explanations is vital: 'If we do not "like" the explanation we must find
the theory *inadequate*, false, or trivial. It simply will no longer serve the
science of religion verbally to abuse other approaches to religion as
"reductionistic". All approaches to religion are reductionistic in that all
approaches assume either implicitly or explicitly some theory of interpretation or explanation' (Penner 1976: 15).

In the discussion on the evaluation of previous methods in the study
of religion at Turku a similar point was made in emphasizing the
important distinction between the widely held wish to understand and
the pursuit of science. Human understanding as the fulfilment of a basic
need might be attained in a number of ways but the difficulty arises over
the way in which understanding is transposed into scientific statement,
i.e., over epistemology:

The second step was then to arrange the perceptions—science was, indeed, merely the
ordering of perceptions—since if the understanding remained unordered, there would

be no science of religion. The difficulties, then, were twofold: the epistemological aspect, i.e. the gathering of information, and the problem of what scientific system could be built up on the basis of the information thus gathered. If, as had repeatedly been stated, the science of religion was an empirical science, then it must be pursued according to the rules imposed on empirical science by epistemology and the theory of science. Scientists of religion, after all, could not be an exclusive group with a unique epistemology, or they would never be accepted as partners in scientific discussion (in Honko 1979: 219 f.).

But as another participant in the discussion, W.H. Capps, pointed out, there are at present a great number of 'varieties of operational definitions' and 'multiple methodological interests and intentions' to be found in the study of religion. One may rightly ask 'is the science of religion a subject or a field? Is it a discipline or is it multi-disciplinary? Does it have a proper subject, or does the multiplicity of its interests prohibit a common focal point?' (in Honko 1979: 180). A great deal of further reflection is required to clarify these questions. One of the most important issues which remained perhaps unexamined at Turku, is the question of what model of 'empirical science' and which 'theory of science' are used as a basis for discussions about the science of religion. Sometimes one must question whether the underlying model itself may be out of date as far as recent developments in the social and natural sciences are concerned.

Closely modelled on the social sciences and particularly influenced by developments in cultural anthropology are some Dutch discussions on the science of religion. This is apparent from the papers of the 'Groningen working-group for the study of fundamental problems and methods of science of religion' (founded in 1968), published under the title *Religion, Culture and Methodology* (Van Baaren and Drijvers 1973). In his contribution 'Science of Religion as a Systematic Discipline. Some Introductory Remarks' (1973: 36–56) T.P. van Baaren argues that religion is a function of culture (meaning a way or form of expression), connected with and interacting with other forms of culture. Religion ought to be studied as a function of culture and this does not imply an attempt at reduction but a strong emphasis on an empirical study of religions which excludes questions of the philosophy of religion. Van Baaren holds the view that the fourfold distinction between the history of religions, phenomenology of religion, psychology of religion, and sociology of religion refers to four different approaches rather than disciplines in the study of religion but has little systematic value. For him, the systematic study of religion is not a historical discipline but a systematic one of a non-normative character: 'science of religion is not concerned with discovering the essence of *the* or *a* religion; this is a task of philosophy or theology.... It only studies religions as they are empirically and disclaims any statements concerning the value and truth of the phenomena studied' (1973: 47). 'Science of religion in all its forms consists of describing, classifying and explaining the material studied, and if need be of understanding it' (1973: 48). That means science of religion is no more subjective than other *Geisteswissenschaften* but 'it aims at reaching a maximum of objectivity and a minimum of subjectivity' (1973: 50). Similar arguments are found in Van Baaren's earlier article 'Systematische Religionswissenschaft' (1969).

Van Baaren's views are critically discussed in H. J.W. Drijvers' contribution 'Theory Formation in Science of Religion and the Study of the History of Religions' (Van Baaren and Drijvers, 1973: 57–77) which further illustrates the strong dependence on cultural anthropology, particularly on Spiro's view that religion has a cognitive, a substantive, and an expressive function and is to be explained in terms of society and personality. According to Drijver, the social sciences 'supplied the principal material for theoretical renovation in the systematical science of religion' and they 'also prove useful for history of religions in their historical aspect' (1973: 73).

The 'faith of the believer' can no longer be a legitimate subject of the science of religion. The current development is away from an earlier phenomenology of religion and a mainly historical and literary approach to the study of religion towards more strictly defined systematic and comparative research which seeks explanations rather than mere *Verstehen* in terms of an intuitive grasp: therefore the strong emphasis on correct terminology and on the formal character and descriptive precision of all terms employed. The science of religion investigates religious conceptions, values and behaviour. Whilst traditional research has been primarily concerned with religious conceptions, it is open to discussion whether renewed attention to religious behaviour is the starting-point of an entirely new science of religion based on the methodic primacy of behaviour (for a detailed discussion of these complex issues see the 'Epilogue' in Van Baaren and Drijvers 1973: 159–68).

The influence of the social sciences, particularly of cultural anthropology, was also very marked at the Turku conference where a subsection was specifically devoted to the 'religio-anthropological approach' (including a paper by M.E. Spiro on 'Symbolism and Functionalism in the Anthropological Study of Religion'). Moreover, a substantial part of the conference dealt with 'religion as expressive culture' (examining theories concerning the ritual process, the language of religion, and depth structures of religious expression). One of the main organisers, Professor Lauri Honko, summarized the discussion about anthropology as follows:

> Cultural anthropology still enjoys a strong position within the scientific study of religion, not least due to its fieldwork techniques and methodology of cultural comparison. A kind of bifurcation appears for instance in the significance which anthropologists investigating religion accord to the relation 'man-the "otherworldly" (god, etc.)' in comparison with the relation 'man-society'. It is this latter relation which has always been central both for cultural and social anthropology.... Discussion arose at the conference as to whether religious symbols are manipulative in nature or not: and the dominant trend appeared to support the opinion that the existence of a symbol cannot be explained anything like exhaustively in terms of economic, social, or similar causes. If symbols are tools, they are so only in a very general sense—i.e. tools of language, thought, and living. The man-'otherworldly' relation continues to hold an important position in the metatheory of religious studies, despite the fact that some anthropologists do not consider it capable of operationalization (cf. the discussion of the term *numen*), while for some historians of religions this appeared to be a question to which different religions would in an inductive approach provide different answers. On the whole it seems that it was precisely the anthropologists and folklorists who most often came in for criticism, sometimes on the grounds that their methods of investigation were those of the natural sciences, sometimes because of their objective typologies, which were even seen as a threat to humanist scholarship (Honko 1979: XXIV).

However, such a strong dependence on the methodology of the social sciences raises the question whether the science of religion ceases to be a field of studies in its own right and is simply identical with the social sciences. The very expression 'the scientific study of religion' has, for some at least, become synonymous with research in the sociology of religion (see, for example, J. Milton Yinger's well-known textbook *The*

Scientific Study of Religion (1970), and also the American *Journal for the Scientific Study of Religion*). But many important issues arising in the study of religions, both with regard to society and individual, cannot be exhaustively dealt with by the sociological approach.

A further narrowing in the understanding of 'science of religion' is found in the quantitative and statistical researches on 'the theory and methodology of the science of religions' undertaken by the Polish Institute of Philosophy and Sociology (Polish Academy of Sciences, Warsaw). The results of these researches are published in the journals *Euhemer* and *Studia Religioznawcze* (with short summaries in Russian, English, German, and sometimes French). One of the editors, Poniatowski, speaks of a '*Metareligionswissenschaft*' and refers to the development of '*scientometrics*' in the study of religion, an approach which implies further analysis of a mainly theoretical and statistical kind of earlier research on religion. However, the heavy emphasis on quantitative data allows for little creative originality and yields perhaps few new results.

In the discussions about the science of religion much depends on whether the term 'science' is understood in a narrow, empirical-positivistic sense or in a wider, more integral manner. One must ask whether the underlying model of 'science' is primarily that of the natural-physical sciences, the life sciences, the social sciences or of the human sciences in the widest sense. If it is the latter, the interrelationship of dialectical and hermeneutical perspectives is of primary importance for the interpretation of the data; moreover, it is also less obvious what constitutes a fact or data in the human sciences. The limitations imposed on the study of religion by particular methodological models, especially those drawn from scientific empiricism, have been examined and strongly critized by several writers in recent years, (for a detailed discussion see A.M. Frazier 1970; J.F. Miller 1975; D. Wiebe 1975 and 1978).

Miller, for example, argues that science, as currently understood, possesses inherent limitations to deal with the phenomena of religion, and this for the following reasons. The scientific *criteria of causality* are unable to be met and are prejudicial to the data of religion as is the very naturalistic reductive methodological *directionality* of science. Also, the meaning criteria employed by the *experimental* scientist, especially the identification of the meaning of a term or symbol with the criterion for identifying the referent of the term or symbol, are impossible to meet in religion if that referent is God; moreover, correspondence is an adequate criterion of truth in religion. In *theoretical* science, where meaning is defined implicitly within the system and truth determined by coherence (as it must be in religion), the scientific theoretical framework is either conceptually incompatible with or inadequate for the fundamental data of religion (see Miller 1975: 147).

R.H. Penner and E.A. Yonan (1972) pointed out earlier that methodological discussions revolving around *Religionswissenschaft* have begun to recognize the essential importance of the problems of definition, reduction, explanation and understanding, but that there has been little explicit analysis of these problems. Drawing on wide-ranging discussions of what contemporary philosophers of science understand by definition, reduction, and explanation, Penner and Yonan apply their results to the science of religion in order to achieve greater clarification about its theoretical premises. Their important article (1972) has been widely discussed in subsequent literature, including G. Dudley's study *Religion on Trial* (1977), which is primarily devoted to a much wider context, namely, that of a critical examination of Eliade's methodology.

Like others, Dudley criticizes current methodological discussions in the study of religion for their undue dependence on outdated theoretical models of the natural sciences (see especially 1977: 112–38). He asks, with some justification, why phenomenologists and historians of religions should especially want to identify their discipline as an empirical science. Instead, he urges contemporary religion scholars to mount a counter-offensive against empirical positivism in the history of religions. Discussing the role of rational criticism in the natural sciences, Dudley writes:

The entire procedure of observation, inductive reasoning, and empirical verification is taken over by empiricist historians of religion from the natural sciences. They regard that procedure as a passport to objectivity that makes *Religionswissenschaft* a true science of religions. The anomaly in this dogma, and indeed in the whole dilemma of *Religionswissenschaft*, is that for nearly three decades, even before the empiricists gained their prominence in the international meetings of the history of religions, empiricism in the natural sciences has been under sweeping criticism. In fact, positivist empiricism in the sciences has been so devastatingly criticized by both philosophers and scientists that it is rather redundant to attack it again (1977: 121 f.).

Based on more recent developments in the philosophy of science, found in the works of Lakatos, Barbour, and Toulmin, Dudley proposes that the field of *Religionswissenschaft* desperately needs a methodology of research programmes built around a core theory (which, he thinks, Eliade's work can provide, a statement which will no doubt be heavily contested by other scholars). Auxiliary hypotheses can be adjusted or rejected, as the case may be, but the core theory can be pursued until all its potentialities have been explored. Such a research programme will be flexible and progressive if it leads to the discovery of new and un-expected phenomena and accounts for phenomena already known but unexplained. At present, empirical positivism is so much in trouble in the natural sciences that historians of religion are inviting problems by importing it into their own field:

To burden *Religionswissenschaft* with all the methodological dogmas of inductive reason-ing and empirical verification is to bring weakness, not strength, into its methodology. What is true for history of religions is true for all the humane sciences. The answer to the sway of empirical positivism in so many university disciplines is not to draw a sharper line between the natural and the humane sciences or between the sciences and the humanities but to seek the same methodological flexibility that has become characteristic in the sciences themselves (1977: 126).

In the various discussions about the most appropriate methodology for the science of religion, however understood, the shared aim of all protagonists is to defend the autonomy of the study of religion and its independence from normative stances derived from philosophical or theological presuppositions. In this sense one can speak of the necessary critical function of the study of religion vis-à-vis established philosoph-ical and religious traditions (for a detailed discussion of this point see K. Rudolph 1978). But from a position of counter-critique one might argue that the claim to methodological neutrality is a myth, that all description involves at least a partial explanation and evaluation. (Dudley (1977) discusses 'the normative/descriptive fallacy' and points out that it is false to suppose that scientific and normative theories are necessarily mutually exclusive. In fact, in many of our most significant scientific theories, normative and descriptive aspects are inextricably related.) Science, as traditionally understood, can only look at religion from a naturalistic point of view; yet claims relating to a supernatural referent or transcendent focus form an integral part of religion. Thus, a narrow scientific understanding of religion might well be a major category mistake if it refuses to consider important philosophical and theological questions which at some point arise in all religious traditions.

One of the most fundamental requirements of any science is that its method must be fully appropriate to its subject-matter. Many approaches to the study of religion are so narrow and reductionist that they may rightly be called 'pseudo-scientific' rather than scientific in the true sense of the word, for they are hardly commensurate with the multidimensional realities found in the institutions, expressions, and experience of religion. Whilst the classical phenomenology of religion with its intuitive approach, its emphasis on the essence of religion and the centrality of religious experience, represents perhaps an 'idealistic-essentialist' reduction of religion against which one must argue that the experiential dimension is only one aspect of religion and that other aspects require other methodologies, the pseudo-scientific limitation of the study of religion to empirical-descriptive 'hard' data represents a reductionism of another kind which has to be equally strongly criticized.

The development of both positions in their extreme form can to some extent be explained as the necessary opposition to and critique of earlier attitudes and enquiries, subsequently considered to be a serious limitation of the study of religion in the wider sense. Whilst it was historically necessary to develop the study of religion in an oppositional mode of thought against the entrenched positions of a narrowly conceived theology or philosophy, we might now be nearer the development of a more relational and inclusive mode of thought which might even recognize the convergence of the questions posed in religious studies and theology. It is perhaps this attempt which is best described as the development of an integral science of religion.

In his description of the '*Panorama des sciences des religions*' Séguy (1970) distinguishes the 'theological sciences' from the 'non-theological sciences of religion' which originally developed in opposition to the theological sciences. He considers the development of the non-theological sciences of religion as an integral part of the process of the modern secularisation of knowledge to which even theologians contribute now. But he also discerns a continuous movement from opposition through composition towards integration in the ever greater interdependence of all aspects of knowledge.

We are far from having reached such a stage of integration in the study of religion but various proposals have recently been made to combine the multiple perspectives and questions of the study of religion in a more integral manner. The vehement exclusion of philosophical questions on the part of many historians of religion is perhaps due to the fact that in practice philosophy of religion has meant a narrowly circumscribed Christian philosophy of religion without taking into account the wide-ranging philosophical questions arising from other religious and cultural traditions.

There exists now widespread dissatisfaction with scientific theories of religion because of their reductionist models. Paul Heelas, in his discussion of 'Some Problems with Religious Studies' (1978), has argued that the study of religion is characterized by competing or incommensurable paradigms. In order to develop a more coherent study of religion, it is necessary to assess these competing paradigms for 'the very nature of the religious alters depending on whether one applies, for example, a positivistic or a theological paradigm.' The fact that religious studies is at present marked by too much paradigm-dependence and faced with an invasive relativism and a phenomenal insecurity makes Heelas say 'that there is an inherent tendency for religious studies (studying the religious as phenomenon) to become something rather different (namely reinterpreting, even reconstituting, the religious in terms of paradigms which cannot be justified with respect to intra-religious criteria)' (1978: 7, 1). The relationship between the different paradigms of religious studies, theology, and a more comprehensive or integral science of religion is frequently being debated but it is impossible to summarize all relevant arguments in detail here. Charles Davis, the editor of the Canadian journal *Sciences Religieuses/Studies in Religion* (SR), which in

1970 replaced the former *Canadian Journal of Theology*, speaks of a reconvergence of theology and religious studies in terms of the further
development of a methodologically coherent, unified field of studies
which unites the historical, scientific, and philosophical levels of studying the data of religion (see Davis 1974–5). He thinks that the empirical,
scientific study of religions cannot be accommodated under the title
'history of religions' or under 'phenomenology of religion.' The latter
should be dropped because of its misleading associations. But he also
argues against the science of religion being merely descriptive: 'Its
descriptive classificatory function is only preliminary. Like sociology
and the other human sciences, the science of religion has to devise
explanatory concepts, models, laws, and theories' (1974–5: 215). In his
distinction between structural and dialectical explanations and between
the reality and existence of the objects of religion Davis depends on
Smart. Reserving the term 'theology' for critical reflection upon religion
(and not applying it to the communicative function of religion so often
confused with theology), Davis suggests that the science of religion is a
more advanced stage of systematic theology, not an essentially different
enterprise. He states:

> The science of religion is an empirical inquiry distinguished from sociology and
> psychology by its primary concern with religious data as religious. Unlike history, it
> deals with what is general or at least recurrent in religious experience and expression. Its
> aim is not just descriptive and classificatory, but explanatory. It should be productive of
> precise, theoretical concepts to make possible a unified grasp of the manifolds of
> concrete religious data and also of explanatory hypotheses and theories. Its task would
> seem to be a more methodical carrying out on a wider range of data of the work of
> ordering done by systematic theology on the data of a single tradition (1974–5: 219).

Davis's suggestion gave rise to further debates and questions which
cannot be reported here but which are evidence of the search for a more
integral approach to the study of religion. For a reaction to Davis's ideas
see *SR* 4, 1974/75 and *SR* 5, 1975/76, as well as B.J.F. Lonergan
(1976–77) and K. Klostermaier (1976–77). Davis (1981) has again
restated his position in the article 'Theology and Religious Studies.'

Davis's ideas are not unlike Pannenberg's discussion (1976) of the
science of religion as a critical theology of religion. Pannenberg argues
that a 'mere phenomenology, psychology or sociology of religion

cannot get to grips with religion's specific object, and the claims of such investigations to be sciences of religion and religions must consequently be described as problematic.' Following to some extent both Heiler and Troeltsch, Pannenberg considers the real thematic of religions to be 'the communication of divine reality experienced in them' which can only be made the object of scientific investigation in a *theology* of religions which would subject the assertions of religious traditions to critical examination and would not depend in its interpretation on a previous religious position. Pannenberg seems to think that this kind of critical theology can bridge the current gap between philosophy of religion and the history of religions (see 1976: 365; 364; 368 n., 689). However, many scholars would rightly fear that the science of religion is not given the necessary autonomy here but is being reabsorbed into theology.

A different and more truly integral approach, less dependent on systematic-critical theology, is found in Georg Schmid's important work (1979). He argues for the necessary role of a critical-reflexive but constructive methodology in the science of religion whose close examination of its own procedure is of central importance. However, methodology does not produce immovable basic laws or complete, self-contained methods but only *principles* in the sense of 'beginnings' or 'first steps leading to other steps and indicating the basic direction of these other steps ... Principles are elements of scientific perception about which science can attain clarity but which science can never hold as unshakable dogmas' (1979: 2 f.). However, Schmid also argues that such critical reflection must be applied to the whole of religion, notwithstanding the enormity of individual data. This reflection on the whole of religion must be combined with the science's reflection upon itself, that is, with a critical consideration of its own task, premises, and methods. It is precisely these three areas which Schmid's work analyses with great subtlety.

Schmid makes a clear and important distinction between *religious reality* and the *reality of religion*. However, this distinction can also appear confusing to the reader as these terms are linguistically too similar to remain sufficiently distinct. He calls *religious reality* the historically demonstrable side of religion which alone can be the object of religious-scientific research:

It means, firstly, *the enormously wide field of religious data*, which include holy writings, and other documents, prayer books, theological treatises, the formation of temples, cultic objects, pictures, symbols, songs, church offices and forms of community. We name religious reality, secondly, the whole manifold of religious life and experience which expresses itself or conceals itself in religious data: sacrifice, prayer, meditation, thanksgiving, worship, search, petition, celebration, experience, remembrance, realization, belief, hope, imitation, astonishment, rebellion, enthusiasm, confession teaching and obedient action.

In what follows, the *reality of religion* means *what is intended in all of this life and experience*, the whence and whereto of all this searching, hoping, believing and worshipping. The reality of religion means the reality for the sake of which all religious reality comes into being. . . .

As science, science of religion knows of no direct access to the reality of religion. The reality of religion is present to the science only in the witness of the religious reality. Only the religious reality is the immediate object of the science of religion, and the science researches this object systematically, this is, in awareness of method and consistent procedure within the chosen method (1979: 11f.).

Not even theology has direct access to the reality of religion. In principle, no aspect of religious reality as datum and event in the life of the individual and society is removed from critical questioning and systematic research. In Schmid's view, the specific characteristic of the modern science of religion is the bringing together of integral reflection and specific research without subsuming the one under the other. Such a systematic science of religion is different from the history of religions and also from phenomenology of religion. However, Schmid's own principles of an integral science of religion might themselves be considered to belong to a new-style phenomenological approach.

Schmid understands the science of religion as the attempt of modern man to overcome his fundamental dilemma with regard to traditional religion by means of systematic research of all religious reality. The strength of his approach lies in the fact that it embraces not only traditional religion but also modern forms of 'secular' and 'anonymous' religion outside all organised religious institutions through its attempt to critically reflect on 'the whole of religion.' As a working hypothesis he states that '*the whole of religion discloses itself in its meaning*' where meaning refers to 'what religion says to one who lives it' (1979: 64).

The major objection to Schmid's work concerns his far too inclusive definition of religion, grounded in a particular philosophical approach which focusses primarily on the individual person and neglects the wider social and historical context of religious data. 'Religion' is here mainly a personal quality rather than an objective phenomenon as when he writes:

Religion is the reality of a person .... Religion is the attempt to find the way beyond the individual thing to the whole. It is the infinitely manifold, continual referal and referring of man to the ground, goal, meaning and middle of all that is real .... Consequently, religion occurs in every human being. A person completely without religion would be a person without reality (1979: 150 ff.).

In principle, the science of religion must investigate and critically examine every form of religion but the only object to which scientific observation has direct access is the broad field of religious data. Schmid distinguishes three dimensions of religion of which religious data is the first, religious experience the second, and the reality of religion the third. Religious experience never comes directly before the eye of the researcher; what the science of religion can say about it, is only based on its research of religious data and their interpretation. The third dimension, the reality of religion (what others have called the transcendent focus or referent) is radically removed from direct scientific observation; it does not lie within the area of religious reality but it is *intended* in all religious reality. 'For the science of religion, this dimension is only present in the religious reality, but it is not part of that reality. Rather, the religious reality refers beyond itself to this dimension. More precisely: the third dimension is present only in the second dimension, which is indicated in the first dimension, the religious reality' (1979: 38). This schema is to some extent reminiscent of Heiler's diagram of three concentric circles (discussed above in the section on phenomenology; see p 91 f.), criticized by Schmid as 'timeless-unhistorical' (1979: 174). In all fairness it must be said that Schmid keeps his dimensions analytically more distinct and makes it clear that the science of religion is strictly limited to the first dimension of religious data. Here, three major methodological steps are clearly distinguished yet interrelated: that of the perception and description of the data (which involves a well delineated phenomenological task); of comprehension (which concerns the relations in which a datum stands, taking into account the historical, cultural, economic, political, and social conditions of a particular time); and that of understanding (which asks about the meaning of the description and setting-in-relation of the data; it asks not only about the relation in which religious data stand but also about the relation which these data are according to their own intentions).

The integral science of religion thus consists of the description, comprehension, and understanding of the broad field of religious data. As a true 'science', however, defined as 'the systematic research of a definite area of the real' (1979: 159), it has no monopoly over research on religion but is closely interrelated with the systematic-scientific tasks of parallel disciplines. Schmid critically examines many recent publications, particularly in German, concerned with methodology and the science of religion (which stands here for *systematische Religionswissenschaft*). Of particular value is his insightful discussion of the demarcation, tension, and interrelationship which exist between the science of religion and systematic theology. His treatment of this issue is conceptually more formalized than that of either Pannenberg (1976) or Davis (1974, 1981), and perhaps more clarifying and helpful in its distinctions. Unfortunately, Schmid mentions neither Pannenberg's nor Davis's discussion of theology and the science of religion; instead, he examines at length Ulrich Mann's 'synoptic method' (1973) as a conscious correlation of theology, science of religion, philosophy of religion, and psychology of religion.

Schmid's *Principles of Integral Science of Religion* (1979) combines systematic and critical reflection with a penetrating analysis of methodological principles, offering at the same time an overall perspective of synthesis. He clearly delineates the areas of study in religion (as the only possible field of the science of religion) from those of experience and reality, yet he also systematically accounts for their interrelationship. This work of analysis and synthesis is an important contribution to greater theory formation as well as to more adequate insight and understanding. It will not doubt find its critics. (A critical review of Schmid's earlier work (1971) is found in U. Tworuschka, (1972)). One must question Schmid's far too inclusive understanding of religion, which does not sufficiently distinguish between 'religion' and 'non-religion';

similarly, his methodological boundaries between philosophy and the science of religion appear to be blurred in places. Much further work is required in working out more adequate criteria for an integral science of religion, taking into account the work of other contemporary scholars. However, criticisms notwithstanding, Schmid's work requires the closest attention as it certainly represents an inspiring challenge for the contemporary scientific study of religion, understood as an ongoing systematic and holistic task.

The foregoing survey has shown that even under the heading of 'science of religion' there exists no common consensus as to the precise nature of the study of religion. Different scholars understand 'science' as well as 'religion' in a different way. The tensions between different methodological stances, objective and subjective factors, as well as between a primarily quantitative or qualitative evaluation of the data, continue to affect much of the methodological discussions about the science of religion. Although several scholars feel that a more rigorous pursuit of methodology may raise more difficulties than it answers questions, it seems evident today that we possess a number of different, but very fruitful approaches to the study of religion which provide helpful alternative methods and levels of interpretation. They each possess particular strengths and weaknesses which need close examining so that their relative usefulness as heuristic tools becomes sufficiently clear. I take the view that this plurality of methods and positions, far from being deplorable, reflects in fact the healthy state of the study of religion and is comparable to the situation in other sciences. It is wholly mistaken to treat science in general or any science in particular as monolithic entities, for there always exists a diversity of theories and schools of thought in the practice of scientific disciplines. What is central, however, is the systematic and orderly accumulation and analysis of data and their interpretation within an overall framework which allows for the development of commonly shared conceptualizations and theories. It is this need for a common body of knowledge, for the development of conceptual skills and the necessary place of methodology in any field of studies which has yet to become more widely accepted in the study of religion. In spite of many wholly justified criticisms regarding inadequate methods, further theory formation and critical methodological reflections are of paramount importance. To proceed further with the study of religion we need to examine as closely as possible what we are doing for 'there is some merit in exhibiting what we study and how we study it with the greatest possible precision; . . . if what we study and how we study it cannot be exhibited with an appropriate precision, then serious questions can be raised not only about our speaking emotive nonsense, but even more devastating than that, about our not saying much of anything worth saying at all' (G. J. Larson 1978: 459).

4. Concluding remarks: present and future perspectives

Our survey has ranged over a great number of publications and authors. It has been concerned with the clarification of current methodological issues and has focussed in particular on the debates regarding the historical and phenomenological approaches to the study of religion. There are many scholars whose contributions have not been discussed here and no injustice is intended by this, for it would seem that most works fall within one or the other category of trends surveyed above. The present article cannot be more than a summary survey of the major developments since 1950; some further publications, not explicitly referred to in our discussion, will be mentioned in the Bibliography below.

Today the study of religion has access to an immense range of data which require for their systematic study a critical methodological awareness and refined conceptual tools so that the demanding tasks of analysis, explanation, and possibly synthesis, may be undertaken in a more differentiated manner. It is clear that particular data require different methods and approaches. But in the formulation of analytically more precise questions and the ongoing search for more adequate explanations, it also becomes clear that the methodological perspectives represented by the history, phenomenology, hermeneutics, and science

of religion can to some extent be considered as an interrelated con-
tinuum. Whether acknowledged or unacknowledged, we repeatedly
encounter in the methodological debate the intersection of such fundamental questions as 'What is religion?' 'What is history?' 'What is
science?.' The kind of answer given to one of these questions will shape
the answer to the others. The criteria for answering are not provided by
the questions themselves nor by the data grouped under them; ultimately, an answer to each of these questions requires the choice of a
particular hermeneutical and philosophical stance. In fact, one may
argue that there cannot be a final answer to these issues but that the
debate is an ongoing one. Different generations of scholars have given
and will no doubt continue to give different answers to these questions.
Whilst some may consider such a situation as unacceptable, because of
its inherent uncertainty and lack of reassurance, others regard it as an
inviting challenge to continue wrestling with important difficulties in
order to achieve greater clarity and deeper understanding.

In undertaking a survey of the methodological debate one realizes the
importance of the historical dimension for understanding contemporary
arguments about methodology. Particular aspects of current controversies are often deeply rooted in a scholarly tradition extending far before
1950 or even 1930 and, in some cases, even to work done before 1900.
This point is well brought out in Eric Sharpe's wide-ranging historical
survey *Comparative Religion* (1975). A sharper awareness and more accurate knowledge of the historical problematic can also result in the
feeling that certain contemporary works are rather ahistorical and parochial or possess a quality of *déjà vu* about them, largely due to their
ignorance of earlier methodological discussions. On the other hand, an
exaggerated insistence on more rigorous methodological requirements
can result in an unproductive intellectual aridity and a lack of creative
originality, if not to say insight, in interpreting religious phenomena.

If one may characterize the present situation among younger scholars
of religion in terms of a mood, it is primarily a mood of uncertainty
which permeates much of the contemporary debate: mounting criticisms and uncertainty about the achievements of the past; doubts and
uncertainty about the direction of present developments, particularly
when the field of study is conceived in terms of a 'science of religion';

uncertainty and disagreement about the right kind of method(s); uncertainty about the very aims of methodology and theory in the study of religion. Some of the best voiced fears regarding the value of methodology have perhaps been expressed by Wilfred Cantwell Smith. However, many of these may be due to a misunderstanding regarding the nature and role of method in the study of religion. If methodology becomes narrowly circumscribed and arid, an end in itself rather than a helpful means for the most adequate and comprehensive study of the many dimensions of religion, it must be criticized. However, if the fear of methodology is simply based on a lack of intellectual effort or on unexamined assumptions grounded in subjectivity, it must equally be critized.

The history and phenomenology of religion cannot serve as a substitute ontology or soteriology as Eliade and others sometimes seem to think. In order to grow in a dynamic and fruitful way, the study of religion must be conceived as a truly scientific enterprise, understood not in a narrow scientistic-reductionist sense but in a wider and more integral manner as the attempt to develop more refined methods of study truly commensurate to what is being studied. It is open to much debate, however, whether a further development of Eliade's work, for example, would provide the most suitable framework for a future research programme as Dudley (1977) has argued. In fact, one must seriously question whether Eliade's fundamental construct of *homo religiosus*, uncritically taken up as an interpretative category by many epigones, is not more of a hindrance than a help for the further development of the study of religion.

If one considers future prospects in the study of religion, the mood of uncertainty prevailing among the present generation does not only relate to questions intrinsic to the subject area but also to situational factors such as the uncertain status of the study of religion in universities and colleges of several western countries today. Whilst the subject as a whole has considerably expanded and continues to grow, and especially is coming more into its own in Asian and African countries, it is somewhat on the retreat in some western countries. This is linked to the general economic recession, particularly in Britain, the uncertain status of an integral science of religion within the older universities, and the institutional ramifications of traditional theology departments so that it is often difficult, if not to say impossible, to be free from theological tutelage. It may also be due to the extraordinary worldwide growth of the sociology of religion which has resulted in the taking over of research interests and projects belonging to the study of religion in a wider sense. Perhaps it may be due most of all to the general lack of consensus among contemporary religion scholars, the absence of a common core theory, of clearly stated aims and objectives, and the relatively underdeveloped links of international collaboration in spite of the existence of the IAHR. It is a fact worth reflecting on that the attendance of mostly European delegates at the History of Religions Congress in Oxford (1908) was as high or even higher than the international participation at most of the later IAHR Congresses. Although the study of religion has grown globally in many different respects, this is not necessarily reflected in a higher attendance at the IAHR Congresses. There may be many explanations for this, one of which I take to be the lack of a more fully developed international organisational structure. A more efficient network at the regional and global level would facilitate closer scholarly contact, more efficient communication and information, and ultimately perhaps the development of international data-processing in the study of religion.

We are living in an increasingly internationally oriented world where some of the scholarly legacy from the past sometimes appears to be more of a ballast than an enriching heritage. One must seriously ask how far the data presented in some works on the history and phenomenology of religion are too selective and culture-specific instead of being globally representative. What further developments will be necessary for the study of religion to become a truly integral discipline which investigates the religious history of humankind in a systematic and comprehensive manner? Widengren's plea that the study of religion has been primarily historical since its origin is no sufficient reason for pursuing historical studies in the same way as in the past. There is much need for change and especially for a greater integration and synthesis of diverse data within a truly global framework. To achieve such integration it is not enough to bring different disciplines simply together within one university department without attempting a greater theoretical elucidation of the overall

framework and its underlying assumptions. Specialisations will continue to exist side by side if no conscious effort at the interpenetration of
different perspectives is made in the work of individual scholars. Some
past approaches to the study of religion may well be outdated and block
further developments whereas other perspectives are much more open
and promising. If one is primarily interested in fuller integration and
synthesis, one must also ask how far current studies are still affected by a
'conceptual imperialism' developed in the political context of past colonialism. For example, how far are the conceptual and linguistic aspects
of the study of religion in European universities still dependent on
earlier colonial contacts or based on data and theories originally developed by colonial ethnography and anthropology? Also, how far are
many conceptual tools in the study of religion too closely dependent on
specific developments of western Christian theology? Moreover, the not
infrequent use of Latin and Greek terms in the titles of books, journals,
and articles, reflects the continuing influence of the European classical
heritage among a small western intellectual elite. But the time has come
to question whether the underlying assumptions in choosing such a
terminology are not too exclusive and may thus prove a potential
obstacle to a more comprehensive and global development of the study
of religion. The concern for the classical, for religions in the ancient
world rather than religions in their importance for society today, can
become a stumbling-block for communication and make the study of
religion appear as an obsolete pursuit. The more one reflects on present
requirements and future developments, the more one begins to see the
need for a fundamental paradigm-shift in the overall orientation of the
study of religion.

   This applies also to the handling of data relating to the study of
Christianity. Although Christianity has enjoyed a privileged position in
theological scholarship, it has not been satisfactorily represented in
comparative historical studies. It is apparent to many that the study of
Christianity could gain a great deal if it is approached from the perspectives of the history of religions and of phenomenology. Although
Christians have written on religions other than their own for many
years, it is only now that the results of a closer examination and critique
of Christianity by scholars from non-Christian traditions are beginning

to gain attention. It is encouraging to see a greater cross-cultural activity in the examination of different religious traditions. Whereas most histories dealing with non-western religions were until recently written by western scholars, we now find non-western scholars writing on their own religious tradition and that of others. We not only come across scholars of Jewish, Muslim, Hindu, Buddhist or African background writing on Christianity, but Hindus writing on Buddhism and Islam, Japanese on Indian and western religions, and so on. This development is to be welcomed and encouraged, provided sound scholarly standards are maintained.

Considering the growth of the methodological debate and the many publications in this field, particularly since the late 1960s and 1970s, one wonders how the study of religion will develop in the near future. At the moment it remains an open question whether the current state of criticism and uncertainty, the search for new developments and common areas of agreement, will provide a turning-point leading to a new breakthrough or simply prove to be an impasse fixed on a past heritage, yielding few new discoveries. Whilst Eliade and other scholars have primarily been interested in archaic ancient and exotic data of the distant past, a growing number of contemporary scholars are fostering a strong interest in the study of living religions within the wider context of society and culture. It is perhaps here that the possibility of a new breakthrough is most likely to occur in future studies.

To some extent there will always exist a dialectical tension between historical and systematic approaches to the study of religion as well as between the necessary research into specific data at a micro-level and the equally necessary examination of wider perspectives at a macro-level. The study of religion will of necessity be comparative, for it is not only concerned with research into one religious tradition but examines phenomena across traditions and cultures, using cross-cultural data. There has been much acrimonious debate about religion being a phenomenon *sui generis*, particularly in the older phenomenology of religion. This debate still needs further clarification. The study of religion must certainly be maintained as an autonomous subject in its own right. But whatever its own particular characteristics, this does not mean that the study of religion can claim a special or unique status within the wider universe of sciences or the circle of human knowledge. The very existence of religion as lived and practised may well point towards a reality other than itself and thereby raise important philosophical and theological questions, but the study of religion as systematically ordered *knowledge* must be closely interrelated with other areas of knowledge and open to comparable criteria of analysis and synthesis.

In Waardenburg's view (1978b), the study of religion is not a particular discipline with one specific method but rather a field of studies still best described as *Religionswissenschaft*, a term 'encompassing all studies concerned with religious data, their observation, ascertainment, description, explanation, analysis, understanding, interpretation' (1978b: 190). Some of the themes which he lists as commanding attention from contemporary scholars of religion are the following: the various kinds of meaning which religious institutions and religious data possess for communities and individuals; the connection between religious and ideological traditions and movements, and the structural similarity of their internal development; myth and symbolism and the specific meaning they convey to people as well as their relationship to the institutionalization of religion; the relationship between different religious communities and the views specific faiths have of themselves and each other; the connection between religious change and social change, i.e., what role particular values and norms of a religious tradition can play in a specific process of development; what is the role of religion in particular local or regional conflict situations; in what way does religion constitute a particular dimension of creative life, socially or individually, by giving access to deeper levels of intentionality and mobilizing constructive forms of thought and action; the extent to which research in religion is guided by theological, philosophical and ideological aims or is subservient to political or other interests; where and how do ethical questions arise in the study of religion, particularly with regard to the future of mankind? (1978b: 211–3).

All these themes require further exploration. Waardenburg is right in saying that the 'future of the study of religion lies to a great extent in the kind of problems to which it addresses itself' (1978b: 211). At the most fundamental and general level the problem of the definition of religion itself is central to methodological discussion and the self-understanding of religious studies. If one undertook a survey of all the definitions of religion in use, an article as long as this one would have to be written. Other important themes of study relate to the situation of traditional religions and modern 'a-religion' in contemporary society. This raises the question of the transplantation of religion in institutionalised form from one society and culture to another (see M. Pye 1969) and further questions about cross-cultural and interreligious encounter (see J. Pentikäinen 1976). Yet another important area of research concerns the cultural function of religion(s) and, at a second-order level, of the science of religion as an interpreter of religious and social reality. Ninian Smart, in his Gifford Lectures on 'The Varieties of Religious Identity' (1979–80) explicitly devoted one of his lectures to 'The Science of Religion as an Interpreter of Modern History' in which he pointed out that the scientific study of religion with its comparative method and its sensitivity to the symbolic life of mankind is important in the analysis not only of the religious traditions but also of secular ideologies. This view is summarized in his conclusion that 'the science of religion itself may become an important source in the interpretation of modern history and also provide the materials for a new world-view which takes account of the varieties of symbolic identity' (1979–80: 7; see also Smart 1981). This is not all that far removed from Eliade's ideal of a creative cultural hermeneutic even though Smart and Eliade differ widely as to the details and premises of such a cultural task.

The older, more empirically oriented *Religionswissenschaft* collected and accumulated a vast store of data, particularly historical data, for the study of religion. This factual-descriptive, empiricist stance was subsequently counteracted by the development of the phenomenological approach with its emphasis on *epoché* and the search for essences. Many a postulate of phenomenology still has to be taken seriously but phenomenology itself has not provided a theoretical advance nor made a great contribution to methodology. The reaction against the essentialist and subjective accounts of the phenomenologists took the form of a development away from a concern for ideas and essences to a strong emphasis on scientific facts, particularly as understood by certain proponents of the science of religion. By now, however, the validity and relative value of facts has again been called into question both by the philosophy of science and by some new developments in the integral science of religion. It is increasingly being realized that philosophical positions of one kind or another underpin the different methodological stances and to some extent this cannot be avoided. The methodological task must, therefore, always include the examination and clarification of these underlying choices of perspective, whether made explicit or tacitly assumed. In addition, it is being recognized that questions of truth claims, inherent in at least some areas of religious discourse and experience, must also in one way or another be examined and accounted for. If individual scholars choose to ignore or avoid such theoretical requirements, this does not mean they are non-existent.

Without some kind of hermeneutic, some theory of understanding and interpretation, it is impossible to systematically order and account for the variety of religious data. One can consider the history of religions, phenomenology, and hermeneutics as three interrelated approaches and tasks of an integral science of religion. So conceived, and practised in an international, intercultural, and interdisciplinary framework and spirit, an integral science of religion opens new and exciting avenues not only for the area of religious studies, but also for contemporary society and culture.

NOTE: This survey was completed in early 1980 and does not include a discussion of publications which have appeared since then, in particular G. Lanczkowski, *Einführung in die Religionswissenschaft* (1980, Darmstadt: Wissenschaftliche Buchgesellschaft) which presents an introduction to the objects and different disciplines of the study of religion. It also discusses the relationship between *Religionswissenschaft* and theology, philosophy, and other approaches. It is a brief, summary work which mainly relies on well known authors and long established material.

Readers may also be interested in the special survey of *Concilium*, 136 (1980) on 'What is Religion? An Enquiry for Christian Theology' whose guest editors are Mircea Eliade and David Tracy (see particularly N. Terrin, 'On the Definition of Religion in the History of Religions,' pp. 72–7 and L. Sullivan 'History of Religions: The Shape of an Art,' pp. 78–85.

A recent discussion of the work of the IAHR is found in the section 'Is Academic Study Disinterested?' in M. Braybrooke, *Inter-faith Organizations, 1893–1979: An Historical Directory* (1980, New York and Toronto: pp. 9–18).

Important theoretical works continue to appear in the *Religion and Reason* series published by Mouton. The following three titles appeared too late to be considered here: D.A. Crosby, *Interpretive Theories of Religion* (1981); D. Wiebe, *Religion and Truth. Towards an Alternative Paradigm for the Study of Religion* (1981); R.J. Siebert, *The Critical Theory of Religion*. The Frankfurt School (1984).

W.L. Brenneman, Jr., S.O. Yarian and A.M. Olson, *The Seeing Eye*. Hermeneutical Phenomenology in the Study of Religion (1982) raises important points for hermeneutics and must be considered in a discussion of Eliade's methodology.

The above discussion, and the language in which it is expressed, accurately reflects the major issues debated up till the late 1970s. It does not incorporate the more recent feminist critique of the study of religion. This would require a reassessment of the issues in another article.

Bibliography

Allen, D. (1978), *Structure and Creativity in Religion*. Hermeneutics in Mircea Eliade's Phenomenology and New Direction Religion and Reason 14. The Hague: Mouton.

Antes, P. (1979), 'Systematische Religionswissenschaft.' Zwei unversöhnliche Forschungsrichtungen?' *Humanitas Religiosa*, Festschrift für Harold Biezais, 213–21.

Asmussen, J.P., Laessoe, J. and Colpe, C. (1971–2), *Handbuch der Religionsgeschichte*, 3 vols., Göttingen: Vandenhoeck & Ruprecht.

Baird, R. (1968), 'Interpretative Categories and the History of Religions,' *History and Theory* 8: 17–30.

— (1971), *Category Formation and the History of Religions*. Religion and Reason 1. The Hague: Mouton.

— (1975), ed. *Methodological Issues in Religious Studies*. See 'Postscript: Methodology, Theory and Explanation in the Study of Religion.' Chico: New Horizons Press.

Barnhart, J.E. (1977), *The Study of Religion and its Meaning*. New Explorations in Light of K. Popper and E. Durkheim. Religion and Reason 12. The Hague: Mouton.

Benz, E. (1968), 'Die Bedeutung der Religionswissenschaft für die Koexistenz der Weltreligionen heute,' in IAHR Claremont Congress Proceedings, vol. III: 8–22. Leiden: E.J. Brill.

Bettis, J.D., (1969), ed. *Phenomenology of Religion*. Eight Modern Descriptions of the Essence of Religion. London: SCM.

Bianchi, U. (1972), 'The Definition of Religion (On the Methodology of Historical-Comparative Research).' In Bianchi, Bleeker and Bausani: 15–34.

— (1975), *The History of Religions*. Leiden: E.J. Brill. See 'Object and Methodology of the History of Religion,' 1–29; and 'Modern Problems of Methodology and Interpretation,' 163–200.

— (1979), 'The History of Religions and the "Religio-anthropological Approach",' in Honko: 299–321.

Bianchi, U., Bleeker, C.J. and Bausani, A., eds. (1972), *Problems and Methods of the History of Religions*. Leiden: E.J. Brill.

Biezais, H. (1979), 'Typology of Religion and the Phenomenological Method,' in Honko 1979: 143–61.

Bleeker, C.J. (1959), 'The Phenomenological Method,' *Numen* 6: 96–111; also in Bleeker 1963: 1–15.

— (1960), 'The future task of the history of religions,' *Numen* 7: 221–34; also in IAHR Marburg Congress Proceedings, 1961: 229–40. Leiden: E.J. Brill.

— (1963), *The Sacred Bridge*. Researches into the Nature and Structure of Religion. Leiden: E.J. Brill.

— (1969), 'Methodology and the Science of Religion,' in Jurji 1969: 237–47.

— (1971a), 'Comparing the Religio-Historical and the Theological Method,' *Numen* 18: 9–29.

— (1971b), 'Epilegomena,' in Bleeker and Widengren, 1969–71, vol. II: 642–51.

— (1971c), 'Wie steht es um die Religionsphänomenologie?', *Bibliotheca Orientalis* 28: 303–8.

— (1972), 'The Contribution of the Phenomenology of Religion to the Study of the History of Religions,' in Bianchi, Bleeker and Bausani: 35–45.

— (1975a), *The History of Religions 1950–1975*. Monograph produced for the IAHR Congress, Lancaster. Leiden: E.J. Brill.

— (1975b), 'Looking Backward and Forward,' in IAHR Stockholm Congress Proceedings, 23–32. Leiden: E.J. Brill.

— (1978), 'Die Bedeutung der religionsgeschichtlichen und religionsphänomenologischen Forschung Friedrich Heilers,' *Numen* 25: 2–13.

Bleeker, C.J. and Widengren, G., eds. (1969–71), *Historia Religionum*. Handbook for the History of Religions, 2 vols. Leiden: E.J. Brill.

Bolle, K.W. (1967a), 'History of Religions with a Hermeneutic Oriented toward Christian Theology?' in Kitagawa 1967: 89–118.

— (1967b), 'Religionsgeschichtliche Forschung und theologische Impulse?', *Kairos* 9: 43–53.

— (1980), 'Reflections on the History of Religions and History,' *History of Religions* 20: 62–80.

Bottero, J. (1970), 'Les histoires des religions,' in Desroche and Seguy: 99–127.

Brelich, A. (1970), 'Prolégomènes à une histoire des religions,' in Puech: vol. I: 1–59.

Brenneman, W.L., Yarian, S.O. and Olson, A.M. (1982), *The Seeing Eye*. Hermeneutical Phenomenology in the Study of Religion. University Park and London: The Pennsylvania State University Press.

Braybrooke, M. (1980), *Inter-Faith Organizations, 1893–1979: An Historical Directory.* Texts and Studies in Religion. New York and Toronto: Edwin Mellen Press.

Bulletin Signalétique: sciences regligieuses. Paris: Centre National de la Recherche scientifiqure.

Castellani, G., ed. (1970–1), *Storia Delle Religioni.* 5 vols. Turin: Unione Tipografice-Editrice.

Clavier, H. (1968), 'Resurgences d'un problème de méthode en histoire des religions,' *Numen* 15: 94–118.

Cohn, W. (1964), 'What is Religion? An Analysis for Cross-Cultural Comparisons,' *Journal of Christian Education* 7: 116–38.

— (1969), 'On the Problem of Religion in Non-Western Cultures,' *International Yearbook for the Sociology of Religion* 5: 7–19.

Colpe, C., ed. (1974), *Die Diskussion um das Heilige.* Darmstadt: Wissenschaftliche Buchgesellschaft.

— (1979), 'Symbol Theory and Copy Theory as Basic Epistemological and Conceptual Alternatives in Religious Studies,' in Honko: 161–73.

Combs, E. (1976–7), 'Learned and learning: CSSR/SCER, 1965–1975,' *Sciences Religieuses/Studies in Religion* 6: 357–63.

Crosby, D.A., (1981), *Interpretive Theories of Religion.* Religion and Reason 20. The Hague: Mouton.

Culianu, I.P., (1981), 'History of Religions in Italy: The State of the Art,' *History of Religions* 20: 250–60.

Dammann, E. (1972), *Grundriss der Religionsgeschichte.* Stuttgart: 2nd. ed. 1978: Kohlhammer.

Davis, C. (1974–5), 'The Reconvergence of Theology and Religious Studies,' *Sciences Religieuses/Studies in Religion* 4: 205–21.

— (1981), 'Theology and Religious Studies,' *The Scottish Journal of Religious Studies* 2: 11–20.

Desroche, H. and Seguy, J., eds. (1970), *Introduction aux Sciences Humaines des Religions.* Paris: Cujas.

Dhavamony, M. (1973), *Phenomenology of Religion.* Rome: Gregorian University Press.

Drijvers, H.J.W. (1973), 'Theory Formation in Science of Religion and the Study of the History of Religions,' in Van Baaren and Drijvers: 57–77.

Dudley III, G. (1977), *Religion on Trial.* Mircea Eliade and his Critics. Philadelphia: Temple University Press.

Earhardt, H. Byron (1967), 'Toward a Unified Interpretation of Japanese Religion,' in Kitagawa, Eliade and Long: 195–226.

— (1975), 'The Japanese Dictionary of Religious Studies: Analysis and Assessment,' *Japanese Journal of Religious Studies* 2: 5–12.

Eliade, M. (1958), *Patterns in Comparative Religion*. London: Sheed and Ward. *Traité d'Histoire des Religions:* Paris: Payot 1949.
— (1959), 'Methodological Remarks on the Study of Religious Symbolism,' in Eliade and Kitagawa: 86–107.
— (1961), 'A New Humanism,' *History of Religions* 1: 1–18; also in Eliade 1969: 1–11.
— (1963), 'The History of Religions in Retrospect: 1912–1962,' *The Journal of Bible and Religion* 31: 98–109; also in Eliade 1969: 12–36.
— (1965), 'Observations on Religious Symbolism,' in Eliade, *The Two and the One*, 189–211. New York: Harper.
— (1967), 'Cultural Fashions and the History of Religions,' in Kitagawa, Eliade and Long: 21–38.
— (1969), *The Quest*. History and Meaning in Religion. Third ed. 1975. Chicago and London: Collins.
— (1979), *A History of Religious Ideas*. French ed.: Paris 1976. Vol. I: London; Collins; Chicago 1981: Chicago University Press. Vol. II; Chicago 1982: Chicago University Press.
Eliade, M. and Kitagawa, J.M., eds. (1959), *The History of Religions*. Essays in Methodology. Fifth ed. 1970. Chicago and London: Chicago University Press.
Eliade, M. and Tracy, D., eds. (1980), 'What is Religion? An Inquiry for Christian Theology,' *Concilium* 136.
Elsas, C., ed. (1975), *Religion*. Ein Jahrhundert theologischer, philosophischer, soziologischer und psychologischer Interpretationsansätze. München: Piper.

Flasche, R. (1978), *Die Religionswissenschaft Joachim Wachs*. Berlin and New York: Springer.
Frazier, A.M. (1970), 'Models for a Methodology of Religious Meaning,' *Bucknell Review* 18: 19–28.

Goodenough, R. (1959), 'Religionswissenschaft,' *Numen* 6: 77–95.
Goldammer, K. (1979), 'Is There a Method of Symbol Research Which Offers Hermeneutic Access to Depth-Dimensions of Religious Experience?' in Honko: 498–518.
Gualtieri, A.R. (1967), 'What is Comparative Religion Comparing? The Subject Matter of "Religious Studies",' *Journal for the Scientific Study of Religion* 6: 31–9.
— (1972), 'Confessional theology in the context of the history of religions,' *Sciences Religieuses/Studies in Religion* 1: 347–60.

Hayes, V.C., ed. (1977), *Australian Essays in World Religions*. Adelaide: The Australian Association for the Study of Religions.
Heelas, P. (1977), 'Intra-religious Explanation,' *Journal of the Anthropological Society of Oxford* 8: 1–17.
— (1978), 'Some Problems with Religious Studies,' *Religion* 8: 1–14.

Heiler, F. (1959), 'The History of Religions as a Preparation for the Co-operation of Religions,' in Eliade and Kitagawa: 132–60.

— (1960), 'The History of Religions as a Way to Unity of Religions,' in IAHR Tokyo Congress Proceedings, 7–22. Leiden: E.J. Brill.

— (1961), *Erscheinungsformen und Wesen der Religion*. Religionen der Menschheit 1. Stuttgart: Kohlhammer.

Helfer, J.S., ed. (1968), 'Introduction' in *On Method in the History of Religions. History and Theory* 8: 1–7.

Holm, N.G. (1970), 'Der Mythos in der Religionswissenschaft,' *Temenos* 6: 36–67.

— (1971), Review of Eliade and Kitagawa, '*The History of Religions* (1970), *Temenos* 7: 131–7.

— (1972), Review of Bianchi, Bleeker and Bausani, *Problems and Methods of the History of Religions* (1972), *Temenos* 8: 139–42.

Honko, L., ed. (1979), *Science of Religion*. Studies in Methodology. Proceedings of the Study Conference of the IAHR, held in Turku, Finland, Aug. 27–31, 1973. Religion and Reason 13. The Hague: Mouton.

Hultkrantz, A. (1970), 'The Phenomenology of Religion: Aims and Methods,' *Temenos* 6: 68–88.

— (1979), 'Ecology of Religion: Its Scope and Method,' in Honko: 221–36.

International Association for the Study of the History of Religions. (1954a–1980), *International Bibliography of the History of Religions. Bibliographie Internationale de L'Histoire des Religions*. Leiden: E.J. Brill.

— (1954b–), *Numen*. Journal of the International Association for the Study of the History of Religions. Leiden: E.J. Brill.

Isambert, F.A. (1970), 'La phénoménologie religieuse,' in Desroche and Seguy: 217–40.

Jurji, E.J. (1963), *The Phenomenology of Religion*. Philadelphia: Westminster.

— (1969), ed. *Religious Pluralism and World Community*. Interfaith and Intercultural Communication. Leiden: E.J. Brill.

Katz, S.T., ed. (1978), *Mysticism and Philosophical Analysis*. London: Sheldon Press.

Kee, A. (1980), 'The Study of Religion in Poland,' *Religious Studies* 16: 61–7.

King, N.Q. (1973), Review of *Handbuch der Religionsgeschichte* vol. 2, *Scottish Journal of Theology* 26: 377–9.

King, U. (1981), 'A hermeneutic circle of religious ideas,' *Religious Studies* 17: 565–9.

Kitagawa, J.M. (1959), 'The History of Religions in America,' in Eliade and Kitagawa: 1–30.

— (1967), 'Primitive, Classical, and Modern Religions: A Perspective on Understanding the History of Religions,' in Kitagawa, Eliade and Long: 39–65.

— (1968), 'The Making of a Historian of Religions,' *Journal of the American Academy of Religions* 36: 191–201; also translated as 'Die Schulung eines Religionswissenschaftlers,' *Kairos* 11, 1969: 264–74.

Kitagawa, J.M., Eliade, M. and Long, C., eds. (1967), *The History of Religions*. Essays on the Problem of Understanding. Chicago: Chicago University Press.

Klostermaier, K. (1976–7), 'From phenomenology to metascience: Reflections on the study of religion,' *Sciences Religieuses/Studies in Religion* 6: 551–64.

Kristensen, W.B. (1960), *The Meaning of Religion*. Lectures in the Phenomenology of Religion. The Hague: Mouton.

Kryvelev, I.A. (1975), *Istoriya Religii*, 2 vols. Moscow: Mysl'.

Kvaerne, P. (1973), '"Comparative Religion: Whither—and Why?" A Reply to W. Cantwell Smith,' *Temenos* 9: 161–72.

Lanczkowski, G. (1971), *Begegnung und Wandel der Religionen*. Düsseldorf: Diederichs.

— (1974), ed. *Selbstverständnis und Wesen der Religionswissenschaft*. Darmstadt: Wissenschaftliche Buchgesellschaft.

— (1978a), *Einführung in die Religionsphänomenologie*. Darmstadt: Wissenschaftliche Buchgesellschaft.

— (1978b), 'Literaturbericht zur Religionswissenschaft,' *Theologische Rundschau* 43: 285–320.

— (1980), *Einführung in die Religionswissenschaft*. Darmstadt: Wissenschaftliche Buchgesellschaft.

Larson, G.J. (1978), 'Prolegomenon to a Theory of Religion,' *Journal of the American Academy of Religion* 46: 443–63.

Leibovici, M. (1972), 'Méthodologie et développement de l'histoire des religions,' *Sciences Religieuses/Studies in Religion* 1: 339–46.

Ling, T.O. (1968), *History of Religions East and West*. 2nd ed. 1977. London: Macmillan.

— (1980), 'Philosophers, Gentlemen and Anthropologists: Prolegomena to the Study of Religion,' *The Scottish Journal of Religious Studies* 1: 26–30.

Lonergan, B.J.F. (1976–7), 'The ongoing genesis of methods,' *Sciences Religieuses/Studies in Religion* 6: 341–55.

Long, C.H. (1967), 'Archaism and Hermeneutics,' in Kitagawa, Eliade and Long: 67–87.

Mann, U., ed. (1973), *Theologie und Religionswissenschaft*. Der gegenwärtige Stand ihrer Forschungsergebnisse und Aufgaben im Hinblick auf ihr gegenseitiges Verhältnis. Darmstadt: Wissenschaftliche Buchgesellschaft.

Mehauden, M. (1961), 'Un "Musée comparatif des Phénomènes Religieux",' in IAHR Marburg Congress Proceedings, 191–3. Leiden: E.J. Brill.

Mensching, G. (197⁰, *Structures and Patterns of Religion*. Delhi: Motilal Banarsidass.

Meslin, M. (1973), *Pour une Science des Religions*. Paris: Editions du Sevil.

Miller, J.F. (1975), 'Inherent Conceptual Limitations of the Scientific Method and Scientific Models for the Study of Religion,' *Internationales Jahrbuch für Wissens- und Religionssoziologie* 9: 137–47.

Mitros, J.F. (1973), *Religions: A Select, Classified Bibliography*. Louvain and Paris: Editions Nauwelaerts.

Morioka, K. (1975), *Religion in Changing Japanese Society*. See 'List of Major Periodicals in Japan,' 222–3. Tokyo: University of Tokyo Press.

Nenola-Kallio, A. (1973), 'Report on the Study Conference of the IAHR on "Methodology of the Science of Religion" held in Turku, Finland, August 27–31, 1973,' *Temenos* 9: 15–24.

Ogden, S.M. (1978), 'Theology and Religious Studies: Their Difference and the Difference it makes,' *Journal of the American Academy of Religion* 46: 3–17.

Open University (1977), *Man's Religious Quest*. Arts/Social Sciences: An Interfaculty Second Level Course. Course material AD 208, Units 1–32; see also '*Man's Religious Quest*. A review of Open University materials,' *Religion* 9, 1979: 116–39.

Oxtoby, W.G. (1968), '*Religionswissenschaft* Revisited,' in J. Neusner ed., *Religions in Antiquity*, 590–608. Leiden: E.J. Brill.

— (1976), ed. *Religious Diversity*. Essays by Wilfred Cantwell Smith. New York: Harper and Row.

Pannenberg, W. (1973), *Wissenschaftstheorie und Theologie*. See 'Religionswissenschaft als Theologie der Religion,'361–74. English translation *Theology and the Philosophy of Science*, 1976: 358–71. London: Darton Longman and Todd.

Penner, H.H. (1968), 'Myth and Ritual: A Wasteland or a Forest of Symbols?' in Helfer: 46–57.

— (1970), 'Is Phenomenology a Method for the Study of Religion?,' *Bucknell Review* 18: 29–54.

— (1971), 'The Poverty of Functionalism,' *History of Religions* 11: 91–7.

— (1975), The Problem of Semantics in the Study of Religion' in Baird: 79–94.

— (1976), 'The Fall and Rise of Methodology: a Retrospective Review,' *Religious Studies Review* 2: 11–6.

Penner, H.H. and Yonan, E.A. (1972), 'Is a Science of Religion Possible?,' *The Journal of Religion* 52: 107–33.

Pentikäinen, J. (1976), 'The Encounter of Religions as a Religio-Scientific Problem,' *Temenos* 12: 7–20.

Pomian-Srzednicki, M. (1982), *The Politics and Sociology of Secularization in Poland*. London: Routledge and Kegan Paul.

Poniatowski, Z. (1972), 'The scientometrics of the science of religions,' *Euhemer* 3: 3–21.

— (1975), 'Twenty Years of *Numen* in the Light of Statistical Analysis,' *Studia Religioznawcze* 10: 75–99 (in Polish, with summary in English and German).

Problèmes et methodes d'histoire des religions. (1968), Mélanges publiés par la Section des Sciences Religieuses à l'occasion du centenaire de l'Ecole Pratique des Hautes Etudes. Paris: Presses Universitaires de France.

Puech, H., ed. (1970–6), *Histoire des Religions*. Encyclopédie de la Pléiade, 3 vols. Paris: Gallimard.

Pummer, R. (1972), '*Religionswissenschaft* or Religiology?,' *Numen* 19: 91–127.

— (1974), 'The Study Conference on "Methodology of the Science of Religion" in Turku, Finland 1973,' *Numen* 21: 156–9.

— (1975), 'Recent Publications on the Methodology of the Science of Religion,' *Numen* 22: 161–82.

Pye, M. (1969), 'The Transplantation of Religions,' *Numen* 16: 234–9.

— (1971), 'Syncretism and Ambiguity,' *Numen* 18: 83–93.

— (1972), *Comparative Religion*. An Introduction through Source Materials. Newton Abbot: David and Charles. See 'Introduction,' pp. 7–35, for methodological discussion.

— (1973), 'Comparative Hermeneutics in Religion,' in Pye and Morgan: 9–58.

— (1974), 'Problems of Method in the Interpretation of Religion,' *Japanese Journal of Religious Studies* 1: 107–23.

Pye, M. and Morgan, R., eds. (1973), *The Cardinal Meaning*. Essays in Comparative Hermeneutics: Buddhism and Christianity. *Religion and Reason* 6. The Hague: Mouton.

Ratschow, C.H. (1973), 'Methodik der Religionswissenschaft,' in *Enzyklopädie der Geisteswissenschaftlichen Arbeitsmethoden*: 347–400. München: Piper.

Religion in Geschichte und Gegenwart, Die. Handwörterbuch für Theologie und Religionswissenschaft, 7 vols. Tübingen: Mohr 1957–1965.

Religion (1975), Special issue on the occasion of the XIIIth Congress of the International Association for the History of Religions. Lancaster, August 1975.

Religious Studies Review. Council on the Study of Religion. Waterloo, Ont.: Wilfried Laurier University.

Ricketts, M. Linscott (1973), 'In Defence of Eliade. Toward Bridging the Communication Gap between Anthropology and the History of Religions,' *Religion* 3: 13–34.

Ries, J., ed. (1978), *L'expression du sacré dans les grandes religions*. Series *Homo Religiosus*. Louvain: Centre d'histoire des religions.

Ringgren, H. (1970), 'Die Objektivität der Religionswissenschaft,' *Temenos* 6: 119–29.

Ringgren, H. and Ström, A.V. (1967), *Religions of Mankind*. Today and Yesterday. Philadelphia: Fortress Press.

Rudolph, K. (1962), *Die Religionsgeschichte an der Leipziger Universitat und die Entwicklung der Religionswissenschaft. Ein Beitrag zur Wissenschaftsgeschichte und zum Problem der Religionswissenschaft.* Berlin: Akademie—Verlag.

— (1967), 'Die Problematik der Religionswissenschaft als akademisches Lehrfach,' *Kairos* 9: 22–42.

— (1970), 'Der Beitrag der Religionswissenschaft zum Problem der sogenannten Entmythologisierung,' *Kairos* 12: 183–207.

— (1971a), 'Religionsgeschichte und "Religionsphänomenologie",' *Theologische Literaturzeitung* 96: 241–50.

— (1971b), 'Das Problem einer Entwicklung in der Religionsgeschichte,' *Kairos* 13: 95–118.

— (1973a), '"Historia Religionum". Bemerkungen zu einigen neueren Handbüchern der Religionsgeschichte,' *Theologische Literaturzeitung* 98: 401–18.

— (1973b), 'Das Problem der Autonomie und Integrität der Religionswissenschaft,' *Nederlands Theologisch Tijdschrift* 27: 105–31.

— (1978), 'Die "ideologiekritische" Funktion der Religionswissenschaft,' *Numen* 25: 17–39.

— (1979), 'Religionswissenschaft auf alten und neuen Wegen. Bemerkungen zu einigen Neuerscheinungen,' *Theologische Literaturzeitung* 104: 11–34.

Rupp, A. (1978), *Religion, Phänomen und Geschichte*. Prolegomena zur Methodologie der Religionsgeschichte. Forschungen zur Anthropologie und Religionsgeschichte. Saarbrücken: Homo et Religio.

Saliba, J.A. (1974), 'The New Ethnography and the Study of Religion,' *Journal for the Scientific Study of Religion* 13: 145–59.

— (1976), *'Homo Religiosus' in Mircea Eliade*. An Anthropological Evaluation. Leiden: E.J. Brill.

Schmid, G. (1979), *Principles of Integral Science of Religion*. Religion and Reason 17. The Hague: Mouton.

Schlette, H.R. (1970), 'Ist die Religionswissenschaft am Ende?,' *Zeitschrift für Missionswissenschaft und Religionswissenschaft* 54: 195–200.

Schröder, C.M., ed. (1961–), *Die Religionen der Menschheit*. Stuttgart: Kohlhammer. Planned series of forty-two volumes, most of which have been published.

Science of Religion. Abstracts and Index of Recent Articles. Amsterdam; The Institute for the Study of Religion, Free University.

Seguy, J. (1970), 'Panorama des sciences des religions,' in Desroche and Seguy: 37–52.

Seiwert, H. (1977), 'Systematische Religionswissenschaft: Theoriebildung und Empiriebezug,' *Zeitschrift für Missionswissenschaft und Religionswissenschaft* 61: 1–18.

Sharma, A. (1975), 'An Inquiry into the Nature of the Distinction between the History of Religion and the Phenomenology of Religion,' *Numen* 22: 81–96.

Sharpe, E. (1971), 'Some Problems of Method in the Study of Religion,' *Religion* 1: 1–14.

— (1975), *Comparative Religion*. A History. London: Duckworth.

Siebert, R.J. (1984), *The Critical Theory of Religion*. The Frankfurt School. Religion and Reason 29. Berlin: Mouton.

Smart, N. (1973a), *The Phenomenon of Religion*. London: MacMillan.

— (1973b), *The Science of Religion and the Sociology of Knowledge*. Princeton: Princeton University Press.

— (1978), 'Beyond Eliade: The Future of Theory in Religion,' *Numen* 25: 171–83.

— (1979), 'Understanding Religious Experience,' in S.T. Katz ed. *Mysticism and Philosophical Analysis*, 10–21. London: Sheldon Press.

— (1979–80), 'The Varieties of Religious Identity.' Gifford Lectures. Outline of a Series of Ten Lectures. University of Edinburgh.

— (1981) *Beyond Ideology*, Religion and the Future of Western Civilization (Gifford Lectures 1979–80). London: Collins.

Smith, M. (1968), 'Historical Method in the Study of Religion,' in Helfer 1968: 8–16.

Smith, W. Cantwell (1959), 'Comparative Religion: Whither—and Why?,' in Eliade and Kitagawa: 31–58.

— (1964), *The Meaning and End of Religion*. New York: New American Library, Mentor.

— (1965), *The Faith of Other Men*. New York: New American Library, Mentor.

— (1975a), 'Methodology and the Study of Religion: Some Misgivings,' in Baird: 1–30.

— (1975b), 'Religion as Symbolism,' in *Encyclopaedia Britannica. Propaedia*: 498–500. 15th ed. Chicago 1975.

— (1976), 'Objectivity and the Humane Sciences: A New Proposal,' in Oxtoby: 158–80.

— (1977), *Belief and History*. Charlottesville: University of Virginia Press.

— (1979), *Faith and Belief*. Princeton: Princeton University Press.

— (1981), 'History in Relation to both Science and Religion,' *The Scottish Journal of Religious Studies* 2: 3–10.

— (1981), *Towards a World Theology: Faith and the Comparative History of Religion*. London and Philadelphia: Westminster.

Spiro, M. (1979), 'Symbolism and Functionalism in the Anthropological Study of Religion; in Honko: 322–39.

Stephenson, G. (1975), 'Kritische Bemerkungen zu C.H. Ratschows Methodenlehre,' *Zeitschrift für Missionswissenschaft und Religionswissenschaft* 59: 201–8.

— (1976), ed. *Der Religionswandel unserer Zeit im Spiegel der Religionswissenschaft*. Darmstadt: Wissenschaftliche Buchgesellschaft.

Streng, F. (1968), 'What does "History" mean in the History of Religions?,' *Anglican Theological Review* 50: 156–78.

Szolc, P.O. (Scholz) (1971), 'Religionswissenschaft in Polen,' *Numen* 18: 45–80.

Sullivan, L. (1980), 'History of Religions: The Shape of an Art,' *Concilium* 136: 78–85.

Terrin, N. (1980), 'On the Definition of Religion in the History of Religions,' *Concilium* 136: 72–7.

Thrower, J. (1983), *Marxist-Leninist Scientific Atheism and the Study of Religion and Atheism in the USSR*. Religion and Reason 25. Berlin: Mouton.

Tillich, P. (1967), 'The Significance of the History of Religions for the Systematic Theologian,' in Kitagawa, Eliade and Long: 241–56.

Tokarev, S.A. (1966a), 'Principles of the Morphological Classification of Religions (Part I),' *Soviet Anthropology and Archaeology* 4: 3–10.

— (1966b), 'Principles of the Morphological Classification of Religions (Part II),' *Soviet Anthropology and Archaeology* 5: 11–25.

— (1968), *Die Religion in der Geschichte der Völker*. Berlin: Dietz.

— (1976), *Religiya v Istorii Narodov Mira*, 2 vols. third ed., *Moscow: Politizdat*.

Tyloch, W. (1979), 'Polish Society for the Science of Religions,' *Euhemer* 23: 3–8.

Tworuschka, U. (1974), 'Integrale Religionswissenschaft—Methode der Zukunft?,' *Zeitschrift für Religions–und Geistesgeschichte* 26: 239–43.

Van Baaren, T.P. (1969), 'Systematische Religionswissenschaft,' *Nederlands Theologisch Tijdschrift* 24: 81–8.

— (1973), 'Science of Religion as a Systematic Discipline: Some Introductory Remarks, in Van Baaren and Drijvers: 35–56.

Van Baaren, T.P. and Drijvers, H.J.W., eds. (1973), *Religion, Culture and Methodology*. Papers of the Groningen Working-group for the Study of Fundamental Problems and Methods of Science of Religion. Religion and Reason 8. The Hague: Mouton.

Van Baaren, T.P., Leertouwer, L. and Buning, H., eds. (1973–), *Iconography of Religions*. Institute of Iconography, Groningen. Survey of major iconographic expressions of all religions of any importance in the world, both of literate and illiterate peoples.

Waardenburg, J. (1971–), ed. *Religion and Reason*. New Series on 'Method and Theory in the Study and Interpretation of Religion.' The Hague and Berlin: Mouton.

— (1972a), 'Religion between Reality and Idea. A Century of Phenomenology of Religion in the Netherlands,' *Numen* 19: 128–203.

— (1972b), 'Grundsätzliches zur Religionsphänomenologie,' *Neue Zeitschrift für Systematische Theologie und Religionsphilosophie* 14: 315–35.

— (1973a), *Classical Approaches to the Study of Religion*. Aims, Methods and Theories of Research. Vol. 1: Introduction and Anthology; Vol. 2: Bibliography. Religion and Reason 3 and 4. The Hague: Mouton.

— (1973b), 'Research on Meaning in Religion,' in Van Baaren and Drijvers: 109–36.

— (1975a), '*Religionswissenschaft* in Continental Europe,' *Religion*. Special issue, August: 27–54.

— (1975b), 'The Category of Faith in Phenomenological Research' in IAHR Stockholm Congress Proceedings, 305–15. Leiden: E.J. Brill; also in Waardenburg, 1978a: 79–88.

— (1976), '*Religionswissenschaft* in Continental Europe excluding Scandinavia. Some Factual Data,' *Numen* 23: 219–38.

— (1977), 'Religion vom Blickpunkt der religiösen Erscheinungen,' *Neue Zeitschrift für Systematische Theologie und Religionsphilosophie* 19: 62–77.

— (1978a), *Reflections on the Study of Religion*. Religion and Reason 15. The Hague: Mouton.

— (1978b), '*Religionswissenschaft* New Style. Some Thoughts and Afterthoughts,' *Annual Review of the Social Science of Religion* 2: 189–220.

— (1979), 'The Language of Religion, and the Study of Religion as Sign Systems,' in Honko: 441–57.

Wach, J. (1958), *The Comparative Study of Religions*. New York: Columbia University Press.

Werblowsky, R.J.Z. (1959), 'The Comparative Study of Religions—A Review Essay,' *Judaism: A Quarterly Journal of Jewish Life and Thought* 8: 1–9.

— (1960), 'Marburg—and After?,' *Numen* 7: 215–20.

— (1976), *Beyond Tradition and Modernity*. Changing Religions in a Changing World. London: Athlone Press.

— (1979), 'Histories of Religion,' *Numen* 26: 250–5.

Whaling, F. (1979), Review of *From Primitives to Zen*, *Religious Studies* 15: 421–3.

Wiebe, D. (1975), 'Explanation and the Scientific Study of Religion,' *Religion* 5: 33–52.

— (1978), 'Is a science of religion possible?,' *Sciences Religieuses/Studies in Religion* 7: 5–17.

— (1979), 'The Role of "Belief" in the Study of Religion. A response to W.C. Smith,' *Numen* 26: 234–49.

— (1981), *Religion and Truth*. Towards an Alternative Paradigm for the Study of Religion. Religion and Reason 23. The Hague: Mouton.

Widengren, G. (1968), 'Some Remarks on the Methods of the Phenomenology of Religion,' *Acta Universitatis Upsaliensis* 17: 250–60.

— (1969), *Religionsphänomenologie*. Berlin: De Gruyter.

— (1971), 'La méthode comparative: entre philologie et phénoménologie,' *Numen* 18: 161–72; also in Bianchi, Bleeker and Bausani 1972: 5–14.

— (1975), 'The Opening Address' in the IAHR Stockholm Congess Proceedings, 14–22. Leiden: E.J. Brill.

Yinger, J.M. (1970), *The Scientific Study of Religion*. New York: Macmillan.

The Scientific Study of Religion in its Plurality

NINIAN SMART

There has been since World War II, and in particular since the mid-1960s, a great flowering of the study of religion. There has been great growth in institutions offering courses in religion in the English-speaking world; while in Continental Europe and Scandinavia there has, in the period since 1945, not only been a restoration to vigour of the faculties of theology, but also a modest but significant advance in the history of religions, partly in the context of a widened interest in non-European cultures. At the same time, work in the social sciences has increasingly converged, in matters related to religion, upon the work of comparative religionists.

But though we may live during a period when old-fashioned rationalism is declining, and when the importance of the study of religion is more widely recognized, there is not always much clarity in the assumptions brought to bear upon it. Or at least there is much divergence of aim and method in the way in which it is approached.

This is partly because the subject is considerably shaped by the institutions in which it is embedded. Thus the existence of faculties of Christian theology imposes certain categories upon scholarship—for instance the division into such branches of enquiry as New Testament, patristics, church history, systematic theology, philosophy of religion, comparative religion (or history of religions). This builds into the subject already an asymmetry in the way in which Christianity is treated as compared with other religious traditions. This of course reflects the history of scholarship and the fact that classically the study of religion has been tied for the most part to the training of clergy and other specialists; and so the modern universities of Europe and America in some degree inherit the cultural assumption that Christianity should have a privileged place in the curriculum. Conversely, worry about such an arrangement sometimes leads to the exclusion of theology from the secular university. It is not my task here to enter into the controversies surrounding this matter: but rather to look to the way in which the history of the subject affects approaches to it. Undoubtedly for many scholars there remains the assumption that their task is to be understood in the light of Christian (or Jewish or other) truth: that is, in one way or another commitment is relevant to study. We can in respect of all this point to a number of differing models.

First, there is the full-fledged model of what may be called constructive traditionalism. That is, there is the approach to the study of religion from the perspective of a given tradition—most frequently Christianity, and in particular some variety of it (Lutheranism, Roman Catholicism, etc.). Ultimately here the exploration of tests, the undertaking of a critical evaluation of them, the processes of hermeneutics, the systematic exploration of doctrines and so on are geared to the constructive presentation of the tradition as expressing spiritual and intellectual truth. Ultimately the task is one of expressing rather than describing. Thus the work of such figures as Barth, Küng, Bultmann, Käsemann, Tillich, and John Robinson—to put together a variegated selection of recent theological and Biblical scholars—is in the last analysis concerned with working out Christian truth, rather than simply doing history or even debating on both sides of the question (as might happen in the context of the philosophy of religion).

Second, there may be an attitude of seeing the study of religion as primarily concerned with issues in philosophical theology—that is, with the questions arising concerning the nature and existence of God (or of the Ultimate, to use a wider-reaching term) as perceived in the light of the history of religion, etc. This orientation may be called pluralistic theology. The accent is primarily on questions of truth in religion rather than on truths concerning religion.

Third, the theological tradition may be treated positivistically: that is the essential task of the theologian is to explore and describe the history of the faith independently of truth judgments about the content of faith. Still, it is naturally the case that such an approach has its agenda set by some implicit evaluations—for instance, about the importance of particular periods and aspects of Christian, or other, history. We may call this approach theological positivism. The fact of positivism does not preclude such an approach from being critical, and making use of the various tools of modern critical historiography.

It is clear that looked at from a planetary point of view there are questions arising about such models of theology. For one thing, the very word 'theology' is a western one. What does one use for Buddhism? Should we talk of the Buddhologian? Moreover, not all traditions are as hospitable either to pluralism or to critical positivism as is the modern western tradition. Nevertheless, historians of religion have opened up critical questions about the various traditions. I do not wish to argue the point here, but it seems to me clear that every tradition will inevitably have to come to terms with such scrutiny. It matters, of course, less in some faiths than others. For instance, Buddhism is not quite so tightly wedded to history as is Christianity or Judaism, while the facts of early Islam are less in doubt than those of these other religions. But naturally the critical positivist questions necessarily raise issues of truth in the context of what we have dubbed pluralistic theology and thus are liable to generate new approaches within the various forms of constructive traditionalism. Thus neo-Hindu theologies (such as those of Vivekananda and Radhakrishnan) can be seen as ways of coming to terms not merely with western culture but also with modern methods of scholarship, concerning India's deep past.

The modern period has of course seen the opening up more richly than in the past of contacts and conversations between religious traditions. The exchange of insights between faiths has come to have the name of dialogue. It is true that dialogue could simply be a method of exchanging information and so just be a tool of historical research: but more pregnantly it has been a particular style of pluralistic theology, a kind of cooperative spiritual exploration of truth. Because however it does differ in style and tradition it may be useful to have a different name for it. I shall call it constructive dialogue.

But none of all this so far is what may be thought of as the scientific study of religion. It is quite true that sometimes so-called scientific studies of religion (say in sociology) conceal value- or truth- assumptions which are of an essentially theological or philosophical nature (e.g., projectionism makes certain assumptions about the truth of religious belief, typically). It is quite true also that pluralistic theology, constructive traditionalism and so forth may in fact use scientific methods in the course of their enquiries. Certainly, such great theologians as Karl Barth made use of much plain historical material and critical method. But the main thrust of their concerns was not descriptive and scientific but expressive, proclamatory, philosophical: presenting a faith-stance or a worldview.

It may be thought that there is a 'science of God.' In a sense perhaps there is (and to that sense I shall later come). But I think in a more obvious way the idea that there is a 'science of God,' a kind of theological science, uses the term in a Pickwickian way. Belief in God is highly debatable, only indirectly (at best) testable, a question of reaction and commitment, much bound up with value questions. Since the alternative views of the Ultimate are so various, and even include the view that there is no Ultimate, it would be rash to define a theological science by postulating to start with a personal God. At best we might think about a 'science of the Ultimate.' Now it is clear that some men claim to experience the Ultimate, and it would be wrong to neglect such experience. But because of the vagaries and strangenesses of issues about interpretation it would be better in the first instance to confine the use of the word 'scientific' to the relatively neutral investigation of phenomena, including those comprised by religious experience. In brief, then, I think it is reasonable to say that the various models I have listed above (constructive traditionalism through to constructive dialogue) do not fall, essentially, within the purview of what may be called the scientific study of religion, though they may overlap with it.

Those overlaps actually are important. How can one really get the feel of a faith except by mingling among its adherents? A religion is more than texts, and the past: it is living history. This being so, a kind of dialogue with people is necessarily part of the fabric of enquiry into religion, whether scientific or otherwise.

Again, the philosophical skills which are fashioned in the philosophy of religion are important in the empirical investigation of religion. For one thing, descriptions have to be scrutinized for assumptions. Often our categories come not in utter nakedness but trailing clouds of theory, often inappropriate theory. Again, philosophy is much bound up with questions of verification and method. Moreover the whole enterprise of hermeneutical enquiry is one which requires philosophical debate. So it is idle to think one can simply do the history of religions, or the sociology of religion, or whatever, without in fact bumping up against philosophical and conceptual problems.

Moreover, the processes of critical history concerning, for example, Christian origins, vital in the task of constructive Christian theology, are relevant to other areas of religio-historical enquiry.

In brief, there is an overlap between the value-laden models for the study of religion and the relatively value-free scientific study of religion.

One has, however, to be clear about this notion of the relatively value-free. It is sometimes said that it is not possible (or even desirable) to be perfectly value-free, perfectly 'objective.' The term 'objective' is an unfortunate one, because actually all science and all unravelling of the world involves a kind of interplay, a struggle even, between the inquirers and that which they are concerned to understand. Nature is mean about her secrets. The right questions have to be posed: and she is a great slaughterer of theories. Objectivity is important only in two ways—one being that by being relatively free of prejudice the inquirer may show imagination in developing new questions to pose to nature; and secondly objectivity implies the acceptance of the possible death of one's pet ideas. One should be adventurous and sagacious, but also stoical in defeat. When we come to the human sciences, however, there is a difference of a profound kind: for it is no longer a mute nature that addresses us, but living and communicative beings. Empathy becomes important. And that means somehow adopting the American Indian proverb: 'Never judge a man till you have walked a mile in his moccasins.' Or rather: 'Never describe a man until you have walked a mile in his moccasins.' The term 'objectivity' is not usually taken to include much in the way of feeling or empathy.

So though the scientific study of religion should be relatively value-free, it has got to enter somehow into the world of values. This is part of what has come to be called the phenomenological method, as practised by for instance Kristensen and van der Leeuw. However, it happens that partly because of its particular philosophical origins in the tradition of Husserl, phenomenology of religion has also come to be bound up greatly with the search for essences: that is, with describing types of religious phenomena, and classifying them. This is to be seen in *Religion in Essence and Manifestation* and in Widengren's phenomenological work, and represents part of the whole enterprise known as the comparative study of religion. It is thus probably useful for the sake of clarity to distinguish between what I have referred to above as the phenomenological method, which involves 'entering in' to the thought world of the believer, and typological phenomenology, which is an attempt to anatomize the forms of religion in a comparative manner.

The use of the term 'phenomenology' implies, as it is usually employed, a suspension of belief, a prescinding from the worldview which the investigator may happen to hold, except in so far as he may think that the investigation of religious phenomena is important, which may imply something about a worldview, though at a higher logical level. (It is in general important to pay attention to levels: thus to say that we should use empathy to enter into people's various positions is a position about positions, i.e., it belongs to a higher level.) This sometimes obscures the fact that structures are important as well as empathy. That is, since the believer views his activity against the background, (or should we say from within the background?), of a whole web of beliefs and resonances, the person who wishes to understand the meaning of his action needs to unravel that structure or web. For instance, what are we to make of the Buddhist laying a flower before the statue of a Buddha in Sri Lanka? To understand her it is necessary to understand her understanding of the world, and that constitutes quite a complex structure. So empathy has to be more than imaginative feeling: it has to include a delineation of structures. So there is a certain tension between the phenomenological method or structured empathy, and typological phenomenology, which tends to try to cut through the organic particularities of a given cultural milieu.

This tension is something which runs deeply through the territory of the history of religions. For while some of the scholars in the field are more concerned with the comparative study of religion (a phrase which comes in and out of vogue—out of vogue in so far as comparisons could be thought to be odious, and redolent of whiffs of western imperialism and Christian superiority, the phrase falls on evil days; yet in vogue in so far as we wish the study of religions to make use of the opportunities for comparison and contrast, opportunities which are useful in testing various hypotheses about religion)—others again are concerned more with the history of a given tradition or culture. Thus the study of religion contains among other things the histories of various traditions, which may or may not be at one time or another in mutual historical interaction; but it also contains attempts at comparative treatment, which is necessarily cross-cultural. It is at different times important to stress uniquenesses of historical development and similarities of phenomena and elements in differing cultures. The danger of separate histories is that each may fail to see certain aspects of the dynamics of religion which can be gleaned from cross-cultural comparison. The danger of the comparative study of religion is that it may crassly bulldoze the particularities of the traditions.

Basically the comparative study of religion as it is practised tends to comprise first an attempt at a world history of religions; and second various kinds of typological phenomenology (for instance the comparative study of mysticism, sacrifice, worship and so on). To complicate matters, it has become usual to substitute the phrase history of religions for the comparative study of religion. Sometimes, as in the work of Eliade, such history of religions includes a special scheme of typological phenomenology. Actually Eliade's scheme has been remarkably fruitful, especially in raising issues about the religious and human meaning of space and time. But in addition Eliade's work, like Otto's and Wach's— to name two important forerunners—includes a general theory of existence: a kind of philosophy, one might say, compounded out of various sources including Eliade's own historical experience. Thus his typological phenomenology, especially in regard to views of history, is in part determined by a kind of philosophical theology. This does not mean that we have to discard the typology, but it does mean that we have to be aware, critically, of assumptions open to question and lying behind the more empirical presentations of the data. It would perhaps be ironic if having escaped from theological dogmatism as inappropriate for the scientific study of religion we met it in new and more heavily disguised form in a philosophy of existence unquestioned behind the shamanism. The point is that the science of religion should welcome imaginative ways of looking at the data, including Eliadean ones, Marxist ones and so on; but that is not to say that what counts as the scientific study of religion should be determined and defined by any one theory. For each theory should be testable in relation to the data in the field. Assuming any one theory to define the field destroys its true testability and gives it a spurious authority.

Because of the institutional evolution of the subject the comparative study of religion has not always existed in close relationship to such scientific or social-scientific disciplines as the sociology of religion, anthropology of religion and psychology of religion. True, in the late nineteenth century especially the influence of anthropology was very considerable, partly because it was fashionable to speculate about the origins and evolution of religion and 'primitive' cultures were thought of also as somehow primeval and so containing clues to the earliest phases of human culture and spirituality. Actually there seems no intrinsic reason why the history of religions and the sociology and anthropology of religion should not be treated as a single investigatory enterprise. The divergences are somewhat fortuitous. Thus the difference between sociology and anthropology represents a crude division between large- and small-scale societies, a difference of style of founding fathers and gurus, and a certain distinctness of methodological emphasis. But as for the scale question, this is hardly in the last resort relevant to overall theorizing about society; as to the styles, well, they add up to differing and often competing theories which have to be tested in the same empirical marketplace; and as for methods, differences are to do with feasibilities—cancer research may employ different techniques from research into the brain, but we do not thus artifically divide human functioning. Further, though obviously the concern of the social scientists is primarily with social relationships and dynamics, this is after all a major aspect of a religion and its cultural expression and milieu, so that there is in principle no absolute divide between history of religions and the social sciences of religion.

Similarly one may see history of religions as somewhat like economic history: the latter is history with the accent on economic aspects of existence, and the former is history with the accent on religious aspects of existence. It would be as artificial to deal with the economic history of 1979 without mentioning Khomeini as it would be to treat of the religious history of the Amish without dealing with the economics of small-scale agriculture.

It may be noted also that some of the major figures in the sociology of religion have also been concerned with typology. To take two examples: Weber and his theories of the relationship between religious and socio-economic development; and Bryan Wilson and his attempt to classify various sects and new religious movements. This work is relevant to the often neglected point that one can have a typology of historical changes—e.g., what happens in cases of culture contact.

Though one might consider, reasonably, that the difference between the various disciplines (history, sociology, anthropology of religion) is somewhat artificial, it does create one advantage, in that the institution-alization of differing approaches leads to effective intellectual lobbies against the neglect of certain areas. Thus it is easy to do the history of religions in a rather textual and 'unliving' way. The social scientists pressure us to restore balance here. A result is the renewed modern interest in the sociology of early Christianity, the attempt to look at Buddhism from the perspective of modern Asian societies, the need to analyse rites of passage in context and so on. The same can be said about some recent and rather adventitious developments. Thus in North America especially the advent of women's political activism has resulted in a burgeoning of women's studies and with that a renewed interest in the female in religion; likewise recent concerns about Blacks, Chicanos, and Native Americans have led to something of a revival in the study of the religions of these people.

One major methodological issue arises especially in regard to the sociology of religion, and in a differing form regarding the psychology of religion. The tendency in these fields is for theories to be developed which are in general projectionist. Thus God and the Ultimate and the lesser entities and symbols of religious belief tend to be seen as uncon-scious or social projections, which then act reflexively upon society and individuals. Thus a highly sophisticated modern form of projection theory is to be found in Peter Berger's *The Sacred Canopy* (British title: *The Social Reality of Religion*), in which he claims to espouse 'methodological atheism.' It is taken as axiomatic that a scientific approach to religion cannot accept the existence of God. But the non-acceptance of the existence of God is not equivalent to the acceptance of the non-existence of God. What should be used in approaching religion is not so much the principle of methodological atheism as the principle of methodological agnosticism. It is not useful for the investigator of religion to begin by imposing assumptions drawn from his own worldview upon the subject matter. Thus the suspension of belief here required is a kind of higher-order agnosticism. Thus God or the Ultimate need neither be affirmed nor denied, but seen as something present in human experience and belief, wherever it is so present. It is only in this sense that there is a 'science of God.' It is important that the power of religious experience and belief and the way God serves as a focus of human activity and feeling should be recognized as factors in history and society and in individual psychology. Often the power of the Ultimate-as-experienced is underestimated by modern rationalist historians and social scientists. How important it is is not a question of validity of experience, but a matter of empirical impact. Conversely it may be that on occasions religionists have overestimated the actual impact of the Ultimate-as-experienced. So though there is not a science of God there is a sort of science of God-as-experienced. This is the advantage of speaking of religion as a phenomenon.

Since impacts are in principle measurable it is not surprising that much attention has been paid by some social scientists to statistical data: we can see one manifestation of this approach in the *Journal for the Scientific Study of Religion*. One of the problems arises from the way in which a suitable wedding between this and more impressionistic but empathetic phenomenology can be achieved. We see a like chasm in the psychology of religion between much of the interesting work being done in typological phenomenology, e.g., over the classification of mysticism and other forms of religious experience, and the measurement of attitudes, etc., which occupies much of psychology-oriented psychology of religion. Frits Staal's sketch on how to deal with mysticism in his *Exploring Mysticism* goes some way towards achieving a synthesis;

but there remain important philosophical problems not fully resolved either by him or by others in regard to the ways to classify inner experiences—an issue much bound up with the important, but vexed, question of the relationship between experience and interpretation. Considerable conceptual problems enter into this discussion, which has recently been carried on in the context of philosophical analysis. Lack of concern with the problem has vitiated some influential works on religious experience, e.g., by Stace and Zaehner.

For various reasons, the interplay between anthropology, depth psychology and history of religions has proved fruitful in the variety of ways myth and symbolism can be approached. There are certain congruences between structuralism, Eliade, and Jung, which suggest that the analysis of religion may be a vital ingredient in any theory of human psychology. And this in turn raises an important question as to what the comparative and phenomenological study of religion ultimately aims at. Though it may be methodologically unsound to try to define the study of religion in terms of some theory within the field, and the data should be so far as possible presented in a way which is not theory-laden—for this would lead too easily and cheaply to 'confirmation' of the theory by the data,—yet it may remain important for the history of religions to supply material which can be used theoretically. Thus the following are important, though difficult areas for speculation and research: Are there in fact archetypal symbols which are liable to appear independently in different cultures? If so, what kind of explanation of this would be in order? What kinds of patterns can be found in the processes of syncretism and the creation of new religious movements in the third world (as the many thousand in Africa) and in parts of the western world? If the mythic mode of expressing existential relationships to the cosmos and to society has been widespread among peoples in the past and to some extent in the present, what other changes are liable to accompany the erosion of this style of thinking? To what extent do non-religious ideologies function in similar ways to traditional religious belief-systems? Can any form of projection theory be empirically confirmed? Most importantly, the confluence of anthropological and religio-historical approaches may be vital in giving us a better modern understanding of human symbolic behaviour.

Curiously, though religions obviously have a vital interest in the arts and music, there has been relative neglect of the visual, musical, and literary dimensions of religious consciousness. This is perhaps in part due to the kind of training typical of western scholars—concerned often with texts as evidences, and fascinated often by doctrinal and intellectual aspects of faith. An interesting methodological question arises in regard to literature, in that novelists especially are devoted to a kind of fictional 'structured empathy' such as I described earlier. They bring out the feel of what it is like to be a given person looking at the world and at others in a certain way (consider, for instance the divergent expressions of attitude delineated by Dostoievsky in the case of the brothers Karamazov). To what degree would new forms of literary presentation be relevant to the task of phenomenology? One thinks here of the novels of Eliade and Sartre as cases where more abstract analyses are clothed in particular flesh.

One can discover, in the evolution of the study of religion, a series of stages. One stage is represented by the discovery and decipherment of other cultures (I look here at the matter inevitably from the standpoint of the western culture which gave rise to the modern study of religion). This process is still going on. There are still large numbers of important texts not yet edited and understood, and the recording of oral traditions is still only very partial. Access to the records of differing religious traditions made possible the process of comparison. Classificatory comparisons form ideally the second stage in the study of religion as a human phenomenon. The third stage is where theories whether sociological (e.g., Weber), anthropological (e.g., Tylor) or psychological (e.g., Jung) can be formulated. We remain at a rather early stage in the development of theorizing about religion. Perhaps also we are at the beginning of a harvest, in which the many fruits of the extensive expansion of research since World War II can be gathered, and when the history of religions—and in a more general way the study of religion—may enter a period of greater influence, in the broader world of learning.

So far we have looked at the scientific study of religion as being plural in scope, for it concerns the many traditions and the plethora of forms of religion to be discovered on the planet and in history; and as being multidisciplinary—for it must include not just the techniques and processes of structured empathy and typological phenomenology, but also methods drawn from history, sociology, anthropology, iconography, and so on. But there remain problems concerning the boundaries of the field. Notoriously an agreed and useful definition of religion is hard or impossible to find. Yet at the same time often scholars seem unnaturally confident as to what they mean by the study of religion. It is a real question as to whether the subject should consider the symbolic systems usually held in the West to lie beyond religion proper—e.g., nationalism, forms of Marxism, and so on. There does seem an incongruity in treating the Taiping rebellion (or revolution) in the category of the history of religions and Maoism in another quite separate category of political history. After all, both movements were trying to resolve much the same problem of China's national identity in a time of crisis, and they have many other properties in common. It is interesting to note that in the account of one of the discussions at the History of Religions Study Conference in Turku Finland (see Lauri Honko, editor, *Science of Religion Studies in Methodology*, (1979: 30) the following passage occurs:

Similarly picking up van Baaren's remark, he—sc. Zwi Werblowsky—suggested (not facetiously) that comparative religion ought also to look at the current process of formation of secular canons, e.g., the works of Chairman Mao.

What is interesting is the disclaimer 'not facetiously.' For it is a result of perhaps an ideological rather than a scientific divide that we put traditional religions in one basket and secular ideologies in another. My own plenary paper, 'From the Tao to Mao,' at the Lancaster Congress of the IAHR in 1975, was itself a protest against the rigid division between traditional and modern secular worldviews. It is after all ultimately an empirical matter to discover if theories worked out in regard to traditional religions also work in the case of their secular counterparts.

Thus there is an argument for saying that the scientific study of religion is non-finite—that is, there is no clear boundary which we can draw around it. It simply has to be discovered in practice how far theorizing goes beyond the traditional faiths. Incidentally it is quite clear that the methods of structured empathy are as necessary in the exploration of secular worldviews as in the case of religions proper.

Though there is increasing reason to hold that the scientific study of religion should be so far as possible value-free, save in so far as in the nature of the case it has to evoke values, via the processes of empathy and phenomenology, there is little doubt that it has a reflexive effect *upon* values. For one thing, the historical approach to scriptures is bound to (and has) affected attitudes to their authority, and can nibble at their contents. Similarly knowledge of other religious traditions is bound to affect attitudes to one's own tradition. Thus a lot of ink has been spilled on the question of the uniqueness of Christianity, since from the perspective of certain theologies there is a motive to stress the difference between Christianity and other faiths; while there is something of the opposite from the perspective of modern Hinduism. The question of Christianity's likeness or unlikeness to other traditions in this or that respect is strictly an empirical question (though it may remain a debatable one). In this way empirical theses may have evaluative consequences.

The fact that the scientific study of religion can have such effects is one reason why it takes a special kind of temperament to be devoted to its pursuit—a kind of passion for evocative dispassion. It is, though, one of the noblest of human enterprises to try to enter imaginatively into the feelings and thoughts of others. This is an ingredient in religious methodology which has many lessons to teach in the modern world and the multicultural ambience of the planet. This is one among a number of reasons why the study of religion and religions should play a widening part in the educated person's understanding of the world. Eliade is right to call for a creative role for the history of religions. Better, this role should be played not just by the history of religions, but more widely by the whole set of disciplines which in interplay make up the study of religion. All this is only perhaps a second-order way of saying that religious sentiments, ideas, and institutions remain a pervasive aspect of the human world. That so often the wider study of religion—what I have called the scientific study of religion—has been suspected from the side of faith and neglected from the side of reason has contributed to the lopsidedness of the human sciences.

The Study of Religion in a Global Context

FRANK WHALING

This is not the sort of book from which any one straightforward conclusion can emerge. It would be strange if this were to be the case, granted that a number of contributors have written in detail and in depth about practically the whole gamut of the study of religion. This chapter will not attempt to arrive at normative and definitive conclusions.

Instead we will complete this study by examining the implications for the study of religion of our present global context—this involves breaking new ground as well as treading ground that has already been covered.

The term 'global context' can mean a number of different things. At an obvious level, it can mean simply 'worldwide,' implying that the study of religion should involve the study of *all* religions, not just those of a particular part of the globe. Although anthropology of religion tends to focus upon primal religion, and sociology of religion and psychology of religion tend to focus upon western religion, there are historical reasons for these limitations of subject matter. These limitations are not necessarily inherent within these disciplines and, as we have seen, they are certainly not inherent within the other approaches to the study of religion, the overall context of which is implicitly planetary.

At another level the notion of 'global context' implies the need to take seriously insights and scholarship from other parts of the globe so that the study of religion may become global rather than 'western' in outlook. The reader, in working through this book, may perhaps have become aware that the contributors, the approaches they have described, the scholars they have mentioned, and the concepts they have used, have been primarily western. Unease at the seeming western monopoly of the study of religion has been growing throughout our period. A recent book by a non-westerner, Edward W. Said (1978), dramatically, if somewhat one-sidedly, highlights a similar point in regard to the study of Orientalism. However, it is part of the purpose of this chapter to make the point that non-Christians in the West such as Buber, and non-westerners such as Coomaraswamy, Radhakrishnan, Suzuki, Mbiti, Nasr, and Wing-Tsit Chan, have already made significant contributions to the study of religion from the perspectives of their own cultures. Advances in knowledge and understanding have emerged not merely from western studies of and contact with other religious traditions, but also from the work of scholars of other traditions who have studied their own culture and reflected upon their contact with the West. Indeed signs are already beginning to emerge of non-westerners (such as Izutsu) studying other non-western religions, and therefore by-passing the West as an omnipresent factor in the study of religion. The process whereby other religious traditions are studying themselves and others, as well as being studied by the West, is being hastened on by religious developments such as the renewal of the other major religious traditions and by extra-religious developments such as the emergence of independent countries, the oil crisis, the rise of communist nations, and so on.

Indeed at another level, the study of science and the study of religion are part of a greater whole. As we survey the 'global context' since 1945 it is clear that during that period the world has become one in a way that was not so evident before. The growth of world population, the spread of nuclear weapons, increasing pollution, the problem of world poverty, and the diminishing of non-renewable energy resources affect the whole planet. What Toffler has called the 'Third Wave' (1980), the new technological revolution centred upon space exploration, the development of the riches of the sea, the increasing use of micro-technology, and the extension of the genetic sciences has consequences for the whole globe. And these consequences are not merely scientific. As Ervin Laszlo puts it, 'The dominant consensus in Western societies is that such problems are mainly physical and ecological in nature, and that they can be overcome by more and higher technology' (1979: 1). He points out, however, that, 'The root causes even of physical and ecological problems are the inner constraints on our vision and values' (1979: 3). In other words, there is a growing awareness of the interconnectedness of our global problems. They are not only physical and scientific, they are also human and cultural. They have to do with the vision, values, the worldview of men, and to that extent they have to do with 'religion.'

One of the important themes in this book has been that of the interrelationship between the different approaches to the study of religion. Implicit in our discussion has been the question as to whether the various methods of studying religion are complementary or opposed. We have suggested in general that the approaches we have outlined are interconnected parts of a wider whole. We have suggested that anthropology of religion, sociology of religion, psychology of religion, history and phenomenology of religion, comparative religion, the study of myths and texts, and the scientific study of religion are all elements within the wider study of religion, and that apparent clashes between the different methods are provisional rather than final. However, any serious grappling with our global context must involve us in a wider discussion centred not only upon the relationship between the different approaches within the study of religion but also upon the relationship between the study of religion and the study of other fields.

In western intellectual history, three dominant educational models have emerged. The Graeco-Roman model was that of *humanitas*, what we would call the humanities, and its main stress was upon literature and man; the medieval European model was that of *theologia*, what we could call theology, and its main stress was upon theology and God; the modern model has until recently been that of the natural sciences, with its main stress upon the analysis of nature, and with its penchant for minute specialisation. The impingement upon scholarship of the modern global context has opened the way for an intensified discussion about the very nature of science, the humanities, and theology, and the relationship between them. There is a growing awareness of the need to redefine areas of human knowledge both for the sake of the disciplines concerned and for the sake of gaining a more integral view of human knowledge with a view to coping more adequately with our global problems. The major part of this book has attempted to summarise the contemporary position in religious studies in order to aid this field of knowledge in its own self-awareness. In this chapter we shall glance briefly at the wider question of the place of religious studies within the whole spectrum of human knowledge. How does it fit into the three areas that have been predominant in western thought? Is religious studies complementary with other areas of knowledge, and, if so, in what way? Has religious studies any part to play in the search for a wider integration within the total academic enterprise?

Clearly all the questions we have raised under the heading of 'the study of religion in a global context' are important. Limitations of space prevent us from dealing with them at length. Insofar as these questions are attempting to chart partly unexplored territory there remains an element of prophecy about them. In ten years time it will be easier to exercise a mature judgment in regard to them. Nevertheless to ignore them completely would be unwise. They represent possible growing-points for the field of religious studies. Insofar as they are so basic, one may reasonably predict that the response made to them (whether it be active or passive, creative or negative) will be significant for the future development of religious studies, and possibly for wider scholarship as well.

In the first place, then, we shall look briefly at the work of certain influential non-Christian or non-western scholars of religion, and attempt to estimate their impact upon the study of religion. A related and important topic concerns the effect of non-western studies upon the field of religious studies: do they relativise or fragment an area of study formerly united by its western provenance, or does it remain a recognisable but perhaps transformed area? Second, we shall place the study of religion within a wider academic spectrum, and attempt to understand its nature by reference to its differences from and its relationship to other academic fields.

We may usefully begin our examination of non-western studies of religion by reflecting upon the implications of Edward W. Said's *Orientalism* (1978). This book is a study of the genesis, growth, and continuation of a western (mainly French and British) tradition of knowledge concerning the Orient (mainly the Arabo-Islamic world). According to Said there was a convergence between Orientalism and western imperialism whereby the western scholars of the Orient, wittingly or unwittingly, aided and abetted the European colonial advance throughout the Orient. As Said puts it:

Orientalism came to signify: a systematic discipline of accumulation. And far from this being exclusively an intellectual or theoretical feature, it made Orientalism fatally tend towards the systematic accumulation of human beings and territories. To reconstruct a dead or lost Oriental language meant ultimately to reconstruct a dead or neglected Orient; it also meant that reconstructive precision, science, even imagination could prepare the way for what armies, administrators, and bureaucracies would later do on the ground in the Orient (1978: 123).

Although he traces this process back into the eighteenth century, Said also mentions respected modern scholars such as Louis Massignon and Sir Hamilton Gibb as exponents of French and British Orientalism. Indeed, in his final chapter, 'Orientalism Now,' Said analyses the supposed role of American Orientalism in influencing or implementing American government policy, and in aiding international business interests. Perhaps Said gets to the heart of the matter in his comment:

The real issue is whether there can be a true representation of anything, or whether any and all representations, because they are representations, are embedded in the language and then in the culture, institutions, and political ambience of the representor (1978: 273).

The implication is that the notion that a university is an academic community committed to the unbiased and disinterested pursuit of knowledge as an end in itself is a chimera. According to Said, western academics, consciously or unconsciously, created an image of the Orient that served the interests not of pure scholarship but of western culture.

Said's thesis is so important in its possible implications that we must first offer a brief critique of it before going on to investigate its ramifications in regard to the study of religion. In the first place, Said's thesis is limited in its terms of reference to Orientalism. This term, as interpreted either by Said or western orientalists, is both wider and narrower than the study of eastern religions—wider because it comprehends the study of the language, literature, and total culture of the area concerned, narrower because it tends to see religion as a facet of the total culture rather than as significant in its own right. Orientalism is therefore both related to and different from the study of eastern religions. In the second place, Said's notion of the Orient refers in practice to Islam rather than to the whole eastern world, indeed it refers in particular to the eastern part of the Arabo-Muslim world. It is difficult, if not hazardous, to draw general conclusions about western studies of the whole world east of Suez from studies of such a specific nature. In the third place, Said's references are mainly to French and British Orientalism. He says relatively little about the work of scholars from other European countries and American scholars who also played key roles in oriental studies. In the fourth place, Said is ambivalent about what should be the approach of one culture towards another. Was the rise of Orientalism inevitable because the West could not avoid seeing other cultures in the light of its own interests, or should the West have known better? Now that the Orient is becoming economically and politically more powerful, does this mean that scholars within resurgent Muslim countries, Japan, China, India, Israel and so on must inevitably view other cultures in the light of their own interests? Or is this not merely a form of political and cultural reductionism? In the fifth place, although Said does not ignore historical data, his method is basically synchronic and structural, and his approach is reminiscent of that of Michel Foucault (1971, 1976). Orientalism as it developed historically was far more diverse, complex, multifaceted, and dynamic that Said gives it credit. For example, early British Orientalists in India such as William Jones, Charles Wilkins, Colebrooke, and H.H. Wilson helped Hindus to reconstruct their own past by researching the Veda, the six systems of Indian philosophy, the Vedānta, and the *smṛti* texts; and it was the Orientalists who *opposed* the cultural arrogance of Macaulay and the Christian imperialism of Grant, and helped to pave the way for the Indian renaissance.

It is easy to analyse the drawbacks in Said's thesis. It is evident also that he is saying something important. Said claims that he has written to help contemporary students of the Orient 'to criticise—with the hope of stirring discussion—the often unquestioned assumptions on which their work for the most part depends' (1978: 24). In this respect his advice is valuable not only for Orientalists but also for students of religion. Western scholarship may have freed itself from excesses of cultural arrogance, yet it is sometimes betrayed by its own presuppositions. For example, the *Journal of the History of Ideas* for 1979 contains forty-five papers: forty-three deal with the history of ideas in the West, one deals with medieval Jewish literature (in the West), and one with the confluence of Chinese and western intellectual history. Has the history of ideas really been centred so exclusively upon the West?

In addition to pointing to the presuppositions underlying western studies of eastern cultures, Said asks a further important question: 'Can one divide human reality, as human reality seems to be genuinely divided, into clearly different cultures, histories, traditions, societies, even races, and survive the consequences humanly?' (1978: 45). His implicit plea is that firstly we should recognise, conceptualise, and genuinely realise the self-awareness of different cultures, histories, traditions, societies, races, and religions but that secondly we should situate them within the one human reality. This summarises in a nutshell the problem put to religious studies by the present global context. How can western scholars and scholars from other cultures authentically represent and transmit a mutually verified knowledge of the various religions of the world in their difference while at the same time recognising that they are part of a wider whole, namely humanity? The first step is to free or allow other cultures and religions to free themselves from western stereotypes; the second step is to see and academically conceptualise the global unity lying behind the religious diversity. In former times the global unity was imposed by the western stereotypes; in the present context it must be interculturally conceptualised by academic colloquia no longer constrained by western sovereignty.

In fact, a number of non-western scholars have already made noteworthy contributions to the study of religion. We shall analyse the work of seven such scholars now before attempting to estimate the implications of their work.

Ananda Coomaraswamy

Coomaraswamy was born in 1877 in Colombo, the son of a Sinhalese father and a British mother. Ananda was only two years old when his father Sir Mutu Coomaraswamy died, and he was educated in Britain at Wycliffe Hall and University College London. He was a Doctor of Science by the time he was thirty, his thesis being centred upon the geology of Ceylon, but during his scientific research in Ceylon and India he became intensely aware of the aesthetic and religious values of those areas and he was destined to spend the rest of his life researching, expounding, and defending those values.

Most of his productive work was done when he was researcher or curator at the Boston Museum of Fine Arts, a period that lasted for thirty years. When he died in 1947, he left behind a wealth of correspondence, books, and notes. Roger Lipsey has recently published two large volumes of papers by Coomaraswamy on traditional art and symbolism and on metaphysics, together with a volume on his life and work (1977), and although it is true to say that Coomaraswamy lived mainly before our period the fact remains that his influence has been more recent.

In his *Modern Indian Thought: A Philosophical Survey*, V.S. Naravane lists Coomaraswamy along with Ram Mohun Roy and his followers, Ramakrishna, Vivekananda, Tagore, Gandhi, Aurobindo, Radhakrishnan, and Iqbal as exemplars of modern Indian thought. Most of these thinkers would rank as advocates for rather than scholars of Indian religion. Coomaraswamy, although he never held a university post in the study of religion, can be classed primarily as a student of Indian art and religion, and his researches in this wide area were both comprehensive and minute—comprehensive in the sense that they covered a wide range of art, metaphysics, religion, and symbolism comparatively as well as regionally, narrow in the sense that he was willing and anxious to tackle particular philological points, as in his comments on entries in the Pali Text Society Dictionary such as *vyañjanā*, and in his essay on *saṃvega* in connection with Buddhist art (Rykwert 1979).

For our purposes, Coomaraswamy's work is important for three reasons. In the first place, he was concerned to reflect, academically, culturally and religiously, upon the Indian experience. He did so both as a scholar and as one who had made 'an unspecified but formal gesture of allegiance to Hinduism' (Rykwert (1979: 107). His reflection upon the Indian experience was neither narrowly Hindu nor narrowly Indian. He had a deep interest in the Buddhist tradition; he wrote on Mughal art showing how it integrally fused Persian and Indian motifs; he wrote on the art and culture of wider India, for example Indonesia; and he traced also the continuity between pre-Aryan, Vedic and Buddhist India. Romain Rolland claims, in his preface to Coomaraswamy's *Dance of Shiva* (1957) that the author's purpose in that book is:

to show the power of the Indian soul, to show all the riches that it holds stored up. . . . The vast and tranquil metaphysic of India is unfolded: her conception of the Universe, her social organisation . . . the magnificent revelation of her art. The whole vast soul of India proclaims from end to end of its crowded and well-ordered edifice the same domination of a sovereign synthesis.

In his small book on *Hinduism and Buddhism* (1943, 1971) Coomaraswamy examines again the main categories of those traditions, claiming that western scholarship had not fully grasped the meaning of the Veda, *karma, māyā*, reincarnation, and the six philosophical systems of the Hindu tradition, nor the Buddha's message within the Buddhist tradition. As he puts it, 'few indeed are the translations of Indian books into European languages that can yet come up to the standards set for themselves by the Tibetan and Chinese Buddhists' (1971: 49). Our concern is not to examine the minutiae of Coomaraswamy's analysis of Indian religion, but to point out that, even before our period began, he was stating for an academic and indeed western audience:

The heart and essence of Indian experience is to be found in a constant intuition of the unity of all life, and the instinctive, ineradicable conviction that the recognition of this unity is the highest good and the uttermost freedom (*Dance of Shiva*, 1957: 22).

Coomaraswamy, secondly, while examining and interpreting Indian religion from his own viewpoint saw it as part of a perennial philosophy embodying universal truths exclusive to no one tradition or period. He writes:

Who that has breathed the pure mountain air of the Upanishads, of Samkara and Kabir, of Rumi and Lao Tse and Jesus—to mention Asiatic prophets—can be alien to those who have sat at the feet of Plato, Kant, Tauler, Ruysbroeck, Whitman, Nietzsche, Blake? (*Dance of Shiva*, 1957: 152).

Religious traditions may therefore be extrinsically different and unique, intrinsically the essential spiritual language of their perennial philosophy remains the same. Coomaraswamy surmised that, due to the problems associated with the rise of industrialisation, the West had partially broken away from the moorings of its own perennial philosophy (see Schmitt 1966) and was in danger of leading the rest of the world in the same direction. And so, before the appearance of Aldous Huxley's well-known book *Perennial Philosophy* in 1946, and before the rise of the 'school' of Philosophia Perennis, an eastern thinker was already uttering these thoughts, and unlike his western contemporary, Guénon, he was unwilling to surrender the tools of scholarship to 'esotericism' in so doing (see Eliade 1979).

In the third place, Coomaraswamy stressed the role and importance of art in Indian religion and life as a support to contemplation, as an evocation of religious archetypes, and as an aid to deeper understanding. The art that he had in mind was not naturalistic presentation, individualistic assertion, 'art for art's sake,' or art for enjoyment's sake, but the significant and liberating art of those 'who in their performances are celebrating God ... in both of his natures, immanent and transcendent' (1977: vol. 1, 40). In many of his works, Coomaraswamy worked out his theories about the aesthetic and religious value of such art. In books such as *Christian and Oriental Philosophy of Art*, he applied his theories comparatively. For him, true works of art are religious icons rather than merely useful objects and they direct the attention of the receptive observer away from outward things to the inward realisation of what he *is*.

Coomaraswamy has been criticised on a number of counts. As Rykwert points out (1979: 104) there were contradictions within his own life between the 'traditional' philosophy and religion he stressed and his own western life-style. The dichotomy he saw between the fragmented life of the industrial West and the integrated pattern of life in the East was too simplistically conceived. It is not clear that the picture he draws of Indian metaphysics and aesthetics can be verified within the actual life-experience of Indian villages. Moreover, his notion of a Philosophia Perennis is a hermeneutical presupposition rather than a verifiable principle. Nevertheless it is clear that, even before the Second

World War, here was an eastern thinker who was ready academically to reconceive the nature of eastern religion without denying the authenticity of other religious traditions. To return to Said's thesis, Coomaraswamy was not willing to accept the western academic stereotype (as he saw it) of Indian religion. He produced an alternative to it, or perhaps we should say an extension of it, and in so doing introduced an eastern dimension into the study of religion.

Sarvepalli Radhakrishnan

Our second non-western scholar, Radhakrishnan, is both similar to and different from Coomaraswamy. By comparison with Coomaraswamy, Radhakrishnan was more interested in philosophy than art, more deeply involved in university concerns, more engaged in Indian national and political life, more concerned with inter-religious relationships than with 'perennial philosophy,' and just as academically engrossed in reinterpreting for the present the Indian (and other) traditions as in recovering and recapitulating their past. Like Coomaraswamy, Radhakrishnan was responsible, because of his intellectual calibre, for the academic promotion of an Indian view of the nature of Indian religion; like Coomaraswamy he was at the same time both a genuine scholar and a committed Hindu.

Radhakrishnan was born in 1888 at Tirutani in South India and (unlike Coomaraswamy) he was brought up in India within a Hindu family. His education at Christian institutions, notably Madras Christian College, influenced him both positively and negatively. A critical study of Hindu ideas was forced upon him but the need for philosophy that arose when his faith in tradition was shaken served only to fuel an interest in both philosophy and Indian religion that became a life-long concern. From 1909 to 1926 Radhakrishnan lectured at Madras, Mysore, and Calcutta. He returned to India briefly to be Vice-Chancellor of Andhra University after a spell as professor of comparative religion from 1929 at Manchester College Oxford, but went back to Oxford in 1936 to take up the Spalding professorship of Eastern religions and ethics. By the time R.C. Zaehner succeeded him in the Spalding chair,

Radhakrishnan was launched upon a more political career that was to culminate in his being President of India from 1962 until 1967.

A number of Radhakrishnan's writings became and continue to be influential, and the impact of their clarity of thought was enhanced by the beauty of their style. In relation to Said's thesis, they constitute, to use one of Professor Joad's terms, a counter-attack from the East. Indeed the writings of Radhakrishnan and Coomaraswamy reassert academically the importance and role of the Indian tradition, and they perform at the academic level the task accomplished in different ways by figures such as Ram Mohun Roy, Sen, the Tagores, Saraswati, Ramakrishna, Vivekananda, Gandhi, and Aurobindo.

Radhakrishnan's serious writing career began in 1918 with his book on the *Philosophy of Rabindranath Tagore*. His treatment of Tagore, by whom he was influenced, in whom he saw a Upanishadic concern for the unity of things rather than Tagore's equal stress on Vaishnavite theism, and through whom his concern for modern India and philosophy were strengthened, fore-shadowed a number of his future interests. His *Reign of Religion in Contemporary Philosophy* (1920) proved to be a temporary aberration in the development of his basic approach. In this book he tried to separate the roles of religion and philosophy. He argued that religious systems should not govern philosophy which was an in-dependent activity in no way dominated by religion. In retrospect this book may be seen as the parting of the ways for Radhakrishnan. Had he continued down the path indicated in this work it is likely that his academic stance would have been more western. In fact much of his later work endeavoured to show not only the close interrelationship between philosophy and religion in India but also their close connections else-where. His *Indian Philosophy* (1923, 1927) became an academic classic, combining as it did a lucid style, a historical overview of Indian philosophy, and a penetrating (if neo-Vedāntist) insight into the nature of the Indian religious and philosophical tradition. Radhakrishnan's next two works, *Hindu View of Life* (1927) and *Kalki* (1929) veered towards an implicit apologetic of Hinduism over against the West. He attempted to summarise the positive aspects of Hindu thought in order to portray Hinduism within the wider context of Indian values as a worldview based upon tolerance and spiritual vision; at the same time he warned against the long-term implications of technological growth and material progress unaccompanied by religious idealism. *An Idealist View of Life* (1932) was the culmination of Radhakrishnan's earliest period of writing. In it he was not afraid to express his own commitment to an idealist view of life. Although his outlook was clearly eastern he also wrote comparatively about western philosophy and western idealism, and he claimed that idealism, broadly conceived, had an important part to play in modern thought. It contended, he wrote (1932: 15):

that the universe has meaning, has value. Ideal values are dynamic forces; they are the driving power of the universe. The world is only intelligible as a system of ends. Such a view has nothing to do with the problem whether a thing is only a particular image or a general relation.

Radhakrishnan wrote a great deal after 1932, but there is a sense in which the main themes of his work were set by then and his later writings merely widened patterns that were already there. He continued to write on Indian religion, and became especially interested in the role of Buddhism as part of the total development of the Indian tradition; he continued to write comparatively on the integral relationship between religion and philosophy; he continued to write on Indian cultural renewal; and he continued to write upon the contribution religion can make to heal the problems of the modern world (see Bibliography for references).

Radhakrishnan is especially interesting, in the context of our present discussion, for three reasons. In the first place, he represents, even more clearly than Coomaraswamy, a 'counter-attack from the East.' Not only was he not content passively to continue western patterns of scholarship in regard to Indian religion, he also brought into the bloodstream of western scholarship an Indian outlook in regard to the study of religion. He approached religion from the viewpoint of philosophy in contrast to the classical western approaches which had been more inclined to stress anthropology, history, sociology, psychology, or phenomenology. In this he is not untypical, scholars such as T.R.V. Murti (1955) would follow him in this, and even today religion is studied mainly within the philosophy departments of Indian universities (only the Punjabi

University at Patiala has a religious studies department in its own right).
Moreover, he had a wide view of philosophy which made him unable to
restrict it to epistemological or parochial issues. As Naravane puts it
(1964: 242):

> Radhakrishnan expects of philosophy that it should be dynamic and practical, that it
> should broadly accept the wholeness of reality and the unity of the different aspects of the
> universe, and that it should help in the recognition, conservation and furtherance of
> value.

In short, he had both a broad notion of the nature of philosophy and a
conviction that religion and philosophy were integral rather than separate studies. In addition to this, he had an Indian insight into the way
philosophy operates. He saw the world as mysterious as well as rational,
as graspable by intuition as well as intellect. But he regarded intuition as
being a way of knowledge rather than an alternative to it, he accepted it
as being a form of thought rather than a flight from thought. In all this,
his approach was clearly Indian.

In the second place, Radhakrishnan was not afraid to lay bare his own
religious commitment. He was unashamedly an idealist, and therefore
not a naturalist, a scientific materialist, a doctrinaire nationalist, or a
humanist. Within idealism, his predilection was towards Śaṅkara's
school of Advaita Vedānta, although his allegiance to Śaṅkara was by no
means uncritical. This meant that one of his main concerns was to
enquire into the nature of ultimate reality which he saw as 'the Beyond
who cannot be comprehended by our concepts or recognised by our
understanding.... He can only be described negatively, or through
seemingly contradictory descriptions' (1939: 298). He states (Schilpp
1952: 671):

> It is my opinion that systems which play the game of philosophy fairly and squarely, with
> freedom from presuppositions and with religious neutrality, end in Absolute Idealism.

In spite of his use of the words 'freedom from presuppositions' and
'religious neutrality,' his approach is not the phenomenological one of
using *epoché* and *Einfühlung* in order to describe and understand the

position of others. His approach is predetermined and his commitment undisguised. Although he asserted that students of religion should 'treat all religions in a spirit of absolute detachment and impartiality' (1933: 16), his own notion of impartiality arose from his partiality for a philosophical approach to religion derived from his Indian background.

Thirdly, and in contrast to Coomaraswamy, Radhakrishnan had a keen interest in the dynamics of the present global religious situation. He was not content, with Coomaraswamy, to attempt to recapture and conceptualise the perennial philosophy of· religions that the modern world was in danger of losing (although his search for the continuity and centrality of idealism approximated to this), his concern was also for the present-day dialogue of religions. This concern revealed itself in two ways. As far as Indian religion was concerned, Radhakrishnan was keen to describe and interpret it in such a fashion as to make it relevant to the contemporary world, and to make it contribute to dialogue. An example of this was his continuing attempt to reinterpret the concept of *māyā*. On the wider scene, he saw the dialogue of world religions as an important element in the building up of a new world culture. He wrote (in Rouner 1966: 296):

The different religions are to be used as building stones for the development of a human culture in which the adherents of the different religions may be fraternally united as children of one Supreme. All religions convey to their followers a message of abiding hope. The world will give birth to a new faith which will be but the old faith in another form, the faith of the ages, the potential divinity of man which will work for the supreme purpose written in our hearts and souls, the unity of all mankind.

Sentiments such as these were contrary to the more historically oriented tendencies of the western study of religion. It seemed to western scholars that the academic status of the study of religion was being subordinated to the laudable, humanitarian, but not directly academic aim of building up world peace and harmony. Moreover, Radhakrishnan's work fed into a movement towards dialogue that was beginning to become manifest within Christian theology, and which was equally suspicious to western scholars of religion. However, the point is that Radhakrishnan's work represented a distinctively non-western contribution to the study of religion which brought into prominence not only an Indian view of the study of Indian religion but also an Indian view concerning the general study of religion. Before the imperial age was over, Radhakrishnan's work was already begun, and the tradition he represents has continued in being right up to the present day.

D.T. Suzuki

Our third non-western scholar, Suzuki, brought a Buddhist and Japanese perspective to the study of religion. His influence upon that study was exercised within his own culture and in the United States rather than in Europe. Although he ranks as a genuine scholar, Suzuki also bears some of the attributes of a guru. Indeed he is similar in certain respects to Radhakrishnan in that he combined a concern for the renewal and defence of his own tradition, a concern for scholarship, and an ability to represent his own tradition with the authority of an academically respected 'father-figure.' He differs from Radhakrishnan by virtue of his relative lack of interest in philosophy, and by virtue of his relatively greater interest in his own religion and indeed his own language.

Suzuki died in 1966 aged ninety-five, and his career divides naturally into three periods. Up to the mid-1920s, he was involved in the defence and presentation of the Buddhist tradition in the West, and in the reformulation and renewal of the Buddhist tradition in the East. From the mid-1920s to about 1949, he was engaged in the more specifically academic task of translating and exegeting Buddhist texts from India, Japan, and China. From 1949 to 1966, Suzuki continued to reinterpret the Buddhist tradition but at the same time he was called upon to represent the views of Buddhism upon various contemporary issues, especially in the United States where his influence led to an increasing interest in Buddhist studies.

Suzuki's first major work, *Outlines of Mahāyāna Buddhism*, appeared in 1907. His assumption was that the Buddhist tradition was a living organism arising out of the Buddha's experience of enlightenment and growing ever since. Although interested in the whole Buddhist tradition, both academically and ecumenically, his main concern was to interpret Chinese and Japanese Mahāyāna Buddhism. In this early work his concern was for Mahāyāna Buddhism in general, later he would become more directly interested in Pure Land and Zen Buddhism in particular. Already there were premonitions of his later ideas. He saw Mahāyāna Buddhism as an integral part of the Buddhist whole, and he saw religious experience as important in the understanding of religion as a whole. He wrote in an eastern ahistorical vein (1907: 15):

Mahāyānism is not an object of historical curiosity. Its vitality and activity concern us in our daily life. It is a great spiritual organism; its moral and religious forces are still exercising an enormous power over millions of souls; and its further development is sure to be a very valuable contribution to the world-progress of the religious consciousness. What does it matter, then, whether or not Mahāyānism is the genuine teaching of the Buddha?

Suzuki sought an ecumenical reconciliation within Buddhism between the moral disciplines of Theravāda and the more speculative disciplines of Mahāyāna, but he stressed within Mahāyāna the priority of mystical intuition in contrast to merely philosophical speculation. He wrote (1914: 272–3):

Vidya must now give way to *dhyana* or *prajna*; that is, intellection must become intuition, which is after all the ultimate form of all religious discipline. Mysticism is the life of religion. Without it religion loses her reason of existence; all her warm vitality departs, all her inexpressible charm vanishes, and there remains nothing but the crumbling bones and cold ashes of death.

It is not our concern to examine in detail the writings of Suzuki which have been collected in over thirty volumes (1969). In addition to his works in Japanese, his technical writings on Indian, Japanese and Chinese Buddhist texts, and his interpretative writings upon Buddhism in general and Mahāyāna Buddhism in particular, he gave his special attention to two other themes. Firstly, he was fascinated by the topic of mysticism. In a Japanese work of 1916 *Zen no tachiba kara* (see *Works*, Vol xiv) he wrote on 'Zen and Mysticism,' 'Tauler's Zen,' and 'Kabir's Zen.' These titles indicated that his interest in mysticism was comparative as well as parochially Buddhist, and this was born out in his *Mysticism: Christian and Buddhist*, which appeared in 1957, in which he compared Meister Eckhart as a representative Christian mystic with some Zen masters and some Pure Land *myōkōnin*, notably Asahara Saichi. Suzuki recognised five common factors in mysticism: intuitive inner experience, a new kind of inner life flowing out of that experience, paradoxical linguistic description of mystical experience, necessarily negative conceptualisations of essentially positive experience, and realistic symbolism. He noted four classifications of the forms of mysticism: the mysticism of faith, including much Christian, Muslim, Hindu, and Pure Land Buddhist mysticism; contemplative mysticism, including Christian prayer, Hindu *yoga*, and Buddhist *dhyāna*; intellectual mysticism, including neo-Platonic and German Christian mysticism, Vedānta Hinduism, the Taoist mysticism of Lao-tze and Chuang-tze, and Mahāyāna Buddhist mysticism; and superstitious mysticism (Hiroshi 1977). Suzuki was more interested in mystical experience and the inner life resulting from it than in the systematic expression of mystical doctrines, and this is evidenced in his treatment of Christian, Zen, and Pure Land mysticism which are outwardly and doctrinally different but 'can be grouped together as belonging to the great school of mysticism' (1957: xix).

Suzuki is remembered secondly for his researches into, and his renewal of, Zen Buddhism. As Dornish comments 'the present vitality of Zen and Western interest in it demonstrate how well he argued his case' (1970: 60). Again his aim was not logically to reconstruct the Zen system or to develop the concept of Emptiness lying at its heart in any thoroughgoing way. As Shimomura Toratarō points out, Nishida Kitarō and Tanabe Hajime did this far better than Suzuki. His concern was rather with the religious psychology of Zen experience, and although he admired the work of William James and Jung, and was indeed a member of Jung's Eranos Circle, he could not stay at what he considered to be the outward level of the psychology of religion. As he wrote in *An Introduction to Zen Buddhism* (1961: 44):

The basic idea of Zen is to come in touch with the inner workings of our being, and to do this in the most direct way possible, without resorting to anything external or superadded ... Zen professes itself to be the spirit of Buddhism, but in fact it is the spirit of all religions and philosophies. When Zen is thoroughly understood, absolute peace of mind is attained, and a man lives as he ought to live.

It remains to be seen whether Lynn White's daring prophecy will have any validity (1956: 304–5).

it may well be that the publication of D.T. Suzuki's first *Essays in Zen Buddhism* in 1927 will seem in future generations as great an intellectual event as William of Moerbeke's Latin translations of Aristotle in the thirteenth century or Marsiglio Ficino's of Plato in the fifteenth. But in Suzuki's case the shell of the Occident has been broken through.

Whether such vast claims are meaningful or not, it is clear that the work of Suzuki is in itself a partial refutation of some of Said's notions, and that Suzuki ranks with Radhakrishnan as a major eastern scholar who realised in his own person the fruits of his intellectual and spiritual quest.

Like Radhakrishnan, Suzuki had his own personal religious commitment. He had an early training in Zen; his second Zen master, Soyen Shaku, enabled him to advance spiritually and also to go to America; his study of Bankei's Zen awakening and teaching of the 'Unborn' had a deep spiritual influence upon him after the death of his wife in 1939. And so, like Radhakrishnan, he was not only the detached scholar objectively exegeting his texts. His scholarship was also an exercise in communicating a way of life he believed to be true.

Suzuki followed Radhakrishnan secondly in creatively reinterpreting his own tradition with the double aim of reforming it to serve his own culture and communicating it to the West to serve western culture. He had a lively sense of the organic continuity of the Buddhist tradition, but this meant that it was always developing, and its modern development had to take account of the global situation which demanded the presentation of Buddhism in both East and West. Suzuki's reformulation of Buddhism and Buddhist studies was therefore geared to the global situation and not only to internal Buddhist needs in the East. His main work was done in relation to Mahāyāna Buddhism, especially in his reinterpretations of Zen, but he was also influential within Buddhist ecumenical circles and in the wider interpretation of Buddhism as a whole.

Suzuki differed from Radhakrishnan in that he was responsible not only for promoting the creative study of his own tradition but also for presenting Zen Buddhism in such a way that it came to command the emotional allegiance of a number of people in the West. Through Suzuki's work, Zen Buddhism found a new vitality in Japan, and a new arena of influence in the United States of America. It became for a number of western students not merely a new area of study but also a new possibility for commitment. Suzuki might state in theory that 'Buddhism and Christianity and all other religious beliefs are not more than variations of one single Faith, deeply imbedded in the human soul' (1921: vol. 1, 156), in practice his stress upon spiritual experience and his interest in Zen studies led some western students to see in Zen an avenue of religious fulfilment as well as academic endeavour. Suzuki therefore achieved the status in some quarters of a guru in a more than academic sense. This kind of western response to Suzuki was viewed with very mixed feelings by western historians of religion, especially European scholars who were trying to establish the study of religion along academically recognisable lines. However, it probably remains true to say that more western scholars of Buddhism would be willing to view themselves (however vaguely) as 'Buddhists' in contrast with western scholars of other religions. Indeed the practical and theoretical implications of Suzuki's work are still working themselves out.

Martin Buber

Our next scholar, Buber, is non-Christian but not non-western. In some ways Buber is similar to Suzuki. The latter introduced a knowledge of Zen Buddhism into the West, Buber did the same for Hasidic Judaism; Buber had a great influence outside the confines of his own tradition, just as Suzuki had done; like Suzuki, Buber's motivation was religious and mystical rather than rationalistic and secular. The principle difference between them is that Suzuki was revered within his own community as an interpreter and exponent of Buddhism, whereas Buber's practical influence upon his tradition was more limited. As Epstein comments:

Buber ignores Talmudic teaching and, in fact, does not consider the observances of Jewish practices as essential to the ideal of society which he advocates. Nor does he attempt to formulate a programme indicating how these ideas are to be realized, which accounts for the limited influence of Buber on Jewish practical life (1959: 314).

Martin Buber was born in 1878 in Vienna, but brought up by his grandparents at Lemberg in Poland where he was educated, and where he had early contacts with the Hasidism that was to form part of his life. His main university studies were at the University of Vienna where he gained his Ph.D. in 1904. During this period he had contacts with, and worked for, the Zionist movement, although he eventually withdrew from active Zionist work in 1921. In addition to this, he began three very important activities during his student days: he commenced intensive studies of the Bible and the Hebrew language that would lead eventually to his completion of a German translation of the Tenach (Hebrew Bible) in 1961; he discovered the Hasidic writings which were to occupy his attention for much of his career; and he developed an interest in foreign epics and myths, including those of China, which were to give an eastern dimension to some of his thought. His first significant book on Hasidism came out in 1906 namely *Die Geschichten des Rabbi Nachman*; his important article on the Tao appeared in 1910; in 1913 his book *Daniel* was published which contained his first poetic formulation of man's duality; and in 1922 his epoch-making *Ich und Du* (I and Thou) appeared. From 1923–33 he was Professor at the Freies Jüdisches Lehrhaus in Frankfurt and at Frankfurt University, but he eventually left Germany in 1938 and became professor of social philosophy at the Hebrew University in Jerusalem, and it was in Jerusalem that he died in 1965. His books continued to appear throughout this period of teaching including his important work of biblical interpretation, *Königtum Gottes* (Kingdom of God) in 1932, to which he applied some of Max Weber's ideas, and his only novel *Gog and Magog* which he wrote in Hebrew in 1943.

Our first comment upon Buber must be that he was a genuinely global figure. His global outlook arose mainly out of his Jewish background, but he was also influenced by Christianity and eastern religions. We have mentioned his work for Zionism, his Hasidic interpretations, his lecturing for a Jewish institute in Frankfurt and a Hebrew University, his work on Biblical translation and interpretation, and the Jewish flavour of his work: yet these served to feed into a wider global vision. The influence of Buber's *I and Thou* upon Christian thinking is clear. Indeed this most famous of Buber's works may well have had a greater influence upon Christian than upon Jewish thought, and he himself was in continual dialogue with Christianity. It is perhaps less well known that Buber was also influenced by eastern thought. As Friedman puts it (1976: 411) 'his concern with mysticism in Taoism, Hasidism, and Zen, and with Eastern thought, became a steady dialogue; it was an integral part of his path, of his being.' Friedman is right to mention the word 'dialogue' in connection with Buber's development. He did not merely accept Hasidism as a block of ideas, he engaged in dialogue with it throughout his life, and the same is true to a lesser extent in relation to Taoism and Zen. It is easier to understand two important notions of Buber's *I and Thou*: those of the I-Thou relationship with nature and of the free man who wills without arbitrariness, if we see the emergence of these ideas against the background of his wrestling with Taoist conceptions of the Tao of nature and *wu-wei*. Moreover, Buber's impressive contrast between Zen and Hasidism in his essay on 'The Place of Hasidism in the History of Religions' shows how his grappling with Zen enabled him to understand Hasidism better and vice versa.

In the second place, Buber like Suzuki was engaged in his studies existentially as well as academically. They were not merely textual or historical researches. Indeed Gershem Scholem attacked Buber for interpreting Hasidism existentially as well as academically. In so doing, claimed Scholem, Buber had overstepped academic boundaries and therefore not helped the cause of a true understanding of Hasidism. Zwi Werblowsky is another representative of a branch of Jewish scholarship that would insist upon separating the History of Religions as a discipline from existentially Jewish considerations. For Buber the separation was not so clearly desirable or possible. His researches involved a dialogue with as well as a study of Hasidism and the Bible. His stress upon dialogue in *I and Thou* was no accident. It was both an academic category and an existential concern.

In the third place, Buber's main concern was with man, and his basic approach was philosophical. His methodology, if we can call it such, was that of philosophical anthropology. His primary interest was in man's relationships with other men, with nature, and with God. These relationships could take the form of an I-It relationship with others as objects, or an I-Thou relationship with others in the immediacy of encounter. Built into this approach was an emphasis upon the primacy of personal I-Thou relationships which could not be objectified and therefore could not be studied as phenomena. For Buber, interpersonal or intrapersonal encounter could not be quantified but was nevertheless crucial. And so, as in the case of Radhakrishnan and Suzuki, Buber's philosophical and indeed mystical interests took him beyond the normal historical, sociological, psychological, and phenomenological horizons of the history of religions.

Seyyed Hossein Nasr

By contrast with the last four scholars we have examined, our fifth scholar, Nasr, is still living. He bears certain resemblances to Coomaraswamy, Radhakrishnan, Suzuki, and Buber. Like Coomaraswamy, he espouses the approach of 'perennial philosophy.' Like Suzuki and Buber, he is responsible for making a particular section of studies of his own tradition, namely Ṣūfī studies, more academically popular in the West. Like Radhakrishnan, he combines an interest in philosophy with an interest in religious experience.

Seyyed Hossein Nasr was born in Tehran in 1933, and he received his early education in Iran with its Shīʿite background. He pursued his academic studies in North America, gaining a B.Sc. in Physics from M.I.T. in 1954, an M.A. from Harvard in 1956, and a Ph.D. in the History of Science and Philosophy from Harvard in 1958. His interest in science and philosophy continued when he returned to Iran to lecture in 1958. Increasingly he became active in the field of Islamic science and philosophy as well as in the problems related to the introduction of western science and technology into the Muslim world. Not only so, he also became prolific in his writing on Islam in general and Ṣūfism in particular. His latest academic post is as Professor of Islamics at Temple University, Philadelphia.

Nasr has already written twenty books and two hundred articles.
They divide into four main sections: Ṣūfī studies (*Sufi Essays* 1972, *Jalal
ad-Din Rumi* 1974); more general Islamic studies (*An Introduction to
Islamic Cosmological Doctrines* 1964, *Three Muslim Sages* 1964, *Ideals and
Realities of Islam* 1966, *Islamic Studies* 1967, *Science and Civilisation in Islam*
1970, *Islamic Science, An Illustrated Study* 1967, *Histoire de la philosophie
islamique* [with Corbin and Yahya] 1964); cultural studies (*Iran* 1966,
Persia, Bridge of Turquoise [with Beny] 1975); and analyses of the plight of
modern man containing an implicit stress upon Philosophia Perennis
(*The Encounter of Man and Nature, The Spiritual Crisis of Modern Man* 1968,
Islam and the Plight of Modern Man 1975, and the forthcoming Gifford
Lectures entitled, *Knowledge and the Sacred*).

The keys to Nasr's thought are indicated by the basic concerns of his
writings. In the first place, he is concerned for Islam and he interprets it
through a perspective derived from (Shīʾite) Ṣūfism. In his *Ideals and
Realities of Islam* he probes beneath the externals of Islamic practice and
symbolism to the inner truths that lie beneath those externals, and he
finds them reflected in Ṣūfism. As he puts it (*Islam and the Plight of Modern
Man*, 1975: 58):

Sufism, being the inner dimension of Islam, shares, in its formal aspect, in the particular
features of this tradition. Since Islam is based on Unity (al-tawhid), all of its manifestations reflect Unity in one way or another; this is especially true of Sufism, in which the
principles of the revelation are most directly reflected.

Indeed, for Nasr, Ṣūfism is also the key to an understanding of comparative religion whereby the inner truths of other religions can be
understood without their outward forms being compromised. He therefore claims (*Sufi Essays*, 1972: 38):

Sufism provides the metaphysics necessary to carry out the study of comparative religion
in depth so that man can accept the validity of every detail of the authentic religions of
mankind and at the same time see beyond these details to the transcendent unity of these
religions.

According to Nasr, Islam and the other religious traditions of the world
can be described and compared in their outward forms. These forms are

unique and different, and there is no need to modify them (as he considers John Hick to do in the case of Christianity) in a misguided attempt to heal religious or cultural divisions. Religions, Nasr asserts, can also be studied in their essence 'which leads to their inner unity because the source of all reality and therefore all religion is God who is One' (1972: 130). Religions are therefore 'relatively absolute:' absolute according to the traditional doctrine of the universality of revelation, and relative according to the particularities of each revealed form. The hermeneutical key to Nasr's analysis of both Islam and other religions is therefore Ṣūfism.

He is careful to state however that Ṣūfism *as such* is intrinsic to Islam and cannot be practised outside it. Nevertheless, according to Nasr, something akin to Ṣūfism exists in other religions according to the nature of things. At the heart of intelligence there lies a divine spark which unites man with the sacred and this doctrine lies at the heart of the religious traditions of mankind. This is the perennial philosophy which amounts to knowledge of the sacred; it is 'metaphysics in its real sense, which is a sapiental knowledge based upon the direct and immediate experience of the Truth' (1975: 29). At the basis of Nasr's work there is the aspiration to extend and widen not only a knowledge of Ṣūfism but also a knowledge of the perennial philosophy previously expounded by Ananda Coomaraswamy. The point is not to extend Ṣūfism itself, as Suzuki's work had extended Zen, but to awaken an awareness of the equivalent of Ṣūfism in other religious traditions.

Like our previous four scholars, Nasr is keenly aware of deficiencies in western culture. In his *Man and Nature, The Spiritual Crisis of Modern Man* (1968), he warned about what is now termed the ecological crisis before it had become fashionable to do this. He traced it back to the secularisation of knowledge in the West whereby the study of nature had been divorced from the sacred and therefore from the Reality which is the source of all that is sacred. He points out that the same kind of divorce has occurred in relation to the study of art, history, philosophy, and even theology. As he puts it (1975: 4):

The inner history of the so-called development of modern Western man from his historic background as traditional man—who represents at once his ancestor in time and his

centre in space—is a gradual alienation from the Centre and the axis through the spokes
of the wheel of existence to the rim, where modern man resides.

Nasr's work therefore is motivated partly by an attempt to heal the
disintegration in western culture caused by the weakening of its religious roots, and partly by an attempt to prevent the same thing happening in non-western cultures.

Although Nasr approaches his work from a Muslim angle, we see in
him a similar emphasis upon philosophy, upon the inwardness of religion, upon the spiritual need of the West, and upon a particular strand
within his own tradition as a key to wider understanding that we
discovered in our other thinkers. Clearly by no means all scholars,
western or Muslim, would agree that Ṣūfism is the key to Islam, or that
the perennial philosophy is the key to understanding world religions.
Many students of religion would be reluctant to agree that the study of
religion must go beyond the study of religious phenomena and forms to
the inner realities that lie behind them. Nor would a number of scholars
feel that the study of religion has, as part of its task, the motive of
diagnosing or healing the ailments of the West or of other parts of the
world. These concerns would be seen to be outside the purview of the
scholar of religion. It is nevertheless significant that the non-Christian
and non-western scholars we have examined *do* dwell upon these themes.

John Mbiti

John Mbiti, like Nasr, is still an active and developing scholar. He is
African and Christian, and he is devoting his energies to an investigation, from an African perspective, of African traditional religion and
African Christianity. This development in ·African studies of African
religion is distinctively post-war, and it is almost certain to grow in
importance. As we shall see, although scholars of African religion such
as Mbiti are aware of wider initiatives in Christian theology they are less
likely to be cognisant of studies of other world religions, especially
eastern ones.

John Mbiti was born in Kenya. His studies began at Makerere

University College and after a spell at Barrington College, Rhode Island, he eventually took a doctorate of theology at Cambridge. He served for a time in an Anglican parish, and was a visiting Lecturer at Selly Oak Colleges, Birmingham and at Hamburg University. However, he returned to Africa in 1964 to become lecturer and later professor of religious studies at Makerere University in Uganda. More recently he has served as Principal of the Ecumenical Institute at Bossey in Switzerland. Like Radhakrishnan, Suzuki, and Nasr he has therefore taught both within his own culture and in the West.

In addition to his many articles Mbiti has written a number of books, including *Akamba Stories* (1966) in the Oxford Library of African Literature, *African Religions and Philosophy* (1969), *Concepts of God in Africa* (1970), *New Testament Eschatology in an African Background* (1971), and *The Prayers of African Religion* (1975). Mbiti's method can best be seen in an analysis of his *African Religions and Philosophy*. He begins this work by pointing out the all-pervasive nature of religion in Africa, and the many varieties of African traditional religion which constitute 'a reality which calls for academic scrutiny' (1969: 1). He reflects upon past methods of studying African religion. He dismisses earlier attitudes which assumed that African beliefs and culture were borrowed from elsewhere, that African religion was 'animism,' that African religion could be termed 'primitive religion' and put at the lower end of a religious evolutionary scale, and that African religions amount to ancestor worship or magic. He comments, 'it is only around the middle of the twentieth century that these subjects have begun to be studied properly and respectfully as an academic discipline in their own right' (1969: 6). Mbiti then goes on to trace four modern approaches to the study of African religion. The first of these approaches is represented by P. Tempels (1946, 1969), J. Jahn (1958, 1961), and J.V. Taylor (1963) writing respectively in French, German, and English. They are more sympathetic than earlier western scholars in their attitude towards African religion. Tempels, in his book *Bantu Philosophy*, analyses Baluba religion and philosophy and interprets it in terms of the 'vital force,' the essence of which is being. Jahn, in his book *Muntu*, points out that Africa has something of philosophical value to offer to the world, and in his reflection upon Muntu and three other categories he widens Tempels' notion of 'vital force.' Taylor, in his book *The Primal Vision*, attempts to get inside the primal world of African religion from a Christian perspective, and largely succeeds in doing this, albeit somewhat uncritically. He, Tempels and Jahn see African religion as an integral part of the whole life of African people.

The second modern approach, represented again in English, French, and German by Parrinder (1954), Deschamps (1960), and Dammann (1963), attempts to treat African religions systematically and to bring together material from various African peoples. Parrinder's book *African Traditional Religion* was especially important, as an early example of this genre, as valuable in its own right, and as a spur to African scholars such as Mbiti who followed a basically similar method.

The third current approach is that of fieldwork oriented anthropologists such as Evans-Pritchard (*Nuer Religion*, 1956) and Lienhardt (*Divinity and Experience: the Religion of the Dinka*, 1961). They represent a strand of western anthropological scholarship that concentrates upon the religions of individual peoples and treats them in depth and in relation to the integral situation of the people concerned.

The fourth approach is that of African scholars themselves who may either take a particular religious topic and treat it in depth within a single area (Danquah 1944, Nketia 1955, Kagame 1956, Idowu 1962), or, like Mbiti, take an overview of a single topic throughout African religion. Mbiti's approach is 'to treat religion as an ontological phenomenon, with the concept of time as the key to teaching some understanding of African religion and philosophy' (1969: 14). His thesis is that it is misleading to think of Africans classifying time into past, present and future in a western fashion. Using two Swahili terms, *sasa* and *zamani*, he divides time into two categories: *sasa* the 'now-period,' the micro-time, of immediate experience; *zamani* the past events, the macro-time, that *has* been experienced. He claims that the African view of time is backward-looking, with the future having no significance, and he works out this thesis in great detail as being relevant to a true understanding and a full comprehension of African religion.

Certain premises underly Mbiti's general thinking. First, he stresses the importance of religion as a key to understanding Africa and as a force for creating a new Africa. 'Singly, jointly or in comparison,' he writes, 'the religions in Africa should be able to exert a force and make a contribution in creating new standards, morals and ethics suitable. for our changing society' (1969: 274). It is only religion that is truly sensitive to the fullness of man's dignity, nature and potentialities; man cannot live by politics and science alone. Second, Mbiti treats African religions as a whole. He emphasises the unity of African religions and philosophy and gives an overall picture of their situation. He considers that there is a basic understanding, mind-set, perception and logic behind the manner in which Africans think, speak, or act that makes it meaningful to. talk about African religion as a generic phenomenon. Third, he is not content to describe and deal with the beliefs, ceremonies, rituals, religious leaders, and other data of African religion. He is concerned with the philosophy that lies behind the words and actions and outward data. That philosophy is not present as a 'philosophical system,' it is arrived at by interpretation, and yet it is crucial. Fourthly, while being sympathetic to Islam and African indigenous religions, Mbiti stresses the role of Christianity in Africa. He claims that it is traditionally African and indigenous and that it therefore has a greater potentiality for 'meeting the dilemmas and challenges of modern Africa, and of reaching the full integration and manhood of individuals and communities' (1969: 277). Once again, therefore, we have in Mbiti a thinker who recognises his own religious commitment, and who is concerned that religion, his own and that of others, should be ready to tackle the problems and challenges of the modern world.

It is possible to criticise Mbiti on five different but interrelated counts. His interest in ascertaining the concepts of God, the prayers, or the view of time in African religion in general makes him vulnerable in relation to the exceptions that inevitably occur within particular areas. He stands on firmer ground when he speaks about the Bantu African religion of south and east Africa, but he has less knowledge about west Africa which in subtle ways is different from Bantu Africa. His concern to determine the general nature of African philosophy and religion tends to involve him in statements that are not only general but also abstract and therefore a stage removed from the concrete particularities of actual peoples. His efforts to understand and engage in dialogue with African religion are applauded by Christian theologians, but the liberation theologians among them tend to question what they consider to be Mbiti's over-concern with religious theory and underconcern for everyday praxis. Finally, his basic thesis that there is no future time in African thought, and his implied notion that there is a monolithic view of time of African thought, have both been brought into question (Horton 1967: 177; Parratt 1977). However, Mbiti is representative of a new movement among Africans to comment academically upon their own religion. He is typical of an increasing endeavour among African scholars to research their own religion both for its own sake and for the light it throws upon the wider religious scene.

Wing-Tsit Chan

One of the most representative scholars of Chinese religion in recent times has been Wing-Tsit Chan. He was born at Canton, and obtained his B.A. degree at Lingnan University. He later finished a Harvard doctorate, and after teaching in China he became professor of chinese culture and philosophy at Dartmouth College in 1942. He subsequently became professor of philosophy at Chatham College, Pittsburgh and during his long teaching career in the United States he has written many articles and books.

Wing-Tsit Chan's writings fall into three broad categories. He has been notable firstly for the quality and prolific nature of his translations. The most widely-known example of this translation work is *A Source Book in Chinese Philosophy* (1963), the whole of which was translated and compiled by Chan. This work covers the ancient, medieval and modern periods of Chinese philosophy and includes material from the Confucian, Taoist, and Buddhist traditions, and it represents a monu-mental feat of translation requiring not only linguistic but also her-meneutical expertise. As Chan comments, his new translations provide consistency of style and language, he is able to make use of recent research works and commentaries, and he is able to render more exactly a number of problematical Chinese technical philosophical terms. Other important translations by Chan include: *Instructions for Practical Living, and Other Neo-Confucian Writings of Wang Yang-Ming* (1963), *The Way of*

Lao Tzu, a Translation and Study of the Tao-te ching (1963), and *The Platform Scripture, The Basic Classic of Zen Buddhism* (1963).

In the second place, Wing-Tsit Chan has written on the whole gamut of Chinese religion and philosophy. In his *Historical Charts of Chinese Philosophy* (1955), he gives a chronological chart of the whole development of the Chinese philosophical tradition. *A Source Book in Chinese Philosophy* covers, in forty-four sections, the entire unfolding of Chinese thought from pre-Confucianism to present-day communist China. He deals in succession with the ancient period (from Confucius to c. 200 BC) which includes various Confucian strands, early Taoist thought, Mo Tzu, the Logicians, Yin Yang, and Legalism; the medieval period (covering the thousand years to about 800 AD) which includes Han Confucianism, Taoist, and Neo-Taoist strands, the various Buddhist schools, and the Confucian revival under Han Yu and Li Ao; and the modern period in which he examines Sung Neo-Confucianism, Ming Neo-Confucianism, Ch'ing Confucianism, and eventually Communism. It is worth noting that he has a real concern for the contemporary period within China. His *Religious Trends in Modern China* (1953) analyses developments within the present century up to the time of the communist revolution, and his *Chinese Philosophy in Mainland China, 1949–1963* brings the story closer to present-day. A more detailed review of Chan's works than we have time for now would show a general interest in various aspects of Chinese religion and thought throughout its history.

In addition to his broad concerns, Wing-Tsit Chan has concentrated wherever possible upon the neo-Confucian element in Chinese philosophy. He has helped to develop a wider academic interest in the neo-Confucian giants, Chu Hsi and Wang Yang-Ming, as well as in lesser-known facets of neo-Confucian thought. He sees the development of neo-Confucianism as being in continuity with earlier developments of Confucianism, with the added advantage that it incorporates within a new synthesis elements taken from the Buddhist and Taoist traditions. The titles of a number of his articles indicate the importance Chan attaches to neo-Confucianism: 'The Evolution of the Confucian Concept *Jen*' (1955), 'How Buddhistic is Wang Yang-Ming?' (1962), 'The Neo-Confucian Solution of the Problem of Evil' (1957), 'Neo-Confucianism and Chinese Scientific Thought' (1957), 'Synthesis in

Chinese Metaphysics' (1951), 'Wang Yang-Ming' (1960), 'Chu Hsi's Completion of Neo-Confucianism' (1973), 'Patterns for Neo-Confucianism: Why Chu Hsi Differed From Ch'eng I' (1978), 'The Evolution of the Neo-Confucian Concept Li as Principle' (1964), and 'Chinese and Western Interpretations of Jen (Humanity)' (1975). It is especially interesting to reflect upon the way Chan develops the neo-Confucian interpretation of the Confucian concepts of *Li* and *Jen*. He regards the concept of *Li* as principle to be the most important in Chinese thought in the last eight hundred years, and yet there is discontinuity in its interpretation because the concept of *Li* had not been 'central in Confucianism from the very beginning' (1964: 123). By contrast, 'the concept of *Jen* (humanity, love, humaneness) is a central concept of Confucian thought and has gone through a long evolution of more than 2,000 years' (1975: 107). One has the feeling, in reading Wing-Tsit Chan, that he sees neo-Confucianism as the syncretic fulfilment of earlier Chinese religion, as the basic religion of the Chinese intelligentsia, and as an ongoing phenomenon in China in that it is 'extremely naturalistic, rationalistic, and humanistic ... free from myths, supernatural deities, and irrational miracles' (1953: 260). For him, neo-Confucianism is the intellectual equivalent of Vedānta for Radhakrishnan, Ḥasidism for Buber, Ṣūfism for Nasr, and Zen for Suzuki.

In reviewing Chan's thought we see that, like our other thinkers, he has a concern for philosophy. His concern for the technicalities of philosophy converges with that of Radhakrishnan in that they both take seriously the history as well as the structure of philosophy, they both review their philosophical tradition in length as well as in depth, and they both have a critical predilection for a particular philosophical viewpoint (Vedānta for Radhakrishnan, neo-Confucianism for Chan). Chan's interest in philosophy is not as existential as that of Buber, Nasr, or Suzuki. He sees it rather as an academic area of interest and an academic tool.

Like Coomaraswamy, Chan's academic career has been exercised mainly in the West. This has been necessitated by practical considerations and for this reason he does not rank as a typical representative of contemporary Chinese scholarship in the cultural sense. Nevertheless, unlike Coomaraswamy, he is concerned about the contemporary religious situation in his own land as it is developing indigenously *now*, and he is less inclined to react unfavourably to western culture or religion. 'No one doubts the positive character of the Christian teaching,' he states (1975: 120).

There is a certain resemblance between Wing-Tsit Chan and Mbiti in that their objects of study, Chinese religion and African traditional religion, have undergone an ostensible decline in the contemporary situation. It is hardly as feasible for members of other cultures to become adherents of Confucianism or African religion as it is for them to become adherents of the major renascent religious traditions. Moreover, the element of mysticism is not as present in neo-Confucianism and African religion as it is in Hasidism, Sufism, Vedanta, or Zen. It is therefore more likely that Chinese religion and African religion will be seen as objects of study rather than vehicles of commitment or religious experience.

The value of the work of Chan and Mbiti, although they are not uninterested in other religions, lies mainly in their ability to use their knowledge of the language, literature, and ethos of their own religious traditions to interpret them academically in a way that would be difficult for western scholars who lack their indigenous background.

Implications of the Work of non-western Scholars of Religion

We have analysed briefly the work of seven scholars: Coomaraswamy, Radhakrishnan, Suzuki, Buber, Nasr, Mbiti, and Chan; they are respectively Celanese, Indian, Japanese, Austrian, Iranian, Kenyan, and Chinese; their expertise lies respectively in Indian religion (the first two), Buddhism, Judaism, Islam, African religions, and Chinese religion. All are clearly important scholars. Opinions may differ as to whether they are truly representative of scholarship in their traditions. It is also true to say that four of them, Coomaraswamy, Radhakrishnan, Suzuki and Buber, did some work before World War II and that their work therefore covers a long time-span. The conclusions that we draw from their work must therefore be limited. Nevertheless, because they are eminent scholars who approach the study of religion from (except for Buber) a non-western standpoint, it is instructive to examine the implications of their work. Our findings must be tentative, they will not necessarily be unimportant.

(1) All these scholars study, first and foremost, their *own* religion. This may seem a trite point to make, it is nevertheless a significant one. As Ursula King points out in an earlier chapter, much western study of religion has stressed the study of religions other than Christianity. On the whole the study of the main western religion, namely Christianity, has been seen as the province of theology and the findings of theology have been *used* by students of religion rather than systematically re-searched by them. Insofar as this is the case, the time is now ripe for a religious studies perspective to be brought to bear more directly upon Christianity and for scholars of religion to study more closely its ideas and values as well as its social structures, rituals, denominations, and scriptures. Although our seven scholars may have had an interest in the study of other religions, their primary concern has been with their own. All of them have combined a general interest in the whole of their own tradition with a particular concern for part of it: Indian art (Coomaraswamy), Vedānta (Radhakrishnan), Zen (Suzuki), Ḥasidism (Buber), Ṣūfism (Nasr), Bantu Africa (Mbiti), and neo-Confucianism (Chan). Many of them have been active in the translation of important texts of their own religion or in the providing of collections of stories in translation. Suzuki, for example, did important work on the *Laṅkāvatāra Sūtra* (1930, 1932), on Aśvaghosa's *Discourse on the Awakening of Faith in the Mahāyāna* (1900), and on exegeting Zen texts, in addition to provid-ing hermeneutical insights into the Buddhist tradition. One of the values of their work has been to enrich our knowledge of the language, texts, and interpretation of their own traditions through a personal concern in what they were studying. In smaller or greater degree, they have not only advanced but transformed the academic study of their own religion.

(2) Our seven scholars share an interest in and a concern for the major living religions of the world. All of them belong to living world religions and these world religions delimit the scope of their studies. In other words, they have little or no academic curiosity about archaic religions that are dead. With the partial exceptions of Mbiti and Chan

who concentrate more narrowly upon their regional (yet still multi-religious) concerns, the others have a wider interest in other world religions. This is in contrast to much western study of religion which tends to focus more upon archaic religion, primal religions (which although living are not major and are not usually able to respond in dialogue), and the historical, sociological, psychological, and more outward aspects of western religion.

(3) A third and related point is that our eminent authors have a creative awareness of the present situation of their own and other religions. All of them are interested in speaking to the present age. Their expertise and research are not confined to an investigation of the past history or ancient texts of their tradition. They are concerned creatively to re-interpret their own religion in the light of the modern situation. The contexts may differ. For Chan, it is communist China, for Mbiti independent Africa, for Coomaraswamy and Radhakrishnan renascent Ceylon and India, for Suzuki modern Japan, for Buber pre- and post-holocaust Judaism, for Nasr modernising Islam, and for all of them the secularising West. They diverge over the nature of their attempts to reinterpret the classical forms of their religious traditions. Coomaraswamy and Nasr aim to recover the perennial philosophy of past tradition to transform the present, Mbiti desires to create an indigenous African theology, Chan wrestles to see the continuity between neo-Confucianism and the developing China, and Radhakrishnan, Suzuki and Buber imaginatively renew important aspects of their developing traditions to speak to contemporary needs. The point is that their academic concern is with the present as well as with the past.

(4) All of them share a relationship with the West. Each of them has studied or taught in the West: Coomaraswamy in England and Boston, Radhakrishnan at Oxford, Suzuki in the United States, Nasr at Harvard and Temple, Mbiti at Cambridge and Bossey, Chan at Dartmouth and Chatham. Although to some extent influenced by the West, to a greater or lesser degree they·all react against it. This reaction is less obvious (although still there) in Chan and Mbiti. It is extremely complex in Buber who was a German Jew before and after the Nazi Holocaust in the West. Coomaraswamy, Radhakrishnan, Suzuki, and Nasr are responding noticeably to what they consider to be the weakening effects upon religion

of western secularisation. It is significant that the response towards the
West adopted by these scholars is threefold. In the first place, they are
commenting implicitly upon western approaches to the study of their
own tradition. While generally not disapproving of the work of western
scholars, their suggestion is that this work needs to be supplemented by
that of scholars belonging to the traditions themselves. Their strictures
upon western scholarship are less radical than those of Said. They are not
implying that western scholars are influenced by quasi-political concerns
but that western cultural presuppositions make it less easy for westerners to understand the language and world-view of the people concerned. In the second place, they are responding to the general educational ethos of western scholarship. Their feeling is (less obviously so
in Chan) that the western tendency to stress empirical and rational
categories derived from a science-based model makes it less easy for
western scholars to understand what Vedānta means to a Hindu, Ṣūfism
to a Muslim, Zen to a Buddhist, or ancestor worship to an African.
Third, and relatedly, they are responding to the general impact upon the
wider world of western civilisation with its basic emphasis upon technology, material progress, scientific specialisation, the accumulation of
data, and so on. At this point, their concern is not so much with the effect
of the West upon the study of religion but with the effect of the West
upon religion as such.

The implications of the ambivalent attitude towards the West on the
part of these seven scholars are both varied and debateable. We have
time to mention only two. The first implication revolves around the
thorny topic of dialogue. All of these scholars see the need for 'dialogue'
although they are not united in their view of what it means. At one level,
dialogue simply means academic dialogue between western and non-
western scholars in order to clarify intellectually and comparatively the
meaning of terms, and the place of those terms within wider
worldviews. An example of this approach is Chan's comparative analysis
of *jen* and humanity within the Chinese and western traditions. At
another level, dialogue may involve a debate between scholars who
consider themselves to be in some degree representatives of their religions. With the possible exception of Chan, our seven scholars have

sometimes engaged in this type of discussion. The aim of this kind of exercise is to clarify areas of agreement and disagreement between religious traditions seen as such. This view of dialogue converges with a similar notion present within Christian theology, and 'dialogue' in this sense is sometimes viewed as a Christian theological approach. This is not necessarily the case, and it is a moot point as to whether dialogue in the Christian theological sense was initiated by Christians or was a response to the work of men such as Radhakrishnan, Suzuki, and Buber. In this type of dialogue, the scholar operates as Christian, Buddhist, Muslim, Hindu or Jewish scholar rather than as 'neutral' scholar. At a third level, dialogue may involve a dialogue between scholars as representative of cultures. When Coomaraswamy, Radhakrishnan, Buber, Nasr, Suzuki, Mbiti, and occasionally Chan operate in this fashion they are not in debate with Christianity but with western culture which is seen to have partly abandoned its roots in Christianity. They are concerned to portray the spiritual crisis of western culture and to suggest by implication how non-western religions and cultures can alleviate the western cultural crisis. Dialogue may be seen, fourthly, as the internal dialogue within the scholar. This view is especially evident in the work of Buber who placed the notion of dialogue within and between persons at the centre of his thinking. According to this view, the scholar cannot remain completely detached from the material or the tradition he is studying: he or she will be influenced by the very fact of engaging in dialogue with the data (as well as the people) of other traditions. Failure to differentiate between these different meanings of 'dialogue' is sometimes responsible for lack of mature academic discussion of this topic. It is likely that the increasing realisation that 'dialogue' has to do with the study of religion as well as with religion, and that the motivation for dialogue arises not only from within Christian theology but from within the ranks of academics of other religions, will lead to a fresh definition of, and interest in, the concept of dialogue.

The second implication of the involvement of non-western scholars of religion in the West revolves around the notion that the study of religion in our global context should have some relevance in regard to the pursuit of world harmony. The recognition that western science has unified the world materially, but that the world is not yet united humanly and spiritually, is seen to be a global problem that cannot be shirked by the study of religion.

(5) The scholars we have studied all have an interest in philosophy. They are not content to remain at the levels of sociology, psychology, history, phenomenology, comparison, science, anthropology or mythical and textual studies. They ask wider questions of their material, and they are interested in philosophy as such. Three of them, Radhakrishnan, Chan, and Nasr, are specialists in philosophy; three others, Suzuki, Buber, and Coomaraswamy have a concern for metaphysics in a more general sense; and Mbiti, although studying the non-philosophical African tradition, is exercised to discover the basic ideas, the 'African Philosophy,' lying behind that tradition. As we have implied, their concern for philosophy is a dual one. They are interested in the religious concepts of the religions they are studying; they are also interested in what those concepts mean to the people concerned, they are interested in *meaning*. They are generally unconcerned about the social sciences with their emphasis upon action and social behaviour. They are more stimulated by ideas-related areas such as spirituality, ethics, and (with Coomaraswamy) aesthetics. Although most of our scholars have done their fair share of translation or textual work, their major concern is for the philosophy, meaning and value lying behind religious texts.

(6) With the exception of Chan who does not parade his religious commitment, our scholars are not concerned to hide their own religious position. It is clear that Coomaraswamy and Radhakrishnan are Hindus, Suzuki a Buddhist, Buber a Jew, Nasr a Muslim, and Mbiti an African Christian. They approach their work from a viewpoint of religious commitment, and although their ideas have been in constant evolution that evolution has advanced within a religious framework that is 'given.' This does not mean that their commitment is narrow or unhelpful. Indeed their commitment may well be part of the reason for the fruitfulness of their theories. That commitment is twofold. It is first to the study of religion itself, for they are primarily students and scholars; it is second a personal religious quest fulfilled through the medium of their study of religion. There is a dialectical relationship between their study of religion and their religion. They see no necessary separation between

commitment and academic responsibility, personalism and objectivity, and *homo religiosus* and *homo academicus*. This is reflected partly in their academic concerns. We have mentioned already their interest in philosophy. This is accompanied, in general, by an interest in religious experience as an area of academic research.

(7) Finally, they all express an interest in what we may term the 'transcendental' as well as the historical structures of religion. The greater part of this book has concentrated upon an investigation of what we may call the historical-immanental structures of religion or religions. The historical, sociological, anthropological, psychological, and textual approaches bracket out transcendental categories; likewise the phenomenological approach, although it classically conceived of a single fundamental essence common to all religions, does not depend upon a transcendent reality revealing itself through religion. In contrast, transcendental structures are more basic to the thinking of the seven scholars we have discussed. Coomaraswamy and Nasr stress the perennial philosophy they see lying at the heart of all religions; they regard it as revealing the Truth as a living reality which provides the archetypal categories whereby men and women can live transcendently as well as immanently. For Radhakrishnan, idealism is the key whereby the structure of ultimate reality can be unfolded. In Suzuki's case, mysticism is the life of religion and the key to its understanding. Buber prefers to stress the I-Thou relationship as central to a true insight into the nature of God and man. Mbiti's framework of thought either stresses or presumes that all African people have a notion of God as Supreme Being. For Chan, Chinese life and culture are closely related to Chinese philosophy the perennial problems of which, knowledge, human destiny, human nature, heaven, and the like, provide the 'transcendental' structure for his thought.

And so we see, with the partial exception of Chan, that our seven scholars conform to a general pattern. They research their own religion, their interest is in the living religions, they have a concern for the present as well as the past, they have an ambivalent relationship with the West, their general approach is philosophical, they do not hide their own commitment, and the structures they investigate are 'transcendental' as well as historical.

Our conclusion must be that in general they do not substantiate Said's thesis. His contention is that Orientalism served the interests of western imperialism rather than pure scholarship. Our findings are that the work of these seven scholars does diverge from some of the presuppositions of western historically-oriented scholarship but on academic and cultural rather than imperialistic grounds. Moreover, their work has begun to bear fruit within the general discipline of the study of religion, especially in the United States. One example of this is the notion that the study of a particular religious tradition can gain useful and even necessary help from scholars of the tradition concerned. This principle was first incorporated effectively into an ongoing project by Kenneth Morgan of Colgate University. In his *Religion of the Hindus* (1953) Morgan used his extensive personal contacts to persuade a number of Hindu scholars to write about various aspects of their own religion. He used the same principle in his *The Path of the Buddha* (1956) and *Islam—The Straight Path* (1958) which were books on their own religious traditions written by Asian Buddhists and Muslims respectively. Wilfred Cantwell Smith has introduced the allied principle of verification whereby he suggests that members of religious traditions that are studied should be consulted in regard to works written on their own traditions. The point at stake is whether western scholars should be able to comment with impunity upon other religions without being subject to the informed opinion of members of those other religions concerning the general appropriateness and accuracy of those comments. This verification principle goes further than the general phenomenological emphasis upon *Einfühlung* which encourages empathy on the part of the scholar for the religious tradition he is studying—it requires that the scholar should keep in mind the fact that he is writing for a wider than western audience. His criteria for writing are not confined, then, to a consideration of how western scholars will respond to his thought; he will have to bear in mind also what scholars and members of the tradition he is studying will have to say about his ideas. If taken seriously, this would involve a subtle change of perspective and orientation. A further sign of the times is the practice in some universities, especially in North America, to appoint adherents of certain religions to teach those religions.

A second example of the implicit or explicit influence of foreign scholars such as those we have examined is the rise of centres for study of religion in different parts of the world. While stressing the academic nature of the study of religion these centres have drawn together experts on different religious traditions and often from different parts of the world to share together in the scholarly task of studying and interpreting religion. The assumption of these centres is often that the major living religions of the world are the main focus of the academic study of religion. They also symbolise by implication the view that academic dialogue is a desirable thing. One of the leading exponents of this viewpoint is W.C. Smith. In a celebrated article, 'Comparative Religion: Whither—and Why?' (1959), Smith outlined his position by tracing the progress of the history of religions in various stages. The first stage saw the accumulation and analysis of facts. At first this was the impersonal accumulation of facts about 'it,' a religion so-called. Then it became the accumulation of facts about 'they,' the people of a religion, by people still personally uninvolved. The next stage saw the personalisation of the work so that 'we' as scholars were studying 'they' as people. A further step came when it was seen that personal contact with others was an important part of the study of religion, and that discussion with others not as 'they' but as 'you' was relevant. This was the stage of dialogue. The final step involved going beyond dialogue to 'colloquium,' the academic co-operation of an international group of scholars writing for a world audience and if possible studying together. The implicit idea of Smith's work was that centres should be set up around the world where such groups of scholars could work together. This has not proved to be possible in any major way, but in a number of places around the world including McGill, Chicago, Ankara, Ibadan, Patiala, Tokyo, and Harvard centres of one sort or another have been formed to accomplish similar aims. Indeed it is difficult to be unaware, in reading Smith's work, of the similarity between some of his ideas and some of those of the seven scholars we examined earlier; it is hard to imagine his work unless it had been preceded and accompanied by theirs.

The influence of non-western thought upon the study of religion is a complex topic and there is not the space in this present work to discuss it more deeply. Any discussion of it is made more difficult by the fact that this thought is neither concentrated within one academic discipline nor confined to the study of one particular religion, and therefore its impact is diffuse rather than concrete. We shall remain content with three final comments.

A. It is clear that the main influence of non-western scholarship upon the study of religion has been in the Anglo-Saxon world of North America and Britain rather than in continental Europe. European scholars have generally remained satisfied with the textual, sociological, anthropological, psychological, historical, and phenomenological approaches we have described in this book. The more daring hermeneutical theories have emerged in North America, and to a lesser extent in Britain, in the work of scholars such as Smith and Eliade who lived in non-western countries and knew their thought. An alternative stream of European thought arising out of the work of Otto and van der Leeuw has maintained closer links with theological work than is commonly found elsewhere in Europe, but this theological work is western. It is outside Europe that the impact of Asian and African thought has been most obvious. The influence of cultural factors, such as the residual contacts forged by the British Empire, the force of the English language, and the Asian links established by the United States after the second world war, should not be minimised in this context, neither should the impact of the thinkers we have described who were influenced by the Anglo-Saxon world. To this extent, Said's thesis is susceptible to radical reinterpretation in the light of the apparently reverse influence of the religions of other cultures upon the scholarship of the imperial forces that worked upon them, whereas the less imperial continental European countries remained more wedded to the presuppositions of western scholarship.

B. A second comment is that western scholarship and indeed western culture has provided the agenda and the framework for reactions from thinkers outside the West. Perhaps this is the hidden thrust of Said's work in contrast to some of the more flamboyantly explicit remarks that he makes. The present global situation is witnessing the rise of other spheres of political and cultural influence in other areas of the world such as Japan, China, the Muslim world, the Soviet block, and the third world which are no longer subject to western hegemony in the old sense. The question implicitly raised by Said is whether scholarship in these developing regions will continue to respond to western problems and concerns or whether scholars from these parts will wish to provide their own agenda and framework independently from the West. To phrase the problem in a different way, to what extent is the western framework for the study of religion western rather than universal? Can scholars from other cultures fit with adjustments into a framework that is universally valid, or are the presuppositions at present governing the study of religion so hidebound by western thought-forms that they must be radically modified in order to become universal? Dr. King in her chapter distinguishes five major areas with different cultural, religious and scholarly traditions which are involved in the study of religion: western Europe, North America, the socialist countries, Africa, and a cluster of Asian countries. She rightly states that it is regrettable that we have so little information about what is going on in some of these areas. This chapter has attempted to fill part of the gap by summarising the work of seven of the well-known scholars of religion from other cultures. We have not tried to summarise *all* the work done by Hindu, Buddhist, Jewish, Muslim, African, and Chinese scholars; we have selected some of the most eminent and shown how their work has been dialectically related to western scholarship especially in the Anglo-Saxon world.

It is difficult to answer the question we have asked as to whether the western superstructure for the study of religion is too culture-bound or whether it is universally applicable. Perhaps four things can be said.

(a) Insofar as we do live in a global world, it is vital that we have more information about what is happening globally in regard to the study of religion, and that there is more scholarly dialogue between scholars from different cultures. It is not just a matter of discovering what scholars from different regions are writing in their own languages about the minutiae of their own traditions but also of examining their general approach to their studies. In other words, it is important to extend the exercise begun in this chapter of analysing seriously the implications of the work of non-western scholars. And from now on they are less likely to be working in the West than was once the case.

(b) There is a glaring lack of information about the study of religion in socialist and communist lands. Diligent gleaning of magazines can turn up articles such as: 'Religion and the Marxist Concept of Social Formation' by Marko Kersevan, '*Une lecture marxiste du prophétisme*' by Daniel Vidal, 'A Marxist Analysis of the Religion of East African Herdsmen' by Pierre Bonte, 'Marxist Analysis and Sociology of Religion' by Otto Maduro (*Social Compass*, XXII, 3–4, 1975), 'Investigate Religion and Criticize Theology' by Ren Jiyu (*Ching Feng*, 20, 1977), and so on. More needs to be done by way of research, exchange, and academic dialogue to increase our global knowledge in this area, especially through the medium of a growing knowledge of the works of scholars in communist lands (as a complement to the work of western scholars on communism, for example, see Thrower's forthcoming book on 'Marxist-Leninism').

(c) Insofar as trends are becoming apparent, there appear to be three developments. On the one hand, there is a tendency among some scholars in countries such as East Germany, in part of the Jewish world (as seen in the work of men such as Neusner), and in Chinese scholarship outside China, to emphasise the critical-historical 'scientific' approach; on the other hand, there is the further development of the tendency we have seen in Coomaraswamy, Radhakrishnan, Suzuki, Buber, Nasr, and Mbiti for scholars of other cultures to use the treasures of their own tradition in order to inform their academic work, and this holds true in a different way of Ren Jiyu's article which is informed by dialectical materialism. In addition, as we have seen, non-western scholars may eschew their own cultural tradition and follow a critical-historical method, they may utilise their own tradition and yet share in a theory of the study of religion that has wider valency, as Coomaraswamy and Nasr share the approach of Philosophia Perennis, or they may study their own tradition less critically. The global situation is therefore a shifting one containing different cultural centres for the study of religion, fluid approaches to the study of religion, and a centre of gravity derived from but no longer stationary within the West.

(d) It is vital that there should be more intercultural and interdisciplinary knowledge and discussion about the whole gamut of problems in religious studies, especially method and theory. One of the reasons why the researches of foreign scholars have not revolutionised the study of religion in the West to the extent that might have been imagined is the fact that western approaches to the study of religion have themselves been uncoordinated. Specialisation in particular religious traditions or particular approaches to the study of religion has countered the possibility of obtaining an overview of the contemporary approaches to the study of religion within the West. So non-western scholarship has not been responding to a monolithic western approach but to a plethora of western approaches depending upon whether a particular approach favoured a sociological, anthropological, historical, phenomenological, philological, psychological, textual/mythical, or even philosophical (or theological) slant—or a combination of them. Western presuppositions concerning academic study have been present in the field of religious studies; an overarching synthesis, such as Said's idea of western Orientalism, was not. The lack of such a sovereign synthesis may, in some quarters, be regretted. By the same token, this lack presents the opportunity to construct a general view of religious studies that can incorporate insights from other cultures.

C. A third and brief comment upon non-western study of religion is that there remains a difference between apologetic defence of one's own religion or proselytisation and the study of religion. In some instances, for example, in some of the work of Suzuki and Radhakrishnan we described, there was evidence of a tendency towards apologetic or proselytisation or both. At this point, they crossed an invisible boundary separating the study of religion from another enterprise that would come more properly under the general heading of 'theology.' Equally, to the extent that they dwell explicitly upon the nature of ultimate reality, they are engaging in a more 'theological' enterprise. It is legitimate to employ hermeneutics, to research from a position of commitment, to engage in academic dialogue with scholars of other religions, to engage in philosophy, and to use 'transcendent' structures, provided that in so doing one is not engaging in advocacy or defence of a particular religious tradition or a particular view of transcendence over against other religious traditions or other views of transcendence. As I have written upon this topic elsewhere in the volume there is no cause to dwell upon it now.

The Global Context of the Study of Religion

In this chapter we have glanced at the contribution of non-western or non-Christian scholars to religious studies. Our final assignment is to look more directly to the global context of that study. In attempting this task, we will concentrate not so much upon the global situation *per se*, with its escalation of nuclear weapons, growth of world population, increasing gap between richer and poorer nations, urgent problems of medical ethics, ecological crisis, and so on (although increasing attention is beginning to be devoted to the study of 'applied religion' in religious ethics), but rather upon the global educational situation within which the study of religion is purveyed. It is clear that given the fact of our global problems, there is the need for sensitive interdisciplinary investigation in depth; there is the need for acute minds from different cultures to wrestle with these questions. There is the need for intellectual agonising, for rigorous scholarship, for academic commitment, in the realisation that the 'we' involved in this discussion is not just our family, our community, our nation, our religious tradition, our academic discipline. This is a global matter, and the 'we' involved is mankind.

Considerations of space permit us to glance only briefly at this complex topic. In order to situate the study of religion in its contemporary educational framework, we shall trace it back briefly to its basic educational roots. We begin our analysis with a consideration of the rise of learning in the western world, a rise that produced, for better or for worse, the modern notion of a university. The beginnings of this development go back to Greece and it was continued and put into clearer form by Rome (*Graecia capta Romum captum ferit*). For 2,500 years Greece and her successors have thrown up a number of areas of study, of disciplines, of specialisations, but at different periods three dominant models have emerged that have suggested implicitly or explicitly the superiority of one area of knowledge over the others. The first dominant model was the Graeco-Roman one of *humanitas*, what we would call the humanities or liberal arts. The main stress in this model was upon literature and man, and the studies of religion and science were subsumed within this wider category. Philosophy was not neglected either, but, as Otto Bird has pointed out (1976: 12–15), Cicero's quarrel with

Socrates was not that the great man was lacking in wisdom, but that Socrates had elevated philosophy into a 'discipline' independent of man's general literary-humanistic, social, and political concerns. The danger was that philosophy would become a specialisation in its own right and if that were to happen truth would be seen to lie not in man nor in the public weal but in philosophy as an intellectual pursuit independent of its practical influence upon humanity and public affairs. It is hard not to interpolate at this point an anticipation of the rise of modern disciplines wherein truth is seen to lie in the discipline, wherein one writes 'for the discipline and one's peers in the discipline' rather than for man. In a classical phrase, Aristotle, describing a person with *paideia* (the Greek equivalent of *humanitas*), comments that he is one, 'who in his own person is able to judge critically in all or nearly all branches of knowledge and not merely in some special subject' (see Bird 1976: 15). The Graeco-Roman model then was that of *humanitas*, with its stress upon the aesthetic value of words both written and spoken, with its stress upon the cultural value of studying another language, with its stress upon the value of the great traditions of the past, with its stress upon the moral and political value of true learning.

This model was inherited and not completely lost during the Christian medieval period. The fall of Rome, the symbol and upholder of the ancient ideal, was responded to by St. Augustine in his *City of God*. St. Augustine and Thomas Aquinas were representative figures of the new European model of learning which was based upon theology rather than *humanitas* as such. As a preparatory means for understanding, Augustine outlined the *humanitas* model that he had inherited (grammar, languages, history, geography, astronomy, dialectic, mathematics, and rhetoric) together with the philosophy of Plato (who had influenced him through Plotinus). However, there was no disputing that the basic axis of his model had now changed: it was God rather than man. The theological nature of the model became even clearer in the thought of Aquinas, who architectonically incorporated Aristotle's system into his full-blown model of theology which became known as the queen of the sciences. As religious thought and the natural sciences had remained the handmaids of *humanitas* during the Graeco-Roman period, *humanitas* and the natural sciences remained the handmaids of theology during the medieval

European period. There was a certain integration of thought during both these periods but within the overall sovereignty of a dominant model.

The third dominant model in the development of western thought was that of the scientific ideal of the modern age. As we have seen, the notion of science is not a purely modern notion (and as we have seen throughout this book 'science' can have different meanings). Nevertheless, the fact remains that the seventeenth century breakthrough in science (Butterfield 1949) constituted, for better or worse, one of the turning-points in the development of human thought. The notion that effective knowledge is available through induction by experiment rather than deduction from given premises; the notion of scientific verification of hypotheses and theories by continual experiment; the notion of isolating particular problems for specialised solution; the notion that pure science can be applied at the technological level; the notion that scientific research is necessarily good come what may; the notion that the modern is new and the new must become newer—have constituted until recently the presuppositions, even the myths, of western thought. And these presuppositions have spilled over into research in the arts and social sciences. The basic source for the application of the scientific ideal was nature, just as the basic source for the application of the literary-humanistic ideal was man, and the basic source for the application of the theological ideal was God. Just as the *humanitas* model had been dominant in Graeco-Roman thought, and the theological model had been dominant in medieval thought, so the natural scientific model became dominant in modern western thought.

However, for a number of reasons, a humbler and more self-conscious attitude towards science as an intellectual model is arising in our own day. There is the realisation that applied science has not only solved some human problems but that it has also fed into other emerging problems of mankind such as those highlighted in a spectacular way by groups such as the Club of Rome in regard to issues such as energy, natural resources, population, food production, urbanisation, climate, pollution, and ecology. There is the sense that it is no longer good enough for scientific research to go 'whither it may' on the supposition that scientific research must be either helpful to mankind or at worst neutral. There has been the thought-provoking research of non-conformist prophets such as Schumacher (1974), Mumford (1970), Illich (1973), Heilbroner (1974), and the like. More importantly, as we have seen, scientific positivism has been eroded partly by the soul-searching work of scientists themselves: for example in Einstein's comments about 'the free creations of thought which cannot inductively be gained from sense-experience' (Schilpp 1944: 287); in Bohr's realisation that the only way for a scientific observer to be uninvolved with his apparatus is if he observes nothing at all; and in Heisenberg's statement that 'we cannot observe atoms as they are in themselves ... we can only seize them in the act of observation, and we can say meaningful things about this relationship only' (see Urban and Glenny 1971). The awareness has also arisen that the dominance of the scientific model, unlike those of the *humanitas* and theological models, was not achieved within a wider integrated intellectual framework but that the accompanying scientific stress upon isolating particular sets of problems for solution within discrete disciplines led to specialisations within knowledge that detracted from its wholeness. Knowledge is ultimately integral and overleaps the disciplinary boundaries that we erect around it. Finally, although natural science claimed, and in technological practice achieved, universal significance, it remained an ineluctably western creation. It contains little sympathetic awareness that our planet contains other cultural and spiritual universes not centred upon western notions, and the fact that this mind-set, though accepted everywhere, is changing is another example of the passage of the times. We therefore stand at a point in intellectual history when our global problems are pressing and evident, when the scientific process that helped to produce them is less self-confident in its ability to solve them, when human knowledge is multidimensional and yet requires greater integration, and when western hegemony of the mind can no longer be taken for granted.

It may be asked, what has this to do with the study of religion? The answer is that, in prospect, it has a great deal to do with the study of religion because it represents the general climate and context within which the study of religion must continue to evolve. It is not our purpose to enter into prophecies of the future. Each chapter of this book has attempted a review of future prospects in its own particular area, and

it would be hazardous to predict confidently developments at the global
and integral educational levels which are necessarily more complex. Our
comments must therefore remain tentative.

We have talked explicitly about the rise of *western* dominant models of
knowledge as though they were by definition universal, and implicitly
about the influence of western universities. Much hings upon what we
mean by a 'university.' A case of sorts can be made for the existence of
'universities' prior to those in the West at the Buddhist centre of Nālanda
in the early centuries of the Christian era, at al-Azhar in Muslim Cairo in
the tenth century, or possibly (but less convincingly) at the Greek
Academies before the Christian era, or at the Confucian centres in early
medieval China. It would be interesting to look at the question of the
history and dominance of educational models through the eyes of those
of other cultures and other religions, and it is part of the task of
comparative religion to enable us to do this. The present educational
problem produced by the spread of western science and by the disintegration of knowledge into discrete specialisations within western universities is not merely a western problem but a global problem. In order
to solve it we need a global vision and a global integration in which
western disciplines, western universities, and western science may play
an important but not a lone part. It is not enough to think in terms of
integrating western educational models and their parts that have become
sundered; the global problem is wider than that. Insofar as the study of
religion is intrinsically global in that it includes the study of *all* the world
religions, it is in a better position that most other academic endeavours
to assimilate insights from the educational and spiritual universes of
other cultures and religions and therefore to enable us to obtain a global
vision. In this book, the present chapter and the previous chapter by
Whaling, and the chapters by Bolle, Smart, and King make preliminary
references to this topic.

It seems reasonable to assert that the three models we have outlined,
although western in provenance, refer to three basic areas of educational
and human concern, namely man, transcendence and nature. It is significant that the study of religion, although primarily a human 'science'
centred upon man has a stake in the other two areas as well. The social
scientific approaches to the study of religion make a partial use of natural

scientific methods of experiment and quantitative analysis, and the study of religion has a direct interest in man's ecological and cultural perspective on nature; the phenomenological view of *Einfühlung* intimated by Ninian Smart, the hermeneutical view of myth intimated by Kees Bolle, and the phenomenological and comparative chapters by King and Whaling, all make reference, in different ways, to the notion of transcendence. Clearly 'transcendence' can mean different things. It can refer to the notion that our own human nature has a transcendent dimension; it can refer to human intentionality in regard to transcendent reality whether this be viewed as God, Allah, Yahweh, Brahman, or whatever; it can refer to an ontology of the sacred; or it can refer to the western post-positivistic search for transcendence in thinkers such as Reich (who sees transcendence as personal liberation, 1970). Marcuse (who sees transcendence as the possibility of historical alternatives, 1968), Laing (who sees transcendence as a psychological creation *ex nihilo*, 1960), Bloch (who sees transcendence as future, 1970), and Jung (who sees transcendence as self-realisation, 1938). The study of religion can hardly eschew any concern for 'transcendence' and therefore, although its basic concern is with man, it straddles the models that deal with natural, human, and transcendent dimensions. This gives it a potentially creative educational role as a catalyst of thought. We referred earlier to the fact that the study of religion operates more as a field of studies than as a watertight academic discipline. This may give it an advantage in the contemporary global situation insofar as, if it were a circumscribed discipline, it would be less able to exercise a mediating, catalytic and integrating function.

The study of religion, however, remains primarily the study of man, rather than the study of nature, or the study of transcendence—even though it retains an interest in man's view of nature and man's view of transcendence. To conceptualise (or reconceptualise) who he is, man is called upon not merely to renew his imaginative powers and his vision of himself through the traditional western humanities of literature, history, geography, art and philosophy, and through the social sciences of sociology, psychology, anthropology, economics, and politics, he is also called upon to take seriously the worldviews existing in other cultures. Seeing the universe empathetically through the eyes of one's fellow men in other cultures is helpful in renewing one's own world view and it is also helpful in seeking a unity within the diversity of global world views. The study of religion is likely to be significant in conceptualising both the multifacetted nature of man's complex being and mankind's global unity in diversity insofar as its work straddles many of the disciplines that deal with man and all of the religions that lie at the heart of human cultures.

Finally, we have implied the need for a greater integration within and between the educational areas that focus upon nature, man, and transcendence. On the one hand there is some force in Heidegger's statement (*Existence and Being*, 1970, p. 326):

The fields of the sciences lie far apart. Their methodologies are fundamentally different. This disrupted multiplicity of disciplines is today only held together by the technical organisation of the universities and their faculties, and maintained as a practical unit of meaning by the practical aims of those faculties.

On the other hand there is equal force in Winston King's comment (1954: 19), 'Religion may be considered to be the most ambitious of all human attempts to unify the diversity of experience.'

During the course of this book, we have summarised in detail a number of diverse contemporary approaches to the study of religion. These approaches are different in the ways that we have analysed within these pages. At the same time as we have summarised these differing approaches to the study of religion we have also sought for new integrative points within this total area of human concern. There is a sense in which the search for integration within the study of religion represents in microcosm the more macrocosmic search for integration within the university of knowledge as a whole.

We have stressed within this chapter the important links that can and should exist between the study of religion and wider areas of academic concern. Ancillary to and complementary with this wider task, there is the need to gather together, at various places around the world, experts within the different areas of the study of religion: scholars in Christian studies, Buddhist studies, Hindu studies, Jewish studies, Muslim studies, Chinese religious studies, African religious studies, primal religious studies, history and phenomenology of religion, comparative religion, mythical and hermeneutical studies, anthropology of religion, sociology of religion, psychology of religion, philosophy of religion, integral science of religion. Through the teamwork of those trained in different specialisations within the study of religion but possessing some overview of and a desire to integrate the whole there will be benefit not only for the study of religion itself but for a far wider academic audience. There is a continous task of reconceptualising through interdisciplinary and interreligious teamwork what we mean by the study of religion, and how we carry it out in our global context. This book is a contribution towards that end. As we wrote in the introduction, the study of religion should play a creative role in contemporary scholarship not only for the sake of the study of religion itself but also for the sake of the world of learning in general, especially during this period when we are confronted with global issues affecting the whole planet earth.

Bibliography

Apel, K.O. (1980), *Towards a Transformation of Philosophy*. London: Routledge.

Ayer, A.J. (1936), *Language, Truth and Logic*. London: Gollancz.

Bachelard, Gaston (1934), *Le Nouvel Esprit Scientifique*. Paris: Presses Universitaires de France.

Bird, Otto (1976), *Cultures in Conflict*. Notre Dame, Indiana: University of Notre Dame Press.

Bloch, Ernst (1970), *Man On His Own*. New York: Herder and Herder.

Bloor, D. (1971), 'Two Paradigms of Scientific Knowledge?' *Science Studies* 1: 101–15.

Bohm, David (1971, 1973), 'Quantum Theory as an Indication of a New Order in Physics' in *Foundations of Physics*, Part A: 359–81; Part B: 139–68.

Bohr, Niels (1958), *Atomic Physics and Human Knowledge*. New York: Wiley.

Bonte, Pierre (1975), 'Cattle for God: An Attempt at a Marxist Analysis of the Religion of East African Herdsmen.' *Social Compass* XXII (3–4): 381–96.

Buber Martin (1906), *Die Geschichten des Rabbi Nachman*. Frankfurt: Rütten and Loening.

— (1908), *Die Legende des Baalschem*. Frankfurt: Rütten and Loening. (1955: The *Legend of the Baal-Shem*, tr. M. Friedman, New York: Harper.)

— (1913), *Daniel. Gespräche von der Verwirklichung*. Leipzig: Insel. (1964: *Daniel. Dialogues on Realisation*, tr. M. Friedman, New York: Holt, Rinehart and Winston.)

— (1922), *Ich und Du*. Leipzig: Insel. (1937: *I and Thou*, tr. R. Gregor Smith, Edinburgh: T. and T. Clark.)

— (1932), *Königtum Gottes*. Berlin: Schocken. (1967: *Kingship of God*, tr. R. Scheimann, New York: Harper and Row.)

— (1948). *Hasidism*. New York: Philosophical Library.

— (1949), *Gog und Magog. Eine Chronik*. Heidelberg: Lambert Schneider. (Hebrew edition, 1943.)

— (1962–63), *Complete Works*: I. *Schriften zur Philosophie*. II. *Schriften zur Bibel*. III. *Schriften zur Chassidismus*. Munich: Kösel; Heidelberg: Lambert Schneider.

— (1965), *Nachlese*. Heidelberg: Lambert Schneider.

Butterfield, Herbert (1949), *Origins of Modern Science*. London: Bell.

Chalmers, A. (1978), *What is This Thing Called Science?* London: Open University Press.

Chan, Wing-Tsit (1951), 'Synthesis in Chinese Metaphysics,' in Moore (ed.), 163–77.

— (1953), *Religious Trends in Modern China*. New York: Columbia University Press.

— (1957), 'The Neo-Confucian Solution of the Problem of Evil.' *Bulletin of the Institute of History and Philology Academica Sinica* 28: 773–91.

— (1957), 'Neo-Confucianism and Chinese Scientific Thought.' *Philosophy East and West* 6: 309–32.

— (1960), 'Wang Yang-Ming,' in *Encyclopaedia Britannica*, vol. 23, 320–21.

— (1962.), 'How Buddhistic is Wang Yang-Ming? *Philosophy East and West* 11: 203–16.

— (1963), *A Source Book in Chinese Philosophy*. Princeton: Princeton University Press.

— (1963), *Writings of Wang Yang-Ming* (translated with notes). New York: Columbia University Press.

— (1963), *The Way of Lao Tzu, A Translation and Study of the Tao-te Ching*. New York: Bobbs-Merrill.

— (1963), *The Platform Scripture* (translated with introduction and notes). New York: St. Johns University Press; (also 1971).

— (1964), 'The Evolution of the Neo-Confucian Concept of Li as a Principle' *Tsing Hua Journal of Chinese Studies*, 123–48.

— (1966), *Chinese Philosophy in Mainland China 1949–63*. Honolulu: East-West Center Press.

— (1967), *Reflections on Things at Hand, the Neo-Confucian Anthology, Compiled by Chu Hsi and Lu Tsu-ch'ien* (translated with notes). New York: Columbia University Press.

— (1969) *The Great Asian Religions: An Anthology*. New York: Macmillan.

— (1973). 'Chu Hsi's Completion of Neo-Confucianism,' in *Études Sung in memoriam Etienne Balazs*. Series II, Part I, ed. Francoise Aubin, 59–90.

Droscher, Vitus B. (1971), *The Magic of the Senses*. New York: Harper and Row.

Duhem, P. (1962), *The Aim and Structure of Physical Theory*. New York: Atheneum.

Eliade, Mircea (1979), 'Some Notes on Theosophia Perennis: Ananda K. Coomaraswamy and Henry Corbin.' *History of Religions*, 167–76.

Epstein, Isidore (1959), *Judaism: A Historical Presentation*. Harmondsworth: Penguin.

Evans-Pritchard, E.E. (1956), *Nuer Religion*. Oxford: Oxford University Press.

Feyerabend, Paul K. (1968), 'On the Improvement of the Sciences and the Arts, and the Possible Identity of the Two,' in *Boston Studies in the Philosophy of Science*, vol. 3, ed. R.S. Cohen and M.M. Wartofsky. Dordrecht: Reidel.

— (1975), *Against Method: Outline of an Anarchistic Theory of Knowledge*. London: New Left.

Foucault, Michel (1971), *The Order of Things*. New York: Random House.

— (1971), *The Archaeology of Knowledge*. New York: Tavistock; (also 1976 New York: Harper and Row).

Friedman, Maurice (1955), *Martin Buber: The Life of Dialogue*. London: Routledge and Kegan Paul.

— (1976), 'Martin Buber and Asia.' *Philosophy East and West* 26: 411–26.

Gadamer, Hans Georg (1975), *Truth and Method* (translation edited by Garrett Barden and John Gunning). New York: Seabury. (Original *Wahrheit und Methode*. Tübingen: Mohr. 1960.)

Habermas, Jurgen (1963), *Theorie und Praxis; sozialphilosophische Studien*. Neuwied am Rhein: Luchterhand. (*Theory and Practice*, tr. J. Viertel, Boston: Beacon. 1973.)
— (1968), *Erkenntnis und Interesse*. Frankfurt: Suhrkamp. (*Knowledge and Human Interests*, tr. J.J. Shapiro, Boston: Beacon. 1971.)
— (1973), *Legitimationsprobleme im Spät Kapitalismus*. Frankfurt: Suhrkamp (*Legitimation Crisis*, tr. T. McCarthy, Boston: Beacon. 1973.)
Hanson, N.R. (1958), *Patterns of Discovery*. Cambridge: Cambridge University Press.
Heidegger, M. (1970), *Existence and Being* (translated by Werner Brock). Chicago: Regnery (Gateway).
Heilbroner, R.L. (1974), *An Inquiry into the Human Prospect*. New York: W.W. Norton.
Heisenberg, Werner (1971), 'Rationality in Science and Society,' in Urban and Glenny (eds.), 73–88.
Hesse, Mary (1980), *Revolutions and Reconstructions in the Philosophy of Science*. Brighton: Harvester.
Hiroshi, Sakamoto (1978), 'D.T. Suzuki as a Philosopher,' *Eastern Buddhist* XI(2): 33–42.
Horton, R.F. (1967), 'African Traditional Thought and Western Science,' in *Africa* 37: 155–87.
Huxley, Aldous (1946), *The Perennial Philosophy*. London: Chatto and Windus.

Idowu, E.B. (1962), *Olodumare: God in Yoruba Belief*. London: Longmans.
Illich, Ivan (1973), *Celebration of Awareness*. Harmondsworth: Penquin.

Jahn, Jankeinz (1961), *Muntu: an Outline of the New African Culture* (translated by M. Greve). New York: Grove. (Original *Muntu: Umrisse der neoafrikanischen Kultur*. Dusseldorf: Diederichs, 1958.)
Jiyu, Ren. (Chi-Yü, Jen) (1977), 'Investigate Religion and Criticise Theology,' *Ching Feng* 20: 170–76.
Jung, C.G. (1938), *Psychology and Religion*. New Haven: Yale University Press.

Kagame, Alexis (1956), *La Philosophie Bantu-Rwandaise de l'Être*. Brussels: Académie royale des sciences coloniales.
Kerseven, Marko (1975), 'Religion and the Marxist Concept of Social Formation,' *Social Compass* XXII (3–4): 323–42.
King, Winston Lee (1954), *Introduction to Religion: A Phenomenological Approach*. New York: Harper.
Koertge, Noretta (1971), 'Inter-theoretic Criticism and the Growth of Science,' in *Boston Studies in Philosophy of Science*, vol. 8, ed. R.C. Buck and R.S. Cohen, 160–73. Dordrecht: Reidel.
Kuhn, Thomas (1962), *The Structure of Scientific Revolutions*. Chicago: Chicago University Press.

Laing, R.D. (1960), *The Divided Self*. London: Tavistock.

Lakatos, Imre, (ed.) (1968), *The Problem of Inductive Logic*. Amsterdam: North-Holland Publishing Company.

— (1974), 'Falsification and the Methodology of Scientific Research Programmes,' in I. Lakatos and A. Musgrave (eds.), *Criticism and the Growth of Knowledge*. Cambridge: Cambridge University Press.

Laszlo, Ervin (1978), *The Inner Limits of Mankind*. Oxford: Pergamon.

Lienhardt, G. (1961), *Divinity and Experience, the Religion of the Dinka*. Oxford: Clarendon.

Lipsey, Roger, (ed.) (1977), *Coomaraswamy*. Vol. 1, *Selected Papers: Traditional Art and Symbolism*; Vol. 2, *Selected Papers: Metaphysics*; Vol. 3, *His Life and Work*. (Bollingen Series LXXXIX). Princeton: Princeton University Press.

Maduro, Otto (1975), 'Marxist Analysis and Sociology of Religion.' *Social Compass* XXII (3–4): 305–22.

Magee, Bryan (1973), *Popper*. London: Collins Fontana.

— (1974), 'Karl Popper: The World's Greatest Philosopher?' *Current Affairs Bulletin* 50(8): 14–23.

Manheim, Werner (1974), *Martin Buber*. New York: Twayne.

Marcuse, H. (1968), *Negations: Essays in Critical Theory*. Boston: Beacon.

Mbiti, John (1966), *Akamba Stories*. Oxford: Clarendon.

— (1969), *African Religions and Philosophy*. London: Heinemann.

— (1970), *Concepts of God in Africa*. London: SPCK.

— (1971), *New Testament Eschatology in an African Background*. London: Oxford University Press.

— (1975), *The Prayers of African Religion*. London: SPCK.

Medawar, Peter (1969), *Induction and Intuition in Scientific Thought*. London: Methuen.

Moore, Charles A. (1944), *Philosophy East and West*. Princeton University Press.

— (1951), (ed.) *Essays in East-West Philosophy*. Honolulu: University of Hawaii.

— (1962), *Philosophy and Culture—East and West*. Honolulu: University of Hawaii.

Morgan, Kenneth (1953), (ed.) *Religion of the Hindus*. New York: Ronald.

— (1956). *The Path of the Buddha*. New York: Ronald.

— (1958), *Islam—The Straight Path*. New York: Ronald.

Mumford, L. (1970), *The Myth of the Machine: The Pentagon of Power*. New York: Harcourt Brace Jovanovich.

Murti, T.R.V. (1955), *The Central Philosophy of Buddhism: A Study of the Mādhyamika System*. London: Allen and Unwin.

Musgrave, Alan E. (1974), 'Logical Versus Historical Theories of Confirmation,' *British Journal for the Philosophy of Science* 25: 1–23.

Nagel, Ernest (1961), *The Structure of Science*. New York: Harcourt Brace.

Naravane, V.S. (1964), *Modern Indian Thought: A Philosophical Survey*. Bombay: Asia Publishing House.

Nasr, Seyyed Hossein (1964), *Three Muslim Sages*. Cambridge: Harvard University Press.
— (1964), *An Introduction to Islamic Cosmological Doctrines*. Cambridge: Harvard University Press.
— (1964), *Histoire de la philosophie islamique* (with H. Corbin and O. Yahya). Paris: Gallimard.
— (1966), *Ideals and Realities of Islam*. London: Allen and Unwin.
— (1966). *Iran*. Paris: UNESCO.
— (1967), *Islamic Studies: Essays on Law and Society, the Sciences, and Philosophy and Sufism*. Beirut: Librairie du Liban,
— (1968), *Science and Civilisation in Iran*. Cambridge: Harvard University Press.
— (1968). *The Encounter of Man and Nature; the Spiritual Crisis of Modern Man*. London: Allen and Unwin.
— (1968), *Sufi Essays*. London: Allen and Unwin.
— (1974), *Jalal ad-Din Rumi. Supreme Persian Poet and Sage*. Tehran: High Council of Culture and Arts.
— (1975), *Islam and the Plight of Modern Man*. London, New York: Longman.
— (1975), *An Annotated Bibliography of Islamic Science*. Vol. 1. Tehran: Imperial Iranian Academy of Philosophy.
— (1975), *Persia, Bridge of Turquoise* (with R. Beny). Toronto: McClelland and Stewart.
— (1976), *Islamic Science—An Illustrated Study*. London: Thorsons.
— (1981), *Knowledge and the Sacred*. Edinburgh: Edinburgh University Press.
Nketia, J.H. Kwabena (1955), *Funeral Dirges of the Akan People*. Accra.

Parratt, John (1977), 'Time in Traditional African Thought.' *Religion* 7 (2): 117–26.
Parrinder, E.G. (1954), *African Traditional Religion*. London: Hutchinson's University Library.
Polanyi, Michael (1946), *Science, Faith and Society*. Oxford: Oxford University Press; (also Chicago University Press, fifth impr. 1973).
— (1951), *The Logic of Liberty*. London: Routledge.
— (1958), *Personal Knowledge*. London: Routledge.
— (1969), *Knowing and Being*. London: Routledge.
Popper, Karl. R. (1935), *Logik der Forschung zur Erkenntnistheorie der modernen Naturwissenschaft*. Wien: J. Springer. (*The Logic of Scientific Discovery*, London: Hutchinson, 1968.)
— (1962), *Conjectures and Refutations*. New York: Basic Books.
— (1972), *Objective Knowledge*. Oxford: Oxford University Press.

Radhakrishnan, Sarvepalli (1918), *Philosophy of Rabindranath Tagore*. London: Macmillan.
— (1920), *Reign of Religion in Contemporary Philosophy*. London: Macmillan.
— (1923, 1927), *Indian Philosophy*, 2 vols. New York: Macmillan.
— (1927), *Hindu View of Life*. London: Allen and Unwin.
— (1932), *An Idealist View of Life*. New York: Macmillan.

— (1933), *East and West in Religion*. London: Allen and Unwin.
— (1938), *Gautama the Buddha*. London: H. Milford.
— (1939), *Mahatma Gandhi*. London: Allen and Unwin.
— (1939), *Eastern Religions and Western Thought*. Oxford: Oxford University Press.
— (1947), *Religion and Society*. London: Allen and Unwin.
— (1948), *Kalki*. Bombay: Hind Kitabs; (original, 1929).
— (1949), *Great Indians*. Bombay: Hind Kitabs.
— (1950), *Dhammapada*. Oxford: Oxford University Press.
— (1966), 'Fellowship of the Spirit,' In Rouner (ed.) *Philosophy, Religion and the Coming World Civilisation*.
— (1967), *Religion in a Changing World*. London: Allen and Unwin.
Reich, C. (1970), *The Greening of America*. New York: Random House.
Rescher, Nicholas (1973), 2nd. ed. (1979), *Conceptual Idealism and Cognitive Systematization*. Oxford: Blackwell.
Rouner, Leroy, ed. (1966), *Philosophy, Religion, and the Coming World Civilisation*. The Hague: Martinus Nijhoff.
Rykwert, Joseph (1979), 'A.D. Coomaraswamy.' *Religion* 9: 104–15.

Said, Edward W. (1978), *Orientalism*. London: Routledge.
Scheffler, Israel (1967), *Science and Subjectivity*. New York: Bobbs-Merrill.
Schilpp, Paul Arthur, ed. (1944), *The Philosophy of Bertrand Russell*. Evanston and Chicago: Northwestern University.
— (1952). (ed.) *The Philosophy of Sarvepalli Radhakrishnan*. New York: Tudor.
— (1974). (ed.) *The Philosophy of Karl Popper*. La Salle, Illinois: Open Court.
Schmitt, Charles B. (1966), 'Perennial Philosophy: From Agostino Stenco to Leibniz.' *Journal of the History of Ideas* 27: 505–32.
Scholem, Gershom G. (1946), *Major Trends in Jewish Mysticism*. New York: Schocken.
Schumaker, Ernst Friedrich (1973), *Small is Beautiful: A Study of Economics as if People Mattered*. London: Blond and Briggs; (also Abacus, 1974).
Smith, Wilfred Cantwell (1959), 'Comparative Religion: Whither and Why?' in M. Eliade and J.M. Kitagawa (eds.) *The History of Religions: Essays in Methodology*. Chicago and London: University of Chicago Press.
Stove, D.C. (1973), *Probability and Hume's Inductive Scepticism*. Oxford: Oxford University Press.
Suzuki, Daisetz Teitaro (1900), *Translation of Aśvaghosa's 'Discourse on the Awakening of Faith in the Mahāyāna'*. Chicago: Open Court.
— (1907), *Outlines of Mahayana Buddhism*. London: Luzac; (also New York: Schocken, 1963).
— (1914), 'The Development of Mahayana Buddhism,' *Monist* XXIV: 565–81.
— (1916), *Zen no tachiba kara (From the Standpoint of Zen)*. Tokyo: Kōyū-Kan.
— (1927), *Essays in Zen Buddhism*. First Series. London: Luzac.
— (1930), *Studies in the Lankāvatāra Sūtra*. London: Routledge.

— (1932), Translation of '*Laṅkāvatāra Sūtra*'. London: Routledge.

— (1949), *The Zen Doctrine of No-Mind*. London: Rider.

— (1953), 'Zen: A Reply to Hu shin,' *Philosophy East and West* 3: 25–46.

— (1955), *Studies in Zen*. New York: Philosophical Library.

— (1957), *Mysticism: Christian and Buddist*. New York: Harper.

— (1969), *Suẓaki Daiseṭẓ Zenshū (Complete Works of Suẓuki)*. Tokyo: Iwanami Shoten.

Takakusu, Junjirō (1947), *The Essentials of Buddhist Philosophy* (ed. Wing-Tsit Chan and C.A. Moore). Honolulu: University of Hawaii.

Taylor, John V. (1963), *The Primal Vision*. London: SCM Press.

Tempels, Placied (1946), *Bantoe-filosofie*. Antwerp: De Sikkel. (*Bantu Philosophy*, Paris: Presence africaine, 1969—translation of French version of Bantoe-filosofie.)

Toffler, Alvin (1980), *The Third Wave*. New York: Morrow.

Urban, G.R. and Glenny, M., eds. (1971), *Can We Survive Our Future?* London: Bodley Head.

Vidal, Daniel (1975), '*Une lecture marxiste du prophétisme,*' *Social Compass* XXII (3–4): 355–80.

Waardenburg, Jacques (1973), *Classical Approaches to the Study of Religion*, 2 vols. The Hague: Mouton.

White, Lynn. T. (1956), *Frontiers of Knowledge in the Study of Man*. New York: Harper.

Psychological Approaches

DAVID M. WULFF

The realm of religious experience and practice is indisputably one of fundamental psychological importance. Just as psychologists who would truly understand living human beings must take into account the religious dimension, so scholars of religion seeking to comprehend the extraordinary diversity of religious expression must recognize the pervasive influence of the psyche's structure and dynamics. The psychology of religion ought therefore to be a thriving enterprise, fostered by the interest and collaboration of a large number of variously trained scholars.

The situation is in fact quite otherwise. Throughout its erratic development, the field has been widely neglected if not also disparaged, and even today many psychologists and scholars of religion look upon it as a field unworthy of serious interest. Psychologists, the evidence suggests, tend to be indifferent or antagonistic toward religious faith and its expressions, and many apparently see no need to include in their investigations what to them is unimportant. Scholars of religion, on the other hand, fear that psychological analysis of religion will likely be insensitive and reductionistic; some even declare it to be irrelevant, regardless of its spirit or quality.

In this climate of indifference and distrust a small number of scholars have nonetheless specialized in the psychological study of religion. The field arose as a self-conscious endeavor late in the nineteenth century, the offspring chiefly of liberal Protestant theology and the aspiring, newly independent discipline of empirical psychology. In America, where the psychology of religion is said to have been founded, it has been pursued most often by psychologists, typically of Protestant background and largely sympathetic to the religious life. In the German-speaking world, a majority of the field's proponents have been Protestant theologians or historians of religion; Freud and Jung are, of course, important exceptions. In French-speaking countries, religiously uncommitted specialists in psychopathology early played a leading role, but today Catholic psychologists interested in the dynamics of normal religious faith are at center stage.

Although the American, German, and French literatures have to this day remained relatively discrete, they show notable parallels in their development. In each are found two fundamental trends: a *descriptive* one, which emphasizes sympathetic phenomenological analysis, commonly undertaken to aid religious education and pastoral care; and an *explanatory* one, which seeks to uncover the causal connections presumed to be responsible for the experience and conduct of religious persons, some of whom, at least, are thought to be deluded. Understandably, the descriptive approach has been preferred by religiously committed researchers, whereas the explanatory one has been advanced chiefly by outsiders.

These radically different agenda are undoubtedly a factor in the psychology of religion's precarious status: the descriptive trend suggests to some psychologists that the field is not a science but merely a branch of practical theology and apologetics; the explanatory trend, on the other hand, confirms for many scholars of religion that the psychologist is less interested in illuminating the religious life than in destroying it. These suspicions, in combination with the radically disruptive effects of the two world wars as well as certain intellectual developments hostile to the field, in both theology and psychology, eventually led to the field's decline on both sides of the ocean—in the 1920s in America and the 1930s in Europe.

Trends in Present-Day Psychology of Religion

Today, all three literatures are undergoing revival. On the one hand, reevaluation and even reprinting of some of the early works evinces growing recognition that there is much to be learned from the scholarship of the inaugural period. On the other hand, a considerable variety of new studies have appeared, employing a broad range of recently developed methods and insights. The literature in fact has burgeoned dramatically since World War II, especially in America.

The American Literature

Discerning trends in this literature is greatly complicated by the diversity of topics that have been subsumed under the rubric 'psychology of religion.' The outcome, as Capps, Ransohoff, and Rambo (1976) observe, is a field that appears hopelessly diffuse. Some scholars, such as Meissner (1961), prefer to label the literature as a whole 'psychology *and* religion,' reserving the *of* variant for those studies that employ psychological theories and methods to illumine specific religious phenomena. The remaining works would fall, then, under such topic areas as pastoral psychology, religious education, research on religious professionals, and dialogue between theology and psychology. The trend analysis that Capps and his associates carried out on the basis of their broadly comprehensive though somewhat idiosyncratic bibliography of chiefly American works reveals that six of the eight top-ranking subdimensions fall outside the more strictly defined psychology of religion. Moreover, for the period from 1950 to 1970, these subdimensions show a sharper increase than the less sectarian and applied ones.

The diffuseness of the literature on psychology and religion reflects the diversity of contributors who are drawn to it. Psychologists, psychiatrists, anthropologists, historians of religion, theologians, and religious educators, among others, bring with them widely varying backgrounds, assumptions, and interests. Furthermore, as Strommen

(1971) points out, the typical contributor makes but a single, incidental incursion into the field, commonly without a guiding theory or hypothesis. Rarely, observe Capps and his colleagues, do contributors demonstrate familiarity with more than a single area of research.

Within the psychology of religion proper, one may discern two outstanding trends in the work of American investigators. Among those trained in the research methods of contemporary social science, on the one hand, there is a strong tendency to emphasize quantitative research. The first task of such an approach is the development of a measure of religiosity, which most researchers today agree is multidimensional. One may then seek to establish piety's correlates by calculating the degree of relation between one's scales of religiosity and established measures of other variables, including various social attitudes, personality traits, and demographic factors (Argyle and Beit-Hallahmi 1975). Research of this type is featured in the *Journal for the Scientific Study of Religion*, a publication sponsored by the Society for the Scientific Study of Religion, an organization founded in 1949 by a group of sociologists and psychologists. It also appears regularly in the *Review of Religious Research* and sporadically in a wide range of specialized psychology and sociology journals.

To many scholars of religion, on the other hand, elaborate statistical analysis of questionnaire data seems both unnecessarily mystifying and inevitably trivial. Far more promising from their point of view are the depth psychologies of Freud, Jung, and their successors. The psychiatric approach to religion tends also to emphasize the dynamic viewpoints of these Europe-derived theories. Anthropologists occasionally draw on them as well. The resulting literature is widely scattered throughout journals of religion, psychiatry, and clinical psychology, among others. The viewpoint is represented, too, in a variety of books, many of them critical investigations or interpretations of Freud or Jung (e.g., Homans 1970, 1979; Philp 1956, 1958), but an occasional one using depth psychology as a tool of analysis (Campbell 1959–1968, Carstairs 1957; O'Flaherty 1980). Both the depth-psychological and the quantitative approaches, as the references here may suggest, are current in the British literature as well.

A third, somewhat less obvious trend in American scholarship also has roots, often unrecognized, in European thought. Prominent humanistic psychologists such as Gordon Allport (1950), Erich Fromm (1950), and Abraham Maslow (1964) not only have articulated an appealingly positive model of human nature that more or less accords with liberal theology but also have written small, widely read books on psychology and religion. Allport in particular has been influential. On the one hand he has restated and developed several of James's (1902) themes, emphasizing anew the diversity of religious experience, distinguishing mature from immature forms, and defending the value of mature religious faith. On the other hand Allport has contributed two widely used scales to the correlational literature: the Study of Values, based on Spranger's typology, and the Religious Orientation scale, which distinguishes intrinsic and extrinsic attitudes. Allport's approach to religion, like that of other humanistic psychologists, is essentially descriptive and typological rather than explanatory.

A significant outgrowth of Maslow's reflections on peak experiences is yet another trend, broadly labeled transpersonal psychology. Interested as they are in mystical experience, meditation, and other altered states of consciousness, the transpersonal psychologists have naturally turned to the various religious traditions, especially Eastern ones, for insight into transcendent, egoless experience. Related to the human potential movement, transpersonal psychology aspires not only to nurture exceptional individual development but also radically to transform society (Boucouvalas 1980). Seeming at times to be more a new religious movement than a disinterested scholarly discipline, transpersonal psychology has nonetheless inspired a corpus of research useful to a comprehensive psychology of religion (e.g., Tart 1969).

A final trend of note likewise lies on the boundaries of the psychology of religion, strictly defined. From the beginning, contributors to this field have actively sought to aid religious education by studying the course of religious development, noting especially the capacities and needs of each age group and making recommendations for successfully guiding individuals into a life of (usually Christian) faith. Today such research has grown far more sophisticated, drawing on advances in research methods and developmental theory. This voluminous literature is helpfully reviewed by various authors in Strommen's (1971) handbook on religious development. Among the studies they cite, British educator Ronald Goldman's (1964) investigation of the development of religious thinking deserves special mention for its careful design, rich findings, and the import of its author's recommendations for a child-centered religious education. A recent descriptive and normative study by James Fowler (1981) is likewise well grounded in empirical research and will doubtless be highly influential. Drawing on the seminal work on faith of Wilfred Smith (1963) and the developmental thinking of Piaget, Erikson, and Kohlberg, Fowler found evidence in his interview data for six sequential stages of faith, ranging from the intuitive-projective faith of the young child to the universalizing, self-transcending faith of the rare person of full maturity.

Excellent though some of the recent research on religious development is, its normative character may well trouble those who aspire to a strictly objective psychology of religion that is free of sectarian concerns. Yet such concerns are pervasive in the field as a whole. One sees them reflected, for example, in the prophetic spirit of the research on prejudice in the churches; in the articles of the *Journal of Psychology and Theology*, which are expected to be consistent with the Evangelical Christian point of view; and in the curious paucity of negative findings in the research reports of the practitioner-researchers of Transcendental Meditation. Evidence of various kinds demonstrates that in fact persons interested in the psychology of religion or fields allied with it are likely to describe themselves as religious, and indeed, many have had a theological education. It is apparent that, for many contributors, involvement in the psychology of religion is a direct expression of a personal religious commitment.

Occasionally, of course, the opposite situation holds true: the psychology of religion also serves as a forum for the religiously hostile to attack piety and its expressions. Perhaps best known is Freud's reduction of religion to infantile wish-fulfillment. British analyst Ernest Jones, one of Freud's most faithful disciples, channeled his own, violent atheism into a series of papers that blithely banalize some of the Christian tradition's most treasured symbols. American psychologist George Vetter (1958), after disdainfully documenting the sorry side of the Christian tradition, accounts for its beliefs and rituals through a simple associationist theory of learning. Less sweeping but no less incisive are some of the criticisms voiced by the humanistic psychologists.

No doubt Smith and Fowler would be right in pointing out that *every* psychology of religion—indeed, any scholarly effort whatsoever—is a statement of faith, an expression of the coherence and meaning that its author perceives in the world. It becomes a question, then, of the degree to which the dimensions of that faith set limits upon one's endeavor. The psychologist of religion must steer a course between two great dangers: the Scylla of apologetics and the Charybdis of psychologism. Where the psychology of religion has not simply become an instrument of a particular, often narrow theological outlook it has too often claimed the last word on religious truth. Even among those who successfully avoid these twin dangers, parochialism in psychological conception or religious perspective is so common as to be the rule.

Warning long ago against these and other dangers, Schaub (1926) observes that the diversity in viewpoint and method evident even then might be read equally as a sign of immaturity and promising vitality. That diversity remains to this day, as illustrated by Vande Kemp's (1976) survey of American college courses on or related to the psychology of religion. Given the paucity of introductory textbooks and the tendency of their authors to be methodologically or religiously sectarian,[1] teachers of such courses usually resort to a selection of works available in paperback. Among her respondents Vande Kemp found astonishingly little consensus on basic reading in this area. Of 49 such courses, only 17 required James's acknowledged classic *The Varieties of Religious Experience*, 14, Freud's *The Future of an Illusion*, and 10, Allport's *The Individual and His Religion*; only 8 other titles were chosen by 4 or more of the 49 instructors. The great majority of these courses, furthermore, were taught in religion departments, presumably by persons relatively untrained in contemporary psychology's theories and methods. Psychologists, on the other hand, are almost invariably unschooled in the history and theory of religion. Representatives of either group, of course, may exhibit parochialism within their own domain.

The German Literature

The prominence of Freud in Vande Kemp's findings is a reminder of the major, even leading role that European perspectives have come to play in the American psychology of religion. The importance internationally of the depth psychologies of Freud and Jung is underscored in a trend analysis carried out by the late Danish theologian and psychologist of religion Villiam Grønbaek (1970). Using 24 'important' books in the psychology of religion published in America and Europe between 1950 and 1967, Grønbaek found that the following names occurred most frequently and in this order: (1) William James, (2) Sigmund Freud, (3) Gordon Allport, (4) Werner Gruehn, (5) Edwin Starbuck, (6) Carl Jung, (7) Karl Girgensohn, (8) Philipp Lersch, (9) André Godin, and (10) Rudolph Otto. It is striking, first of all, that the top three contenders in Grønbaek's list are the same as those Vande Kemp found. It is telling, moreover, that six of Grønbaek's list of ten are from the German literature; three others are Americans—all of whom had studied in Europe—and one, André Godin, is a Belgian who has published in both French and English. If the psychology of religion was first set into motion in America, it would appear at present to have its intellectual center of gravity in Europe.

Freud's views on religion, expressed in a series of books and papers (e.g., 1913, 1927, 1939) and echoed in the writings of a number of his disciples, are well enough known to require only the briefest summary here. Religious beliefs and practices, he said, are rooted in the fears and wishes of childhood, foremost those that constitute the Oedipus complex. God the father is a re-creation of the omniscient and omnipotent father of infancy, who first inspired the love and fear that characterize the religious devotee's attitude toward the divine. The irrationality of religion's motives and the repression that keeps hidden its all-to-human origins are betrayed, Freud argued, by the air of inviolable sanctity that surrounds religious ideas and by the compulsive qualities of sacred rites reminiscent of neurotic 'ritual.'

The literature inspired by Freud's writings on religion has today grown to enormous proportions, easily exceeding a thousand books and articles in German, English, French, and a number of other languages

(Beit-Hallahmi 1978, Meissner 1961, Nase and Scharfenberg 1977, Spiegel 1972). At first this literature consisted chiefly of elaborations or criticisms of the themes that Freud enunciated. Over time, however, increasing attention was given to pre-Oedipal elements in religion, to religious traditions and phenomena neglected by Freud, and to the potentially constructive character of the psychoanalytic critique. Today, major revisions in psychoanalytic theory have brought in their train new and essentially positive efforts to clarify the psyche's role in religion. Foremost among these are Erik Erikson's (1958, 1969, 1977) studies from the viewpoint of ego psychology; a number of works from the perspective of object-relations theory (e.g., Guntrip 1969, Henderson 1975, Rizzuto 1979); and a growing international literature inspired by the 'new narcissism' of the late Chicago psychoanalyst Heinz Kohut (Heimbrock 1977, Homans 1979, Kakar 1978, Randall 1976, Spiegel, 1978). Also noteworthy is the spate of critical studies advocating dialogue between theology and psychoanalysis (e.g., Homans 1968, Müller-Pozzi 1975, Preuss 1971, Scharfenberg 1968, 1972, Zahrnt 1972). As Meerwin (1971) points out, however, the invitation to dialogue has come, with few exceptions, from theologians, not psychoanalysts.

Although Jungian psychologists may be no more inclined than the Freudians to initiate exchange with theologians, analytical psychology's fundamental interest in religious symbols guarantees a continuing and explicit basis for dialogue. In sharp contrast to Freud, with whom he was associated for a limited period of time, Jung argues that religion is an essential psychological function that one neglects only at considerable risk.

Underlying the personal unconscious, according to Jung, is a deeper-lying region, the collective unconscious, out of whose depths arise the myths and symbols that constitute humanity's religious traditions. Over millennia of time, Jung hypothesizes, recurrent experiences have gradually formed the structural elements of the collective unconscious, the archetypes, which have come to serve as the basis for recognizing and experiencing anew the persons and situations that compose human reality. In the individual psyche the archetypes are at first wholly unknown and undifferentiated. With time, however, as a result of external events as well as natural inner tendencies, the archetypes tend to be projected into an indefinite variety of corresponding images, among the most important of which are the various religious symbols. By means of these images, the individual gradually differentiates and comes to terms with the archetypes, which represent both dangers and opportunities in the human situation. Complementary to differentiation is the tendency toward integration, toward the equilibrium and wholeness that is represented by the archetype of the self and its multifarious images, including the Buddha and Christ.

In the past, says Jung, the process by which one moves toward the actualization of the self, the individuation process, was directed and promoted above all by religious rituals and teachings. An understanding of the content of these traditions is thus essential if one is to grasp, as Jung and his disciples sought to do, the dynamics of this fundamental psychic activity. The rather considerable international literature that is the outcome of this effort, along with the responses of theologians and other scholars, is helpfully reviewed by Heisig (1973) in an exhaustive and highly critical survey of 442 books, chapters, and articles. The bibliography to Hummel's (1972) comparative study of analytical psychology and theological anthropology, though limited to the German literature, is also valuably comprehensive.

Although Jung's psychology has not yet stimulated the multitude of revisions that Freud's has prompted, the work of James Hillman, formerly the Director of Studies at the C.G. Jung Institute in Zurich, deserves mention here as a promising further development. Hillman advocates an 'archetypal psychology' that is chiefly concerned with 'soul-making,' that is, with the nurturing of the deepest possibilities of our natures. By 're-visioning' psychology, Hillman seeks to free the soul from partial identifications—most notably with the heroic ego—and to foster the soul's life through a non-interpretive understanding of the imaginal process. Among the soul's diverse images are the Gods, and thus psychology, if it is to be genuinely one of depth, must be religious and theistic—polytheistic, in fact, given the soul's 'native polycentricity' (Hillman 1975: 167)—though not in any literal sense. Such a psychology, Hillman adds in direct criticism of Jung, must also be wary of any literal understanding of its own concepts and techniques, so that what in reality are archetypal structures in process are mistaken for universal axiomatic laws. Largely ignored just as Jung's work has been by academic psychologists, Hillman's archetypal psychology is gaining increasing attention from scholars of religion (Moore 1980).

An Austrian and a Swiss, respectively, Freud and Jung retain to this day their leading positions of influence within the German psychology of religion. Independent of their work, however, and sometimes in opposition to it, is an equally significant descriptive literature, contributed by both psychologists and scholars of religion. In the seven volumes of the revived *Archiv für Religionspsychologie* published between 1962 and 1978, Freud and Jung are hardly more frequently cited than Karl Girgensohn (1921) and his student Werner Gruehn (1960), both Protestant theologians renowned for applying Oswald Külpe's method of systematic experimental introspection to religious experience. Although Girgensohn and his associates, collectively known as the Dorpat school of religious psychology, maintain that their 'experimental' method sets their program apart from all others, they share with other descriptive investigators a reliance on self-observation, an emphasis on individual uniqueness, and a desire to foster a mature religious life.

Members of the Dorpat school presented to a variety of subjects a series of religious stimuli—most often hymns, poems, or brief, striking sentences. The subjects were asked to report as accurately as possible their experience of these materials. In his own classic study, Girgensohn (1921) concluded that religious experience is not simply a vague or undefinable feeling, but that it consists, rather, of two essential elements: (1) intuitive thoughts of the divine that are recognized or accepted as one's own, and (2) the personal conviction that the object of these thoughts constitutes an unquestionable reality. The religious experience is marked, Girgensohn also observes, by certain transformations of the self. In proportion to the advancement of the experience, the self undergoes enlargement and intensification, to the point, in exceptional cases, of becoming extinguished as it merges with the divine.

Occasionally modified to accommodate a more diverse group of subjects, the Dorpat school's method was assiduously employed for more than a decade by an international group of scholars, including Grønbaek. World War II, however, drastically curtailed the work of the school, and today it is considered by many to be nothing more than a curious historical phenomenon. Its program is nonetheless still actively advocated and widely discussed (Bolley and Clostermann 1963, Gins 1976, Godin 1959, Müller-Pozzi 1975, Vëto 1971).

Most descriptive psychologists of religion have considered a range of methods to be more or less equally valid, so long as religious experience remains well in view. Their common goal is to 'understand' (*verstehen*) religious experience, not by means of reductive causal explanation, but by 'reliving' the experience empathically, in order to discern the meaningful connections that give structure and coherence to the human world as it is lived by each individual. Valuable in itself, such an understanding is thought to provide a vital foundation for all further scholarly study of religion. Some emphasize as well its potential for enriching individual religious lives.

Outside German-speaking circles probably the best known of the German descriptive studies are Rudolph Otto's *Das Heilige* (1917, translated as *The Idea of the Holy*) and Friedrich Heiler's *Das Gebet* (1918, in English, *Prayer*). Numerous other studies belong here too. Most of the investigations of childhood and adolescent piety are primarily descriptive, including Spranger's (1924, 1925) enduring contributions and the more recent works of Thun (1959, 1963, 1969), whose investigations extend to the piety of old age. Self-consciously phenomenological studies are represented by Albrecht (1951) and Walther (1976) in two parallel inquiries into mystical experience, and the *verstehende* approach of Dilthey and Spranger has been employed in a noteworthy and wideranging work by Trillhaas (1953). Although religiously somewhat parochial, Pöll's (1965, 1974) systematic analysis of religious experience is representative of much of this literature. Among American humanistic psychologists, Allport (1950), who was a student of Spranger's, shows most clearly the influence of the German descriptive tradition.

The current of influence flows the other way as well. The correlational and factor-analytic procedures that are today a *sine qua non* for the conduct of research among certain American psychologists and sociologists of religion have been adopted by some German investigators, including Boos-Nünning (1972), Fuchs and Oppermann (1975), and Holl and Fischer (1968). Given, however, the continuing dominance in the German literature of theologians and other scholars of religion, it is unlikely that the quantitative approach will soon displace the dynamic and descriptive ones.

Mention should be made, finally, of the relatively modest German literature on religion and psychiatry. As Heimann's (1961) essay demonstrates, the psychiatric interest in religion is linked historically and conceptually with the trends we have just surveyed, as well as with the field of pastoral care. In fact, however, it has developed in relative isolation, reflecting its specialized interest in exceptional states and pathological processes. Weitbrecht's (1948) standard work focuses in particular on conversion, treating it as a subtype of personality change. One of Weitbrecht's students, Günter Schüttler (1971, 1974), traveled to India and Japan to carry out field observations and psychiatric evaluation of a group of Tibetan oracle priests and another of Zen masters. The phenomena considered in these and other works include asceticism, inspiration, possession, mystical ecstasy, stigmata, and speaking in tongues. Attention is also given to peculiarities of religiousness that mark certain well-defined forms of psychopathology.

The French Literature

Historically, the best known work on the psychopathology of religion was carried out by French psychiatrists and psychologists, including Charcot, Ribot, and Janet. It was their sometimes too facile reduction of exceptional religious experience to pathological states, in fact, that inspired James's famous refutation of 'medical materialism.' The same tendency prompted in the French literature a spate of critical Catholic works that urge subtler discriminations among religious states and challenge the presumption that psychology is able to comprehend the whole of mystical experience. Room must be left, they argue, for the activity of God, which only philosophy and theology are said to be competent to discuss.

The Catholic response to the efforts to develop a psychopathology of religion has not, however, been limited to criticism. Long sensitive to the subtleties of the spiritual life, the complications that can distort it, and the difficult task of directing it, Catholic scholars have undertaken a variety of positive investigations that fall well within the psychology of religion. Particularly noteworthy is the series *Études Carmélitaines*, founded in 1911 as a serial and reconstituted in 1936 as a succession of monographs, most of which record the proceedings of a series of conferences on psychology of religion sponsored by the Discalced Carmelites. The latter volumes, containing contributions from philosophers, theologians, historians of religion, psychologists, and medical specialists, are organized around such themes as stigmatization, mysticism, Satan, contemplation, the boundaries of human capacity, the role of sensation in religious experience, and the relation of liberty and structure (e.g., Jésus-Marie 1948, 1954). Interrupted during the war, this series of monographs finally came to an end in 1960 after the retirement of its long-time editor, Father Bruno de Jésus-Marie.

The volumes in the *Études Carmélitaines* evince the trend among Catholic psychiatrists and psychologists to retain supernatural causes among their diagnostic categories. Unlike Charcot, Ribot, and Janet, accordingly, they are inclined to distinguish 'true' and 'false' religious occurrences, including conversion, mystical experience, miraculous cures, and possession (e.g., Lhermitte 1956). Yet at least a few have been reluctant to employ supernatural explanation, as Siwek (1950), a Jesuit who was a student of Janet's, demonstrates in his study of the twentieth-century stigmatist Theresa Neumann of Konnersreuth.

Although the significant French work of the most recent decades remains largely in the hands of Catholic scholars, the themes that now dominate the literature are familiar to us from the American and German traditions: the theories of Freud and Jung, the use of questionnaires and statistical analysis, an interest in religious development and education. As in the other major literatures, we find here systematic studies of the background, principles, and implications of the depth psychologies of religion, including that of Jung (Hostie 1955, van de Winckel 1959) and especially that of Freud (Beirnaert 1964, Bellet 1973, Pohier 1972, Tauxe 1974). Where depth psychology is not found wanting by these authors, they are likely to see it as a means of purifying and promoting the Christian faith. The practical concerns underlying many of these works are even more explicit in a second area of reflection and research, religious development and education. Most notable are the *Lumen Vitae*

Studies in Religious Psychology edited by the Belgian Jesuit psychologist of religion André Godin (e.g., 1959, 1964, 1972), in which appear numerous reports of empirical research as well as articles of theoretical import. On the Protestant side are two works by scholars associated with the University of Geneva: the widely cited book on the child's religious sentiment by former director of the J.J. Rousseau Institute Pierre Bovet (1925), a work augmented in its second edition (1951) by chapters on religious education; and a more recent investigation of adolescent piety by Edmond Rochedieu (1962), the successor to Georges Berguer (1946), a Protestant pastor in France and Geneva who was the first scholar anywhere to occupy a chair in the psychology of religion.

The widespread respect among French-speaking psychologists of religion for the quantitative research techniques developed chiefly in America is evident not only in the *Lumen Vitae* series but also in the works that have won the Lumen Vitae Quinquennial Award in the psychology of religion, administered by the recently reconstituted *Commission internationale de psychologie religieuse scientifique* (Deconchy 1967; Dumoulin and Jaspard 1973; Rulla, Imoda, and Ridick 1978). Statistical methods akin to those employed in these works, including factor analysis, have also found a home at the Center for the Psychology of Religion of the Catholic University of Louvain. The work of this Center, which was founded by Father Antoine Vergote, is represented in a special issue of the bilingual journal *Social Compass* (Vergote et al. 1972) as well as in a series of studies exploring the relation of parental figures to the representation of God (Vergote and Tamayo 1981).

The possibilities of employing in religious research the even more exacting techniques of experimental and quasi-experimental psychology are being explored in a series of investigations of religious orthodoxy by Catholic theologian and psychologist of religion Jean-Pierre Deconchy (1977, 1980), who is Director of Research of the Paris-based National Center for Scientific Research. Experimentation of a rather different sort, employing physiological measures and non-Western practitioners of yoga, has been carried out over many years by Thérèse Brosse (1963), once head of the cardiology clinic of Paris University's faculty of medicine.

A Worldwide Endeavor

It is probably safe to say that there are today works on the psychology of religion in most of the world's major languages. One may confidently add, however, that the great majority of these works are dependent in fundamental ways on the literatures we have just reviewed in brief—though they are, of course, no less valuable in their own right for being so. An Italian textbook by Milanesi and Aletti (1973), for example, features the views of James, Allport, Freud, Jung, and Fromm. In Spain, a modified version of the Allport and Ross intrinsic-extrinsic Religious Orientation scale was employed by Jesús Amón (1969), a Jesuit psychologist at the University of Madrid, to assess the relation of extrinsic religiousness and anti-Protestant prejudice. The intrinsic-extrinsic distinction likewise plays a role, along with measures of authoritarianism, dogmatism, and rigidity, in Lange's (1971) correlational studies in Amsterdam of the religious practices and social attitudes of a sample of Jews, Catholics, and Protestants. In Sweden, the related perspectives of James, Allport, and Clark (1958), along with the role theory of Swedish theologian and psychologist of religion Hjalmar Sundén (1959), are brought to bear on the religious development of Nathan Söderblom by Hans Åkerberg (1975). In Japan and India, finally, the physiological and quantitative techniques of Western psychologists have been used to study representatives of Eastern religious traditions (Akishige 1977, Hirai 1974, Rajamanickam 1976). Although such publications as these may employ familiar theories and methods, there is nevertheless much to be learned from their application to different phenomena and in other cultures. Some of these works, moreover, such as Sierksma's (1956) incisive analysis of religious projection from the viewpoint of the psychology of perception, offer fresh perspectives of fundamental importance.

The spread internationally of most of the leading theories and methods in the psychology of religion and the occasional appearance of collaborative works (e.g., Godin's volumes, and Brusselmans et al. 1980) have not yet changed the reality of the three major traditions, nor have they diminished the value of acquaintance with all three. Indeed, the problem of the language barrier seems only to grow, given the recent work, for example, in the Scandinavian countries and the Netherlands. There is the further difficulty simply of gaining physical access to the myriad journal articles and books in which the literature has appeared over the decades, for few libraries are likely to have more than a small fraction of these widely scattered sources.

Some Fundamental Issues in the Psychology of Religion

The barriers of language and geography are not, unfortunately, the only problems that trouble contemporary psychologists of religion. There is, of course, the fundamental contrast already observed between understanding and explanation, between empathic comprehension from within and causal analysis from without. Implicated in this issue are other, more specific ones, upon which well-informed and thoughtful scholars continue to disagree.

The Definition of Religion

The task of defining religion, some scholars have maintained, is in the end a hopeless one. Yet not to undertake it is to risk proceeding on the basis of a seriously inadequate understanding of the object of one's study. Most psychologists of religion agree that religiousness involves a combination of cognition, emotion, and action, though one or another of these three traditional elements is commonly emphasized. The conviction is widespread, for example, that religious experience is primary and that its articulation in words and outward actions is a secondary expression that, if taken alone, would allow little discrimination between the 'truly religious' and those whose piety is, however well-intended, largely imitative or derived. One identifies religious persons primarily, then, in terms of the experiences they report, not through what they believe or the religious rituals in which they report participation. Although some argue that religion necessarily entails experience of the divine, others have identified it with any intensified and deeply serious attitude toward the world of experience, out of which emerges, however inchoately, a sense of life's meaning.

Beyond the task of formulating a general definition of religion lies another one, no less problematical: devising some means by which one may observe it in the lives of particular persons. How does one assess the piety of an individual, especially in a way that allows comparison with that of another? Modern positivistic psychology's distrust of introspective and empathic modes of research has led to the development of a complex science of psychological assessment, an essential element of which is the attitude scale (Shaw and Wright, 1967). Scales of this type usually consist of a series of statements with which respondents are asked simply to agree or disagree. Their answers allow the calculation of quantitative scores as well as the carrying out of a variety of statistical manipulations. Beyond providing an operational definition of religion for correlational studies, these scales have served, when subjected to the complex statistical technique of factor analysis, as a means for testing assumptions about religion's dimensionality. Although a few-investigators continue to hold that religiousness is a single dimension, however it may be measured, most have concluded that multidimensional scales approximate reality more closely. At the same time, there is growing appreciation for the element of arbitrariness in the whole undertaking (Dittes 1969, King and Hunt 1972).

The measurement of piety's dimensions has become the keystone for most of the research carried out in England and America. Questions about the adequacy of the various means of quantification, therefore, are critical for an evaluation of this literature. Although it is a truism that all psychological measurement devices are at best *relatively* reliable and valid, depending in part on the context in which they are employed, those assessing religious attitudes seem peculiarly vulnerable to criticism. There are of course those who doubt that quantification of piety is a legitimate or useful enterprise in the first place. To quantify, they argue, is invariably to distort and mislead. The reduction of religious faith to numbers on a scale, they aver, is the final triumph of the banality of modern technology.

A more moderate view might assert the usefulness of quantitative research at the same time that it recognizes the dangers it involves, especially if misinterpreted. The strength of the quantitative approach lies in the explicitness with which it carries out its operations, and thus the ease with which they can be reproduced by other researchers and their results compared. Yet this approach is at the same time far less sensitive to the object of its investigation, for it radically restricts the individual's opportunity to respond and thus reduces the investigator's basis for interpretation. Scales measuring religious belief in particular have been unnecessarily limited, for most of them give the respondent only two alternatives: literal belief and literal disbelief. Even the addition of one or two more subtle alternatives, however, beyond increasing the risk of suggesting the 'right' answer to those eager to impress the investigator, is unlikely to provide sufficient latitude for the diverse populations that will be evaluated by these questionnaires. Furthermore, even if it were possible to represent every theological position, one would need in addition some indication of how important the selected belief is to the respondent's total outlook.

The same problems hold true for scales measuring other dimensions of religiousness. The more specific the inquiry about one's religious practices or the extent of one's knowledge, say, of the Scriptures, the narrower the concept of religiousness the scale is able to operationalize. Too general a set of items, on the other hand, so reduces the variability of scores in some populations that the scale will be useless in the search for piety's correlates. The task facing the operationalists, in sum, is an enormously difficult one. They must compose scales of a specificity precisely appropriate to the populations they wish to study, with alternatives acceptable to every respondent (if not also to the historian of religion). This collection of scales, moreover, must be sufficiently diverse to allow each respondent to indicate the ways in which he or she gives expression to the personal faith—the inner experience of transcendence—that lies at the heart of the religious life (Smith 1963). At the same time psychometric evidence must be forthcoming that demonstrates a level of reliability and validity sufficient for the purposes intended. The fact is, of course, that research proceeds apace even though these standards have nowhere been approximated. Its value is accordingly a matter for considerable discussion, as at least some of those who carry it out realize.

The quantitative psychologists are not the only ones with definitional problems. Freud is another who set limits on his analysis by adopting too narrow a definition of religion. For him, religion is two things only: a set of dogmatic and unchallengeable beliefs, above all belief in a father-God who is loved and feared, and the unreflective carrying out of rigidly prescribed ritual. When his friend Romain Rolland suggested to Freud that he had overlooked the true origin of religious sentiments, the 'oceanic' feeling of unboundedness, Freud (1930: 72) could only speculate that such feelings, wholly unknown to him, might represent the ego's defensive 'restoration of limitless narcissism' in the face of a threatening world. More than that he was unwilling to say. It has been the task of the psychoanalysts following him to expand the range of religious phenomena to which the theory has been applied, though their efforts have not always been convincing.

The Selection of Subjects

The religious persons Freud had in mind when he wrote *The Future of an Illusion* are clearly not the same ones that James assembled in the pages of the *Varieties*. Nor are the typical respondents to the quantitative psychologist's questionnaire. How one defines religion, it is apparent, determines in large measure where one will look for its representation. One has the choice, first of all, between religious persons and religious contents. Whereas Starbuck and James elected to focus on persons, albeit rather different classes of them, Stratton (1911) based his analysis primarily on the sacred writings of the world's religious traditions. Jung likewise opted for a psychology of religious contents—what he calls 'the psychology of religion proper' (Jung 1952, in 1969: 464)—while recognizing the legitimacy of a predominant interest in individuals.

If one is convinced, on the other hand, that religion is known best of all through its manifestation in personal lives, there is yet the question of which persons will tell us the most about its nature. Much like the French alienists, James (1902: 6, 39) argues for studying the 'unmistakable and extreme' cases, the '"geniuses" in the religious line,' who indeed commonly show signs of pathological disturbance. It is in their experience, he maintains, that piety first springs into life, and through them above all that one can hope to clarify the nature of religion's fruits, positive and negative.

Although interest in exceptional religious experience remains alive today, many contemporary psychologists of religion are convinced that a general psychology of religion must be founded on the study of ordinary piety, however habitual or second-hand it may be. Samples are drawn wherever they can be found—in college and seminary classrooms, local churches, homes for the delinquent or the aged, and so on. Data may also be compiled from national surveys or public records. In every case, statistical or content analysis is directed to the end of characterizing trends in piety and its correlates that may be generalized to larger populations, though precisely who constitutes these populations is often unclear.

If there is today a preference for the assessment of unexceptional piety, there is nevertheless hardly a category of person whose religiousness has not been explored, at least in the Western world. The field as a whole has been surprisingly catholic, though one may regret the lack of balance and integration. Unfortunately, however, many persons have been chosen for study simply because they were close at hand. It is noteworthy, therefore, when researchers such as King and Hunt (1972) make exceptional efforts to assemble carefully selected and well-specified samples. In such cases one knows at least to whom the results may be legitimately generalized. Their efforts should also remind one that the question of whom (or what) one studies is fundamental to the investigation of religion.

The Faith of the Investigator

No less fundamental is the researcher's own faith. We have already noted the marked tendency for psychologists of religion themselves to be religious, embracing in some cases a conservative Christian theology that plays an explicit role in their professional work. Even those of a more liberal bent have made plain that their research is shaped and directed by their personal religious concerns. Conservative or liberal, the critics will say, the religious psychologist cannot be trusted to be a disinterested investigator of religion. The ideal standpoint, it has been suggested, is that of the skeptic or agnostic: both the religiously committed and the atheist are thought likely to impose the character of their own perspectives on their research.

It is surely no coincidence that negative evaluations of religion have come from psychologists who have personally and vehemently rejected traditional religious forms and expressions (e.g., Leuba, Watson, and Skinner), whereas analyses essentially favorable to religion have been carried out by scholars known for the depth of their piety (e.g., Otto, Heiler, and Pratt). Must both groups therefore disqualify themselves? Otto and Heiler have each argued that the fruitful study of religion is impossible for individuals who have never known religious feelings. Such persons, agrees Pfennigsdorf (1927: 15), will risk getting lost in the complexities of the material, mistaking insignificant elements for major ones, for example; they are also likely to make uncritical use of measures that are inappropriate to religious experience. The meaning of religious phenomena is in large measure subjective, he argues, so that one must approach them first of all on the basis of one's own experience.

The objective psychologist, who in principle eschews all subjective modes of comprehension, is not likely to agree. Psychologists have studied a host of subjects, including animals, human infants, and the mentally ill, whose subjective experience remains largely or wholly unknown to normal adult human beings. Careful observation, experimental manipulation, and cautious interpretation have nevertheless made it possible to gain some understanding of the lives of these subjects. Might not these techniques serve equally well in the study of religious persons?

If the investigation of religion is possible by certain means without one's having "been there" oneself, surely first-hand acquaintance is the best safeguard against presumption and insensitivity. It may be that certain forms of religious experience or practice can in fact be comprehended by the psychologist who claims to be irreligious, but just as surely other forms lie beyond such a researcher's unknowing grasp. Yet the same may be true of the religious psychologist, if such an individual is similarly characterized by a narrowly bounded faith. At bottom, it would seem, it is a matter of where one's limits lie, for no one is capable of fully understanding another person, a fact that Otto and Heiler would be among the first to acknowledge.

The Choice of Basic Categories

The defining of religion and the choosing of subjects for study are undoubtedly influenced by how intimately the psychologist of religion knows the religious life. So too, perhaps, is the task of selecting the categories one shall use for analysis. Dittes (1969) suggests that in this regard there are two fundamental strategies. On the one hand, the investigator may employ the descriptive language of the person of faith; one accepts for scholarly use, at least at the outset, the traditional categories of religious experience and conduct. On the other hand, one may deem it more useful to begin with the categories of psychology as they have been developed in the study of other phenomena. This starting point, says Dittes, is likely to be chosen by persons who, seeing no essential difference between religious and nonreligious phenomena, seek to demonstrate that general theories of behavior are adequate for the religious varieties as well. To one impressed above all by the unparalleled richness of the religious life, however, such an approach will likely appear crassly reductionistic and procrustean.

Elsewhere Dittes has himself opted for giving priority to psychology's categories. 'Until we can use these more scientific constructs,' he says, 'our understanding of what religion is will be impoverished' (Havens 1968: 7). The same point of view is advanced by Pruyser (1968), who maintains that the reliance on religion's own categories has led the psychology of religion into an intellectual cul-de-sac. Goodenough (1965), by contrast, argues for a fundamental rethinking of psychology in the light of a sympathetic understanding of the diverse manifestations of religion. 'The business of the "psychology of reli-

gion,"' he says, 'is not to fit religious experiences into the pigeonholes of
Freud or Jung or into the categories of *Gestalt* or stimulus-response or
any other, but rather to see what the data of religious experiences
themselves suggest' (1965: xi).

The issue is largely the one with which we began this chapter:
description versus explanation. It is also a question of where one locates
the psychology of religion within the scholarly arena. Is it primarily a
subfield within psychology, so that one is justified in giving priority to
the methods and theories of contemporary psychology, or is it more
properly considered a helping discipline within *Religionswissenschaft*,
where the emphasis will likely be placed on faithfulness to religious
phenomena? In the American and French literatures, the accent has been
on the field's psychological roots; among German writers, by contrast,
the psychology of religion has been viewed primarily as an aid to
scholars of religion, who are generally suspicious of any theoretical or
methodological imperialism. Although a balance between respect for
religious manifestations and astute employment of psychological categories would seem to be possible, it has proved so far to be an exceptional achievement.

The Question of Truth

Profoundly implicated in every issue we have reviewed here—if
indeed it is not the fountainhead of them all—is a final and most difficult
question: what may the psychologist of religion say on the matter of
religious truth? Freud won the disapprobation of theologians for pre-
suming to judge religion an illusion, albeit one that by chance may
happen to be true. Jung has likewise been sharply criticized for foreclos-
ing the question of religion's objective validity.

The problem here, according to Scheler (1921), is not one of a
particular theorist's point of view, but of the whole enterprise of an
explanatory psychology of religion. By its very nature, Scheler maintains, such a psychology inevitably calls into question the reality of
religion's object. Beyond this 'spurious' and 'atheistic' approach is
another, however, the descriptive one. Yet even the 'merely descriptive'

psychology of religion, he claims, is possible only within individual religious communities. 'There are therefore as many psychologies of religion as there are *separate confessions*' (1921: 159).

Scheler's counsel of despair, however, seems not to have discouraged others from seeking to develop a generally valid psychology of religion, be it descriptive or explanatory. Yet his concern with psychology's attitude toward the religious object is widespread, especially on the continent. In a well-known and highly praised paper that is still discussed today, University of Geneva psychologist Theodor Flournoy (1903) set forth as one of the psychology of religion's fundamental principles the 'exclusion of the transcendent.' The psychologist of religion, according to this principle, must leave aside all judgments about the existence of religion's transcendent objects, neither affirming nor denying their reality. Wobbermin's (1928) added warning that one nevertheless must somehow take into account the decisive significance of the transcendent in the fundamental structure of religious consciousness seems, on the other hand, to have gone largely unheard. As Müller-Pozzi (1975: 37) observes, Flournoy's principle has given the psychology of religion a purely negative disposition: it specifies only what lies outside the field's competence, not what its positive contributions may be.

Agreeing that the question of truth is not the psychologist's to answer, Heimann (1961) notes that contemporary researchers are nonetheless concerned with distinguishing genuine religiosity from spurious or pseudoreligious forms. The question is in part a practical one, for its answer, however tentative, will shape the decisions and conduct of psychotherapists and pastoral counselors. Genuine piety, according to Heimann, is marked by a correspondence between the spiritual aspirations of the person and the likelihood of their realization, given the individual's capacities and determination. To make such a judgment, clearly, one must possess in large measure both perspicacity and wisdom.

Separable from the question of genuineness is the even more perplexing matter of pathology. Worldwide, a large portion of the literature in the psychology of religion concerns itself with pathological phenomena; in most cases the fact of psychic disorder is unmistakable. Occasionally, however, the subject of these studies is a person whose 'madness' has inspired a significant religious movement. The followers of such a person may themselves come in for scrutiny. 'One must be capable of distinguishing the pathological and the useless from what is valuable and worth preserving,' writes Jung (1943: 45), 'and that is one of the most difficult things.' Toward the end of making such a discrimination, Trillhaas (1953: 177–179) offers seven criteria. Pathological religiousness, he says, is characterized by (1) unusually long and intense episodes; (2) unclear and illogical thought patterns combined with remarkably self-confident faith; (3) behavior that violates general legal and ethical ideals; (4) marked egocentricity, with the conviction that the revelation, which may include special instructions, is one's private possession; (5 striking variation in the content of religious experience from one phase to the next in the underlying disorder, without continuity between phases; (6) incommunicability of the highly personal experience to the empathic understanding of others; and (7) partialness in the degree to which the experience fills the person's life, with corresponding inconsistency in behavior.

Even while seeking to distinquish genuine piety from spurious forms or healthy varieties from pathological ones, the psychologist of religion must bracket the reality of faith's object. To make reference to that object, however, without at the same time taking some evaluative stance toward it seems nearly impossible. Our very language, including the word religion itself (Smith 1963), misleads us. Simply to point out that someone 'believes' something is subtly to imply that the belief in question is subject to doubt. To speak of God without qualification or comment is to give the impression that one is taking for granted a particular theological viewpoint.

The difficult issues that we have reviewed here spring in large part, according to Ulrich Mann (1973: 39), out of the troublesome nature of religion itself. If Heimbrock (1978) is right that in scarcely any other field of study have the questions of object, method, and goal received more diverse answers or been the source of more controversy than in the psychology of religion, it nevertheless shares these difficulties to a large degree with other subfields in the study of religion. The 'situation of crisis' in which the psychology of religion has found itself since its earliest days, concludes Mann, is inherent in the field. There is simply no way to escape it.

Methods in the Psychology of Religion

The unavoidability of these difficulties is most evident in the practical matter of choosing one's methods. For psychology in general, the question of method has been bound up from the beginning with a fundamental dilemma. Unlike the chemist or physicist, who may be able to point with ease to the phenomenon under investigation, the psychologist's object, the human psyche, appears frustratingly private and intangible. Furthermore, the human capacities that make possible the planning and carrying out of research are in psychology the very focus of investigation. The instrument of research is itself the object. On the one hand, then, what one is investigating, impalpable though it be, has already a familiarity that may beguile the unsuspecting; on the other hand, every deliberate effort to rise above the familiar and start anew, scientifically, seems doomed to fall back into hopeless subjectivity. Psychology, some have argued accordingly, can never be a science, at least not one on the model of physics or chemistry.

The century-long search for methods universally acceptable for psychological research remains to this day unfulfilled. The situation as Stern described it many years ago is little changed:

There is hardly a psychological method the correctness or usefulness of which might not be contested in principle or practice, while on the other hand there is a strong tendency to elevate some one method to the status of the sole means of salvation. Both acts, the proscribing of methods and the dictation of methods, are alike harmful to the progress of the science (1935: 47).

Wisdom lies, according to Stern, in remaining task- and problem-centered, drawing undogmatically on whatever methods promise to deepen one's comprehension. Although methodological imperialism is not unknown in the psychology of religion, the field as a whole has been strikingly pluralistic in its quest for understanding.

Whereas in principle the psychology of religion is distinguished from other forms of psychological research only by its object, not its methods, it has proceeded in fact with relative independence from methodological trends in general psychology. Like the psychology of personality, to which in some respects it is closely related, it has been less influenced by positivistic notions of science than has laboratory psychology in America. As in the case of personality psychology, its concerns are thought by many to be too complex and holistic to brook the stringent demands of the experimentalist's methods and theories, though especially in America there has been of late considerable accommodation. As might be expected, it is particularly among scholars whose training is primarily in the study of religion, not psychology, that the field has been promoted with relative indifference to fashions in general psychological research. Some researchers, on the other hand, seem to follow these fashions unquestioningly, with little apparent regard for the difficulties that may be created by doing so.

Observing Individual Piety

From the beginning, the psychology of religion has been said to have two fundamental methods: the observation of religious individuals and the study of traditional content from the history of religion. The first of these has received by far the greater emphasis, though of course the two are intimately related. Both are still employed today.

Self-Observation. The way of observation, many have thought, must begin with one's own experience. Self-observation or introspection was for psychologists at the turn of the century the chief means of psychological research. With the rise of both behaviorism and psychoanalysis, however, the usefulness and reliability of introspective reports were sharply called into question. New, more objective methods of observation were developed by the behaviorists, who were determined to eliminate introspection altogether from their science. The psychoanalysts, by contrast, set about to augment introspection through free association, which emancipates self-observation from the conscious control of the observer. The always-reluctant surrendering of control and the analyst's carefully timed interpretations of the hidden meanings transform traditional introspective evidence, so the psychoanalysts claim, into a vital source of insight. Although the psychoanalysts thus preserve a place for self-observation, they, like the behaviorists, consider it virtually useless in itself.

To those unconvinced by the behavioristic and psychoanalytic viewpoints, however, disciplined self-examination of naive experience remains a major avenue of knowledge. The advantages of self-observation are easy to see, says Pöll:

> It demands no elaborate preparations or safeguards, as is often the case in the psychological experiment. Introspective concentration on the matter at hand is enough, an achievement requiring, to be sure, practice, care, and self-criticism but not apparatus, tests, or statistical calculations. What is decisive, however, is the fact that only self-observation leads one directly to the psychic life. Only in self-observation do we encounter experience as it is in itself and not as it is expressed in words, gestures, and other forms of behavior. By this means we come upon religious awe, joy, and repentance themselves. Moreover, self-observation alone can clearly reveal at least the fundamental forms of experience and therewith likewise the psychic life of others. The same is true in the religious sphere (1965: 45).

A proper understanding of the basic forms of religious experience requires, therefore, that one know them at first hand. Such intimate knowledge of certain forms may serve, furthermore, as a basis for empathically re-living, or at least sensing the character of, those experiences in which one has not oneself directly participated.

Detractors of self-observation, on the other hand, have repeatedly pointed out the difficulties and dangers of such a method. They argue, first of all, that it is impossible to observe psychic events as they are occurring. Intrusion into ongoing experience with the intention of observing it seems inevitably to disturb or transform it. A man earnestly praying to God, for example, who suddenly attempts to observe himself in prayer will at that instant cease praying. If he waits to make his introspective effort until after his prayer has come to a natural conclusion, what will follow, according to Traxel's (1968) argument, will consist only of reflection and interpretation, not observation.

There are other, no less serious problems. There is always the possibility of self-deception, especially when feelings of self-regard are
implicated in the experience under observation. A theologically sophisticated person whose introspective gaze is turned, say, to the idea of God
may unwittingly overlook the vital substratum of naive images and
associations that linger from early childhood. Yet even if the role of such
elements is recognized, one may be reluctant to share that awareness
with others, fearing that they will judge one's faith immature. Where
self-deception, then, has not robbed the literature of a full and balanced
account of religious experience, circumspection may bring about the
same result.

The vagueness of experience, discussed with unsurpassable eloquence
by James (1890) in his famous chapter on the stream of consciousness,
presents the would-be self-observer with still another difficulty. The
problem lies not only in bringing these fleeting and ill-defined portions
of consciousness before the mind's eye, but also in finding words that
adequately describe them. We overlook these vague yet important
aspects of our experience, says James, because they are unnamed. Our
language, in the end, is inadequate to articulate these subtleties. Even
when a label is found for some aspect of experience, that label is bound
to misrepresent it. 'As soon as we name anything and thus assign it to
some definite psychological category, it *is* no longer the same thing that
it was before,' writes Stern (1935: 11); it acquires a peculiar rigidity and
fixity that cannot be ascribed to mind itself.'

Proponents of self-observation have proved to be no less aware of the
risks and shortcomings of this technique. Yet one abandons a method,
they argue, not because its application is fraught with difficulties but
because a better, more certain one has come along. The fact is, they
maintain, self-observation is not simply one method among others, one
that we may set aside at will. It is, rather, 'a prerequisite for every [other]
method in the psychology of religion' (Stählin 1912: 395). If self-
observation has not been employed by the researcher in the quest for
hypotheses and the design of the study, it surely enters into the subjects'
responses. As Boring (1953: 169) indicates, 'introspection is still with us,
doing its business under various aliases, of which *verbal report* is one.'
Where its use is unrecognized or unacknowledged, however, it is likely

to be employed only casually or to be hamstrung by too-severe limitations. It is time, Bakan (1954) argues, to move toward a 'careful and avowed use' of self-observation, especially if we are to have a psychology appropriate to the tasks at hand—in this context, the study of religion.

Advocates of introspection have long recognized the difficulty, if not the impossibility, of observing experience as it is occurring. In most cases, certainly, observation will have to be indirectly carried out, either immediately after the experience—in a form that Stern calls primary self-remembrance—or sometime later, when of course recollection is likely to be far less reliable. The vicissitudes of memory, however, are variable enough to disallow any simple generalizations about what is possible. Pöll (1965) observes that experiences involving no obvious stimulus—dreams, fantasies, as well as many religious states—possess, like sensory experiences, short-lived 'after-images,' to which one may for a brief time give one's attention. Longer enduring after-effects, more fragmentary in character, may permit a fuller study of certain elements. Such residues, furthermore, along with certain occurrences consequent to the experience, may serve sometime later to awaken anew the original experience, in part or in whole. Marcel Proust's famous recovery of his childhood days in Combray, from the taste of cake soaked in tea, vividly illustrates this possibility. Proust's voluminous remembrances demonstrate as well, it would seem, that language can go a long way in communicating the private transport of so lively a recollection.

Yet how does one verify such a report? Only those phenomena that can be made public and hence observable by two or more investigators are capable of verification, say many contemporary researchers, thereby ruling out all self-observation. Bakan (1954) argues to the contrary, maintaining that verification can be achieved without meeting the 'naive criterion of publicity,' through the introspective reports of other investigators. One may even seek to create, as Girgensohn and his associates did, a uniform set of conditions, so that one observer's report is easily comparable to a series of others. Should one discover that each of these replications produces essentially the same result, and that such verification, furthermore, cannot be attributed to suggestion, one may be confident that the findings have a degree of generality. How large a degree is another troublesome question, yet it is not unique to self-observation, as Bakan points out.

In effect, verification and the assessment of generality occur, however informally, whenever findings from self-observation are examined. One automatically checks another's introspective report against one's own experience. If the two are consistent, the report will immediately appear self-evident. Having the quality of self-evidence does not mean, of course, that the report cannot also be penetratingly original or existentially helpful. Smith (1971) has suggested, in fact, that the social sciences and the humanities substitute for the natural sciences' principle of verification one that might be called the principle of existential appropriability; that is, no statement would be considered true if it cannot be meaningfully appropriated into the lives of those about whom it is made. Such a principle is employed less easily in the case of introspection, where it may not be clear to whom, beyond the self-observer, the statements pertain. Bakan provides, however, a possible corollary: the value of an introspective report may be assessed by the degree to which its suggestion of possibilities enhances the sensitivity of its reader. Knowledge of such possibilities may lead further—to the deepening of the reader's own experience, the goal of much spontaneous self-observation in the history of religion.

Indeed, Pöll maintains that psychologists will find religion a particularly fruitful area for self-observation, especially given the long history of merciless self-examination on the part of religious aspirants. Such unrelenting concern for the quality of one's spiritual life entails, of course, certain presuppositions, goals, and value judgments that must be set aside by the disinterested psychological observer. Yet the object of study—the inner psychic life—is in both cases the same. Each for its own purposes, moreover, is peculiarly aware of the tendencies toward self-deception and self-justification. Together with the unusual familiarity and the complex personal associations that accrue with ritual practice, this long-standing concern with accurate introspection, Pöll concludes, allows the application of self-observation in the psychology of religion with exceptional proficiency and reliability.

Yet even in this field there are no proponents of the exclusive use of introspection. Findings obtained in such a way, it is agreed, must be checked and supplemented by other methods, though most of them bring the investigator or the subjects back, at some point, to the task of self-observation. Even when one employs physiological indices, such as EEG recordings, or certain unobtrusive measures requiring no verbal response from one's subjects, one is likely to be forced to rely on introspective evidence, if only when it comes time to interpret the meaning of one's results. Limited though they are, therefore, by human subjectivity, most of these techniques nevertheless sufficiently increase the degree of control and accuracy to make their use highly desirable. They are more objective, many would say, for they separate the observer from the object of study. Yet it must be remembered that the more distance that is placed between a phenomenon and the individual who observes and records it, the more opportunity there will be for error. None of these further methods is as direct as unalloyed self-observation.

Self-Report. The first and for a time most widely used method of studying the religious life of others, the self-report, obviously relies heavily on the subjects' own introspective capacities as well as their willingness to employ them. Although self-report is a term ordinarily used to refer to any data or information provided by the subject, it will be used here in a more restricted sense. For our purposes, a self-report is a precise record of any freely expressed verbal communication, whether written or spoken, that is intended by the subject to represent a defined range of personal experience or reflection. So delimited, this rubric excludes standardized tests, which typically allow only agreement or disagreement with a series of standard questions, as well as projective techniques, which by design seek to circumvent the subject's intentions.

Among those sources of data that constitute self-reports as defined here, the most important distinction is between the spontaneous and the elicited. Spontaneous reports have the great virtue of having come into being independent of the investigator's inquiry. Unshaped by leading questions and less commonly burdened by perfunctory prose, these writings are a rich source of exceptional self-observation. Yet such reports are available from only a limited range of persons and, far from being truly spontaneous, they are often written for specific purposes, ones not always evident to the reader. Moreover, they often leave out much that a researcher would want to know. It is common, therefore, for psychologists of religion to elicit self-reports from a broader, more typical range of subjects and, on some occasions, to follow up the subjects' responses with a series of individualized and more probing questions.

Virtually all 'spontaneous' self-reports constitute what are called human or *personal documents*, including letters, journals, and topical or comprehensive autobiographies, as well as certain artistic productions (Allport 1942). It is possible, of course, to elicit such documents as well, by assigning the keeping of a diary, say, or by distributing open-ended questionnaires. Yet unless the subjects are involved in the task as an end in itself, the results may well be disappointingly pedestrian. At their best, however, personal documents are unrivaled as a source of intimate, accessible, and fascinating data. For James (1902: 501–502), they alone promise entrée into the private recesses of personal feeling, 'the darker, blinder strata of character, . . . the only places in the world in which we catch real fact in the making, and directly perceive how events happen, and how work is actually done.'

If the personal document is the means *par excellence* by which one may become acquainted with the concrete reality of individual lives, it is at the same time a source of data with potentially serious shortcomings. At the time it is recorded, the personal document is already shaped and edited by the perspective, motives, and verbal abilities of its writer. Every document is necessarily selective, and whether or not it is so intended, such selectivity will likely help to cast a particular light on the author. It is not uncommon, for example, for diarists to exercise their art primarily at times of frustration or unhappiness. What is included, moreover, may be designed, unconsciously or deliberately, to deceive the reader. Simple lapses of memory may serve the same end. Even in cases of penetrating self-awareness and radical honesty, however, one must still contend with the conceptual framework employed by every writer, which serves not only as a basis for selecting and emphasizing certain elements but also for formulating their relations to one another, filling in gaps, and interpreting, finally, the significance of the whole. Such interpretation may in fact be largely arbitrary. If one is nevertheless determined to meet these difficulties, especially by drawing on supporting evidence from other sources, there is still the problem of scarcity. In spite of the diverse motives that prompt the formulation of personal documents, obtaining useful ones is ordinarily difficult and expensive at best (Allport 1942).

In reviewing the case against the personal document, Allport emphasizes that its insufficiencies must not be evaluated apart from either the measures that can be taken to compensate for them or the limitations of other methods. From Allport's point of view, the personal document's relative advantages greatly outweigh its shortcomings. Above all, it provides the psychological investigator with 'the needed touchstone of reality' (1942: 143), especially in the domain of subjective meaning, a region of particular importance for the psychology of religion. 'It is safe to say,' writes Allport, 'that [the religious life] has never been studied with even partial adequacy by any means other than the personal document' (1942: 38). In it, one has preserved the organismic wholeness that is commonly lost with other research techniques in psychology. Where the document has been written over time, moreover, as in the case of the diary and some autobiographies, one has an unparalleled opportunity for longitudinal study. Personal documents, Allport argues, provide the particulars upon which all general psychological understanding depends. Indeed, he hypothesizes that the goals of science—commonly thought to be understanding, prediction, and control—can be achieved more effectively by means of the 'idiographic' study of single cases than by traditional 'nomothetic' methods, those designed to establish general laws.

Allport does not, however, advocate the abandonment of nomothetic techniques. Rather, he emphasizes the value of employing both approaches to psychological events. The manner in which idiographic study of personal documents and nomothetic analysis of highly structured questionnaire responses can complement each other is illustrated by two investigations published nearly a half century apart, both bearing on the personal rejection of a traditionally religious outlook. On the one hand is Vetter and Green's (1932) questionnaire investigation of 320 male members of the American Association for the Advancement of Atheism; on the other is Åkerberg's (1978) study of Swedish political scientist and newspaper editor Herbert Tingsten, who, when he died in 1973, left behind a corpus of autobiographical writings that describes a life of profound nihilism, chronic anxiety, ill-defined guilt, and deep fear of personal annihilation in death. The outstanding trends in the lives of Vetter and Green's atheists are astonishingly confirmed in nearly every respect in Tingsten's own life: the position of the first-born; a parent of more than ordinary piety (his mother); a troubled childhood (debilitating illness in Tingsten's case); the death of a parent within the first two decades (his mother, when he was 14), an adolescent 'conversion' to atheism (by about age 16), a high degree of education, and politically liberal views.

Without knowing that a disproportionately high percentage of members of an atheist organization share these life trends, one might not think to consider their role in forming Tingsten's own atheist views. Indeed, Vetter and Green's avowed atheists themselves seemed not to recognize the influence of early personal and social factors in their anti-religious attitudes, but credited instead their later reading and reflection. Tingsten, it should be said, noted both the role of his scientific education and his mother's death in his own growing conviction that life is without meaning.

Yet Åkerberg's study of Tingsten is not simply one more instance to add to Vetter and Green's statistics. On the contrary, only in this study, and especially in the deeply moving autobiographical passages that are used to illustrate the themes in Tingsten's life, do we encounter a living personal reality. From Vetter and Green's study we have no idea what place atheistic sentiments have in the total economy of each subject's life, nor do we learn, for example, how those subjects who lost a parent in childhood or adolescence reacted to that event. There is no mistaking these matters in Tingsten's case. From Åkerberg's study, too, we learn something of the course of Tingsten's nihilistic dread throughout his life and the measures he took in his efforts to escape it. One has, then, an opportunity to gain insight into the dynamics of the atheistic outlook in one person's life, an opportunity that Vetter and Green's anonymous and static data do not provide.

One can well imagine that Vetter and Green would have designed a somewhat different questionnaire had Tingsten's writings been available to them. They would surely have wanted to know if other atheists share his inexplicable sense of sin and dread of annihilation. Are they haunted, too, by 'an impetuous seeking without a goal'? Under what circumstances is equanimity found or 'grace' experienced? Is their 'atheism' merely hostility toward particular traditional religious ideas or is it, as in Tingsten's case, a thoroughgoing loss of a sense of life's meaning? A more open-ended questionnaire would undoubtedly be required, and from it would most certainly issue a new collection of personal documents underscoring crucial if sometimes subtle variations in life circumstances and personal outlook. One would come to understand more of the life experiences of 'atheists' at the same time that one would grow more cautious in generalizing about them.

Early in the century the *open-ended questionnaire* was the chief means by which psychologists of religion gathered their data. Sharing most of the advantages of the spontaneous self-report, the replies to such a questionnaire have several additional virtues: they are parallel to each other in content and structure, which are determined beforehand by the investigator; they are potentially available in large numbers and from persons of nearly every walk of life; and they may be obtained under a great variety of circumstances, as the need arises. On the other hand, the questionnaire reply is no less dependent than the spontaneously produced document on its writer's introspective capacities, memory, self-knowledge, verbal ability, and candor. Although one has more opportunity to ask what one wants to know, there is no guarantee that the answer, if it is forthcoming, will be full and reliable. Moreover, with certain populations the questionnaire will tend to elicit largely conventional expressions or orthodox declamations. Yet even if the response is formulated in relatively original terms, it is likely to exhibit a clarity and order that misrepresents the respondent's experience. The very posing of questions will likely suggest a particular form and content for the answers and may at the same time yield a document misleading in its emphases.

To these problems must be added one more: the fact of selective returns. Even with a relatively undemanding questionnaire and a group of subjects actively interested in promoting their own viewpoints, Vetter and Green received replies from fewer than 60 percent of the persons in their random sample—a percentage, as they note, that is exceptionally *high* for a mailed questionnaire. By contrast, of the 550 questionnaires that Pratt (1907) distributed, only 15 percent were returned. Today, a 50 percent return rate is considered good, though it is clearly low enough to require special efforts to determine how representative that proportion of respondents may be.

If one has the time and opportunity, *interviewing* one's subjects may serve as a way around some of the difficulties of the questionnaire. In face-to-face conversation, one's subjects will likely give answers that are fuller, more spontaneous, and less subject to editing for syntax, consistency, and coherence. Moreover, even if one carefully employs a standard series of questions, one may also gently encourage the reticent subject to expand on certain points, just as one may probe for the personal meaning of conventional or obscure expressions. One also has the opportunity to observe the subject's expressive behavior as the answers are given; facial expressions, gestures, and posture, along with the subject's manner of speaking, can give to the astute observer important clues to the attitudes that lie behind the words, thereby providing leads to further questioning. The interview is thus potentially more sensitive to individual differences at the same time that it casts light on the adequacy of the prepared questions themselves.

The interview yields a self-report as defined in this chapter only when the subject's own words are faithfully recorded, today most commonly by electronic means. Apart from this requirement, the interview as a means of gathering self-reports may be conducted in a variety of ways. Piaget's semi-clinical interview, which combines a standard set of questions with the clinician's technique of free inquiry, has been employed by Elkind (1964) to explore the spontaneous meanings that children between the ages of 5 and 14 ascribe to their own religious denominations. A similar technique was used by Goldman (1964), whose questions were directed to reveal his six- to seventeen-year-old subjects' thinking about three pictures with religious content and three Bible stories. In Germany, Thun (1959, 1969) has employed less structured forms of interviewing as a means of eliciting reports of religious experience and reflection. With children he conducted the interviews as class discussions on particular topics; his interviews with elderly subjects, by contrast, were carried out individually and in most cases in two lengthy sessions, the second of which was directed to such themes as past experience, interests, ideals, conscience, death, prayer, church, and the nature of God. Even less structure and more intense personal association was the rule in Coles's (1971) remarkable interview study of the poor in the northern cities of the United States. Eschewing representative samples and statistical analysis on the one hand and insensitive reductive interpretation on the other, Coles relies heavily on the words of three informants—two women and the minister of one of them—to make evident how intimately the poor and suffering have come to know God and Jesus Christ, and how changes in life's circumstances can affect that intimacy.

Whether one limits one's interviews to the posing of a few selected questions to anonymous respondents or extends it to the point of becoming a participant-observer in the subjects' lives, this manner of gathering self-reports is obviously time-consuming to an exceptional degree. The problem of establishing rapport, moreover, which comes into play whenever a subject's cooperation is required, becomes especially critical in the context of an interview. The advantage of the extended interview lies not only in the longer protocols that result but also in the opportunity it provides for the growth of familiarity and trust, vital ingredients for the development of rapport. Yet one must also be certain that interested encouragement, whether in the form of further questions or simple gestures of acknowledgment, does not become a major factor in shaping the content of the interview. The task of the interviewer becomes increasingly difficult as the subject matter comes to deal less with factual matters and more with questions of attitudes and values.

The often large quantity of material gathered by means of self-report can be handled in any of several ways, depending on the character of the data as well as one's purposes. Where the number of subjects is small, it is possible to allow each of them to emerge as a separate personality, represented by lengthy quotations and supplementary life-history material (e.g., Coles 1971, McDowell 1978, Thun 1969). More commonly, the self-reports of a relatively large number of subjects are used in an essentially inductive manner to identify fundamental stages or types, or to illuminate the structural elements of an experience, around which, then, the research report is organized. Brief excerpts from the docu-

ments of several different writers, who are likely to be identified by little
more than age, sex, and perhaps school year or occupation, serve to
illustrate each type or element (e.g., Goldman 1964, Guittard 1953,
Schmid 1960). It is possible, of course, to combine these approaches, as
Schüttler (1974) demonstrates in his interview study of enlightenment in
Zen Buddhist practice.

An idiographic approach requires by definition an emphasis on particular personalities, though the individual case study can also serve the
nomothetic goal of explanation in terms of one or another theory. In a
few cases, personal documents have been allowed to stand virtually
alone, with little commentary or interpretation. As Girgensohn (1921)
discovered, however, self-reports that seem to the investigator to be
unequivocally clear in their significance may be far from transparent to
other readers. Whether one's purposes are idiographic or nomothetic,
then, some structure and interpretation would seem to be highly desirable. When one is elaborating the personal documents into a formal
life history, organization and conceptualization are essential (Watson
1976).

A full and accurate understanding of one's documents—if such is
ever possible—requires far more than a casual reading of them. Many investigators have relied upon some form of systematic intuiting, whether
it be genuinely phenomenological in character or guided by some set of
presuppositions. An intuitive approach relies heavily, of course, on an
intimate knowledge of one's materials as well as on highly developed
capacities for empathy and discernment. Other researchers have sought
more objective means of dealing with the extended document's idiosyncratic subjectivity, employing techniques of content analysis, rating
scales, and a variety of statistical procedures (e.g., Pahnke 1966).

Standardized Questionnaire. The difficulties both of obtaining detailed
and usable self-reports and then of analyzing their content have led to
the widespread substitution of the standardized questionnaire and related measurement devices. Not only do these techniques require far less
time and effort from the respondent, thus making cooperation more
likely, but they also eliminate altogether the subjective evaluation process. Indeed, it is possible to have one's respondents enter their agreement or disagreement with the questionnaire statements on a machine-

scorable answer sheet, so that each respondent's answers pass directly from that page to the computer. Sophisticated statistical analysis is then possible, including structural analysis of the questionnaire itself as well as calculations of the degree of relatedness between the questionnaire's scales and other social and personality variables, once they too have been operationally defined.

Questionnaires assembled to measure individual differences in religiousness range from very brief scales such as Yinger's (1977) scale of non-doctrinal religious attitudes to far more complex instruments, including King and Hunt's (1972) factor-analytically derived scales of diverse religious attitudes and behavior and Mallory's (1977) questionnaire on spirituality, a large part of which consists of quotations from the writings of St. John of the Cross. For convenience's sake, if not also out of conviction, many investigators have assumed that religiosity is a single dimension along which people are widely scattered. According to this point of view, a variety of indices—such as church attendance, frequency of prayer, attitudes toward 'religion' or 'the church,' religious beliefs, occurrence of religious experience, knowledge of the Scriptures, and adherence to religious norms—are effectively measuring the same thing, though perhaps not equally well. It is of no great consequence, then, which measure one uses.

The relatively low correlation typically found among these measures, however, and their failure to show the same pattern of relation to other variables, raises serious doubts that the unidimensional assumption is correct. The application of factor analysis—a complex statistical procedure that, since the development of the high-speed computer, has been commonly used to evaluate the interrelation of items on a questionnaire—has in many cases confirmed the hypothesis that religiousness is multidimensional. Yet an occasional factor-analytic study reasserts the existence of a single religiosity factor or at least a general one. As Dittes (1969) points out, the dimensionality of a questionnaire depends in large measure on the kinds of items that compose it and the nature of the subjects who respond to it. A questionnaire that is made up of items expressing conventional religious attitudes, that contains as well a number of non-religious items, and that is completed by a religiously heterogeneous group of respondents will likely yield a single 'religious factor.' If, however, the questionnaire is wholly composed of sophisticated religious items and is administered to a homogenous group of religiously knowledgeable and committed persons, one may expect the questionnaire to yield a more complex factorial structure. King and Hunt (1972), for example, found 10 meaningful factors and Mallory (1977) discovered 13.

Once religiousness has been operationally defined by means of a standardized questionnaire—one, we may hope, that has proved itself acceptable in terms of reliability and validity (see Standards 1974)—the main task of this approach in the psychology of religion can be undertaken: the identification of piety's correlates. The easiest way of uncovering such relationships is the technique of contrasting groups. Two or more classes of people are identified that differ on some fundamental dimension: sex, age, educational attainment, socioeconomic status, profession, denominational affiliation, psychiatric history, criminal record, country of citizenship, and so on. Where such differences are not obvious or a matter of record, one may ask acquaintances of one's subjects to assign them to one group or another. After obtaining scores on one's questionnaire from a representative sample of persons in each of these groups, one may look for mean differences that are 'statistically significant,' that is, that are great enough in comparison to the variability of scores within the groups to allow one to conclude with a high level of confidence that the samples one has drawn are not, in terms of piety, from the same population. Such group differences may provide important clues to the nature and dynamics of religious faith, clues sufficiently ambiguous, however, to allow a range of interpretations.

Useful though group membership has proved to be, it is at best a crude measure of individual differences. More subtle discriminations are made possible by the use of standardized personality and attitude questionnaires, many of which have been formally published and widely researched. By such means one may explore the relation of piety to intelligence, prejudicial attitudes, dogmatism, neurotic tendencies, introversion-extraversion, locus of control, fear of death, achievement orientation, political attitudes, as well as a host of other, less commonly employed variables.

Although consistent findings have issued out of this research, their generality is an important but neglected question. The tendency toward fundamentalist literalism in the writing of items for religiosity questionnaires has prejudiced the results from the outset, practically guaranteeing, for example, a negative correlation with intellectual capacity or a positive one with dogmatism. Hunt (1972a) has argued for adding a 'mythological' dimension to these scales, and Greeley (1972) urges yet another, a 'hermeneutic' one, which would more clearly refer to the transcendent. In fact, every questionnaire option raises the question of hermeneutics, as Hunt (1972b) points out. It is a matter, in the end, of how many interpretive options are required to accommodate a diverse group of respondents. Given the extraordinary range of individual differences in human piety, one can well imagine that no existing questionnaire is wholly satisfactory.

Many of the personality and attitude questionnaires used in these correlation studies are similarly problematical. For example, Shostrom's (1966) Personal Orientation Inventory, a putative measure of self-actualization that is today one of the most widely—and uncritically—used personality tests in the correlational psychology of religion, is in fact a test of dubious value. The extreme, categorical statements that compose this questionnaire represent an undefended ethical and metaphysical position, many elements of which would win a sociopath's happy approval. The negative correlations often found between measures of piety and the POI's scales, coefficients that are commonly interpreted to religion's disadvantage, may in fact be accounted for by the test's emphasis, not on genuine self-actualization, but on loosely principled self-interest and power. In a correlational study with the Allport-Vernon-Lindzey Study of Values, for example, an investigation that Shostrom himself cites, the POI scales proved to be most positively related, on the average, to the Political or power scale, and most negatively correlated with the Social scale, which is intended as a measure of altruistic love. No attitude or personality questionnaire should be used in any context without first carrying out a well-informed and thorough evaluation of the evidence for what it measures. One should be particularly wary of the test manual's claims in this regard as well as of the labels attached to the test's various scales. Regrettably, much of the correlational literature in the psychology of religion suffers

from too casual a use of measuring instruments, including those designed to assess the diverse expressions of religious faith.

The use of one or another form of self-report or standardized questionnaire to evaluate an individual's religiosity presupposes that most
people are capable of providing a reliable account of their inmost
feelings and attitudes. Yet it is precisely this assumption that Freud and
the clinical psychologists who have followed him have most vigorously
called into question. Comparative religionist W.C. Smith (1959: 39)
likewise challenges any simple reliance on self-report: personal faith, he
avers, 'cannot adequately be expressed in words, not even by a man who
holds it devoutly.' To comprehend the faith of others, he says, 'we must
look not at their religion but at the universe, so far as possible through
their eyes. It is what the Hindu is able to see, by being a Hindu, that is
significant' (Smith 1963: 138).

Projective Methods. Coming to know how another perceives the world,
albeit in a rather more limited sense, is precisely the goal of projective
techniques. In order to encourage individuals to disclose the chief
elements, organization, and meanings of the personal world in which
each of them lives, an ambiguous or relatively unstructured set of
complex stimuli is presented to each of them for organization and
interpretation. Because no particular responses are compelled by these
materials, it is assumed that the order imposed by the subject inevitably
reveals something of the character of that individual's private world of
experience, a world that may otherwise remain wholly inarticulate.
Furthermore, because the purpose of the projective test is more or less
disguised, it is thought by its users to be less vulnerable than other
assessment techniques to efforts to create a deliberate impression. By
those of psychoanalytic persuasion, it is also thought to tap unconscious
layers of the psyche and thus to provide material unavailable to introspection. Whereas the standardized questionnaire presents a sharply
limited range of predetermined and conventional meanings from among
which the respondent must choose, the projective test allows for an
indefinite number of meanings, including the most highly idiosyncratic
and richly elaborated. The task of interpreting an individual's responses
is correspondingly more complex and the subject of considerable
controversy.

On the relatively rare occasions when projective methods have been introduced into the psychology of religion, they have most often been used in one of two ways: to assess the psychological status of persons of a particular religious outlook or to explore the religious views of individuals of a particular general class (e.g., children). The first of these approaches employs standard projective techniques, chiefly the Rorschach inkblot test and the Thematic Apperception Test (TAT). The Rorschach has served, for example, to evaluate Protestant seminarians (Helfaer 1972), Pentecostal adherents (Wood 1965), and psychotic patients with religious delusions (Lowe 1953). It has also been used to explore group differences, such as those between religious conservatives and liberals (Dreger 1952) and those among groups varying in level of meditation experience (Brown and Engler 1980). The more highly structured pictures of the TAT are commonly used in conjunction with the Rorschach, as in Lowe's and Dreger's studies, but they have also been employed separately, as in Schüttler's (1971) investigation of Tibetan monks. A variety of other standard projective methods have been drawn into the psychology of religion as well, including the Rosenzweig Picture-Frustration Study, the Szondi Test, Koch's Tree Test, the animal test, the Draw-a-Person Test, and sentence completion.

The reasonable expectation that ordinary projective methods might occasionally yield explicit religious imagery or themes, especially from unusually pious individuals, has in most cases not been fulfilled (Attkisson, Handler, and Shrader 1969; Pruyser 1968). Accordingly, when projective methods are utilized to assess religiousness *per se*, rather than some other personality trends, they are usually modified to ensure that religious themes will be forthcoming. Thus TAT-type pictures with obvious religious elements have been used by several investigators (Goldman 1964, Godin and Coupez 1957), word association has been carried out with religious concepts (Deconchy 1967), 'letters to God' have been elicited from parochial elementary school children (Ludwig, Weber, and Iben 1974), and drawings of God or other religious themes have been sought from children, adolescents, and psychiatric patients (Bindl 1965, Rizzuto 1979). The texts and pictures so obtained provide a basis for judgments about religious concerns and development, both for individual subjects and for particular groups as a whole.

Correlations between religiosity scores derived from projective methods and those of existing standardized questionnaires are low enough—
Ludwig and Blank (1969), for example, report ones ranging from 0.22 to
0.37—to suggest that the two methods are assessing different aspects or
dimensions of piety. Whether or not the projective approach presently
comes closer to assessing how an individual sees the universe is surely a
moot question. In principle, however, it would seem to have the advantage. One must nevertheless remember that the partial abandonment
of structure, while reducing the likelihood of dissimulation and response set and providing more latitude for individual response, also
reintroduces the complicated problems of scoring and interpreting
idiosyncratic personal content. It is these difficulties that standardized
questionnaires are designed to minimize.

Naturalistic Observation. Except for spontaneous personal documents,
all the methods we have so far considered depend upon a measure of
cooperation from the individual observed. Yet informing potential
subjects of one's plans to study them, especially when self-reports are
required, is most likely to introduce a degree of self-consciousness, if not
also defensiveness, that may seriously distort one's findings. One is
usually dependent, moreover, on the limited capacities of one's subjects
for systematic and accurate self-observation. The events observed, finally, commonly lie in the past, so that one must also contend with the
vicissitudes of memory and recall.

To catch phenomena when and where they spontaneously occur,
while minimizing as much as possible the disturbing presence of the
observer, is the goal of naturalistic observation. Although this rubric is
associated more commonly with sociological investigation, it has been
employed on occasion by psychologists as well. Indeed, one may view
some forms of psychotherapy as a variant of it, as Rapaport (1959) does
when he identifies the basic method of psychoanalysis as participant
observation. That is, the phenomenon of transference brings vital relationships from the past into the consultation room and casts the
therapist into the dual role of 'significant other' and trained observer. By
means of participant observation and the use of such techniques as free
association and dream analysis, the therapist seeks to make these transferred relational patterns conscious and thereby to give the patient

insight into them. For the psychology of religion, the outcome has been a series of case studies that serve at least to illustrate, if they do not also test, the principles of the psychoanalytic viewpoint (see, for example, Edelheit 1974; also Lubin 1959).

The method of participant observation in its more usual sense can be found in a study by Festinger, Riecken, and Schachter (1956), who observed at close range a small millennial group convinced that a great flood was shortly to inundate a large portion of the Western hemisphere and that the group's members, as faithful believers, would be carried out of harm's way by superior beings from another planet. The observers that Festinger and his associates managed to insinuate into the group feigned conviction at the same time that they tried to avoid acts of participation that would shape the group's conduct and destiny. Exhausting though their impossible task proved to be, the observers managed to learn much about the group members and to document in considerable detail the long wait for orders, the final preparations, and the reactions to disconfirmation. In a similar if somewhat less dramatic study in which intentional deception was not employed, Lofland (1966), who was himself the participant observer, was for a time cast in the role of 'studying the precepts.' Once it became evident, however, that he was not likely to convert to the viewpoint of the Korea-based doomsday cult, which was later to achieve considerable notoriety, its members forced his withdrawal. For yet another naturalistic investigation, in which participation would have been virtually impossible, Schüttler (1971) gained permission to observe and photograph a Tibetan oracle ceremony, as well as to interview several high-ranking priests. The Dalai Lama apparently assented to this research because of his disdain for such folk practices.

The problem of observing phenomena in their natural setting without changing or shaping them has impelled some social scientists to search out 'non-reactive' measures, for use in combination with other techniques. Work of this sort is rare in the psychology of religion, but a study of TeVault, Forbes, and Gromoll (1971) illustrates what can be done. Five of the most liberal and five of the most conservative Protestant congregations in a midwestern city in America were carefully chosen to assure that they constituted an otherwise homogeneous sample of middle-class churches in predominantly or exclusively white residential neighborhoods. Sunday morning during the main service, the investigators determined the proportion of cars in each church parking lot that had a locked driver's door. They found that the percentage of locked cars was significantly higher in the lots of the conservative churches than in those of the liberal churches (41 percent as compared to 33). If one is not inclined to accept this finding as evidence that 'conservative church members, repressing their own unacceptable urges, project them onto others,' one cannot deny that it is suggestive of how the religious conservative views and relates to the world.

Unfortunately, naturalistic observation is rarely so unobtrusive or so clearly defined and quantified as in this study. The complexity, unpredictability, and transiency of the phenomena studied by Festinger and his associates are far more typical. It is these very qualities that deter many psychologists from undertaking this form of observation. Too many unmeasured and thus statistically uncontrollable variables play simultaneous roles in the proceedings, and one seldom has the opportunity—or, when it presents itself, feels justified in taking it—to modify any of these variables. Rokeach's (1964) experimental manipulation of the interactions and delusions of three mental patients each of whom believed he was Christ is a rare instance of intrusion into naturally occurring (if also abnormal) processes.

Experimentation. According to some psychologists, the degree of control and accuracy of measurement that is required for truly scientific research, including the testing of hypotheses about cause and effect, can never be achieved in a natural setting. Even the correlational approach, though it adheres more faithfully to contemporary standards of psychometric practice, falls short of the ideal, for it too disallows firm conclusions about the causal ordering of events. Only experimentation as it is understood in the physical sciences—not, for example, as the Dorpat school uses it—is capable of establishing beyond a doubt the cause-effect relations that lie at the heart of psychological explanation. Proponents of this point of view, which constitutes one of the 'two disciplines of scientific psychology' (Cronbach 1957), by and large disdain the concern for individual differences that characterizes the other, correlational discipline. They seek, rather, to observe the effects of systematically controlled changes in laboratory conditions on selected dependent variables. Subjects are chosen in a manner that minimizes the role of individual differences; committed as the experimentalists are to the most rigorous standards of observation and measurement, they are inclined to emphasize the effects of highly accessible, environmental factors and to discount or ignore the more vaguely defined and roughly measured variables that concern the personality psychologist.

Many persons simply take it for granted that experimental methods are not applicable in the psychology of religion. Even if it is possible to introduce aspects of religiousness as experimental variables—and a relatively large literature stands as testimony that it is—there is strong sentiment in many quarters that experimentation with religion for scientific purposes is unethical if not also sacrilegious. Even the benign 'experimentation' of the Dorpat school was undertaken with some trepidation: to preserve the sanctity of the proceedings, some members of this tradition began and ended the 'experiments' with prayer (Vetö 1971).

The size of the experimental literature in this field depends upon how one defines both experimentation and religion. If one is willing to include only those studies in which the independent variables are genuinely under the experimenter's control and the dependent variable is an unmistakable dimension of piety, one will be hard pressed to find more than one or two examples. Undoubtedly the best known of these is Pahnke's (1966) study of the potential role of drugs in mystical ex- perience. In this experiment, careful efforts were made to control for personality factors, religious background, past religious experience, as well as the subjects' expectations and the setting of the experiment itself. The experimental group was presumed to be distinguished from the control group only by the fact that its members were given 30 milligrams of psilocybin, whereas the control group subjects received an identical- appearing capsule of nicotinic acid, the side effects of which were intended to give the control subjects the impression that it was they who had received the psychedelic drug. The dependent variable, elaborately measured by a lengthy questionnaire and content analysis of essay and interview data, was the subjects' experience during a Good Friday service. The self-reports of the experimental group proved indeed to show significantly more of the hallmarks of mystical experience than did those of the control group.

If, on the other hand, one casts a net large enough to include experimental studies of meditation (which most American psychologists of religion, curiously, seem not to associate with their domain of research) as well as studies where religion is among the *independent* variables or where the independent variables are to a large degree *not* under the experimenter's control—so-called quasi-experimental studies—one will discover a literature of considerable proportions (e.g., see Bock and Warren 1972, Darley and Batson 1973, Deconchy 1980, Funderburk 1977).

Yet however one sets the boundaries, complications and doubts remain. The ethical and epistemological issues are only now gaining an adequate hearing (Batson 1977, Batson and Deconchy 1978). There are practical difficulties, too: a woman who agrees to speak in tongues for a scientific observer discovers that, under these circumstances, she experiences no inner exhilaration; a Zen monk finds that the electrodes attached to his scalp are a distraction that prevents his usual course of meditation; a widely respected yogi, reputed to have attained the rare state of *samadhi*, rejects experimental investigation as presumptuous and trivial; the subjects in an elaborately double-blind study—Pahnke's—suddenly realize which group they are in. According to Koepp's (1920) argument, searching for other subjects or redesigning one's system of controls, helpful though they might be for such particular difficulties as these, will not solve the fundamental dilemma of all experimental research in the psychology of religion: any religious phenomenon brought into the laboratory—that is, any such phenomenon that is called forth, not for its own sake, but for scientific purposes—will inevitably be changed, to the point, says Koepp, that it will lose its essentially religious character. At the very best, he concludes, the experiment may indirectly touch upon matters that are of secondary importance in the religious life. Yet research design today is far more sophisticated than Koepp most likely anticipated. It has proved possible, for example, to conduct quasi-experimental research in naturalistic settings (e.g., Hood 1977). Recent trends, both in research and in discussions of method, suggest that the last word has yet to be spoken on these issues.

Studying Content and Tradition

The research interests of many psychologists of religion are by and large limited to the varied expressions of personal faith. Committed to the contemporary understanding of empirical investigation, which is defined in terms of established observational techniques, these researchers assume that historical materials lie outside the arena of psychological investigation (e.g., see Girgensohn, 1921: 5–12). Others, however, see in the cumulative materials of the world's religious traditions a rich mine of data for psychological analysis. Koepp (1920), for one, has argued that the comparative history of religion is an essential source of phenomena for psychological investigation, given especially the impossibility, in his view, of any direct observation of living religious experience. From Jung's (1969) perspective, it is not simply a matter of finding data where one can; rather, he distinguishes two kinds of psychology of religion, one concerned with the religious person, the other, with religious contents. Still others emphasize the reciprocal dependence of the history and the psychology of religion, the former providing the materials, the latter, the modes and categories of analysis (see Hellpach 1951, van der Leeuw 1926).

Comparative and historical materials have been used by psychologists of religion in a variety of ways. Early in the century, the work of some scholars in this field showed a convergence of psychological and anthropological perspectives. Wundt's (1905–1909) massive study entitled *Mythus und Religion*, which centers on a psychology of mythic apperception, is entirely dependent for its data on historical and anthropological research. Psychological interest in religion's origins and the testimony of comparative data likewise arose in England and America as well as in France, where the psychology of religion was to claim Durkheim's classic work *The Elementary Forms of the Religious Life*, published in 1912, as a major resource of its own.

The authors of such works were fascinated above all by reports on the practices of 'primitive' tribes. Stratton (1911), by contrast, was drawn chiefly to the sacred literatures of the world's religious traditions. Rejecting in a brief aside his contemporaries' reliance on the questionnaire, especially given the narrow range of persons reached by it,

Stratton turned instead to 'the prayer, the hymn, the myth, the sacred prophecy,' which, he believed, 'still furnish to the psychologist the best means of examining the full nature of religion in its diverse forms' (1911: v–vi). Stratton concludes in this strikingly original work that at religion's heart is the struggle with the conflict of psychic opposites, a conflict laid to rest in some but still a present reality in others.

Yet another variety of historical investigation draws thematically on the records of particular religious events as its primary source of data, records that occasionally include personal documents and eye-witness accounts, as in the famous seventeenth-century case of possession at Loudun. Not surprisingly, as this example illustrates, these studies focus chiefly on exceptional phenomena, including—in addition to demon possession and exorcism—speaking in tongues, religious revivals, and a variety of ecstatic practices. One may also find investigations of one or another religious movement, including case studies of their leaders and perhaps psychological evaluations of their adherents.

Whereas one might expect the psychoanalytic literature on religion to consist largely of individual case studies, in fact the bulk of it focuses on religious contents, not on individual persons. One may find psychoanalytic interpretations of religious rituals, shamanism, biblical stories and figures, religious movements, concepts of divinity, religious symbols, holidays, and sacred art. The overrepresentation of Jews among psychoanalysts is reflected in a preponderance of elements from the Jewish tradition, although there are also occasional works on themes from the Christian, Hindu, and a scattering of other traditions. Analytical psychology, beginning with Jung, likewise strongly emphasizes religious content, but in this case the accent is on Christian rather than Jewish elements. Jung and his followers were especially interested in Gnostic and alchemical symbols, particularly in their connections with the Christian tradition.

Widespread though the use of historical materials and traditional content therefore is in the psychology of religion, no generally accepted methods for their evaluation or interpretation have been established. Not uncommonly, depth psychologists introduce individual case material in conjunction with historical content, the psychoanalysts to emphasize the putative infantile dynamics of the traditional elements, the Jungians to demonstrate the timeless, archetypal, even religious qualities of individual dreams and fantasies. However fascinating such comparisons may be, experimental psychologists consider them far from adequate tests of the respective theories. At best, it is argued, they serve an illustrative function. By those who have found the depth-psychological approaches illuminating, however, the clinical and comparative studies, whatever their technical shortcomings, have produced far more suggestive accounts of the psychodynamics of religion than have the efforts of the correlational and experimental psychologists. The clinical viewpoint, argue Hiltner and Rogers (1963), is an essential source of hypotheses, derived both systematically and heuristically; the experimentalists, as they take on these more complex problems, can provide the needed checks and controls.

The possibility of a more systematic approach to traditional content is illustrated by Young's (1926) analysis of Protestant hymns. Young classified 2922 hymns from seven conservative-Protestant hymnbooks in terms of their dominant appeal or motive. The most common theme proved to be 'infantile return,' a turning back to God the all-powerful father who protects and consoles; second most common was 'future reward,' the joyful anticipation of heaven, often expressed in quite literal terms. Together these themes account for nearly 58 percent of the hymns, and many others bear a close relation to one or the other of these motifs. Here is evidence, says Young, for the validity of the psychoanalytic claim that religion reflects the conflict between infantile wishes and the demands of reality. This investigation also illustrates how historical materials may be used to test hypotheses derived from the study of individual piety.

Techniques or Hermeneutics: Some Reflections on Method

There is little doubt that concern with method can have a salutary effect on the conduct of research. It encourages investigators to think more critically about the means by which they make their observations and, in that light, the significance and limits of their findings. More self-conscious about the potentially distorting roles of their own points of view and personal needs, they are better able to appreciate the discipline of using precisely specified techniques shared by a scientific community. These common procedures, moreover, allow the comparison of one study with another and thus the accumulation of evidence bearing on a single area of investigation.

Yet absorption in the technicalities of method can too easily lead to a methodological imperialism that blindly denies legitimacy to other approaches. It can likewise result in a rigidity of technique that unknowingly violates, through insensitive intrusion or misrepresentation, the phenomenon it seeks to comprehend. Grønbaek (1970) warns particularly against unthinking appropriation of modern scientific techniques by the psychology of religion; there is a danger, he says, of becoming *less* scientific, so that one fails to do justice to the uniqueness of the religious life. A truly scientific attitude, thoughtful scholars have emphasized again and again, does not simply adopt methods that have proved successful in one domain and use them in another; rather, it seeks to identify the means of investigation that are most appropriate to its object.

It may also be the case that such means will have none of the appearance of conventional methods. Coe (1916) makes this point in discussing the third, psychological part of Höffding's *The Philosophy of Religion* (1901). Höffding, he says,

makes little use of anthropology, or of sacred literatures, or of religious biographies, or of question-list returns; yet his analysis of the religious experience is among the most noteworthy. The reason is that, though he adduces few new data, he sees far into common facts. Now, this far-sight of his is not an accident; it is rather the ripe fruit of long experience with psychological facts and problems (1916: 55–56).

Höffding's 'method,' then, is an extraordinary mind both richly furnished and discerning, one capable of seeing the commonplace in a new light, of making connections between facts previously thought unrelated. A world-famous psychologist and the outstanding Danish philosopher of his day, Höffding counted himself a methodological pluralist. His broad sympathies are likewise reflected in his sensitivity to a wide range of individual and historical differences in piety as well as to a great diversity of nuances that he says lie beyond the abstractions of psychological analysis.

Höffding's example underscores for the psychology of religion the critical importance of human understanding, of an interpreting mind. Although portions of the field are today still burdened by the literal-mindedness of positivistic psychology as well as its conviction that operational procedures are an adequate solution for the problem of meaning, there is growing recognition of the centrality of hermeneutics to any genuine psychology of religion. In Germany, where hermeneutics has its deepest roots, psychologists of religion, especially those of the *verstehende* tradition, have long recognized the importance of interpretive understanding (see Pöll 1965). More recently, the essentially hermeneutical character of the depth psychologies has become the subject of close analysis, above all by Ricoeur (1965) in his widely discussed study of Freud, but by others as well, including Heimbrock (1977, 1978), Homans (1970), and Müller-Pozzi (1975), who are concerned chiefly with the psychoanalytic interpretation of religion, and Heisig (1979), Homans (1969), Hummel (1972), and Wehr (1974), who explore the Jungian perspective. Worthy of note, too, is a somewhat earlier work by Sierksma (1950), who discusses the *verstehende* approach in relation to Freudian psychoanalysis and Jung's analytical psychology.

Although they may be loathe to admit it, correlational and experimental psychologists are no less involved in the process of interpretation. Elaborate instrumentation and statistical procedures, far from solving the hermeneutical question, only compound it, by removing human (and animal) responses from their natural context of meaning and transforming them into highly abstract graphs and numbers. When researchers report that their results are statistically 'significant,' or, in a flight of interpretive fancy, that their animal subjects are exhibiting 'superstitious' or 'ritual' behavior, they are using language in a way that serves to obscure rather than clarify meaning. Regardless of theoretical or methodological commitment, in sum, the psychologist is at some point engaged in the task of interpreting evidence, and thus in hermeneutics. To ignore the important issues of interpretation in psychology, argues Hudson (1975: 12), 'is to do our best to ensure the triviality of whatever research we undertake.' In the psychology of religion, regrettably, concern with hermeneutics has come almost exclusively from the side of theology and religious studies, not from psychology.

A LOOK TO THE FUTURE

So unreciprocal a concern with hermeneutics—that is, with the theory of interpretation, not merely the exegetical task of applying a particular interpretive standpoint—calls to mind other important differences among the practitioners of the psychology of religion. Some insist foremost on precision and clarity; others, on speculative depth and mystery. The former are likely to emphasize the creedal and behavioral sides of religion; the latter, the experiential and mythic. For some, 'religion' calls up all the features of a particular Christian denomination, whereas for others it signifies nothing less than the sum total of the elements composing the world's religious traditions, or perhaps some essence underlying these. In some quarters, the search comes to an end when piety, thought finally to be unmasked, is proved to follow the same laws as other psychic events; in others, satisfaction lies only in the sudden opening outward of a new vista, when one finally sees how the world can appear from another, perhaps radically different perspective. The ultimate test and fulfillment of the psychology of religion, some would say, lies in its capacity to promote the spiritual life, by aiding religious education and pastoral care. Such practical and too-often sectarian concerns, others would reply, are a serious hindrance to any truly comprehensive psychology of religion.

Such differences as these are inevitable, given the multiplicity of perspectives in psychology itself, the enormous complexity of religion, and the diversity in educational background and professional identity of scholars in the field. The personal equation surely plays an important role as well. One's own religious outlook, even if it is a relatively inchoate one, cannot but influence the questions one asks, the theories and methods one adopts, the conclusions one draws. At another level, religious outlook implies a host of personal characteristics, such as temperament, quality of intellect, dominant motives, and degree of empathy and social concern, that combine to shape one's vision and hence one's conduct of research.

According to Jung, the personal factor in psychology is a reality as significant as it is unavoidable. One's psychology constitutes a 'subjective confession,' Jung says; it is testimony to what one has seen and heard within the vast range of human experience. To emphasize the subjective factor in psychology, however, is not to deny the possibility of meaningful communication or even agreement on essential matters. Yet dialogue among researchers of differing persuasions, if it is to yield genuine progress, requires that its participants recognize the relativity and limitations of their own points of view. One might expect psychologists of religion before all others to appreciate the multitude of factors that condition any fundamental commitment, whether it be religious or scientific. Among such specialists, however, explicit recognition of the personal element in their own work, including discussion of both its potential contributions and its dangers, is still far too uncommon. It is even rarer among the amateurs—coming usually from the side of psychology—who, for reasons of their own, are momentarily given to holding forth on the nature of religion or to applying a favorite theory or technique to one more area of human experience.

There is nevertheless evidence of progress. The cause of dialogue among psychologists of religion promises to be well served, for example, by the recent transformation of two formerly Catholic associations into officially non-sectarian ones. One of these, known today as Psychologists Interested in Religious Issues, was accepted in 1975 as a division of the American Psychological Association. The other, the *Association internationale d'études médico-psychologiques et religieuses*, draws the majority of its members from French-, Spanish-, and Italian-speaking countries. Along with the *Internationale Gesellschaft für Religionspsychologie*, a small organization of scholars from Germany and a dozen or so other countries, these groups provide a forum for researchers of diverse backgrounds and persuasions.

Yet to whatever degree these organizations succeed in transcending their parochial origins and promote the informed scholarly dialogue upon which true advancement of the psychology of religion will depend, they cannot hope to compensate for a lack of support within educational institutions. Formal graduate study in the psychology of religion is today hardly possible anywhere outside schools of theology, the traditional setting in which almost all appointments in this field have been made. Departments of psychology or of religious studies, where the psychology of religion would far less likely be associated with pastoral care and other applied or sectarian concerns, have by and large failed to provide alternative contexts. Given the typical psychologist's attitude of suspicion or even hostility toward religion, it is not surprising that departments of psychology are loathe to hire psychologists interested in religion, let alone ones who might inaugurate special programs in the area. Would-be students of the psychology of religion often return the compliment: most of the courses in the standard curriculum in psychology, they judge, are useless for any genuine comprehension of the deepest and most interesting aspects of humankind. Departments of religious studies, if they do not tacitly share this sentiment, are in any case rarely prepared to offer intensive work in the psychology of religion. Limited budgets and long-standing departmental priorities, often shaped by a sectarian past, do not permit the hiring of a specialist broadly trained both in the history of religion and in psychology, if indeed such a person can be found. At best, a single introductory-level course, sometimes in the department of psychology but more often in religious studies, is offered by persons without training beyond that level themselves.

One should not wonder, then, that at least in America hardly anyone has assayed more than a small, accessible portion of the field's voluminous and wide-ranging literature; that standards of scholarship in the psychology of religion are generally lower than in psychology or religious studies; that there is a corresponding disregard for the field and its practitioners; that in turn there are few professorships or chairs in the area; that financial support for advanced work and research likewise is hardly to be found; and that those promising young scholars who might reverse these trends too often elect another, less problematical area of study. The situation in England and on the continent is apparently little different (see Deconchy 1970, Grønbaek 1970, Scobie 1977).

On balance, it must be observed that some of the world's most eminent psychologists have actively contributed to the psychology of religion. Moreover, several of the leading graduate psychology programs in America have in recent years awarded the Ph.D. for dissertations in the area. It is clear that a good measure of the prejudice against the field is of the uninformed and reflexive type, with which the study of religion in general has long had to contend. There are signs, too, that scholars of religion are increasingly turning to psychology for leads to a fuller comprehension of piety's diverse manifestations. The leads are in fact there: the challenge lies in finding and developing them.

To meet this challenge, students of the psychology of religion will need to become well acquainted with a large portion of the field's own literature; to master the theories and methods of psychology, past and present, with a critical eye to their strengths and weaknesses; to inform themselves to the fullest degree possible in the history of religions; to witness at first hand, and sympathetically, a broad range of contemporary piety; and to prepare themselves for critical reflection upon every aspect of their undertaking, from the statement of goals to the final interpretation. Beyond instilling in the individual researcher a healthy sense of humility, the awesome demands of such an agenda should serve to underscore the dependence of the psychologist of religion upon other specialists, in psychology and in the study of religion, as well as the importance of cooperative effort among scholars who share a commitment to broad, flexible, and disinterested investigation. By means of such collaboration, the psychology of religion may yet fulfill its promise, both as a field of scholarly inquiry and as a source of practical insight.

[1] The author has sought to provide a more adequate balance of viewpoints and phenomena in his own forthcoming book, tentatively entitled 'Psychology of Religion: An Historical Introduction.' Many of the themes and issues mentioned here are discussed in greater depth in this longer, more comprehensive work.

Bibliography

Åkerberg, H. *Omvändelse och kamp: En empirisk religionspsykologisk undersökning av den unge Nathan Söderbloms religiösa utveckling 1866–1894.* Lund: Studentlitteratur, 1975.

Åkerberg, H. 'Attempts to Escape: A Psychological Study on the Autobiographical Notes of Herbert Tingsten 1971–1972.' In T. Källstad (ed.), *Psychological Studies on Religious Man.* Stockholm: Almqvist and Wiksell, 1978, 71–92.

Akishige, Y. (ed.). *Psychological Studies on Zen* (2 vols.). Tokyo: Komazawa University, 1977. [Volume 1 first published in 1968.]

Albrecht, C. *Psychologie des mystischen Bewusstseins.* Bremen: Schünemann, 1951.

Allport, G.W. *The Use of Personal Documents in Psychological Science.* New York: Social Science Research Council, 1942.

Allport, G.W. *The Individual and His Religion: A Psychological Interpretation.* New York: Macmillan, 1950.

Amón, J. *Prejuicio antiprotestante y religiosidad utilitaria.* Madrid: Editorial Aguilar, 1969.

Argyle, M., and Beit-Hallahmi, B. *The Social Psychology of Religion.* London: Routledge and Kegan Paul, 1975.

Attkisson, C.C., Handler, L., and Shrader, R.R. 'The Use of Figure Drawings to Assess Religious Values.' *Journal of Psychology,* 1969, *71,* 27–31.

Bakan, D. 'A Reconsideration of the Problem of Introspection.' *Psychological Bulletin,* 1954, *51,* 105–118.

Batson, C.D. 'Experimentation in Psychology of Religion: An Impossible Dream.' *Journal for the Scientific Study of Religion,* 1977, *16,* 413–418.

Batson, C.D., and Deconchy, J.-P. 'Psychologie de la religion et expérimentation.' *Archives de Science Sociales des Religions,* 1978, *46,* 169–192.

Beirnaert, L. *Expérience chrétienne et psychologie* (2nd ed.). Paris: Éditions de l'ÉPI, 1966. (First edition, 1964.)

Beit-Hallahmi, B. *Psychoanalysis and Religion: A Bibliography.* Norwood, Pa.: Norwood Editions, 1978.

Bellet, M. *Foi et psychanalyse.* Paris: Desclée de Brouwer, 1973.

Berguer, C. *Traité de psychologie de la religion.* Laysanne: Payot, 1946.

Bindl, M.F. *Das religiöse Erleben im Spiegel der Bildgestaltung; Eine entwicklungs-psychologische Untersuchung.* Freiburg: Herder, 1965.

Bock, D.C., and Warren, N.C. 'Religious Belief as a Factor in Obedience to Destructive Commands.' *Review of Religious Research,* 1972, *13,* 185–191.

Bolley, A., and Clostermann, G. *Abhandlungen zur Religions- und Arbeitspsychologie; Werner Gruehn zum Gedächtnis.* Münster: Aschendorff, 1963.

Boos-Nünning, U. *Dimensionen der Religiosität: Zur Operationalisierung und Messung religiöser Einstellungen.* München: Chr. Kaiser; Mainz: Matthias-Grünewald, 1972.

Boring, E.G. 'A History of Introspection.' *Psychological Bulletin,* 1953, *50,* 169–189.

Boucouvalas, M. 'Transpersonal Psychology: A Working Outline of the Field.' *Journal of Transpersonal Psychology*, 1980, *12*, 37–46.

Bovet, P. *The Child's Religion*. Trans. G.H. Green. New York: Dutton, 1928. (Original French edition, 1925.)

Bovet, P. *Le sentiment religieux et la psychologie de l'enfant* (2nd ed.). Neuchâtel: Delachaux et Niestlé, 1951.

Brosse, T. *Études instrumentales des techniques du yoga: expérimentation psychosomatique*. Paris: École francaise d'Extrême-Orient (Dépositaire: Adrien-Maisonneuve), 1963.

Brown, D.P., and Engler, J. 'The Stages of Mindfulness Meditation: A Validation Study.' *Journal of Transpersonal Psychology*, 1980, *12*, 143–192.

Brusselmans, C. (ed.). *Toward Moral and Religious Maturity*. Morristown, N.J.: Silver Burdett, 1980.

Campbell, J. *The Masks of God* (4 vols.). New York: Viking Press, 1959–1968.

Capps, D., Rambo, L., and Ransohoff, P. *Psychology of Religion: A Guide to Information Sources*. Detroit: Gale Research, 1976.

Capps, D., Ransohoff, P., and Rambo, L. 'Publication Trends in the Psychology of Religion to 1974.' *Journal for the Scientific Study of Religion*, 1976, *15*, 15–28.

Carstairs, C.M. *The Twice-Born; A Study of a Community of High-Caste Hindus*. London: Hogarth Press, 1957.

Clark, W.H. *The Psychology of Religion: An Introduction to Religious Experience and Behavior*. New York: Macmillan, 1958.

Coe, G.A. *The Psychology of Religion*. Chicago: University of Chicago Press, 1916.

Coles, R. *The South Goes North*. Boston: Little, Brown, 1971.

Cronbach, L.J. 'The Two Disciplines of Scientific Psychology.' *American Psychologist*, 1957, *12*, 671–684.

Darley, J.M., and Batson, C.D. '"From Jerusalem to Jericho": A Study of Situational and Dispositional Variables in Helping Behavior.' *Jounal of Personality and Social Psychology*, 1973, *27*, 100–108.

Deconchy, J.-P. *Structure génétique de l'idée de Dieu chez des catholiques français*. Bruxelles: Lumen Vitae, 1967.

Deconchy, J.-P. 'La Psychologie des faits religieux.' In H. Desroche and J. Seguy (eds.), *Introduction aux sciences humaines des religions*. Paris: Cujas, 1970, 145–174.

Deconchy, J.-P. La Psychologie sociale expérimentale et les comportements religieux. *Annual Review of the Social Sciences of Religion*, 1977, *1*, 103–132.

Deconchy, P.-J. *Orthodoxie religieuse et sciences humaines*. Suivi de (Religious) Orthodoxy, Rationality, and Scientific Knowledge. The Hague: Mouton, 1980.

Dittes, J.E. 'Psychology of Religion.' In G. Lindzey and E. Aronson (eds.), *The Handbook of Social Psychology* (2nd ed., vol. 5). Reading, Mass.: Addison-Wesley, 1969, 602–659.

Dreger, R.M. 'Some Personality Correlates of Religious Attitudes as Determined by Projective Techniques.' *Psychological Monographs*, 1952, *66*, No. 3 (Whole No. 335).

Dumoulin, A., and Jaspard, J.-M. *Les médiations religieuses dans l'univers de l'enfant: Prêtre et*

Eucharistie dans la perception du divin et l'attitude religieuse de 6 à 12 ans. Bruxelles: Lumen Vitae, 1972.

Edelheit, H. 'Crucifixion Fantasies and Their Relation to the Primal Scene.' *International Journal of Psycho-Analysis*, 1974, *55*, 193–199.

Elkind, D. 'Piaget's Semi-Clinical Interview and and the Study of Spontaneous Religion.' *Journal for the Scientific Study of Religion*, 1964, *4*, 40–47.

Erikson, E.H. *Young Man Luther: A Study in Psychoanalysis and History.* New York: W.W. Norton, 1958.

Erikson, E.H. *Gandhi's Truth: On the Origins of Militant Nonviolence.* New York: W.W. Norton, 1969.

Erikson, E.H. *Toys and Reasons: Stages in the Ritualization of Experience.* New York: W.W. Norton, 1977.

Festinger, L., Riecken, H.W., Jr., and Schachter, S. *When Prophecy Fails.* Minneapolis: University of Minnesota Press, 1956.

Flournoy, T. 'Les principes de la psychologie religieuse.' *Archives de Psychologie*, 1903, *2*, 33–57.

Fowler, J.W. *Stages of Faith: The Psychology of Human Development and the Quest for Meaning.* San Francisco: Harper and Row, 1981.

Freud, S. 'Totem and Taboo: Some Points of Agreement Between the Mental Lives of Savages and Neurotics.' In *The Standard Edition of the Complete Psychological Works of Sigmund Freud*, Vol. 13. London: Hogarth Press, 1953, 1–161. (First German Edition in one volume, 1913.)

Freud, S. 'The Future of an Illusion.' *Standard Edition*, Vol. 21, 1961, 1–56. (First German edition, 1927.)

Freud, S. 'Civilization and Its Discontents.' *Standard Edition*, Vol. 21, 1961, 64–145. (Original German edition, 1930.)

Freud, S. 'Moses and Monotheism: Three Essays.' *Standard Edition*, Vol. 23, 1964, 7–137. (Original German edition, 1939.)

Fromm, E. *Psychoanalysis and Religion.* New Haven: Yale University Press, 1950.

Fuchs, A., and Oppermann, R. 'Dimensionen der Religiosität und Bedeutungsstruktur religiöser Konzepte.' *Archiv für Religionspsychologie*, 1975, *11*, 260–266.

Funderburk, J. *Science Studies Yoga; A Review of Physiological Data.* Glenview, Ill.: Himalayan International Institute, 1977.

Gins, K. 'Inhalt oder Anzahl religiöser Erlebnis-Phänomene? Zur Frage nach dem Untersuchungsgegenstand empirischer Religionspsychologie.' *Archiv für Religionspsychologie*, 1976, *12*, 150–175.

Girgensohn, K. *Der seeliche Aufbau des religiösen Erlebens; Eine religionspsychologische Untersuchung auf experimenteller Grundlage* (2nd ed.). Corrected and supplemented by W. Gruehn. Gütersloh: C. Bertelsmann, 1930. (First edition, 1921.)

Godin, A. (ed.). *Research in Religious Psychology: Speculative and Positive.* Brussels: Lumen Vitae, 1959.

Godin, A. (ed.). *From Religious Experience to a Religious Attitude.* Chicago: Loyola University Press, 1965. (First Published, 1964.)

Godin, A. (ed.). *Death and Presence: The Psychology of Death and the After-Life.* Brussels: Lumen Vitae, 1972.

Godin, A., and Coupez, A. 'Religious Projective Pictures: A Technique of Assessment of Religious Psychism.' *Lumen Vitae*, 1957, *12*, 260–274. [Reprinted in Godin, 1959.]

Goldman, R. *Religious Thinking from Childhood to Adolescence.* London: Routledge and Kegan Paul, 1964.

Goodenough, E.R. *The Psychology of Religious Experience.* New York: Basic Books, 1965.

Greeley, A.M. 'Comment on Hunt's "Mythological-Symbolic Religious Commitment: The LAM Scales."' *Journal for the Scientific Study of Religion*, 1972, *11*, 287–289.

Grønbaek, V. 'Die heutige Lage der Religionspsychologie.' *Theologische Literaturzeitung*, 1970, *95*, 321–327.

Gruehn, W. *Die Frömmigkeit der Gegenwart; Grundtatsachen der empirischen Psychologie* (2nd ed.). Konstanz: Friedrich Bahn, 1960. [First edition, 1955.]

Guittard, L. *L'évolution religieuse des adolescents.* Paris: Editions Spes, 1954.

Guntrip, H. 'Religion in Relation to Personal Integration.' *British Journal of Medical Psychology*, 1969, *42*, 323–333.

Havens, J. (ed.). *Psychology and Religion: A Contemporary Dialogue.* Princeton: Van Nostrand, 1968.

Heiler, F. *Prayer; A Study in the History and Psychology of Religion.* Trans. S. McComb. New York: Oxford University Press, 1932. (Original German edition, 1918.)

Heimann, H. 'Religion und Psychiatrie.' In H.W. Gruhle, et al. (eds.), *Psychiatrie der Gegenwart: Forschung und Praxis*, Vol. 3: *Soziale und angewandte Psychiatrie.* Berlin: Springer, 1961, 471–493.

Heimbrock, H.-G. *Phantasie und christlicher Glaube: Zum Dialog zwischen Theeologie und Psychoanalyse.* Kaiser: Grünewald, 1977.

Heimbrock, H.-G. 'Wahrheit in der Wirklichkeit? Ein Literaturbericht zur Religionspsychologie.' *Theologia Practica*, 1978, *13*, 148–158.

Heisig, J.W. 'Jung and Theology: A Bibliographic Essay.' *Spring: An Annual of Archetypal Psychology and Jungian Thought*, 1973, 204–255.

Heisig, J.W. *Imago Dei: A Study of C.G. Jung's Psychology of Religion.* Lewisburg, Pa.: Bucknell University Press, 1979.

Helfaer, P.M. *The Psychology of Religious Doubt.* Boston: Beacon Press, 1972.

Hellpach, W. *Grundriss der Religionspsychologie (Glaubensseelenkunde).* Stuttgart: Ferdinand Enke, 1951.

Henderson, J. 'Object Relations and the Doctrine of "Original Sin."' *International Review of Psycho-Analysis*, 1975, *2*, 107–120.

Hillman, J. *Re-Visioning Psychology.* New York: Harper and Row, 1975.

Hiltner, S., and Rogers, W.R. 'Research on Religion and Personality Dynamics'. *Religious Education*, 1962, *57* (4, Research Supplement), 128–140.

Hirai, T. *Psychophysiology of Zen.* Tokyo: Igaku Shoin, 1974.

Höffding, H. *The Philosophy of Religion.* Trans. from the German edition by B.E. Meyer. London: Macmillan, 1906. (First Danish edition, 1901.)

Holl, A., and Fischer, G.H. *Kirche auf Distanz; Eine religionspsychologische Untersuchung über die Einstellung Österreichischer Soldaten zu Kirche und Religion*. Wien: Wilhelm Braumüller, 1968.

Homans, P, (ed.). *The Dialogue Between Theology and Psychology*. Chicago: University of Chicago Press, 1968.

Homans, P. 'Psychology and Hermeneutics: Jung's Contribution,' *Zygon/Journal of Religion and Science*, 1969, *4*, 333–355.

Homans, P. *Theology after Freud: An Interpretive Inquiry*. Indianapolis, Ind.: Bobbs-Merrill, 1970.

Homans, P. *Jung in Context: Modernity and the Making of a Psychology*. Chicago: University of Chicago Press, 1979.

Hood, R.W., Jr. 'Eliciting Mystical States of Consciousness with Semistructured Nature Experiences.' *Journal for the Scientific Study of Religion*, 1977, *16*, 155–163.

Hostie, R. *Religion and the Psychology of Jung*. Trans. G.R. Lamb. London: Sheed and Ward, 1957. (Original French edition, 1955.)

Hudson, L. *Human Beings: The Psychology of Human Experience*. Garden City, N.Y.: Anchor/Doubleday, 1975.

Hummel, G. *Theologische Anthropologie und die Wirklichkeit der Psyche*. Darmstadt: Wissenschaftliche Buchgesellschaft, 1972.

Hunt, R.A. 'Mythological-Symbolic Religious Commitment: The LAM Scales.' *Journal for the Scientific Study of Religion*, 1972, *11*, 42–52. (a)

Hunt, R.A. 'Reply to Greeley.' *Journal for the Scientific Study of Religion*, 1972, *11*, 290–292. (b)

James, W. *The Principles of Psychology* (2 vols.). New York: Henry Holt, 1890.

James, W. *The Varieties of Religious Experience; A Study in Human Nature*. New York: Longmans, Green, 1902.

Jésus-Marie, Fr. Bruno de (ed.). *Satan*. Paris: Desclée de Brouwer, 1948. [Modified English edition, 1951.]

Jésus-Marie, Fr. Bruno de (ed.). *Nos sens et Dieu*. Paris: Desclée de Brouwer, 1954.

Jung, C.G. 'On the Psychology of the Unconscious.' In *Collected Works*, vol. 7 (2nd ed.). Princeton: Princeton University Press, 1966, 1–119. (Fifth German edition, 1943.)

Jung, C.G. *Psychology and Religion: West and East* (2nd ed.). Vol. 11 of the *Collected Works*. Princeton: Princeton University Press, 1969.

Kakar, S. *The Inner World; A Psycho-analytic Study of Childhood and Society in India*. Delhi: Oxford University Press, 1978.

King, M.B., and Hunt, R.A. *Measuring Religious Dimensions: Studies of Congregational Involvement*. Dallas: Southern Methodist University, 1972.

Koepp, W. *Einführung in das Studium der Religionspsychologie*. Tübingen: Mohr (Paul Siebeck), 1920.

Lange, A. *De autoritaire persoonlijkheid en zijn godsdienstige wereld*. Assen: Van Gorcum, 1971.

Lhermitte, J. *True and False Possession*. Trans. P.J. Hepburne-Scott. New York: Hawthorne, 1963. (Original French edition, 1956.)

Lofland, J. *Doomsday Cult: A Study of Conversion, Proselytization and Maintenance of Faith* (enlarged ed.). New York: Irvington, 1977. (Original edition, 1966.)

Lowe, W.L. 'Psychodynamics of Religious Delusions and Hallucinations.' *American Journal of Psychotherapy*, 1953, *7*, 454–462.

Lubin, A.J. 'A Boy's View of Jesus.' *Psychoanalytic Study of the Child*, 1959, *14*, 155–168.

Ludwig, D.J., and Blank, T. 'Measurement of Religion as Perceptual Set.' *Journal for the Scientific Study of Religion*, 1969, *8*, 319–321.

Ludwig, D.J., Weber, T., and Iben, D. 'Letters to God: A Study of Children's Religious Concepts.' *Journal of Psychology and Theology*, 1974, *2*, 31–35.

Mallory, M.M. *Christian Mysticism: Transcending Techniques; A Theological Reflection on the Empirical Testing of the Teaching of St. John of the Cross.* Assen: Van Gorcum, 1977.

Mann, U. *Einführung in die Religionspsychologie.* Darmstadt: Wissenschaftliche Buchgesellschaft, 1973.

Maslow, A.H. *Religions, Values, and Peak-Experiences.* Columbus: Ohio State University Press, 1964.

McDowell, V.H. *Re-creating: The Experience of Life-Change and Religion.* Boston: Beacon Press, 1978.

Meerwein, F. 'Neuere Überlegungen zur psychoanalytischen Religionspsychologie.' *Zeitschrift für psychosomatische Medizin und Psychoanalyse*, 1971, *17*, 363–380.

Meissner, W.W. *Annotated Bibliography in Religion and Psychology.* New York: Academy of Religion and Mental Health, 1961.

Milanesi, G., and Aletti, M. *Psicologia della religione.* Torino: Elle Di Ci, 1973.

Moore, T.W. 'James Hillman: Psychology With Soul.' *Religious Studies Review*, 1980, *6*, 278–285.

Müller-Pozzi, H. *Psychologie des Glaubens. Versuch einer Verhältnisbestimmung von Theologie und Psychologie.* München: Kaiser-Grünewald, 1975.

Nase, E., and Scharfenberg, J. (eds.). *Psychoanalyse und Religion.* Darmstadt: Wissenschaftliche Buchgesellschaft, 1977.

O'Flaherty, W.D. *Women, Androgynes, and Other Mythical Beasts.* Chicago: University of Chicago Press, 1980.

Otto, R. *The Idea of the Holy; An Inquiry into the Non-Rational Factor in the Idea of the Divine and Its Relation to the Rational.* Trans. J.W. Harvey. London: Oxford University Press, 1923; 2nd ed., 1950. (First German edition, 1917.)

Pahnke, W.N. 'Drugs and Mysticism.' *International Journal of Parapsychology*, 1966, *8*, 295–314.

Pfennigsdorf, D.E. *Der religiöse Wille. Ein Beitrag zum psychologischen Verständnis des Christentums und seiner praktischen Aufgaben* (2nd ed.). Leipzig: Deichert, 1927.

Philp, H.L. *Freud and Religious Belief.* London: Rockliff, 1956.

Philp, H.L. *Jung and the Problem of Evil.* London: Rockliff, 1958.

Pöll, W. *Religionspsychologie; Formen der religiösen Kenntnisnahme.* München: Kösel, 1965.

Pöll, W. *Das religiöse Erlebnis und seine Strukturen.* München: Kösel, 1974.

Pohier, J.-M. *Au nom du Père...; Recherches théologiques et psychanalytiques.* Paris: Les Éditions du Cerf, 1972.

Pratt, J.B. *The Psychology of Religious Belief.* New York: Macmillan, 1907.

Preuss, H.G. *Illusion und Wirklichkeit; An den Grenzen von Religion und Psychoanalyse.* Stuttgart: Ernst Klett, 1971.

Pruyser, P.W. *A Dynamic Psychology of Religion.* New York: Harper and Row, 1968.

Rajamanickam, M. *A Psychological Study of Religious and Related Attitudes of the Student and Professional Groups in South India.* Annamalainagar, Tamilnadu: Annamalai University, 1976.

Randall, R.L. 'Religious Ideation of a Narcissistically Disturbed Individual.' *Journal of Pastoral Care,* 1976, *30,* 35–45.

Rapaport, D. 'The Structure of Psychoanalytic Theory: A Systematizing Attempt.' In S. Koch (ed.), *Psychology: A Study of a Science,* vol. 3. *Formulations of the Person and the Social Context.* New York: McGraw-Hill, 1959, 55–183.

Ricoeur, P. *Freud and Philosophy; An Essay on Interpretation.* Trans. D. Savage. New Haven: Yale University Press, 1970. (Original French edition, 1965.)

Rizzuto, A.-M. *The Birth of the Living God: A Psychoanalytic Study.* Chicago: University of Chicago Press, 1979.

Rochedieu, E. *Personnalité et vie religieuse chez l'adolescent; Étude de psychologie religieuse.* Neuchâtel: Delachaux et Niestlé, 1962.

Rokeach, M. *The Three Christs of Ypsilanti; A Psychological Study.* New York: Alfred A. Knopf, 1964.

Rulla, L.M., Imoda, F., and Ridick, Sr., J. *Structure psychologique et vocation.* Rome: Presses de l'Université Grégorienne, 1978.

Scharfenberg, J. *Sigmund Freud und seine Religionskritik als Herausforderung für den christlichen Glauben.* Göttingen: Vandenhoeck und Ruprecht, 1968.

Scharfenberg, J. *Religion zwischen Wahn und Wirklichkeit; gesammelte Beiträge zur Korrelation von Theologie und Psychoanalyse.* Hamburg: Furche, 1972.

Schaub, E.L. The Psychology of Religion in America During the Past Quarter-Century. *Journal of Religion,* 1926, *6,* 113–134.

Scheler, M. *On the Eternal in Man.* Trans. B. Noble. New York: Harper and Row, 1960. (First German edition, 1921.)

Schmid, L. *Religiöse Erleben unserer Jugend. Eine religionspsychologische Untersuchung.* Zollikon: Evangelischer Verlag, 1960.

Schüttler, G. *Die letzten Tibetischen Orakelpriester: Psychiatrisch-neurologische Aspekte.* Wiesbaden: Franz Steiner, 1971.

Schüttler, G. *Die Erleuchtung im Zen-Buddhismus. Gespräche mit Zen-Meistern und psychopathologische Analyse.* Freiburg: Karl Alber, 1974.

Scobie, G.E.W. 'The Psychology of Religion: A Religious Revival?' *Bulletin of the British Psychological Society,* 1977, *30,* 142–144.

Shaw, M.E., and Wright, J.M. *Scales for the Measurement of Attitudes.* New York: McGraw-Hill, 1967.

Shostrom, E.L. *Personal Orientation Inventory: An Inventory for the Measurement of Self-Actualization*. San Diego: Educational and Industrial Testing Service, 1966.

Sierksma, F. *Phaenomenologie der religie en complexe psychologie*. Assen: Van Gorcum, 1950. [Also published as *Freud, Jung en de religie*, 1951.]

Sierksma, F. *De religieuze projectie; Ene antropologische en psychologische studie over de projectie-verschijnselen in de godsdiensten*. Delft: Gaade, 1956.

Siwek, P. *The Riddle of Konnersreuth; A Psychological and Religious Study*. Trans. I. McCormick. Milwaukee: Bruce, 1953. (French edition, 1950.)

Smith, W.C. 'Comparative Religion: Whither—and Why?' In M. Eliade and J.M. Kitagawa (eds.), *The History of Religions; Essays in Methodology*. Chicago: University of Chicago Press, 1959, 31–58.

Smith, W.C. *The Meaning and End of Religion; A New Approach to the Religious Traditions of Mankind*. New York: Macmillan, 1963.

Smith, W.C. 'A Human View of Truth.' *Studies in Religion*, 1971, *1*, 6–24.

Spiegel, Y. (ed.). *Psychoanalytische Interpretationen biblischer Texte*. München: Chr. Kaiser, 1972.

Spiegel, Y. (ed.). *Doppeldeutlich, Tiefendimensionen biblischer Texte*. München: Chr. Kaiser, 1978.

Spranger, E. *Psychologie des Jugendalters*. Leipzig: Quelle und Meyer, 1924.

Spranger, E. *Types of Men; The Psychology and Ethics of Personality*. Trans. P.J.W. Pigors. Halle: Max Niemeyer, 1928. (Trans. of the 5th German edition of *Lebensformen*, 1925.)

Stählin, W. 'Die Verwendung von Fragebogen in der Religionspsychologie.' *Zeitschrift für Religionspsychologie*, 1912, *5*, 394–408.

Standards for Educational and Psychological Tests. Washington, D.C.: American Psychological Association, 1974.

Stern, W. *General Psychology from the Personalistic Standpoint*. Trans. H.D. Spoerl. New York: Macmillan, 1938. (Original German edition, 1935.)

Stratton, G.M. *Psychology of the Religious Life*. London: George Allen and Unwin, 1911.

Strommen, M.P. (ed.). *Research on Religious Development: A Comprehensive Handbook*. New York: Hawthorn, 1971.

Sundén, H. *Die Religion und die Rollen. Eine psychologische Untersuchung der Frömmigkeit*. Berlin: Alfred Töpelmann, 1966. (Original Swedish edition, 1959.)

Tart, C.T. (ed.). *Altered States of Consciousness: A Book of Readings*. New York: John Wiley and Sons, 1969.

Tauxe, H.C. *Freud et le besoin religieux*. Lausanne: L'Age d'homme, 1974.

TeVault, R.K., Forbes, G.B., and Gromoll, H.F. 'Trustfulness and Suspiciousness as a Function of Liberal or Conservative Church Membership: A Field Experiment.' *Journal of Psychology*, 1971, *79*, 163–164.

Thun, T. *Die Religion des Kindes* (2nd ed.). Stuttgart: Ernst Klett, 1964. (First edition, 1959.)

Thun, T. *Die religiöse Entscheidung der Jugend*. Stuttgart: Ernst Klett, 1963.

Thun, T. *Das religiöse Schicksal des alten Menschen.* Stuttgart: Ernst Klett, 1969.

Traxel, W. *Über Gegenstand und Methode der Psychologie.* Bern: Hans Huber, 1968.

Trillhaas, W. *Die innere Welt; Religionspsychologie.* München: Chr. Kaiser, 1953.

Vande Kemp, H. 'Teaching Psychology/Religion in the Seventies: Monoply or Cooperation? *Teaching of Psychology,* 1976, *3,* 15–18.

van der Leeuw, G. 'Ueber einige neuere Ergebnisse der psychologischen Forschung und ihre Anwendung auf die Geschichte, insonderheit der Religionsgeschichte.' *Studi e materiali di storia della religioni,* 1926, *2,* 1–43.

van de Winckel, E. *De l'inconscient a Dieu; ascèse chrétienne et psychologie de C.G. Jung.* Paris: Editions Montaigne, 1959.

Vergote, A., et al. 'Psychologie de la Religion/Psychology of Religion.' *Social Compass,* 1972, *19,* No. 3.

Vergote, A., and Tamayo, A. (eds.). *The Parental Figures and the Representation of God; A Psychological and Cross-Cultural Study.* The Hague: Mouton, 1981.

Vetö, L. 'Bedeutung und Grenzen der experimentellen Methode in der Religionspsychologie.' *Archiv für Religionspsychologie,* 1971, *10,* 275–285.

Vetter, G.B. *Magic and Religion; Their Psychological Nature, Origin, and Function.* New York: Philosophical Library, 1958.

Vetter, G.B., and Green, M. 'Personality and Group Factors in the Making of Atheists.' *Journal of Abnormal and Social Psychology,* 1932, *27,* 179–194.

Walther, G. *Phänomenologie der Mystik* (3rd ed.). Olten: Walter, 1976. [First edition, 1923.]

Watson, L.C. 'Understanding a Life History as a Subjective Document: Hermeneutical and Phenomenological Perspectives.' *Ethos,* 1976, *4,* 95–131.

Wehr, G. *Wege zu religiöser Erfahrung; Analytische Psychologie im Dienste der Bibelauslegung; Eine Anregung.* Darmstadt: Wissenschaftliche Buchgesellschaft, 1974.

Weitbrecht, H.J. *Beiträge zur Religionspsychopathologie, insbesondere zur Psychopathologie der Bekehrung.* Heidelberg: Scherer, 1948.

Wobbermin, G. 'Die Methoden der religionspsychologischen Arbeit.' In E. Abderhalden (ed.), *Handbuch der biologischen Arbeitsmethoden,* Abt. 6, Teil C/1. Berlin: Urban und Schwarzenberg, 1928, 1–44.

Wood, W.W. *Culture and Personality Aspects of the Pentecostal Holiness Religion.* The Hague: Mouton, 1965.

Wundt, W. *Mythus und Religion* (3 vols., 2nd ed.). Constitutes vols. 4–6 of *Völkerpsychologie: Eine Untersuchung der Entwicklungsgesetze von Sprache, Mythus und Sitte.* Leipzig: Alfred Kröner, 1910–1915. (First edition, 1905–1909.)

Yinger, J.M. 'A Comparative Study of the Substructures of Religion.' *Journal for the Scientific Study of Religion,* 1977, *16,* 67–86.

Young, K. 'The Psychology of Hymns.' *Journal of Abnormal and Social Psychology,* 1926, *20,* 391–406.

Zährnt, H. (ed.). *Jesus und Freud; ein Symposion von Psychoanalytikern und Theologen.* München: Piper, 1972.

Sociological Approaches

GÜNTER KEHRER AND BERT HARDIN

The Founding Fathers

The sociological theories of religion that were typical of the discussion after World War II cannot be reduced to any one dominant approach. In 1964 Talcott Parsons wrote that the main theoretical developments in the sociology of religion had been due to the work of Pareto, Durkheim, Weber, and Malinowski (1964: 197–211). Although, with the exception of Malinowski, the contributions from these authors had occurred before 1918, it can be said without exaggeration that their writings dominated the changes in sociological thinking that took place in the period between the two world wars. It was not only Parsons's 'voluntaristic bias' that led to a high estimation of post-positivistic (or post-Spencerian) sociology. There was also a general shift in the moral, political, religious, and philosophical reasoning that served as a frame of reference for modern sociology. Modern sociology was less interested in the so-called objective trends in the evolution of society and culture, and more interested in the subjective motives and aims of the actors. *Lebensphilosophie* and existentialism were the philosophical expressions of this development, the roots of which dated back to the end of the nineteenth century (cf. Simmel 1912). In this context a very different understanding of religion from that of the 'classical' fathers of sociology became necessary. Comte, Spencer, and Marx had paralleled religion more or less with the past and science with the future although they did have a more favourable attitude toward religion than, for instance, Voltaire, Condorcet, or Holbach. Thus, in some respects, they were not the direct successors of the radical Enlightenment. The generation that included Durkheim, Weber, Pareto, and Malinowski was even less influenced by the philosophy of the Enlightenment. It is not our task to speculate about the social origins of voluntaristic thinking, it is more important for our purpose of describing the present situation of the sociology of religion to draw attention to the fact that there is at least one point that the two generations had in common. It was the problem of order, or to state it in different terms: how can societies be integrated? The same problem (which can, of course, be traced back to the thinking of Machiavelli and Hobbes—if not Aristotle) has become the most prominent theoretical issue for the modern sociology of religion.

It is a very rarely discussed fact that the most important scholars in the field of the sociology of religion—Pareto, Durkheim, Weber, and Malinowski—did not spend their time in systematically exploring the situation of religion in modern societies. They were interested either in the religious life of existing tribal societies (Durkheim, Malinowski), in the role of religion in the history of European societies (Weber), or in the non-logical components of social action (Pareto). Essentially the same limitations had been found in the work of the founders of sociology (Comte, Spencer) but the conclusions their successors drew were totally different. Whereas Comte and Spencer had sought 'functional equivalents' for religion which could fulfil the same integrating functions that religion had had in less differentiated societies, Durkheim postulated that this function is always fulfilled by religion, although the religion of modern societies will have some new features compared with the religion of the past. Pareto and Malinowski (with Weber it is not clear) seemed to believe that religion cannot be replaced at all. Despite these differences it is evident that the founders of modern sociological thinking about religion formulated their theories out of generalizations drawn from non-modern societies. This cannot be explained exclusively by the role of historical thinking before 1918; it seems to be a consequence of an underlying belief that religion had its best time in the past. This belief corresponds to the fact that all four of these men were personally agnostics (cf. Savramis 1968: 39).

Thus it is at least questionable whether the theoretical findings of Durkheim or Malinowski can be used as explanations for the role of religion in modern societies. It is, in any case, impossible to make use of their concepts for theological thinking. The Christian religion which had served as an integrating factor had lost this function by the process of what can be called an 'intellectual' secularisation. The Christian explanations of the world and of life were no longer valid for the majority of the populations in modern societies. There was no doubt for Durkheim and others that the religion necessary for the society of the future was not the Christian religion, indeed Durkheim believed that 'memorial days' celebrating great national events would replace Christian holidays. However, our primary interest is not with the sociology of religion of the famous 1890 to 1920 generation. Instead, some of its features have been mentioned in order to point out a logical problem which prevails even up to the most recent sociological reasonings about religion. On the one hand, sociology (in itself a recent science) is mainly interested in theories about modern societies. In fact, general theory is only useful when it helps towards an understanding of the conditions of modern society. On the other hand, in the attempt to be as broad as possible sociologists must contend with phenomena which also existed in earlier societies, often in other forms. In the case of religion this means that general theory must annihilate important traits of modern self-understanding in regard to religion. This is due, at least in part, to problems with the universe of discourse in the sociology of religion. Concepts which are shared in the general universe of discourse in a linguistic sense are not shared in the ideational sense (see Hardin 1977: 113–116). Although this will occur in every science, in sociology it leads to many misunderstandings because, in general, sociologists are not inclined to use words in a strictly nominalistic sense. We shall show later that a good deal of discussion in the sociology of religion can be reduced to this problem.

After 1945 it seemed evident that the sociology of religion could not be done in the Spencerian way. As Parsons put it, in a famous sentence, 'Spencer is dead' (1942). The dominance of the so-called voluntaristic sociology was not debated. This means that—given the situation of the supremacy of American sociology—the European traditions of Weber,

Durkheim, etc. came back to Europe disguised in Parsonsian sociology. There can be no doubt that after 1945 European sociologists, for the most part, looked to America. However, there were at least two European developments in the sociology of religion of consequence for this time which date back to the pre-war period. The first of these was the phenomenological approach, and the second was *la sociologie religieuse.*

The phenomenological sociology of religion can be analyzed as a combination of the phenomenology of religion and formal sociology. In fact, it is sometimes difficult to distinguish between the sociological approach and that of the religious-phenomenological. The main traditions are to be found in Dutch and German liberal theology. The most prominent theologians who developed a phenomenology of religion are G. van der Leeuw (1933, enlarged 1956, translated 1938) and Rudolf Otto (1919, original 1917). In formal sociology the works of Georg Simmel (1923) and Leopold von Wiese (1955) serve as excellent examples.

The combination of these two traditions is most clearly expressed in Joachim Wach's *Sociology of Religion.* Although it was originally published in America and only later translated into German, it is a thoroughly continental book (1944, German translation 1951). Its German counterpart is Gustav Mensching's *Religionssoziologie* first published in 1947. Wach and Mensching, who were, of course, influenced by Weber, were mostly interested in general patterns of religion. The material from which they drew their conclusions was found in the history of religion, mostly of Greek and Roman origin, and in the descriptions of ethnographers. As far as we can see this kind of sociology of religion did not find any successors in Europe or America. There are, however, many ways in which the modern sociological analysis of religion is influenced by these authors. There are also connections between the phenomenological study of religion and the beginning of voluntaristic sociology. Thus discussion of the typologies of religious bodies (the famous church-sect typology which up to recent times was one of the most debated issues in the sociology of religion) can be found in the works of Max Weber and Ernst Troeltsch (1912) and later in the works of Joachim Wach and Gustav Mensching.

The increased interest in small religious groups (which has never ceased in Great Britain—see Wilson, 1961, 1963) has presented occasions to make use of some of the concepts developed by scholars of the 'phenomenological school.'

Sociologie religieuse was only partly guided by academic interests. It has become common to date this kind of sociology of religion back to Gabriel Le Bras and Fernand Boulard (cf. Le Bras 1955/56 and 1956). Even if this is correct in some respects, it must be noted that there were some predecessors in the nineteenth and twentieth centuries, e.g., Godin and Daniel (1943) and Boulard, Achard, and Emerard (1945). Church organizations were always interested in collecting data about the religious life of their adherents, and about the effectiveness of the mission of the church. Gabriel Le Bras tried to give these ecclesiastical interests a more scientific basis. This meant, first of all, using a historical perspective in analyzing the data about church attendance, baptisms, etc. Before Le Bras it was very common to use concepts such as industrialization, secularization, and urbanization in a simple way to explain the low figures in ecclesiastical statistics. Despite some shortcomings in *sociologie religieuse* it should be mentioned that it was Le Bras who drew attention to the fact that differences in religious behaviour between the regions of France were very old and could in some cases be traced back to the time of Louis XIV. Although Le Bras did little to connect his findings with theoretical approaches in the sociology of religion, it is not difficult to see a resemblance in his work to Max Weber's 'sociology of religion' in the well known seventh paragraph of chapter 5 in *Wirtschaft und Gesellschaft* (1956). Le Bras was more interested in scientific historical research and was less occupied with equipping the ecclesiastical administrations with data.

The reason why church officials—Catholic and Protestant—were suddenly eager to have sociological support in doing their jobs lay only partly in the characteristics of *sociologie religieuse*. To a much greater extent it was due to the general change in the relationship between administrations and the social sciences. The most interesting case is that of industrial sociology. This change was caused by the apolitical attitude of post-war sociology, and the attempts of administrative élites (political, economic, and ecclesiastical) to make use of the techniques and data of the social sciences to aid in decision-making or to legitimate decisions. It can easily be shown that *sociologie religieuse* had its strongholds in the Catholic countries of Europe. This is due to two reasons. First, religious behaviour is better defined in the Catholic church than in the Protestant churches, thus it is easier to develop research techniques for exploring the religiosity of Catholics, or at least it seems to be easier. Second, the authorities of the Catholic church are in a better position to use sociological findings than their Protestant colleagues because normally the legitimation for their authority is independent of the effectiveness of their work. Nowadays no sociologist would admit that he or she belongs to the school of *sociologie religieuse*.

Whereas the phenomenological sociology of religion was only of academic interest, *sociologie religieuse* did have political and ecclesiastical relevance. The situation of the modern sociological analysis of religion can only be understood as a reaction against this *sociologie religieuse*. However, there are limitations which must be placed on the preceding statement, i.e., it holds true for continental Europe, it is only partly true for Great Britain, and it is even less true for the USA. We shall see that one of the few authors who has become prominent in Europe *and* America, Thomas Luckmann, developed his theory of religion, in the beginning, as a critique of *sociologie religieuse*.

Structural-Functionalism

We said earlier that American sociology of religion in the 1950s was Parsonsian sociology. This is particularly true if one regards the great theoretical approaches. However, empirical research work was only partly directed by structural-functional theory. In many cases the old discussion of church-sect typology prevailed, and there were various attempts to prove or to refute the Weber-thesis. The relevance of the structural-functional understanding of religion cannot be denied, because this approach became one of the most important theoretical schemes for the sociological discussion of religion. Therefore it must be presented here at some length.

During Parsons's whole academic life he was interested in religious phenomena. He wrote many papers which fall into the field of religion, yet the space reserved for the discussion of religion in his main contribution to sociology, the *Social System* (1951), is very limited. Only in chapters 5 and 8 did Parsons write in any detail about the functions of religion for the social system. The contribution in chapter 8 is a more systematic discussion of what he had said in the paper 'The Role of Ideas in Social Action' (1938). According to Parsons, religion has two main functions for the maintenance of the social system. First, it gives cognitive meaning to the moral-evaluative sentiments and norms of an action system; second, religion serves to balance out the frustrating discrepancies between the results of action which can be legitimately expected, and the results which can be observed in reality. These two functions are not independent of each other.

There seem to be at least two main problems involved in the structural-functional approach to the sociology of religion. The first problem concerns the role of older approaches within this theory. The second problem concerns the question: what kind(s) of society, and consequently what kind(s) of religion, must be supposed in order to formulate such a theory? We shall present Parsons's theory of religion in such a way that it enables us to discuss these problems.

With Parsons's first function mentioned above, the point in question is 'the cognitive definition of the situation for action as a whole, including the catechetic and evaluative levels of interest in the situation.' Parsons discusses this point with reference to a supernatural order distinguished in some sense from the natural and moral orders of things. Although this supernatural order is separated from the more empirical and moral orders, it is by no means meaningless for them. On the contrary, it serves as a point of reference when such questions are to be answered as why the natural order is what it is, and why we should obey the moral obligations of the moral order. Thus, the concept of order on earth seems understandable when there is also a heavenly order. Parsons cannot overlook the fact that there are only a few societies and a few religions which have developed an order of the supernatural. There may even be cases where the difference between natural and supernatural order cannot be found (Parsons mentions the case of communist societies). In other words: the problem of the universality of religion—

in a logical, not a purely empirical sense—is under discussion. Since Parsons intends to work out a general frame of reference for the understanding of all possible societies, and since religion plays an important role in this frame of reference, he must insist on the logical universality of religion, and, consequently, on the logical universality of the difference between the two orders of things. The possibility of doing this lies for Parsons in the conviction that one can distinguish between things that are scientifically knowable and things that are not knowable in this sense. It is not very difficult to show that Parsons follows here the standards of positivistic epistemology which were only rarely attacked in the first half of this century (1951: 359–63; Adorno et al. 1969). As we stated above, Parsons wanted to overcome the shortcomings of a positivistic sociology that could see in religion only residuals of pre-scientific thinking. However, Parsons is in one important respect a successor to this positivistic thinking, at least in methodology.

The second function of religion, as discussed by Parsons, is that of 'explaining' the discrepancies between what an actor can expect from doing 'good,' e.g., well-being, and the actual result of action. Parsons points to two perennial problems in this context, namely the problem of (premature) death, and the problem of undeserved suffering. These problems refer to the age-old theological and philosophical issue of theodicy. Parsons appears to believe that these problems are universal in a twofold sense: First, that the phenomena of premature death and suffering, though not usually explainable in terms of immoral behaviour, nevertheless exist; and second, that these phenomena need an explanation that goes beyond the realm of scientific and empirical thought. Since Parsons defines religious belief systems as being non-empirical and evaluative, it is evident that every explanation which transcends empirical *and* cognitive (descriptive) thinking is by definition a religious one. The question is, however, whether the problems of this kind of theodicy are universal in the sense of Parsons's theory. We would suggest that it is helpful to relate these problems to a particular stage in the development of religion. The question of theodicy can only occur when there is a very close connection between religion and ethics. It is by no means sure that this connection is universal. It seems more plausible to assume that this kind of 'moral religion' is a very recent product in the history of religion. Events need explanation, some events need more explanation than others, but not every explanation that transcends the average amount of 'theory' is a religious one. But even when the concept of religion is very broad, it is unlikely that the problem of undeserved suffering will be articulated without the frame of reference of an ethical religion. Rather, it is more likely that the problems of suffering and death will be solved by seeking the person who is responsible for them, for example in terms of witchcraft. Parsons relies too much upon the belief systems of the great world religions, particularly upon the Christian belief system in its Protestant form. Within this belief system the moral problem of undeserved suffering (including that of premature death) is very crucial.

It is interesting to see that Parsons' view of religion can also be upheld when the general theory of society moves to evolutionary concepts. In *Societies: Evolutionary and Comparative Perspectives* (1966) Parsons wrote that the legitimation system of every society is 'always related to, and meaningfully dependent on, a grounding in ordered relations to ultimate reality. That is, its grounding is always in some sense religious.' The legitimation system defines the interrelations between a society and a cultural system. Further, even in primitive societies there are at least four analytically defined components of the societal system: religion, kinship, technology, and symbolic communication—the so-called evolutionary universals in society.

It is impossible in this context to refer to every author who has formulated his sociology of religion in accordance with Parsons. We shall mention only two examples: Kingsley Davis's *Human Society* (1948) and Elisabeth K. Nottingham's *Religion and Society* (1954). (See also Nottingham 1971, Goode 1951, Hoult 1958, Schreuder 1962, Lundberg et al. 1963, Goldschmidt and Matthes 1962). Kingsley Davis states frankly: 'So universal, permanent, and pervasive is religion in human society that unless we understand it thoroughly we shall fail to understand society.' Davis postulates at the very beginning of his discussion what should be the result of a careful investigation, i.e., that there is only one theory of religion which is not outmoded, the functional one. 'In making scientific sense of nonscientific belief and practice in explaining religion, myth, magic, and ritual, there has been one trend of social

theory more successful than the rest. This is the functional-structural type of sociological analysis....' The main function of religion is its unique and indispensable contribution to social integration. Four things are most important in this respect. Religion provides:
(1) a justification of the primacy of a group's ends; (2) a constant renewal of common sentiments; (3) a concrete reference for a group's values; and, (4) a source of reward and punishment for conduct.

This theory was very much influenced by Émile Durkheim, whom Davis considers to be one of the most prominent authors in structural-functional sociology. Integration means for Davis the dominance of common ends over private ends, or to state it in another way: how is it that individuals with competing ends and wishes are able to work together and fulfil tasks necessary for the achievement of group ends? This is the problem of order which was the starting-point for the sociological thinking of Auguste Comte. It is the same problem that Thomas Hobbes tried to solve in purely political terms. It can be shown that there is a close relationship between the concept of politics and that of religion in social theory. This relationship is as follows: the more the coercion aspect or the power aspect in politics is dominant, the less important is the role ascribed to religion. Since every consensus-theory of politics needs a field where the consensus must be fixed, it is more than plausible to seek this field in a realm that transcends the empirical world. Although measurement of the degrees of integration seems to be difficult, one can assume that societies have different degrees of integration. However integration is necessary, i.e., a group (a society) must share certain values in common. The sharedness of values and goals needs a non-rationalistic explanation, a religious one. Only a society that had no shared values and goals would need no religion, but such a society could not exist. Davis seems to suppose that, despite the fact of the logical universality of religion, the process of social development from small isolated societies to complex urbanized ones (Davis cannot speak of evolution as the structural-functional theorists did some 15 years later) will weaken the role of religion though it can never disappear. This process of weakening the function of religion is called secularization. The question for Davis is 'how far can secularization go?'. The extreme end of the secularization process would be social disorder. In this state of affairs it is likely that new religious sects will arise. It can happen that one of these sects will prevail and give rise to a new religiously legitimated order or integration. Davis draws our attention to the origin of early Christianity. It would seem, according to Davis, that there is merely a circulation of religion and that secularization could only mean the decline of one religious synthesis and the rise of another one. Usually, however, secularization implies a much broader field of debate, particularly the decline of supernatural thinking in the modern world. Therefore, the question is whether 'the religion of the future may dispense with the supernatural.' Davis answers this question by differentiating the concept of the 'supernatural' into two. The first conceives of a spiritual world peopled by anthropomorphic imagination, and the second consists of beliefs which transcend experience. The second case of the 'supernatural' will never disappear. Davis refers to concepts such as the master race, manifest destiny, progress, democracy, the classless state, etc., as being ideas, whereas Parsons would prefer to classify these ideas as ideologies which can serve as functional equivalents for religion. Thus, Kingsley Davis seems more inclined to have a broader theory of religion.

Elisabeth K. Nottingham discusses the problem of whether or not the modern movements of nationalism, socialism, fascism, and communism should be included in the category of religion. Nottingham stresses the fact that the answer to this question is dependent on one's definition of religion. She uses a very broad—or inclusive—definition and classifies these movements as non-supernatural or secular religions. One can question whether it makes much sense to coin such a concept as 'non-supernatural religion.' This apparent contradiction seems to be reasonable if one considers that the structural-functional theorists do not use the concepts in the old scholastic manner. Words are defined in a 'functional' way; this means that all phenomena that fulfil the same function can be classified under the same heading. It is arbitrary what name is given to it. This procedure seems rather plausible, if the words are used in a purely nominalistic sense. Although most functionalists would pretend to do this, it is questionable whether a nominalistic usage of words can be successful in sociology where every object of research is named by words which have descriptive and prescriptive meanings in ordinary language (see Hare 1967). The unfruitful discussions about 'the' definition of religion, namely the debate between the adherents of an inclusive and an exclusive definition, can never be decided, because both parties have a totally different starting point. Whereas an inclusive definition makes sense only in a functional frame of reference, an exclusive definition is interesting in the comparative analysis of religious phenomena. It is not possible to decide one way or the other which is heuristically more fruitful for the sociology of religion. The main problem with an inclusive definition of religion is that one must label very different things with the same word when these things fulfil the same function. To do this is not a necessary condition for a functional analysis of society.

Conflict theory and evolutionary schemes

As Ralf Dahrendorf (1957, 1967) and later on—in the field of sociology of religion—J. Milton Yinger said (1970), functionalism is very much interested in harmony (integration), but only to a very small degree in conflict. One might speculate whether functionalist sociology laid so much stress on religion because religion integrates society, or whether the functionalist theory leads to a view of religion as an integrative power. Yinger is right when he says, 'there is little by way of research based on a conflict perspective' (1970: 92; see also 1946). Some sociologists see a difference in the sociological theory of religion between theories of integration and theories of change. We believe, however, that this difference is only a minor one, though, of course, theories which emphasize the normality of change place less stress upon the importance of integration. Though social conflict is seen by Dahrendorf as the main cause of social change, there is no necessary connection between theories of change and those of conflict. The famous Weber-thesis explains social and cultural change, but nevertheless it is one of the main witnesses for functional theory. Talcott Parsons demonstrates, by use of the Weber-thesis, the importance of the role of ideas in social action.

The main difference is between an integration theory of religion and a possible theory based on conflict. Although it might seem that Marxian sociology would produce a conflict theory of religion, the very few remarks of Marx relating to religion point to integration rather than to conflict. The reason for religion is to comfort those who live under inhuman conditions. Although religion is for Marx in some way 'protest' against misery, it is first of all the destruction of religion (or the critique of religion) that enables the oppressed to revolt against the real cause of their situation. Genuine Marxism is not interested in religion, because the task of criticizing religion had been done by the philosophers of the radical enlightenment (see Marx and Engels 1958, Marx 1958: 378ff). We shall see later that the so-called neo-Marxist interest in religion is more influenced by existentialism than by Marxism. Thus the question is still open. Is a sociological theory of religion possible which is based on the concept of conflict?

Another point which is no less important is the problem of development, or the concept of evolution. In the years between the two world wars, evolutionary sociology seemed to be completely dead. Parsons's statement in 1937 that 'Spencer is dead' meant also the end of evolutionary thinking. The breakdown of conceptions of evolution in social thinking is without any reasonable doubt a result of the loss of faith in the supremacy of European culture. Whereas in the nineteenth century this faith had prevailed, the emergence of existential beliefs in the twentieth century led to a kind of philosophical and political thinking which saw every culture as unique and not simply a stage in an inevitable process of evolution. Some fifteen years after the second world war we can see the rebirth of evolutionary approaches in the social sciences. The reasons for the emergence of this neo-evolutionism are complex and cannot be reduced to one cause. Keeping this reservation in mind, we believe that interest in the problems of the so-called underdeveloped countries led to reflections about the reasons for underdevelopment, and the forces that are favourable to modernization. Robert N. Bellah was the first prominent sociologist to speak of 'religious evolution' (in 1964, we cite from Birnbaum and Lenzer, 1969: 67–83). Bellah started his career as a sociologist with an analysis of the role of Japanese religion in the modernization process of Japan during the Tokugawa period (1957). At first glance this seems nothing else than a transfer of the

Weber-thesis to the Far East, but this view implies also the conception of an autonomous development of religion (see also 1970, 1975).

The main feature that serves as a key to Bellah's evolutionary scheme is the emergence of religious rejection of the world. Interestingly enough, this emergence is observed not only in the formation of the great empires of Asia but also in the smaller one of Greece. Bellah points out the role of literacy and the role of religious organization at the stage of the 'historic religions' which are the carriers of world rejection. This had not been found earlier in 'primitive religion' or in 'archaic religion,' nor can it be found in the so-called 'modern religion' of the present. The stage of 'early modern religion' serves as a 'missing-link' between historic and modern religion. Bellah draws a line from the stage where 'church and society are one' (primitive religion) through the stage where religion denied the world and in some form society, to the modern world where, despite the fact of religious pluralism, religions offer the opportunity for 'creative innovations in every sphere of human action.' Thus modern culture and modern society, which do not rest on rejection of the world, could only come into existence when the original identity of religion and society was dissolved by the world-rejection of the historic religions. It is nearly impossible to prove the adequacy of Bellah's evolutionary scheme with data from the history of religions. We believe that one of the major problems with Bellah's approach lies in his theoretical insistence on the rather elaborate belief systems of religions. It cannot be denied that in the first millenium BC theological and philosophical thinking—as far as it has been transferred to us—is highly world-rejecting. It must be seen, however, that we possess only the works of religious and/or philosophical specialists who elaborated ideas about the relationship of soul and body, and the possible salvation of the soul. These ideas have in many cases a very real basis in the role of intellectuals in societies. The exclusion of intellectuals from political power and economic wealth—as can easily be shown in the cases of Plato and the priests of ancient Israel during and partly after the exile—leads very often to the path of other-worldly fulfilment.

This perspective is a sociological one, because it links belief systems with the social conditions of the élites who produce the beliefs. We do not want to deny the possibility that religious belief systems have an autonomous power for development. We want to say, however, that a belief system—whether religious, political, or aesthetic—cannot exist without a social carrier (see Borhek and Curtis 1975). It may be possible that in tribal societies the whole society functions as a carrier for a religious belief system, though some elementary forms of religious specialization can be observed in many primitive societies. Since the emergence of religious specialists can be seen as a part of a process of division of labour, it seems necessary to regard developments in religion as being in close relationship with the development of other parts of the societal system. Bellah lays too much stress on religion as such. The reason for this strategy of isolating religion from society as a whole lies in over-emphasizing some ideas of Durkheim and Weber, and neglecting some principles of Marxian social thought, namely that man produces his religion, and that first of all, before producing religion, man has to eat, etc. Thus the way that man obtains food, clothing, shelter, etc., will be of some importance for his religion. This aspect was not new and was never contested. Durkheim and Weber were more interested in another aspect of religion. Whereas Durkheim emphasized the role of religion in integrating society, Weber seemed to develop a theory which showed that religion is a phenomenon *sui generis* which influenced economic and social evolution rather than being influenced by the general development. We would point out, however, that this understanding of Weber is too narrow, and it is too much based on his famous essay on the 'Protestant Ethic.' Some paragraphs of his more systematic sociology of religion in *Wirtschaft und Gesellschaft* look more like a Marxist sociology. This holds true particularly for his conception of the affinity between social classes and some kinds of religious belief systems. Although shifts in religious thinking can occur very easily, the main question remains open: why are some new religious ideas successful and some not? It may be expected that Marxist sociologists will try to find answers to this question.

Marxism, Neo-Marxism, and the Frankfurt-school

The main contribution of Marxists to a sociology of religion should lie in an analysis of existing religious belief systems in order to find out which social groups express their social needs in these belief systems. To some extent there could be a convergence with the findings of the sociology of religion regarding all kinds of crisis-cults. As far as we can see Marxist sociologists are only very rarely interested in the phenomena of religion. In the German Democratic Republic there have been a few attempts to develop a Marxist sociology of religion. These attempts are rather orthodox and primarily try to explain why religion can still be found in socialist countries (Klohr, ed., 1966; Klohr and Klügl 1966). At the same time the so-called neo-Marxism in Czechoslovakia, and in some countries of Western Europe, started a 'dialogue' with left-wing Catholics and Protestants (Kellner, ed., 1966; Stöhr, ed., 1966, Gardavsky 1968, Metz and Rahner, eds., 1966, etc.). This dialogue is, on the one hand, a result of the 'opening' of the Catholic church and communist regimes. On the other hand, it was the common experience of communists and revolutionary theologians in South America that led to a revision of the mutual anathemas. Despite the partial political success of this dialogue, its results for a sociology of religion were poor. Even the most prominent neo-Marxist author in the field of religion, V. Gardavsky, speaks, more or less, about the fundamental functions which religion fulfils and which are dependent on the inherent nature of man. It is quite understandable that this kind of thinking about religion was of great importance for the socialist countries, because the factual denial of all problems of personal suffering was thus attacked. To point out the relevance of religion for human existence means at the same time to lay stress on neglected phenomena of life. The outcome for a more sophisticated sociology of religion in western countries cannot be appreciated in this way. Most of what the neo-Marxists say about religion is not very different from that which is now common-place in functional sociology. Thus the scientific contribution of Marxist sociology is still to be made.

Even the conceptions of religion of the so-called 'Frankfurt-school' of sociology are not of any great interest (Horkheimer in Schatz, ed., 1971: 113–19; Habermas and Negt in Bahr, ed., 1975, Geyer et al. 1970). After 1965 Max Horkheimer became more and more involved in debates about religion and the possible future of religion, but his remarks reflect a more or less pessimistic view of the future development of society and mankind. Since Horkheimer believed that the importance of the individual will diminish, and since he saw the main article of Christian faith as being the importance of the individual as an *imago Dei*, he argued for an alliance between religion and humanist forces in the western world. It is not so much the conception of the counselling function of religion in regard to suffering and death that Horkheimer pointed out, but the promise of a future without suffering, without power, without injustice. This promise is the eschatological part of the Judeo-Christian religious tradition that became politically relevant in the years after 1965 when certain factions of the Christian Churches allied with rebellious youth. In these years some attempts were made to overcome the 'conservative' bias of the functionalist theory of religion. It is interesting to see that the most important theorist of the Frankfurt School, Jürgen Habermas, speaks only very rarely about religion. Many theologians, however, believe that 'dialectical' sociology has some affinity to the kind of theological thinking they prefer. Whereas Adorno saw in the Christian religion of the twentieth century a form of totally neutralized religion that serves primarily as an agent in the process of building false consciousness (1950: 728–38), Habermas said in 1971 that he could imagine that it might be possible for us not to do away with theologians, in that the necessity for theologians lies in their contribution to reflection about the conditions that are necessary for the dignity of man. Habermas thinks primarily of the relevance of exemplary actions, which can often be found in small religious groups, and which have something to do with a kind of witnessing by doing. This conception is, of course, a political one; but the differentiation between sociological, political, and philosophical conceptions is an illegitimate distinction for the adherents of the Frankfurt School.

As far as we can see there has been only one attempt to use the conceptions of the Frankfurt School for a study in the field of the sociology of religion. Even this attempt is only to a certain degree typical of dialectical sociology. In 1973 Rainer Döbert published an essay about 'The Development of Religious Systems:—The Limits of the Frame of Reference of System-Theory.' This can only be understood as part of the controversy between Jürgen Habermas and Niklas Luhmann about 'system-theory' or 'critical theory of society' (Habermas and Luhmann 1971; Maciejewski, ed., 1973, 1974). Döbert wants to show that Luhmann's system-theory cannot adequately explain the stages of religious evolution. Although Döbert is not primarily interested in developing a theory of religious evolution, he points out some reasons for this evolution. He believes that religious development can be understood as a 'manifestation of the unfolding of the competence of communication.' This idea is in line with the general conception of Habermas that communication free of power implications (*herrschaftsfreie Kommunikation*) is the only way of proving scientific and/or moral assumptions. Thus the situation of modern religion, where ethics prevail over dogmatics, and where individuals communicate in an atmosphere of guaranteed freedom of religion, is a model for the desired state in all fields of human action. Since the evolution of religion with its most important stages (which are essentially the same as Bellah's stages) is nothing other than an 'augmentation of a more reflexive form of control of behaviour,' there must be a trend in universal history towards a diminishing of authoritarian control in favour of control by communication and reflection. This trend could only be fulfilled when societies were successful in solving the problems of basic needs. Thus we can see in Döbert's essay a very interesting combination of Marxist thought with some thinking in American sociology. More interesting, however, is the combination of Marxist thought with ideas of moral philosophy, which, however, cannot be discussed in this context.

System Theory

The influence of American sociology can be seen in another sociological theory of religion that has been discussed at least in Germany. Niklas Luhmann's general sociology, the so-called system theory, is in many aspects influenced by structural-functional sociology. Whereas structural-functional thought is part of a general theory of action, Luhmann's general thought belongs to theories that try to explain the emergence or maintenance of system within given environments. Luhmann believes that the categories he introduces in his analysis are able to explain all kinds of social phenomena, including religion (1977). The function of religion is mainly to transform the indeterminable world (environment and system) into a determinable one. Parsons defined religion as a system within the social system that relates society to its ultimate reality. Luhmann's concept is even 'more' functional. According to Luhmann, religion is not necessarily a social system. In many societies (particularly in tribal ones) there is not enough differentiation for a religious system. However, the function of religion is universal. This function is not primarily to stabilize the order of society, but to make it possible for society, as a system, to exist. To explain this approach it is necessary to unfold the basic ideas of Luhmann at some length. One of his central categories is that of complexity. Every environment is complex, this means that many choices—at least more than one—are possible. Vis-à-vis this kind of amorphous environment the act of choosing one possibility and neglecting others is of crucial importance, for this means that complexity is reduced. In terms of Luhmann's theory it is more correct to say that the function of systems is to reduce complexity. Without systems there is no reduction of complexity. This reduction, however, has its own problems, because the choice of alternatives is by no means evident, i.e., it is always possible to choose otherwise. This is the problem of contingency, as it is called by Luhmann. The degree of contingency is itself dependent upon the degree of internal complexity in a society. Societies which are simply segmented may offer only one possibility. Thus the reduction of complexity produces an increasing of contingency which must be determined. Therefore, it is possible to state that the transformation of the indeterminable world into a determinable one is the same as the transformation of indetermined complexity into determined complexity, i.e., to find a formula for ever-existing contingency. 'God' is such a formula of contingency. The problem of contingency is, in some respects, identical with the older problems of undeserved suffering which were discussed by the sociologists of the structural-functional school.

It is also possible to incorporate evolutionary approaches within Luhmann's system theory. He defined evolution, in accordance with Spencer's conception, as a process of differentiation. This means, first of all, that new systems emerge within society. One of these systems is the religious one. Although the function of religion is universal and independent from the stages of evolutionary process, some special problems theologians—and Berger—attacked the societal basis of modern Christian religion. Modern Christianity, they said, was not founded on the teachings of the New Testament, but on the teachings of a secularized social gospel. Sociology of religion serves as a critique of religion; the same function that theology has. The beginning of Berger's sociology of religion is a critique of the church rather than an analysis of the churches. The conceptions used in this critique are theological ones. On the other hand, Luckmann was not influenced by theological thinking. He started his 'career' as a sociologist of religion with a critique of the sociology of religion as it existed in the two decades after 1945, particularly *sociologie religieuse*. Luckmann confronted this school with the great traditions of the sociology of religion of Max Weber and Émile Durkheim. Whereas these authors saw in religion the core of society itself, so that sociology of religion was general sociology, modern *sociologie religieuse* used a very narrow conception of religion which was in fact reduced to some easily observable religious practices, such as church-going, which cannot be regarded as the relevant religious phenomena. Berger's and Luckmann's essays in sociology of religion have been used sometimes as specimens for a sociological critique of the theory of secularization. This usage is superficial, because both authors are very much interested in the change that religion undergoes in modern industrial society. Berger makes use of the word 'secularization' without any hesitation, whereas Luckmann is cautious to avoid any identification with the meaning of 'secularization' as a loss of religion (cf. Lübbe 1965; Martin 1969, 1978). Luckmann is one of the first sociologists to have such a broad definition of religion that many phenomena fall under this category. The point is not whether the so-called secular 'religions,' namely ideologies, particularly political ones, should be summarized as religions, but to find a definition of religion that enables one to have a common name for things that seem to be different, but are really the same. It is evident that this definition can only be a functional one. Thus Luckmann is the most radical fighter for a purely functional definition of religion. His definition is rather simple. Religion is the process of transcending the individual existence of man in a structural meaning, which is, in most cases, a culturally given system of meaning. It can hardly be denied that in every society human existence is shaped by giving transcendent meaning to a mass of 'isolated' facts. In other words, religion can be handled as being equivalent to socialization. Luckmann says that this definition is a direct consequence of Durkheim's sociology of religion, and in some respects this seems to be true. One might think of Durkheim's notions about the future of religion in modern societies. We believe, however, that Luckmann's definition is even broader than Durkheim's. What then are the reasons for such a broad definition of religion? Partly it can be explained by the shortcomings of *sociologie religieuse*. In concentrating on the observable facts of religious behaviour as they were shaped by the norms of the churches and other religious bodies, the authors of this school overlooked the possibility that new forms of religious life might arise in modern society. *Sociologie religieuse* confronted the traditional forms of religious life with so-called secular trends. Thus interests focussed on individualism, or sexuality, or familism were considered not only to be opposed to certain Christian teachings, but also to be against religion in general. The consequence was that modern society was labelled irreligious. It is not difficult to disclaim the procedures chosen by the sociologists of *sociologie religieuse*. They identified one form of religion with religion in general, the result being that the decline of this form was identical with the decline of all religion. This narrow definition of religion was guided by ecclesiastical interests rather than by sociological intentions. If one compares the situation of sociology in the fifties with the works of Max Weber and Émile Durkheim, it is quite understandable that Luckmann demanded a reorientation of the sociology of religion which would start with a more adequate definition of religion. *Sociologie religieuse* narrowed religion to some features of religious practice; Luckmann widened religion to include the constituent phenomena of society in general. Thus sociology of religion could only move between the Scylla of the loss of religion in modern society, and the Charybdis of a state where there is nothing more important than religion. There is no time now to continue discussing Luckmann's concept of religion at length. However it must be admitted that Luckmann's definition proved its usefulness in at least one case, namely in explaining the shifts in the relationship between society and religion. Although Luckmann does not elaborate an evolutionary scheme, he is able to show that some stages in societal development—archaic societies, great civilizations, modern societies—correspond very closely with specific forms of the institutionalization of religion. In archaic societies, the structured cosmos of meaning is very closely knit with the biographies of the individuals living in these societies, and societies in the stage of the great civilizations tend to be differentiated in such a way that religion became an institution and sometimes an organization on its own. The existing churches of our own age are residuals of this period. In modern societies the specialized forms of religion that were typical of the period of great civilizations still exist, but they must compete with emerging religions which can have political forms (ideologies), or a more private form (cults of the individual, and subjectivistic philosophies), etc. These systems of meaning are normally not organized or specialized in distinguishable bodies or organizations. The difference between the situation of religion in modern societies and that in archaic societies is to be found primarily in the fact that the new belief systems are extremely pluralistic. This has the consequence that systems of meanings are not obligatory for every member of society or for every situation. This pluralistic situation leads to an attitude vis-à-vis systems of meaning which is comparable to the situation of a buyer in a supermarket. He or she can choose between different offerings of merchandise, and the goods, once chosen, have no compulsory consequences for the next choice. If this analysis holds true, it is indeed not a very good prospect to do research in the field of ecclesiastically defined religious activities in order to find out what the state of religion in modern societies may be. Although Luckmann believes that some forms of specialized religion will survive in the future and consequently the importance of the churches will only very slowly diminish, one may expect elements of the new religions to amalgamate with elements of specialized religion. This process of amalgamation can be understood as secularization when one is ready to limit the concept of secularization to what happens to specialized religion.

Peter Berger's approach to the sociology of religion is not very different from Luckmann's. As mentioned above Berger prefers a more exclusive definition of religion. In addition to this, Berger seems to have a concept that identifies religion with *sacralized* nomos and this is not fully identical with the system of meaning which constitutes religion according to Luckmann. 'Nomos' is the attempt of man to struggle against the meaninglessness of the world. Because man tends to establish the meaning crystallized in nomos for the entire world, there is always the tendency to connect nomos and cosmos into one entity. It seems evident that Berger could test this approach with examples from tribal societies. It is less likely for modern societies to have such a sacralized nomos linked with a meaningful cosmos. Thus the category of secularization can be adequate for an understanding of the religious situation in modern societies. A more exclusive definition of religion, that would understand religion as the cosmos to which meaning is ascribed by the nomos, prevents a view that sees religion everywhere in society. The 'plausibility structure' which connects cosmos and nomos is not easily found in modern society. Religion is not the core of society itself, but one side of the dialectic between society and religion. It follows from this view that religion can lose its importance in the course of societal evolution. This loss of importance can take place in several ways. One of the most common forms is the total adaptation of religion to society. The earlier books of Berger laid stress on this point. Another very important way in which religion can lose its relevance is by the segregation of religion into discrete institutions within which religion becomes encapsulated. The possibility of influencing the world (including society) outside religious institutions thereby becomes diminished. It would seem that Berger is pessimistic about the future of religion in modern societies. But he believes that the supernatural—which is in some way identical to religion—cannot entirely vanish from the earth. Traces of the supernatural can be found in phenomena that at first glance seem to have little in common with religion in its more traditional understanding. For example the shelter a mother gives to her child when it awakes in the night, the laughter of a clown, etc., are all phenomena which show that man is not completely a victim of the outer world, but that he can overcome this world by his action. It seems to us that Berger enlarges his understanding of religion by these remarks, and that it goes in the direction of Luckmann's definition.

Most recent development and final theses

One of the most recent sociological approaches to religion is the attempt to use the concept of identity for the understanding of religion. The concept of identity has been of great use to psychologists and sociologists, and has served in some cases even for analyzing the individual religious career of some "hero" in the history of religion. An attempt to bring together all these scattered sketches was done by Hans Mol in 1976 (see also 1978). Mol starts with the dialectic between differentiation and identity. Identity is necessary for every kind of existence (individual, group, and societal), and it is always challenged by the likewise inevitable process of differentiation and adaptation. Mol relates religion to the identity side of this dialectic. This does not mean that religion is always on the 'conservative' side of the struggle, because the religiously defined identity of groups can be a source of great societal changes. The most important aspect is, in our opinion, Mol's differentiation between the foci of identity. It can be questioned whether the differentiation between individuals, groups, and societies is sufficient, but even if this were not the case Mol can show that some problems in the field of the sociology of religion may be solved when one considers that the foci of identity are not the same. Thus sacralized group identity can be disfunctional in regard to the identity of a society as a whole. The discussion between the adherents of different definitions of religion could also be ended by Mol's approach. The advantages of Mol's conception lie primarily in the possibility of reinterpreting the findings of studies which were guided by other theories of religion. It is still an open question as to whether it will be possible to inaugurate research following the outline of an identity theory of religion. Because Mol intends to incorporate a sociological understanding of sacralized identity into a much broader frame of reference that can serve as a formula for understanding nearly all the phenomena of life, it is difficult for him to avoid the the pitfall of explaining too much by one theory.

This attempt to give an impression of modern sociological approaches to religion is, of course, subjective, and we do not claim that everybody will accept it. We feel, however, that the most important approaches are mentioned and briefly discussed. We have not tried to give a survey of the findings of empirical research, even though the more sophisticated approaches are not independent of this research. Likewise we have neglected the whole field of anthropological approaches which, particularly in Great Britain and the USA, cannot be separated from sociological theories without difficulty. We have discussed only briefly the problem of secularization which was nevertheless one of the most fruitful and also one of the most important concepts about religion in this century. Further we do not think that the old problem of the typology of religious organizations earns much interest at present, although we do not deny that very much intelligent work has been done in this field. It is primarily shortage of space that has led to the omission of theories which try to explain the several waves of religious 'revival.' The most recent event in this area is the emergence of new cults in the Western hemisphere.

Keeping in mind all of these reservations, one might ask if there are any final fruits in the sociology of religion emerging in the post-1945 period. What is the contribution that sociologists have made toward a better understanding of religion? We believe that these questions can be answered by some theses with which most sociologists of religion might agree:

(1) Modern sociological approaches to the study of religion have shown that religion cannot be understood as an extra-social phenomenon which will diminish in the course of societal evolution.

(2) It has become evident that there must be differentiation between the social function of religion on the one hand and religious belief systems and religious institutions on the other. This differentiation which was sometimes neglected is very important because the two aspects relate to very different social phenomena which must be explained by theories of different ranges.

(3) The question of whether religion is an inevitable part of social life is still open. Since this question belongs to the problem of the definition of religion, the answer will always be arbitrary.

(4) Some old problems have not been solved; it can be shown, however, that they must be redefined in order to obtain a more scientific perspective. For example, this holds true for the question of secularization. After the structural-functional approach it became very

common to ask the old—sometimes theological—questions in a new manner.

(5) Attempts are being made to incorporate the sociology of religion into general sociology. The reason for these attempts lies partly in the situation of the sociology of religion immediately after 1945. As this situation no longer exists, it is unnecessary to fight for a scientific independence which is not seriously denied.

(6) At this time there is no dominating sociological theory of religion. This reflects the situation of sociology in general.

Bibliography

Adorno, Theodor W. et al. *The Authoritarian Personality*, Harper, New York, 1950.

Adorno, Theodor W. et al. *Der Positivismusstreit in der deutschen Soziologie*, Luchterhand, Neuwied-Berlin, 1969.

Bahr, Hans-Eckehard ed. *Religionsgespräche. Zur gesellschaftlichen Rolle der Religion*, Luchterhand, Darmstadt-Neuwied, 1975.

Bellah, Robert N. *Tokugawa Religion*, Free Press, Glencoe, 1957.

— *Beyond Belief. Essays on Religion in a Post-traditional World*, Harper and Row, New York, 1970.

— *The Broken Covenant: American Civil Religion in Time of Trial*, Seabury Press, New York, 1975.

Berger, Peter L. *The Noise of Solemn Assemblies*, Doubleday, Garden City, 1961.

— *The Precarious Vision*, Doubleday, Garden City, 1961.

— *The Sacred Canopy: Elements of a Sociological Theory of Religion*, Doubleday, Garden City, 1967.

— *A Rumor of Angels: Modern Society and the Rediscovery of the Supernatural*, Doubleday, Garden City, 1969.

Berger, Peter L. and Thomas Luckmann *The Social Construction of Reality: A Treatise in the Sociology of Knowledge*, Doubleday, Garden City, 1969.

Birnbaum, Norman and Gertrud Lenzer *Sociology of Religion. A Book of Readings* Prentice-Hall, Englewood Cliffs, N.J., 1969.

Borhek, James T. and Richard F. Curtis *A Sociology of Belief*, Wiley, New York, 1975.

Boulard, F., A. Achard, and H.J. Emerard *Problemes Missionnaires de la France Rurale*, 2 vols., Paris 1945.

Dahrendorf, Ralf *Soziale Klassen und Klassenkonflikt in der industriellen Gesellschaft*, Enke, Stuttgart, 1957.
— *Pfade aus Utopia. Arbeiten zur Theorie und Methode der Soziologie*, Piper, Munich, 1967.
Davis, Kingsley *Human Society*, Macmillan, New York, 1948.
Döbert, Rainer *Systemtheorie und die Entwicklung religiöser Deutungssysteme*, Suhrkamp, Frankfurt, 1973.
Durkheim, Émile *Les Formes Elémentaires de la Vie Religieuse*, Alcan Paris, 1912.
Dux, Günter 'Ursprung, Funktion und Gehalt der Religion', in *International Yearbook for the Sociology of Religion*, Westdeutscher, Opladen, 1973, 7–62.
Gardavsky, Vitezslav *Gott ist nicht ganz tot. Betrachtungen eines Marxisten über Bibel, Religion und Atheismus*, Kaiser, München, 1968.
Geyer, H.G., H.N. Janowski, and A. Schmidt *Theologie und Soziologie*, Kreuz, Stuttgart, 1970.
Godin, H., Y. Daniel *La France, Pays de Mission?*, Lyon, 1943.
Goldschmidt, D. and J. Matthes (eds.) *Probleme der Religionssoziologie*, West-deutscher, Köln und Opladen, 1962.
Goode, William J. *Religion among the Primitives*, Free Press, Glencoe, 1951.
Habermas, Jürgen and Niklas Luhmann *Theorie der Gesellschaft oder Sozialtechnologie*, Suhrkamp, Frankfurt, 1971.
Hahn, Alois *Religion und der Verlust der Sinngebung. Identitätsprobleme in der modernen Gesellschaft*, Herder and Herder, Frankfurt/New York, 1974.
Hardin, Bert *The Professionalization of Sociology. A Comparative Study: Germany -U.S.A.*, Campus, Frankfurt/New York, 1977.
Hare, Richard M. *The Language of Morals*, Oxford University Press, Oxford, 1967.
Hill, Michael *A Sociology of Religion*, Heinemann, London, 1973.
Hoult, Thomas F. *The Sociology of Religion*, Dryden, New York, 1958.
Kellner, Erich ed. *Christentum und Marxismus—heute. Gespräche der Paulusgesellschaft*, Europa, Vienna, 1966.
Klohr, Olaf ed. *Religion und Atheismus heute. Ergebnisse und Aufgaben marxistischer Religionssoziologie*, VEB Deutscher Verlag der Wissenschaft, Berlin, 1966.
Klohr, Olaf and J. Klügl *Grundriss der marxistischen Soziologie der Religion*, VEB Deutscher Verlag der Wissenschaft, Berlin, 1966.
Le Bras, Gabriel *Études de Sociologie Religieuse* 2 vol., Presse Univ. de Paris, Paris 1955/56.
— "Sociologie Religieuse et Science des Religions", in: *Archives de Sociologie des Religions*, 1956, (1): 3–18.
Leeuw, Gerardus van der *Phänomenologie der Religion*, Mohr, Tübingen, 1956.
— *Religion in Essence and Manifestation. A Study in Phenomenology*, Turner, London, 1938.
Lenski, Gerhard *The Religious Factor*, New York, 1963 (3d ed.).
Luckmann, Thomas *Das Problem der Religion in der modernen Gesellschaft*, Rombach, Freiburg, 1963.
— *The Invisible Religion*, Macmillan, New York, 1967.
— "Sammelbesprechung zur Religionszoziologie", in: *Kölner Zeitschrift für Soziologie und Sozialpsychologie*, 1960 (12): 315–326.

Lübbe, Hermann *Säkularisierung. Geschichte eines ideenpolitischen Begriffs*, Freiburg-München, 1965.

Luhmann, Niklas *Funktion der Religion*, Suhrkamp, Frankfurt, 1977.

Lundberg, George A. Clarence C. Schrag, and Otto N. Larsen, *Sociology*, Harper and Row, New York, Evanston, London, 1963 (3d ed.).

Maciejewski, Franz ed. *Theorie der Gesellschaft oder Sozialtechnologie Supplement 1 und 2*, Suhrkamp, Frankfurt, 1973 und 1974.

Martin, David *The Religious and the Secular*, Routledge and Kegan Paul, London, 1969.

— *A General Theory of Secularization*, Blackwell, Oxford, 1978.

Marx, Karl 'Zur Kritik der Hegelschen Rechtsphilosophie', in *Marx-Engels-Werke (MEW)*, Bd. 1, Berlin, 1958.

Marx, Karl and Friedrich Engels *Über Religion*, Dietz, Berlin, 1958.

Mensching, Gustav *Soziologie der Religion*, Ludwig Röhrscheid, Bonn, 1947.

Metz, Johann Baptist and Karl Rahner, eds. *Der Dialog oder ändert sich das Verhältnis zwischen Katholizismus und Marxismus?*, Rowohlt, Reinbek, 1966.

Mol, Hans *Identity and the Sacred*, Blackwell, Oxford, 1976.

Mol, Hans ed. *Identity and Religion*, Sage Publications, London, 1978.

Nottingham, Elizabeth K. *Religion and Society*, Random House, New York, 1954.

— *Religion. A Sociological View*, Random House, New York, 1971.

Otto, Rudolph *Das Heilige*, Trewendt und Granier, Breslau, 1919 (3d ed.).

Parsons, Talcott *The Structure of Social Action*, Free Press, Glencoe, 1949 (2d ed.).

— *The Social System*, Free Press, Glencoe, 1951.

— *Essays in Sociological Theory*, Free Press, Glencoe, 1964.

— *Societies. Evolutionary and Comparative Perspective*, Prentice-Hall, Englewood Cliffs, N.J., 1966.

Savramis, Demosthenes *Religionssoziologie*, Nymphenburger Verlagshandlung, München, 1968.

Schatz, Oskar ed. *Hat die Religion Zukunft?*, Verlag Styria, Graz, Wien, Köln, 1971.

Schreuder, Osmund *Kirche im Vorort*, Herder, Freiburg, 1962.

Simmel, Georg *Die Religion*, Hütten und Löning, Frankfurt, 1912 (2d ed.).

— *Soziologie. Untersuchungen über die Formen der Vergesellschaftung*, Duncker und Humblot, München und Leipzig, 1923 (3d ed.).

Stark, Rodney and Charles Y. Glock *The American Piety: The Nature of Religious Commitment*, Univ. of Calif, Press, Berkeley, Los Angeles, London, 1970 (2d ed.).

Stöhr, Martin ed. *Disputation zwischen Christen und Marxisten*, Kaiser, München, 1966.

Troeltsch, Ernst *Die Soziallehren der christlichen Kirchen und Gruppen*, Mohr, Tübingen, 1912.

Wach, Joachim *Sociology of Religion*, Univ. of Chicago Press, Chicago, 1944.

Weber, Max *Wirtschaft und Gesellschaft*, 2 vol., Mohr, Tübingen, 1956 (3d ed.).

Wiese, Leopold von *System der allgemeinen Soziologie als Lehre von den sozialen Prozessen und den sozialen Gebilden der Menschen*, Duncker and Humblot, Berlin, 1955 (3d ed.).

Wilson, Bryan R. *Sects and Society*, Heinemann, London, 1961.

— "Typologie des Sectes dans une Perspective Dynamique et Comparative", in: *Archives de Sociologie des Religions*, 1963 (16): 49–63.
Yinger, J. Milton *The Scientific Study of Religion*, Macmillan, Toronto, London, 1970.
— *Religion, Society, and the Individual*, Macmillan, New York, 1957.
— *Religion in the Struggle for Power. A Study in the Sociology of Religion*, Duke Univ. Press, Durham, 1946.

Cultural Anthropological Approaches

JARICH OOSTEN

Overcoming ethnocentrism

The word religion is part of our common vocabulary and as a consequence most people assume that they know fairly well what religion is
about. They use the word in their conversation and when someone else
uses the word they usually understand what it means. Many people have
even developed private theories about the nature and origin of religion
and a variety of these private theories exists in western culture. Some
people think that religion consists of a mistaken belief in beings that do
not exist, while other people believe that all religions are essentially the
same. Then we have people who think that all religions are inspired by
divine beings while others think that they were invented by primitive
man to protect himself from fear. These and similar notions are not very
helpful for the development of the anthropological study of religion.
They are usually not based on empirical research, but on a rather
ethnocentric perspective of religion. Since Christianity is the dominant
religion of western culture it is not surprising that these notions are
very much determined by this religion.

Christianity, however, is not an average religion. It is one of the great
religions of the world with a highly developed literary tradition. It has
also a strong missionary sense that was correlated to a negative appreciation of other religions. At first all other religions were considered as
inferior superstitions that had to be exterminated. In Europe

Christianity attained a monopoly position and only Jewish religion was to some extent allowed to exist. In the sixteenth and seventeenth century missionary activities contributed very much to the spread of European economic and political interests over the world. It was only in the eighteenth and nineteenth century that a serious interest in the great religions of the world began to awaken. The religions of non-literate people, however, were still considered as crude and primitive and this view was maintained by many students of religion until the middle of this century (cf. Frazer, Lévy-Bruhl, van der Leeuw, and others). In the course of this century the appreciation of these religions gradually changed and primitive religions were assessed as religions of non-literate peoples (Van Baaren 1964).

Thus it took western researchers a long time to overcome their ethnocentric biasses and to attain an attitude of basic respect for other religions. But we should take into account that these biasses are not only religious, but that they are deeply embedded in western culture as a whole. The superiority of western religion, western political institutions, western arts, etc. was never seriously doubted by most researchers and even now a majority of western people is deeply convinced of the immanent superiority of this civilisation and the ideological export of western religion, values, and knowledge is still a major issue in the relations between western countries and the third world.

The anthropologist is at the same time a member of his own culture and thus subject to its conditioning, and a scientist who attempts to transcend its limitations and to escape its conditionings. Ethnocentrism is not just a problem of the past but a structural impediment to our understanding of other cultures. We can only study other religions adequately if we are prepared to consider the limitations of our own perspective. Since the meaning of the word religion is very much determined by the significance of Christianity in western culture we have to examine this concept more closely before we can apply it to other cultures.

Christianity developed from Jewry and expanded in the Roman empire. While Jewish religion (like Islam) implied a social and political order of society, Christianity was in no position to challenge the social and political structures of the empire. A fundamental change in the order of the world was only to be expected at the end of time when the kingdom of heaven would descend. In the meantime, Christianity adapted to the social and political conditions of existence and developed a powerful organisation in the church. The Roman Catholic Church was an unique institution. No other religious organisation exercised so much power for such a long time. Although it could not prevent the rise of many new churches it maintained its powerful religious and political position until modern times.

The clear distinction between the religious and the political domain, the church and the state, was developed in the crucial stage of the formation of the Christian tradition. It was elaborated theologically (cf. St. Augustine, *De civitate dei*) and it has continued to dominate western culture until the present day. The notion that religion is an autonomous domain that should be separated from the political organisation of the state is generally accepted in western culture. As a consequence many researchers expected a similar situation in other cultures. Anthropological research, however, demonstrated that this is not the case. Both in the great religions of the world (cf. the *sharī'ah* in Islam, the caste system in India, for example) and in non-literate religions a strict distinction between the religious domain and other cultural domains is arbitrary and forced. But even in western culture it is predominantly an ideological value that does not prevent a close connection between both domains. Although the history of the churches or of the Christian dogmas was often presented as an autonomous development relatively independent of other cultural processes, it is quite clear that the history of these institutions was not only determined by their internal dynamics but also by economic and political interests.

The Christian church was the repository of classical culture in western culture until the Risorgimento, and for a long time scientific research and institutions were largely controlled by the church, which opposed all research that contradicted its religious traditions (consider the famous case of Galileo). But it could not prevent itself gradually losing control of scientific developments. Religious studies were a different matter. Here the churches maintained their control much longer. The Christian religion was usually taught in theological departments, faculties of divinity, etc. that were predominantly controlled by the churches.

When the study of other religions developed it was usually integrated into those theological studies and taught in the same institutions. Interest in other religions was often related to missionary activities. Students of religion who did not show sufficient respect for the Christian tradition could endanger their own position (cf. the case of Robertson Smith).

It was often maintained that only people who were religious themselves had sufficient affinity with their subject to study it adequately and this assumption was then often a means to maintain a monopoly of Christian scholars in these institutions. It was not surprising that a critical approach to religion could not flourish very well in these conditions.

These approaches developed in other departments like philosophy (Feuerbach, Marx, and others) and they also developed in the context of the study of social sciences like ethnology, sociology, psychology, etc. (cf. Freud, Durkheim, and many others).

Christian scholars usually considered Christianity as the highest of all religions and tended to measure all other religions by Christian standards, while psychologists, ethnologists, etc, tended to reduce religion to psychological or sociological categories implicitly or explicitly denying its divine origin (cf. Evans-Pritchard's discussion (1965) of those theories and Adam Kuper's assessment (1981) of Evans-Pritchard's own position in this respect).

Both positive and negative assessments of Christian religion deeply influenced the anthropological approach to religion. As long as religion is a crucial and controversial issue in western culture and in its relations with other cultures emotional involvement either positively or negatively is unavoidable. The anthropologist should at least try to become clear about this involvement and try to refrain from value judgments as much as possible. He should not be concerned with the falsity or truth of religion nor with its superiority or inferiority. His main concern is with understanding and explaining.

The anthropological study of religion is in many ways similar to the study of language. No language is false or true, inferior or superior. Each language can be considered as an independent design of the world. First of all the student of language has to learn a particular language.

Once he has a thorough knowledge of it he can attempt to translate it into his own language and to examine its structure in his own terminology. He should be aware that the terminology he uses is not an objective scientific apparatus that transcends the limits of all cultures. It is determined by the history of his own culture.

In the same way the student of religion should become familiar with the religion he is studying before he attempts to translate it into terms of his own culture. Translations easily imply distortions. When we state that the Muslims believe in Allah or the Inuit in Nuliajuk we seem to indicate a similar relation between participants and a divine being, but this is not the case. The word belief in Christianity expresses notions of faith, self surrender, love, etc. while the Inuit consider Nuliajuk as a dangerous spirit that can be controlled by able shamans. We should acknowledge that the relation between Nuliajuk and the Inuit is completely different from that between Christians and God.

The anthropological study of religion is a process of confrontation, translation, and communication. Different cultural perspectives meet in anthropological research: the perspective of the anthropologist and that of the participants. The anthropologist should examine both perspectives and the ways they determine each other. He can never escape the obstacles of ethnocentrism completely, since he is irrevocably conditioned by his own culture, but he should reflect on his own perspective as a methodical requirement of all anthropological research. This implies a careful consideration of his own terminology.

The problem of defining religion

The meaning of the word religion does not cause many problems in ordinary language, because it allows for various interpretations. Everybody can have his own ideas and association when he uses the word. The test of an adequate understanding of the concept in daily use does not consist of a definition of the concept, but of a correct use of the word in various situations. The word religion is best considered as a family resemblance in the sense that this concept was developed by the philosopher Wittgenstein. It refers to a set of complex phenomena. Each of these phenomena shares some features with some other phenomena of this set, but it is not necessary that all phenomena share one particular feature that can be considered as their common essence. No generally accepted rule exists that decides which phenomena have to be included in this set and which have to be excluded.

Wittgenstein's notion of family resemblance helps us to understand how the word religion is used. The anthropologist is not only interested in the use of the concept in his own culture, but he wants to transform it into an analytical tool that can be applied to other cultures. Many definitions of religion have been proposed and none of them is generally accepted in anthropology. Usually different definitions stress different dimensions of religion. Geertz emphasized the cognitive level of religion when he defined religion as: (1) A system of symbols which acts to (2) establish powerful and longlasting moods and motivations in men by (3) formulating conceptions of a general order of existence and (4) clothing these conceptions with such an aura of factuality that (5) the moods and motivations seem uniquely realistic' (Geertz 1965: 4). Spiro on the other hand stressed the action level of religion when he defined religion as an 'institution consisting of culturally patterned interaction with culturally postulated superhuman beings' (1965: 96). Milton Yinger emphasized the significance of religion as a means to deal with ultimate problems: 'Religion then can be defined as a system of beliefs and practices by means of which a group of people struggles with these ultimate problems of life. It expresses their refusal to capitulate to death, to give up in the face of frustration, to allow hostility to tear apart their human associations' (1970: 7).

These three examples give some idea of the variety in religious definitions. Each definition approaches religion from a different angle and stresses a different aspect. As a consequence they are not contradictory. It is the angle from which one views religion that determines the kind of definition one arrives at.

The question: 'What is religion really?' is therefore meaningless. Many approaches to religion are possible and there is no reason to select one of them as the only correct approach. Sociologists, psychologists, anthropologists, all will approach religion from different angles. Here we will be mainly concerned with the anthropological study of religion.

An anthropological approach to the study of religion should be based on the general theoretical framework of cultural anthropology. The key concept then becomes culture. Religion, social organisation, political organisation, are all considered as aspects of culture by the anthropologist and as a consequence religion should be examined in the wider context of culture.

Religion as a cultural order

Many definitions of culture exist (cf. Kroeber and Kluckhohn 1952) but no general agreement is reached about them. The word culture is used on different levels of abstraction. It refers to the ways human beings order and shape their natural world in general, but it also refers to the ways particular peoples order and shape the world. We can speak of western culture, of Greek culture, of the culture of the Athenian nobility in the fourth century BC, etc. The anthropologist selects the level of abstraction that enables him to organise his data most fruitfully in the context of his research.

No human society can exist without order. Every culture can be considered as a particular way of ordering the world. The cultural order is expressed in various ways in different cultural dimensions: religion, art, social organisation, etc. According to Lévi-Strauss all dimensions of culture are determined by the same organising principles that constitute an order of orders (*'ordre des ordres'*), but it is not quite clear why this should be the case. It may be that human beings strive for a homogeneous and consistent cultural order but they will often be subjected to foreign laws, influenced by foreign cultural traditions, etc. An homogeneous and consistent cultural order will therefore usually not exist.

The cultural order determines the life of the participants: concepts, emotions, religious experiences are all shaped by the cultural order. Loss of face can lead to suicide in some cultures while it has few consequences in other cultures. Deep religious experiences are realised through celibacy and asceticism in some cultures and through orgies in others. Different cultural experiences entail different emotional and cognitive associations. The anthropologist who is studying other cultures has to become familiar with other ways of thinking, perceiving, feeling. A culture that attaches much value to visionary experiences will usually have ritual practices that enable their participants to have these visions. The nature of these experiences is clearly determined by the cultural framework. Thus a Christian will see the Virgin Mary or Jesus in a vision while a Buddhist may see a Boddhisattva. Although the cultural order shapes the life of the participants almost completely, it is arbitrary from a logical point of view. There are no intrinsic reasons why a monotheistic religion should be preferable to a polytheistic religion or a matrilineal social organisation to a patrilineal one. The participants are aware of this. They can think of alternative orders and they are often confronted with other people who behave differently and think differently without any serious consequences for themselves or their kinsmen. Therefore the participants need an adequate foundation for their cultural order to protect it from disorder. The rules of the cultural order should be respected by the participants and they should not be changed at random.

In every culture we find a set of beliefs, practices, institutions, that explains the origin and nature of the cultural order and preserves its existence. It is this set of beliefs, practices, institutions, that is usually qualified as religion by the anthropologist.

Religions usually involve belief in personal beings, but this is not necessarily the case (cf. classical Buddhism). It is the cultural domain that is considered to be most fundamental by the participants themselves. It gives significance to their existence and their world and it cannot be reduced to any other cultural order. Thus the nature and organisation of social organisation, political institutions and economic prerogative can be explained in myths, expressed in rituals and maintained by religious institutions. Gods, spirits, ancestors, or cosmic laws are thought to guard the cultural order, and transgressors of its rules are punished in this world or the next.

In many cases the notion of an all encompassing order is clearly expressed in a central religious concept (e.g., Indian Ṛta or Egyptian Maat). In other cases it is reflected in a system of religious laws (cf. Judaism and Islam). Religion does not only constitute the most fundamental order of the world in the perspective of the participants, but it deals also with discrepancies between ideal and reality. Myths explain the origin of suffering and evil, rituals provide means to restore the cosmic order, religious professionals admonish people to maintain the cosmic order. Thus religion is both the last and final order of the world and the means of overcoming transgressions of its rules.

The anthropologist does not have the same perspective concerning a cultural order as do participants in it. He may be convinced that economic or ecological conditions determine a cultural order, but he has to acknowledge that for participants their religion is fundamental. The anthropologist has interests and priorities other than those of the participants. He examines religious beliefs, practices, and institutions, and he will discover many different versions of the religion among the participants. Religion has often been identified with its interpretation by a religious or political élite, but each religion is constituted by a great variety of beliefs, practices, and institutions. Different versions are sometimes contradictory. What is considered as tenets of faith by one group of participants may be considered as superstition by another one. Different versions of a religion are usually related to other cultural differences such as power, status, wealth. These correlations are of great importance to the anthropologist in the explanation of different religious forms and variants. Unlike the participants he is not primarily interested in the truth of a particular interpretation, but he considers all forms of religion as variants that inform him about its structure. He examines these variants and he attempts to construct models that enable him to discover the rules that determine the relations between different variants of a religion in time and space.

Thus the anthropologist arrives at an order that is different from that of the participants. Although the perspective of the participants constitutes the point of departure of his analyses the anthropologist finally attempts to construct models that explain its order in terms of his own anthropological theory.

The division of culture into separate domains is a theoretical construction by the researcher. Most cultures do not have expressions for our concepts of religion, or politics. These words have significance in our own culture and in the context of anthropological theory.

The notion that religion can be considered as a cultural order implies a strategy of research that is directed towards the discovery of that order. Many sociologists and anthropologists have applied this approach to religion (Berger, Douglas, Geertz, Lévi-Strauss, for example). Religion is considered as a complex whole and no particular feature is selected as the most important distinguishing one (e.g., belief in gods, religious (inter) action).

The qualification of religion as a cultural order also implies that its nature is determined by its relative position towards other cultural orders. But although religion is related to these orders it can never be explained completely by its relations to them, since religion is at the same time a relatively autonomous domain with its own internal structure. Both the examination of this internal structure and its dynamics and the study of its relation to other cultural orders are necessary for an adequate understanding of the significance of religion in its cultural context.

Religion and other cultural orders

While other cultural orders should be based on religion the religious order itself cannot be reduced to any other cultural order. This raises major problems. How can the religious order give an adequate foundation to its own existence and validity? From a logical point of view this problem cannot be solved. It is like Baron von Munchhausen pulling himself upwards by his hair. How can any order justify its own existence without reference to another higher order? Nothing can be solved by a process of infinite progression that postulates always higher orders of existence. The participants are aware of this and the paradox is often clearly expressed in religion itself. A good example is given in the book of Job in the Old Testament. Job wants to call God to account for his sufferings, but God is not subject to any higher authority or rules. As a consequence Job has no alternative but to acknowledge God's universal power and this proves to be a satisfactory solution since Job is again well-endowed with worldly possessions. Many variants on this problem can be found in other religions in rituals that inverse the existing order of the world and myths that give a negative proof of the existing order.

Although other cultural orders are ideally founded in the religious order they have often a different structure and origin. Many traditions have contributed to the development of western culture. Jewish religion contributed to Christian religion, Greek religion to western philosophy and science, Roman law to many western codes of law, German social and political organisation to many western social and political institutions, for example. All these traditions merged into western civilisation in a complex process of acculturation. We cannot just assume that they all share the same basic structure. We have to examine how the participants consider different cultural orders to be related and how they are related in our own anthropological perspective.

The participants usually attempt to harmonize different cultural orders on a conceptual level. In many cases theological or ideological superstructures are created to reconcile apparently contradictory principles in different cultural orders. These superstructures become important factors in the process of cultural change.

The participants also attempt to harmonize their social behaviour, status and so on, with their religious convictions. In some cases they give only rationalizations that do not inform us about their real motives, but it also happens that they sometimes cause themselves economic and political hardships for the sake of their religion. Some people forsake their possessions for their religious convictions while others forsake their religious convictions for their possessions. It is impossible to establish an absolute causal priority of one particular cultural order over another one since the relations between them continuously vary. It is clear, however, that different cultural domains are closely related. Weber demonstrated in his well-known analysis of the relation between capitalism and Calvinism how religious and economic factors interacted in the development of capitalism in western Europe (Weber 1922). We usually find correlations between religious convictions and economic and political positions. Thus the poor will be more attracted towards messianistic movements that promise a new order of the world than the rich, who will tend to suppress these movements in order to defend the existing order of the world.

As social, political, economic, and other conditions of existence change in the course of time new questions have to be formulated and answered in the context of religion. If the religious order loses its close connections with other cultural orders which it has to explain, its existence becomes precarious. It becomes an abstract and irrelevant institution for the participants and it is easily replaced by a religion that is more relevant to their conditions of existence.

Religion is in an ambiguous position in another respect. It has to give significance to other cultural orders, but at the same time it participates in these orders as a political institution, an economic institution and so on. Religion cannot escape this ambiguity. In many of the world's religions we find traditions of protest against the wealth and power of the great religious institutions, but once these movements are institutionalized they tend to become sources of political and economic power themselves. The more their members practice poverty as individuals the greater the chance that these institutions accumulate capital as was the fate of many Christian and Buddhist monasteries that practised poverty.

The anthropological study of religion should examine how religion is determined by politics, economics etc. and how at the same time it shapes these cultural orders.

We have now discussed religion as a cultural order that gives significance to other dimensions of culture. But how is religion related to other cultural orders like philosophy, ideology, science, etc. that are often thought to play a similar part in human culture? How is religion related to concepts like magic, superstition, etc. that are usually associated with religion? It is time for some terminological distinctions.

Terminological distinctions

Religion occurs in all cultures while ideology, philosophy, science, etc, are usually confined to the great civilisations. In non-literate cultures we find speculations about the nature of the world and human life that we could qualify as ideological or philosophical but as a rule they do not give rise to philosophical traditions. Oral tradition is a suitable medium for the transmission of tales, lists, proverbs, etc. but it seems to be less suitable for philosophical and ideological speculation. It is only when writing becomes important that philosophical and ideological traditions can develop. In the great civilisations philosophical traditions emerged from religion. Indian philosophy developed from the reflections on religion by the Brahmins. In these philosophical traditions divine beings could be transformed into cosmic essences and atheistic philosophical and religious systems could arise (cf. Sāṇkhya, Buddhism). Similar developments occurred in Greece, China, and other great civilisations.

These philosophical traditions could to some extent substitute for religion. This was only possible when they did not confine themselves to the cognitive level, but also developed practices and institutions similar to those of religion. Since these practises involve some belief in their efficacy the philosophical systems that substituted for religion tended to be transformed into religions again. The founders of the systems were transformed into divine beings (Confucius, Buddha) and the systems themselves could be considered as philosophical and religious systems at the same time.

While religions are based on belief in the fundamental order that was instituted by gods, ancestors and spirits, philosophies usually assume that the understanding of the final order of the world can be gained by rational thinking. Buddhism stresses the importance of meditation that is thought to transcend rational discursive thinking and to prepare the mind for enlightenment.

The word ideology usually refers to the way people conceive of an ideal organisation of their society. Ideologies are usually thought to reflect the natural order of the world and they share with philosophies the notion that true understanding of the nature of the world can be gained by rational thinking. In western societies the great ideological systems developed predominantly from philosophy. In some cases ideologies constitute coherent well-thought-out systems and in other cases ideologies consist of a complex of loosely organised notions about the nature of society. Ideologies usually imply a strategy to realise the ideal state of society. Religions usually have an ideological dimension in the sense that many religious convictions reflect economic and political interests but religion covers a much larger range of problems than that of an ideal society (problems of life and death, the origin of human beings and their world, etc.) and is predominantly based on faith, as we have seen.

Western science also developed from philosophy. The historical opposition between religion and science has induced some people to
consider science as the most true perspective of reality. They think that
religion explains a lot of things that can be explained more satisfactorily
in scientific terms. But we should take into account that religious
explanations serve a different purpose. Religion explains the significance
of things for human beings while science is concerned with both theoretical knowledge for its own sake and its practical applications. Although
scientific explanations help us to understand and explain the order of the
world in theoretical terms they fail to explain its significance for mankind and it is therefore not surprising that science cannot replace
religion—not even in Aldous Huxley's 'brave new world,' where
science can only be supreme by being transformed into religion.

Religion, magic, and superstition are closely connected with each
other. Religion is usually associated with positive values, while those
beliefs and practices that do not seem to be compatible with these values
are usually considered as magic and superstition. The term magic refers
to beliefs and practices that are intended to induce certain effects by
ritual means: procuring of game, making of rain, etc. Magical practices
can be found in all religions. The difference between a rain ritual in
Southern Africa and a prayer for rain in a European church should not
be interpreted as a difference berween magic and religion. Both practices
are magical and derive their meaning from their religious context. The
traditional notion that magical man rules while religious man serves (cf.
van der Leeuw 1933) is an ethnocentric generalisation that is based on
Christian values. The general framework of magical practices is provided
by the religious order and every religion has a magical dimension to the
extent that it attempts to effect certain results by ritual means. Praying
and cursing, curing and bewitching are usually structurally related
techniques that use the same (or inverted) practices to effect opposite
results. In most cultures the distinction that counts is that between black
magic, directed against the interests of society and its members, and
white magic, furthering their interests. Magical practices are thought to
have some effect, but these effects are seldom interpreted in a simple
causal model. The effectiveness of the ritual depends on the moods of the
performer, the attitude and reactions of gods, spirits, ancestors, counter-

magic, etc. Rain rituals will be held in periods when there is some chance of rain and game rituals when the game is approaching. Magic is not irrational. The performer of magical practices decides on a suitable time, place, and situation and he is led by many rational considerations. In many cultures we find specialists who are professionals in magical practices and often they can perform both as white and as black magicians. Some magical practices are rejected while others are accepted and practised by the religious establishment, others again are discussed (cf. the ambiguous position of exorcism in many Christian churches).

The distinction between superstition and faith is also based on religious values. In some periods of western cultural history belief in witches was quite accepted, while it was considered as superstition in other periods. The great religions usually have an élite of religious professionals who decide what is to be considered as superstition and what is not. Their judgments may differ considerably from those of the layman. Gnomes, witches, werewolves are usually considered as supersition in the Christian religion and therefore not included in descriptions of that religion by the anthropologist. This has resulted in a rather artificial distinction between religion and folklore, that is usually not applied to other cultures, where similar beliefs are included in descriptions of their religion. The term superstition is better avoided by the anthropologist, since it often only expresses the value judgments of the participants. When he examines religion as religious order the anthropologist will often have to include many beliefs and practices in that order that are considered as superstition by some participants but not by others.

Literate and non-literate religions

The transformation from a non-literate religion to a literate religion has many implications for its structure and development. In literate cultures philosophies, ideologies, and sciences can develop and the position of the religion itself is changed considerably. When the art of writing is developed it is usually applied to preserve religious knowledge and wisdom, and many of the oldest written texts are of a religious nature. The great religions of the world are literate religions and they possess sacred texts that enable them to spread out into other cultures and yet preserve their unity.

Non-literate religions once were the universal type of religion, but they have gradually been replaced by the great religions of the world. This can to some extent be explained by the differences in the relation between culture and non-literate religions on one side and culture and literate religions on the other side. In order to examine these differences more closely we will now examine the general features of literate and non-literate religions.

Non-literate religions

Since there is no sacred book, the continuity and uniformity of the religion depends on oral traditions that are much more flexible than books. Oral traditions are often sacred and the mnemotechnical skill of the participants is usually considerable, but often political, economic, and other interests cause the participants to adapt their oral traditions and once they have done that the earlier versions are lost irrevocably.

Like a culture each religion consists of a set of variants. Inuit religion consists of the religion of Western, Central and Eastern Inuit. The religion of the Central Inuit consists of different variants of the Netsilik Inuit, the Iglulik Inuit, the Caribou Inuit, etc. The religion of the Iglulik Inuit again consists of different variants: those of the Iglulingmiut, the Aivilingmiut, etc, and each local group of these groupings will have its own version of the religion. These versions will usually depend to some extent on the personalities and interests of influential people like the *angakkut* (shamans). When we take into account that these local groupings are very flexible units that vary each year in size and composition it will be clear that the local versions of religion are also subject to change and variation.

A religion can be described on each level of abstraction. Rasmussen described the religion of the Netsilik and Iglulik Inuit in separate monographs, Boas described the culture and religion of the Central Inuit, and Hultkrantz, Lantis, and others described Inuit religion in general.

The religions of neighbouring peoples like the Chuckchee in Siberia or the Athabascans in northern America are in many respects related to Inuit religion and they can be considered as variants in the wider context of the religions of the hunting and gathering peoples of northern Siberia and North America. It is in this context that the shamanistic complex is often examined (cf. Findeisen, Eliade, and others). In this way the scope can always be extended and this explains why Lévi-Strauss could pursue his mythical analysis all over the Americas. He could have continued over into Siberia and finally have arrived in western Europe. That structural relationships cannot only be found in the structural analysis of myth but also on other levels is demonstrated in many studies, cf. Kretschmar and others on the theme of the dog, or the studies of shamanism in these areas. Structural relations between religions can be explained by an examination of other relations between the cultures concerned. The examination of these relations is in practice very complicated because innumerable historical processes (e.g., migrations, processes of acculturation) influence the relation between neighbouring cultures in many ways. Even then it should be clear that the study of non-literate religions always implies a selection of the level of abstraction of the analysis. The study of a religion as an isolated unit tends to neglect the importance of its relations with other neighbouring religions which often have great value for our analysis. The examination of the relations between different neighbouring religions has too often been neglected. The cause of this neglect can be partially found in an exaggerated confidence in diffusion that proved sterile in the long run. The structural approach of Lèvi-Strauss, however, has opened new and fruitful perspectives for the examination of these relations.

Anthropologists have sometimes argued that religions without literary traditions lack a historical dimension or consciousness. This is a misunderstanding. All cultures have notions about the past that are expressed in their myths and genealogies, but it is clear that the significance of the historical perspective varies in different cultures. As a rule we find myths about the origin of the world and the first human being. Rights on status, land etc. are usually based on myths and genealogical relationships to mythical heroes. Historical traditions tend to become mythical in structure since their function is determined by the interests of the present and no literary tradition can safeguard them against mythical manipulation.

The local variant of a religion can be very much adapted to the specific conditions that determine the life of that group. A ritual transgression can specify which place cannot be passed and which river has to be avoided. While the great religions of the world tend to become rather abstract and ethical in their outlook since they are not confined to the particular conditions of specific groups, non-literate religions can be much more concrete and interwoven with the practice of daily life. This close relation has induced some anthropologists to argue that non-literate people are deeply religious but this is a misunderstanding that is based on an ethnocentric conception of religion and not on an understanding of the religious life of people in non-literate societies. The core of the problem does not rest on different degrees of spirituality but on different structural relations between religion and other domains of culture. The great religions of the world also influence the life of the believers deeply, but in completely different ways. While non-literate religions tend to give a spiritual perspective to the world as it is, many of the world religions tend to preach an alternative to the world of everyday life as a superior and more important dimension of life.

Non-literate religions are very dynamic. Since they are not limited in their development by sacred texts they can adapt more easily to historical processes. Ecological, economic, and other changes have to be accounted for. In all religions a structural field of tensions exists between the preservation of the old traditions and the need to account for and adapt to new developments. The notion that non-literate religions are static is completely false. While there is no need to reinterpret the old texts time and again, the oral traditions themselves can gradually change as need requires.

The complete adaptation of a non-literate religion to other cultural domains also constitutes its weakness. When social, political, and economic conditions change rapidly·the religion becomes vulnerable. Traditional frameworks lose their meaning and the religion disintegrates. This process can often be seen when the non-literate culture comes into contact with a great civilisation. Many reactions are possible (syncretism, messianic cults etc.), but in the long run the traditional religion is usually doomed. When the culture is integrated into a great civilisation the participants usually accept the religion of the dominant culture and adapt it as much as possible to their local needs. Their local customs often constitute an essential core in the practice of the religion. Thus it can be argued that the Christmas tree and other symbols that have nothing to do with Christianity itself have constituted essential elements in Christian rituals, and in some cases they even seem to survive the religion itself when we perceive that many people, who do not consider themselves as Christians anymore, still celebrate Christmas and Easter with traditional symbols.

The literate religions

The great religions of the world have spread from their place of origin in a complex historical process; in some cases they have disappeared from it, but have maintained themselves in other areas (e.g., Christianity, Buddhism). All these religions were deeply influenced by other cultural traditions during their development. Christianity developed from the Jewish religion, was transformed by the Greek and Roman traditions, and was deeply influenced by Germanic traditions in the course of its history. Buddhism proved to be exceptionally adaptable since it tolerated the existence of other religious traditions and considered itself to be a more advanced teaching. Christianity and Islam were less tolerant and Christianity in particular succeeded in almost destroying all rival religious traditions in Europe. Islam faced many more religions with literary traditions (religions of the book) in its territory, and although it persecuted non-literate religions, religions of the book were tolerated. All great religions became related to fixed political and social interests and these determined much of their history. The expansion of Christianity and Islam was usually connected with the expansion of Christian and Islamic political powers. In all the great religions of the world a structural tension exists between the unity of the religion and the cultural diversity between different areas where the religions extend. If regional diversity is stressed the unity of the religion dissolves and when the unity of the religion is stressed it is difficult to adapt the religion to the needs of the local traditions. Within this field of tension many sects and religious variants developed that were usually connected with regional and local interests. The unity of the religion was usually preserved by the literary tradition and the social organisation of the religious professionals.

In the great religions the oldest religious texts (Vedas, Bible, Qur'ān) have most authority. They were created in the stage of formation of the religion and they are usually accepted by all later sects and denominations in that religion. Different comments and interpretations on these texts were developed and these comments gave rise to new comments and interpretations. Thus the literary tradition became more and more complex in the course of time. As a rule the oldest texts are accepted by all believers, while different sects and denominations make their own selections out of the more recent literature and develop their own comments and interpretations as a particular literary tradition. Thus the unity of the religion is preserved by the oldest texts. The great religions all dispose of an élite of religious professionals, who share and preserve the common traditions. Sometimes they are organised in a hierarchical and centralised institution (like the Roman Catholic Church), sometimes they consist of a privileged caste (like the Brahmins), sometimes they consist of specialists in the scriptures whose status depends almost completely on their learning (like the Sunnitic Ulamās).

All these professionals derive their prestige and status from their position in the religious organisation and their knowledge of the great religious traditions. As a rule we find a strong resistance among these élites against deviations from the ideal patterns. They constitute an *avant garde* of the religion against those beliefs that are considered as superstition in the great tradition. They play an important part in the continuous struggle between the great traditions that try to preserve and develop the teachings of the religion and the folk traditions (local traditions) that tend to adapt the religion to local customs.

We should not only distinguish between a great tradition and a folk tradition as two opposed entities but acknowledge the existence of different intermediate levels. The great tradition is usually constituted by rivaling traditions from different areas. Their regional variants can adapt better to the local traditions than the religion as a whole.

Differentiation continues indefinitely until we come to the level of the local variant. In many respects these local variants function similarly to religions without a literary tradition but at the same time they are continuously influenced and determined by the great tradition of their own religion. This is particularly clear in Christianity. The Roman Catholic church always attempted to preserve the unity of the church. Heresies often represented local variations (cf. the Cathars in northern Italy and southern France). The regional variants of religions often gave rise to the development of sects and denominations.

The integration of local traditions within great traditions is often a difficult and painful progress. Christianity, Islam, and other religions gave scope to the integration of local elements on various levels (e.g., veneration of saints that were transformations of local cults from an historical point of view). Christianity succeeded in suppressing some local customs (e.g., wakes, veneration of oak trees, sacrificing of horses) but had to accept other customs (e.g., celebration of Christmas at the winter solstice—the old Jule—celebration of Easter in the context of traditional pre-Christian customs).

As a rule the great tradition gradually supersedes local customs and beliefs that are considered to be superstition by the élites. The believers gradually identify more and more with the great tradition and the development of a world religion usually implies a rather homogeneous civilisation. Thus Hinduism, Christianity, and Islam developed relatively autonomous civilisations with their own traditions in art and science. Buddhism developed differently because it always co-existed with other religions.

We have already seen that the world religions extended over such vast areas that it was difficult for them to adapt themselves to local traditions in the same degree as religions without literary traditions. As a consequence these religions stress those aspects of human life that are considered to be universal. They preach universal ethics for all human beings, and they tend to stress the importance of the unity of the faithful regardless of cultural differences. These teachings should appeal to people of all cultures.

As a consequence the contents of the world religions are usually more abstract and general than those of the non-literate religions. In many cases we find a tendency to stress the ethical dimensions of a world religion to the detriment of cultic rules.

Because the religion has to be directed towards people of different cultures it becomes more individualistic. Every individual, regardless of his cultural background, should find answers to his fundamental questions in the religious teachings.

Thus the world religions tend to develop civilisations that transcend the specific cultures within those civilisations. New groupings arise, often associated with differences in status, wealth, and power, that can sometimes lead to the rise of many different religious organisations corresponding with the social hierarchy. Thus, for example, we see that in the United States most churches have a specific social status that is carefully considered by would-be participants.

The anthropological study of religion should consider very carefully the relations between traditions on different levels in time and space. In most introductions to world religions we read what the Muslim or the Christian believes, practises, etc. But the Muslim in Indonesia in the twentieth century and the Muslim in medieval Persia differ in many respects. At the same time they share a common set of beliefs and practices and their religions can be considered as each other's variants. Structural differences between variants have to be explained by historical and cultural conditions. Anthropological analysis of religion should aim both at the explanation of differences and the explanation of similarities.

The theoretical level of religion

When we study another religion we have to become familiar with its language. Key concepts in other religions (e.g., Tao in Chinese Taoism, Nirvāṇa in Buddhism, Inua in Inuit religion) are very complex notions that cannot be translated unequivocally into the terminology of our own language. Different interpretations of the same word may coexist and often the meaning of the word is subject to change in the course of time. The analyst distinguishes between his ability to understand the concept in terms of its own context and his capacity to translate the concept.

The religious concepts we examine are always part of a complex of religious conceptions and ideas. They may have an exactly defined place in a well-thought-out theological system, or they may be extremely vague. In all cases, however, the problem of translation arises. How do we describe concepts of another culture in terms of our own culture? We do not do this through the medium of an objective terminological apparatus, but by the aid of concepts that play a part in our own culture.

To translate the French word *ciel*, the most important possibilities are 'sky' and 'heaven.' In translating one considers the context of the word, how sky and heaven are used in English, etc. Finally, one chooses the word that most fitly renders *ciel* in that particular context. More difficult is the word *esprit*. The words 'spirit,' 'soul,' 'mind,' 'ghost,' and so on differ entirely in value and meaning, and careful consideration is necessary. We find in practice that one can use words, develop a feeling for language, translate, etc, without being able to give definitions of the words one uses.

In religion we have a good deal to do with terms which are fairly generally agreed to be pretty vague: God, spirit, soul, etc. A French dictionary will offer us the following possible translations of *âme*: soul, mind, spirit, life, conscience, feeling, ghost, person, essence, with additional special meanings such as bore (of a gun), sound-post (of a violin), core (of a bronze cast). These meanings certainly do not make clear what the place of the term *âme* has been in Christian anthropology in France. For that extensive research would be required. When the word is translated, a selection is made from a range of possible translations. The word *âme* does not have meaning as an independent and isolated unit, but in the context of many other related concepts. It has many associations and connotations, and in the process of translation some of these are eliminated while others are added. The translation of Lévi-Strauss' book *La pensée sauvage* into 'The Savage Mind' implied a fundamental change of the subject matter. It is only when the translator is completely familiar with different languages that he is fully aware of the transformations of meaning that are implied in the process of translation. The process of translation does not imply a substitution of one concept for another, but the transformation of one way of thinking into another way of thinking. Thus it is a process of communication.

Although many religious terms appear to be vague, the participants usually feel a clear distinction in the use of those terms. One may speak of a village of a hundred souls, but not of a village of a hundred spirits. At the same time it would be very difficult to fix the limits between the words soul, spirit, conscience, and so on. These concepts may play an important part in a man's personal religious life without his being able to give a clear conceptual definition of those concepts. We can see that the various meanings of *âme* given above are related and that their mutual connections can be described. The word *âme* obviously covers a fairly complex idea with many shades and connotations. It is only when one wishes to assign a well-defined meaning to the concept that one finds it troublesomely vague. The word simply has no unequivocal significance. In everyday languages the word can be used in many ways and its use does not raise any problems for the participants. Thus it is the problem of definition, not the use of these words, that constitutes the vagueness of the concept.

Concepts of the soul can be found in many cultures and usually they are very complex and apparently vague. On closer scrutiny they often appear to express complex ideas about the nature of human beings. The analysis of these concepts should not be directed towards the construction of definitions of these concepts but towards the rules that determine their use. As a rule the participants have only very vague notions about the meanings of these words just like the Christian who can often speak of the soul without having a very clear idea of its meaning. Sometimes philosophers and theologians speculate about the meanings of these concepts and then a new situation arises. The concept becomes a controversial issue and different interpretations of the word can be given at the same time. The anthropologist who examines the meaning of a concept then has to cover the whole range of conflicting and opposing interpretations a word has, while he should be aware at the same time that these rather abstract speculations often have little significance for the way the concept is used by the ordinary believer. Words like *karma*, *māyā*, *mokṣa*, *dharma* are interpreted in many ways in Indian religions, and the anthropologist should not give precedence to the philosopher's interpretations over those of the common believer. Both interpretations are sources of equal value for his understanding of the way a concept is used in religion. Different interpretations of a concept can coexist. The analysis of the theoretical level of religion usually aims at the construction of a coherent model of the beliefs of the participants. Usually, however, these beliefs do not constitute a coherent complex. Contradictory beliefs cannot only coexist in the same culture but even in the same person. Thus we find in many cultures mutually exclusive notions of the fate of deceased people. The participants may believe that they go to the realm of death while they are thought to reincarnate at the same time and sometimes even to haunt other people as bad spirits. Sometimes theologians attempt to harmonise contradictory beliefs, but as a rule many of them coexist in all religions and cause no apparent problems for the participants.

In hymns, theological treatises, etc, the merits of the gods are often extolled. They are described as generous, powerful, righteous. In mythology they often appear as jealous, selfish, deceitful. For the participants this does not raise any problems. Only when philosophical reflection develops, as in Greece and India, are explanations invented for the negative aspects of the great gods. The structure of the pantheon is usually determined by conflicting and competing interests. In Scandinavian religion Odin was the supreme god, but he was also the god of the nobility, while Thorr was considered to be a god of the farmers. Rivalry between the gods is evident in religious texts. In Indian religion Viṣṇu and Śiva both had large followings that exalted their own god and depreciated his rival. In Egyptian religion each town that rose to power tended to raise its own god to the supreme position in the pantheon.

The development and structure of the pantheon therefore have to be related to the social, political, and other interests of the participants.

While religious ideas can usually be organised in more or less coherent systems, myths require a different strategy of analysis. The most important strategies of mythological analysis have been developed in psychological and structural analysis. Psychological methods are rather unpopular in cultural anthropology because they tend to be ethnocentric. Structural anthropology dominates the field of mythical analysis, but it does not offer a consistent method. Thus we find strategies that attempt to reconstruct mythical cycles as ideal types or historical complexes (cf. Dumézil (1952), Ivanov and Toporov (1970), Lincoln (1981)). Structural analysis in the way it was developed by Lévi-Strauss attempts to explain the differences between different variants. Although the latter approach raises many methodological problems it seems more promising than the former, since it does not imply any value judgments concerning the truth or historicity of a variant.

Lévi-Strauss developed the general notion that myths express basic problems in human society. He tends to stress the importance of social problems, particularly problems of alliance. Although there is no need to assume that each myth has one particular meaning or message it seems evident that crucial problems in the order of human culture will be expressed in the structure of the myth and structural conflicts in myths will inform us about structural problems in society. It should be clear, however, that myths are in no way unequivocal expressions or reflections of the structure of society. They can present alternatives to the existing order and often provide negative proof for it.

Myths are tales, and tales do not constitute a consistent logical system in the way religious ideas do. Tales are often bizarre and absurd. They appeal to people because they discuss relevant problems in relevant ways. The anthropologist attempts to discover the rules that determine their organisation and the transformations between different myths in time and space. Myths provide a very interesting perspective on religion because they express the religious order at an unreflected level. The participants do not know why they tell myths in a certain way, although they do know very well how they should be told. It is up to the anthropologist to explain this.

Thus mythical analysis provides an important perspective on the unconscious structures of religion (cf. Oosten 1981 for a more extensive discussion of the problem of the relation between structure and meaning).

Norms and rules of behaviour also belong to the theoretical level of a religion. They express how people think they should behave and are therefore action-orientated. They can be of an ethical and of a ritual nature. The importance of this distinction should not be exaggerated however. Mary Douglas has done important research on the nature of ritual injunctions and she made it quite clear that ritual injunctions can express complex notions about the order of the world. Ritual injunctions mark important boundaries that have to be respected in religious behaviour.

Songs, proverbs, etc, all belong to the theoretical level of religion. They express different notions about the nature of the gods, wisdom and so on. The theoretical level of religion can usually be considered as a system of classification. Male-female, men-animals, right-left, life-death, and so on are ordering principles that determine the organisation of this system. Different domains in the theoretical level, however, can express different notions and sometimes internal contradictions can exist between them. Myths provide room for speculation: many things are possible that cannot be realised in daily life. Ritual injunctions, however, are directed towards religious behaviour and these rules have to take into account the practical conditions of life. Hymns will praise the gods, while myths often place them in quite another perspective.

As a rule, however, we should assume that the theoretical order represents a rather well organised complex. It is not created to confuse people, but to give significance to their lives. At the same time it has to account for conflicting perspectives of different social groups, men and women, nobility and commoners, etc., and the anthropologist should attempt to explain the internal contradictions by an examination of the relations between the theoretical level of a religion and other cultural orders. At the same time he should be aware that the religious system itself can contain contradictions that cannot be solved. The theologians of those religions sometimes try to eliminate these contradictions but in other cases they stress the importance of the paradox. Thus the dogma of Nicaea established the mutually exclusive natures of Christ. He was considered to be both man and god (*credo quia absurdum*).

The theological speculation of the religious élite is an important field of study but we should be aware of the fact that in many cases it has only a limited relevance for the belief of the majority of believers and its importance should therefore not be exaggerated.

The practice of the religion

Ritual practice involves both social and individual religious behaviour. Ritual can be defined as standardised religious behaviour. It can require a group of people, but it can also be practised by an individual e.g., in prayer. Standardised means that the behaviour is determined by certain rules.

While myth can be speculative and discuss alternatives to the existing order of the world, ritual has to take account of this order of the world. It is determined by the categories of time and space. While myth is almost completely verbal, ritual is almost completely action. In ritual words have less importance, and constant repetition of words is a common feature of ritual. The repetition of the words as an action takes precedence over the meaning for the participants who often are not even aware of the meaning of the words they utter.

Myths and ritual are often related. Sometimes a myth is recited in the context of ritual, in other cases the ritual is a re-enactment of a myth. Ritual can also inverse the myth. The Inuit blackened the faces of their sexual partners with soot at the ritual of partner exchange at the new-year's festival, while an important myth relates that Seqineq, the spirit of the sun, once blackened the face of her brother, the moon-spirit Aninga, with soot when he had an incestuous relation with her. Thus men marked women at the partner's exchange and a woman a man in an incestuous relation. It is not clear to what extent rituals constitute systematic complexes similar to those in mythology but this seems to be a fruitful field to explore.

Ritual is action and therefore it involves time, space, participants, and material means. It takes a certain time and it needs a space that is sometimes strictly separated from other places and considered as sacred. Places of worship, churches, temples, etc, often become sacred places and the participants need to perform certain rituals to enter these places if they are allowed to do so at all. Often the place of ritual is determined *ad hoc* and only becomes sacred for a limited period. Sometimes the sacred period is a symbolic representation of the creation and history of the world just as the sacred place is a microcosmic representation of the whole world. These dimensions of sacred place and time have been very much stressed by Eliade. Thus the time and place of a ritual become crucial and we should expect the process of ritual in time and the ordering of ritual in space to express general notions about time and space among the participants. If the West is considered as the region of death and East as the region of life a ritual will usually express these notions. Thus ritual gives us much information about the *Weltanschauung* of the participants and analysis should be directed towards the discovery of its ordering principles. Structures of time and space are not only expressed in ritual, but ritual itself is also directed towards the structure of time and space. Crucial transitions in the year will be accompanied by ritual. The end of the harvest, the beginning of the hunting season, the coming of rain are all periods that can be marked in ritual. Ritual is also related to the human cycles of life. Birth, initiation, marriage, death are all marked by ritual. These rituals often express a basic symbolism of life and death, and van Gennep's important study (1980) of initiation rituals has clearly demonstrated some of the organising principles of these religious practices.

Ritual always requires participants. When a ritual is focussed on specific people, e.g., because it makes an important transition in their lives as in marriage, these people will have a central position in that ritual. When ritual involves a whole society the organisation of a ritual will often involve all significant members of that society. The ordering of a ritual will often have to be explained in terms of the hierarchical and social organisation of a particular culture. Sometimes hierarchical relations will be expressed in the order of a ritual, sometimes they will be inverted (cf. the Saturnalia, Carnival, etc.). In both cases an explanation is required. Complex rituals often involve many symbols and just like myths they cannot be reduced to a single message or meaning. The great rain rituals in southern Africa are often also first fruit ceremonies, kingship rituals, etc. In functionalistic approaches the harmonising aspects of ritual were often unduly stressed. In practice, however, ritual also often expressed antagonism and hostility and could lead to serious quarrels. In Indian societies the Potlatch rituals also offered a ritual domain for competition that could induce bitter conflicts between individuals and groups.

Religious professionals usually play an important part in ritual. Ritual tends to become more and more complex and in many cases only religious specialists are thought to know how rituals should be performed. And these ritual specialists often manipulate the powers they acquire in and through these rituals.

Ritual usually requires sacred objects, which belong to certain groups and persons. The manipulation and exchange of these objects give us important information about the social structure of society. The nature of these objects gives us much information about the religious order. Victor Turner in particular has done very important research in this domain. He demonstrated (1974) how different objects were selected and shaped according to rules that expressed basic notions about the nature of the world. The objects can express notions about color symbolism, elongated versus round, hard versus soft, etc. An interesting approach was developed by Lévi-Strauss in *La Voie des Masques* (1975) to analyse ritual objects. He attempted to demonstrate that masks can be considered as elements in a system and although his results are not always very convincing he opened up a promising perspective.

Ritual requires material objects, individuals, and groups of people that will not always be present in equal measure. While a myth can always be told in the same way, ritual will often be executed in different ways and the ideal way of performing a ritual may never be realised. This constitutes a major problem in the analysis of rituals.

Ritual behaviour is usually very different from everyday behaviour. It is intended to be an alternative behaviour that relates man to another world. Thus we find moods of devotion, exaltation, joy, grief, etc., very strongly expressed in ritual. Huizinga (1958) and Jensen (1960) have linked ritual to play. It is a combination of seriousness and playfulness. The strong emotions that are expressed in rituals have only a limited relevance for everyday life. Sometimes religion seems to constitute an emotional outlet. Victor Turner has stressed the dialectical relationship between structure and nonstructure. Although man has to live in a structured world he longs to turn to a world where structure loses its meaning. He finds this world in ritual in the stage of 'liminality' where the order of the world is temporarily suspended. Structure can be explained as the need to organise human life, liminality as the need to escape that structure. In many ways Turner's notion is reminiscent of Mauss's notion of a pendulum movement between individualistic and social life (1905), but while Mauss stresses a sociological approach Turner often seems close to a psychological reductionism that attempts to find the meaning of ritual in the moods of the participants.

Although the moods and motivations of the participants are important for our understanding of ritual, it seems clear that the structure of ritual can only be explained by its relation to the structure of other cultural domains: notions about the relation between life and death, male-female, etc.

The word religion is usually reserved in our own culture for the great tradition of religion, and belief in witches, gnomes, etc., is usually excluded from it. Similar beliefs in other cultures are often included. In the same way many ritual practices like shaking hands (particularly right hands) and kissing are usually not considered to be religious although similar practices are often considered as religious in other cultures. It should be clear, however, that these practices often give much information about the conception of the world. Thus the shaking of hands has its structural position in a wider context of symbolism of the hands, itself part of an even wider complex of symbolism of the body in western culture.

Individual behaviour can be qualified as ritual behaviour to the extent that it conforms to cultural rules. For example, prayer is a ritual act connected with certain ritual actions like the bending of knees, the closing of eyes, etc.

In cases of social as well as of individual ritual behaviour, the research should focus on the rules that determine that behaviour.

While both the theoretical level and the practical level of religion express ways of ordering the world they use different means. The theoretical level is predominantly verbal. Words convey meaning and emotions to the participants. At the ritual level the participants can actively express the religious order in their behaviour, and performance of ritual itself has significance and conveys strong emotions to the participants. It is interesting to notice that the two levels are not always equally balanced. Thus we find much ritual and little mythology in some cultures, while we find little ritual and much mythology in other cultures. In our own culture the theoretical level is usually considered as more important than the practical level although our own culture is less devoid of ritual than most of its participants often assume.

Conclusions

The anthropological study of religion is a process of communication between different cultures. As our own society develops, our cultural perspective of other cultures will change. The participants in non-literate cultures have been transformed from savages into human beings in the perspective of western culture. The study of religion should be based on an awareness of the relativity of our own perspective and a basic respect for participants in other cultures.

In this chapter I have argued for a systematic approach to religion as a cultural order that gives significance to human beings and their world. This approach can be applied both to the theoretical level and to the practical level of religion. It does not imply a static approach to religion but accounts for variations in time and space. The anthropological study of religion should be directed towards the explanation of religious differences between different religious variants. As a rule these differences will have to be explained by relations between religion and other cultural orders. Since religion is at the same time a relatively autonomous domain that deals in its own way with fundamental human problems like life and death, these explanations will never be completely exhaustive. Both the internal structure of religion and the structure of its relations towards other cultural domains should be examined by the anthropologist.

Bibliography

Berger, P.L. *The Sacred Canopy*. New York: Anchor Books, 1969.
Boas, F. *The Central Eskimos*. 5oth Annual Report of the bureau of ethnology to the secretary of the Smithonian Institution 1884–5. Washington, 1888.
Douglas, M. *Purity and Danger*. New York: Pelican Books, 1970.
— *Natural Symbols*. New York: Pantheon Books, 1970.
Dumézil, G. *Les dieux des Indo-Européens*. Paris: P.U.F., 1952.
— *Les dieux des Germains*. Paris: P.U.F., 1952.

Durkheim, E. *Les formes élémentaires de la vie religieuse.* Paris: P.U.F., 1968.

Eliade, M. *Images and Symbols: Studies in Religious Symbolism.* London: Harvil Press, 1962.

— *Shamanism.* New York: Pantheon Books, 1964.

— *Traité d'histoire des religions.* Paris: Payot, 1964.

Evans-Pritchard, E.E. *Theories of Primitive Religion.* Oxford: Oxford University Press, 1965.

Findeisen, H. *Schamanentum.* Stuttgart: Kohlhammerverlag, 1957.

Frazer, J.G. *The Golden Bough.* London: MacMillan, 1890.

Geertz, C. 'Religion as a Cultural System,' 1–46 in Michael Banton (ed.) *Anthropological Approaches to the Study of Religion.* London: Tavistock Publications, 1965.

Huizinga, J. *Homo Ludens.* Haarlem: Tjeenk Willink, 1958.

Hultkrantz, A. 'Die Religion der Amerikanischen Arktis,' in J. Paulson, A. Hultkrantz, K. Jettmar, (eds.) *Die Religionen Nordeurasiens und der Amerikanischen Arktis.* Stuttgart: Kohlhammer, 1962.

Ivanov, V. et Toporov 'Le mythe Indo-Européen du dieu de l'orage poursuivant le serpent: Reconstruction du schéma,' in *Echanges et communications mélanges offerts à Claude Lévi-Strauss* à l'occasion de son 60ème anniversaire réunis par Jean Pouillon et Pierre Maranda. The Hague-Paris: Mouton, 1970.

Jensen, A.E. *Mythos und Kult bei Naturvölkern.* Wiesbaden: Franz Steiner 1960.

Kretschmar, F. *Hundestammvater und Kerberos.* Stuttgart, 1980.

Kroeber, A. and C. Kluckhohn *Culture: A Critical Review of Concepts and Definitions.* Cambridge: Harvard University. Papers of the Peabody Museum of American Archaeology and Ethnology, vol. 47, 1952.

Kuper, A. 'Evans-Pritchard and the History of Anthropological Thought,' *Times Higher Education Supplement,* 30 October 1981.

Lantis, M. *The Religion of the Eskimos.* Forgotten Religions 5. New York, 1950.

Lévi-Strauss, C. *Le Pensée Sauvage.* Paris: Plon, 1962.

— *Mythologiques I–IV.* Paris: Plon, 1964–1971.

— *La voie des masques.* Genève: Albert Skira, 1975.

Lévy-Bruhl, L. *Mentalité primitive.* Paris: P.U.F., 1960.

— *L'âme primitive.* Paris: P.U.F., 1963.

Lincoln, B. *Priests, Warriors and Cattle. A study in the Ecology of Religions.* Los Angeles, London: University of California Press Berkeley, 1981.

Mauss, M. 'Essai sur les variations saisonnières des sociétés Eskimos (1904–5), in *Sociologie et Anthropologie.* Paris, 1966.

Oosten, J.G. 'The Examination of Religious Concepts in Religious Anthropology,' in Th.P. van Baaren and H.J.W. Drijvers (eds.) *Religion, Culture and Methodology.* The Hague-Paris: Mouton 1973.

— *The Theoretical Structure of the Religion of the Netsilik and Iglulik.* Meppel: Krips Repro, 1976.

— *Religieuze veranderingen in de wereldgodsdiensten.* ICA publication no. 27. Leiden, 1978.

— 'Meaning and Structure in the Structural Analysis of Myth,' in Gretchen A. Moyer,

David S. Moyer and P.E. de Josselin de Jong (eds) *The Nature of Structure*. ICA publication no. 45. Leiden, 1981.

Rasmussen, K. *Intellectual Culture of the Iglulik Eskimos*. Report of the fifth Thule Expedition, vol. VII, no. 1. Copenhagen, 1929.

— *The Netsilik Eskimos. Social life and spiritual culture*. Report of the fifth Thule Expedition, vol. VIII, nos 1 and 2. Copenhagen, 1931.

Spiro, M.E. 'Religion: Problems of Definition and Explanation,' 85–126, in M. Banton (ed) *Anthropological Approaches to the Study of Religion*. London: Tavistock, 1965.

Turner, V. *The Ritual Process*. London: Pelican Books, 1974.

Van Baaren, Th.P. *Menschen wie wir*. Gütersloh: Gerd Mohn, 1964.

Van de Leeuw, G. *Phänomenologie der Religion*. Tübingen: Mohr, 1933.

Van Gennep, A. *The Rites of Passage*. London: Routledge and Kegan Paul, 1980.

Waardenburg, J. *Reflections on the study of Religion*. The Hague: Mouton, 1978.

Weber, M. *Gesammelte Aufsatze zur Religionssoziologie* Tübingen: Mohr, 1922.

Wittgenstein, C. *Philosophical Investigations*. Oxford: Blackwell, 1963.

Yinger, J.M. *The Scientific Study of Religion*. London: Macmillan, 1970.

Cultural Anthropology and the many Functions of Religion

WOUTER E.A. VAN BEEK

Religion has many interpretations, many facts and a host of functions. In the two preceding papers its main function—even if the interpetation varied—was either a sociological or a structural one: religion gives a group cohesion and orders a universe. Yet human life is not always ordered, neither is respect for or obedience to the group everywhere paramount. The erratic individual often moves from the more or less straight and narrow path his culture has laid out for him, not only causing lots of trouble and strife, but paving the way for religious innovation and cultural change. American anthropology in several of its myriad facets, has given ample attention to this dialectic relation between an individual and his religion. The dialectic is quite clear: just as any individual is the product of his society *and* vice versa the society stems from individuals, any religion not only is imposed upon its participants, but to a large extent is moulded by these very personalities it has been instrumental in shaping. Of course this sounds like the age old chicken-and-egg problem; so to avoid any insoluble dilemma let me rephrase the question: what kind of function does religion perform for the individual participant?

Let us start with the first question. The experiment in survival called *homo sapiens* does not live just with his brains, but to a large extent with his glands too. Emotions, though heavily underplayed in religious theory, do form the main motor for most actions. Our general scientific disregard for the 'lower' emotions as explanatory factors is more expressive of our own culture and our academic subculture, than of the religion of our fellow men. Of course, the affluent West can afford to look for the elated feelings of religiosity, nicely ordered wordviews, and coherent belief systems. But in the great majority of societies studied by anthropologists survival is the key word. Harsh surroundings, a merciless physical environment, droughts and famines all take their toll. Hobbes's picture of 'brutish, nasty and short' is an inappropriate description of tribal life surely not to be invoked. On the other hand, Rousseau's noble savage is widely off the mark too. Any field anthropologist knows from his own experience the quiet harmony a rural village offers him. Most of us long to go back to the field, if only for that reason. But as visiting scientists we really have the best of two worlds, the security and—medical—technology of the West and the intensive social interaction of the face-to-face community.

Recently an anthropologist, after having broken his leg in remote Nepal, was flown out by helicopter. No doubt his Sherpa friends were better adapted to the mountains, less clumsy on the steep slopes to say the least, and would not slip as easily; still, they must solve their own problems in their own way, by their own means, and would never in their lifetime be able to send for a helicopter. (Oral communication).

What has this to do with his religion? Well, religion is an important facet of the cultural array of problem-solving devices, either for big calamities or for small nuisances. Wallace, one of the main proponents of this view on religion, cites a charming example:

A Cherokee burning himself, blows fresh water in four parts on the burn reciting: Water is cold, ice is cold, snow is cold, rime is cold. "Relief" I will be saying (Wallace 1966: 117).

Another case comes from our own field experience:

A Kapsiki suffering from headache whirls a discarded potsherd three times around his aching head, and throwing the potsherd away sighs: "Well, that is fixed" (Van Beek 1978: 378).

Religion and personality

Bigger problems call for stronger measures. Long before Lévi-Strauss focussed attention on the *efficacité symbolique* (1958), the role of religious therapy in healing the hodge-podge of so-called psychosomatic illnesses had been acknowledged (e.g., Gillin 1948). Following C.G. Jung's distinction between *anima* and *persona*, Wallace (1966) distinguished social personality (*persona*) and self image (± *anima*). The social identity of a person forces him in a mould in which several personality traits have to be suppressed. One's self image and one's public personality are never identical. In some cases the discrepancy between both can cause a serious clash. The self-image, the weaker of the two, suffers heavily and disillusionment or neurosis results. Now, religion can solve this problem by offering some strong, viable models for personality with which one may identify at least for a short time. Three points are stressed here by Wallace: *some* psychic problems are normal in any culture and, second, each culture has its own brand of problems as well as its own version of normality; definition of mental—or even somatic—illness is culture-relative. Third, some phases in life are more problem-prone than others. Of course religion is not a panacea for all problems, but it sometimes does quite a lot. In ritual people are liberated from the strains their social personality imposes on them, resulting in a healthy catharsis.

The discussion on this issue centers on the question of the shaman. Someone who enters trance easily or with the help of drugs and who in helping clients helps himself too—should he be considered 'psychotic,' 'abnormal' or whatever ethnocentric label western observers may want to attach? In the eyes of many observers the *shaman* shows himself an unstable neurotic person who needs his trance to stay well. In Wallace's terms: a shaman needs regular reidentification with the religious personality model, as his self-image is decidedly at odds with the rights and duties assumed from his social personality. No *artic hysteria* nor any pathological illness, but a relativistic personality conflict. In many respects moreover, shamans are as able farmers, merchants, hunters, or fishermen as any of their compatriots.

Silverman (1967) underlines that there is no reason why shamans should have the same personality traits in all cultures. So Wallace may be right, even if mental defects should not be disregarded so easily. Kennedy (1973) neatly sums up this discussion. Some anthropologists harbour the view that shamans are superbly endowed individuals who have the valuable capacity to put themselves to trance. Castaneda's Don Juan (Castaneda 1968) would have been a splendid example but for the small detail that this material seems to be a fake (de Mille 1980).

Religion, however, is not reserved for special individuals such as shamans; ordinary individuals, too, meet their needs by religion, so in other aspects of religion the expression of not specifically pathological personality traits should be discernible. As an example Spiro's work on the Ifaluk can serve; any society has to build in safety valves for individuals and the Ifaluk society has a lot of inbuilt stress with which the inhabitants have to cope.

Ifaluk is a small Micronesian Island where a few hundred people live at close quarters. All arable land is under cultivation and no population expansion is possible. Living hemmed in like this, Ifaluk have to have a device to get rid of their frustrations, aggression or any kind of negative feeling. Their solution is a supernatural scapegoat. *Alus*, spirits are the core of their belief system, and these *alus* are responsible for anything bad. People hate the spirits, venting agression on them in a way they could never do on their fellowmen. Thus living in disharmony with their supernatural world they can afford to live in harmony with their living kinsmen (Spiro 1952).

Religion and socialisation

One drawback of this elegant reasoning is that it is just *ad hoc* reasoning, and anthropology should not content itself with just explaining the *status quo*. In the 1950s and 1960s a score of researchers and theorists addressed themselves to the problem how an individual is situated in his culture. Most of these researches do not center on religion, as from a theoretical and practical point of view personality development and childhood training are more important. Still, in nearly all studies, religion does play a part. Early stimulus in this direction came from Kardiner and Linton (1945) who developed a scheme of factors influencing personality development, which stimulated some new approaches. Du Bois's Alor study (1944) is the best known of these. In this approach religion is interpreted as a projective system, in which all kinds of residual fears from early childhood may be sublimated on the one hand, and on the other hand training practices and concomitant sociopolitical organisation find a direct expression.

Theoretical and methodological systematisation has come from Whiting and Childe in whose view (1953) a culture consists of a *maintenance system* comprising the basic economic, political, and social organisation. This system is for a large part responsible for the child rearing system, which in its accord shapes 'modal personality'—the standard or desired personality in that particular culture. This personality is a major factor in shaping the projective systems, like art and religion. Whiting and associates set up a huge comparative framework in which half a dozen coordinated field studies were undertaken to be compared later (Whiting and Childe 1953), one of the biggest research endeavours anthropology has ever known. Religious processes feature prominently in the statistical worldwide comparisons that the research team has done. Using a well-known standard sample of all the world cultures, part of the so-called Human Relations Area Files (see Murdock 1969) they extensively checked their theoretical options in operationalised testable propositions. One example: Whiting's neo-Freudian theory postulates a correlation between late weaning and harsh male initiation ceremonies. The reasoning is as follows: Late weaning favors a long *post partum* sex taboo, which incites the husband to have plural wives. This implies virilocality (residence of the couple at the husband's place), resulting in a fixed core of patrilineally related men. The child has a strong mother-bond and will see the father as a rival. Control of insurgent sons can be effected by puberty rites, so this cultural Oedipus situation leads to harsh initiation rituals, to keep the sons in line.

This proposition has been tested with quite positive results. Other projective elements in religion put to the test were interpretations of illness, witchcraft beliefs and accusations, and danger or benevolence in the supernatural world (resp. Whiting and Childe 1953; Spiro and d'Andrade 1958; Lambert, Minturn, Triandis and Wolf 1958).

At the end of the 1960s these studies changed direction; maybe they had run their course. Anyway, Whiting and Childe's massive research program clearly showed that their strict developmental approach yielded only limited results. Thus, one of the major conclusions of the famous *Six Cultures* study (Whiting and Childe 1953) was that the differences in child rearing within one culture surpass the difference between the modal educational ways. So the theory correctly predicts correlations, but those are not overly important. Reliability and validity are high, relevance low. Moreover, other interpretations of the same phenomena are possible.

Religion and social organisation

The covariance of social and religious matters, does not need a personality development scheme as a mediating factor; those correlations can quite easily be explained by the direct dependency of religion on its sociocultural foundation. In fact, this is the leading hypothesis of most of the British anthropological studies of religion, as Jackson shows. The comparative approach, however, is quite feasible too. Young (1962, 1965) showed that the correlation between virilocality and harsh initiation rites can be explained straightaway by pointing at the ways in which 'male solidarity' is organised and has to perpetuate itself. Cohen (1964) using the same approach pointed at the duties and responsibilities of unilineal groups, which necessitate certain ways of initiating boys and girls. The belief system, another projective part of religion, shows considerable covariation with social organisation regardless of child rearing practices. Swanson (1960) showed in another cross-cultural survey how monotheism, polytheism, witchcraft beliefs, and belief in reincarnation were tied in with social variables like level of state formation, social classes, bride prices, and war.

However, the main tide of anthropology has not been in cross-cultural surveys, however fascinating they may be. Thorough and penetrating analyses of individual cases—always the stronghold of anthropology—yield more insight into religious processes and cultural covariation.

General views of religion

A trend towards a more philosophical but still individualistic way of looking at religion can be spotted in several countries. Tying in with the above mentioned theories La Barre, in a giant volume on prophetic movements (La Barre 1972), tries to unravel the 'origins of religion.' For La Barre a religion starts in a prophetic movement, as the source from which all religion springs lies deep within each and'every one of us, to be tapped by someone more fully aware of it than most, a prophet, seer, or revelator. Religion, in his view, is essentially part of the deep, non-charted areas in human experience. Religion is the human way to explain our participation in the unknown. A new religion springs from dreams, dramatic individual experiences, which are interpreted by the dreamer and accepted by groups of people.

Van Baal, in a series of major works on the theory of religion, starts from an existential standpoint (Van Baal 1947, 1971, 1981). Man is a strange phenomenon; he has the unique capability of observing not only the external world around him, but also himself, even his own processes of observation. In this he is out-of-this-world, alien and definitely a stranger. However, at the same time he is very much part of this same universe, part and parcel of his world. Man is subject and object, both stranger and friend. He is a subject longing for participation, longing for a partner. Religion, being an ascriptive way of thinking, is a way to partnership with the universe and the expression of the human condition. Symbols are the means of communication with this universe, which in itself is a cultural creation, imposed upon man by his society.

This approach closely resembles Turner's use of the term *communitas* (1969). Turner discerns two trends in human culture, the first focussing on organisation, with fixed positions, roles, and slots making up the social *persona*, and the other viewing society as a homogeneous community of idiosyncratic individuals who, despite external differences, all share a common humanity. This latter he calls *communitas*: the tendency towards integral humanity. This trend is emphasized in ritual, like in the installation of chiefs, who during the installation ritual are imbued in *communitas* to impress their duties towards the common people upon them. Thus any religion results from a dialectic between individualism and group membership, in which the former has an ethical superiority over the latter, a point mentioned also by Schoffeleers (Schoffeleers and Meyers 1978).

Two other areas of anthropological interest in religion are prominent at the moment. One is the broad specter of conflict, protest, etc., the other the ecological approach to anthropology.

Religion and conflict

Each society has its own tensions and problems which may show in religion. One favorite—i.e., for anthropologists—expression of problems and conflicts is witchcraft. Rituals of rebellion (Gluckman 1954, Norbeck 1963) are another way of expressing inherent insoluble conflicts. In both cases the reasoning closely follows the psychological tracks indicated above: the ritual, beliefs or accusations serve as a safety valve, and perform a catharsis for the society, which by playing on inherent contradictions makes those tolerable, thus preserving the *status quo* of society. However, in the long run this kind of catharsis, can have a negative effect too, as Wallace showed in his Iroquois example:

> The Iroquois channeled aggressive tendencies by means of the so-called Condolence Ceremony, towards other tribes; the Ceremony eliminated intratribal warfare and thus made intertribal warfare possible. However, the retaliation invoked by the surrounding tribes at the end decimated the Iroquois and nearly obliterated them as a tribal unit (Wallace 1966: 205–286).

Conflict, tension or protests often are invoked whenever anthropologists treat new religious movements. The literature on these is very vast but surveys are available (Wilson 1973, La Barre 1972, Köbben 1959). Most authors relate the new movement to some external influence, which plays hazard with the traditional ways of life, Balandier (1955) considers the colonial situation the main factor, the religious movement being a reaction against it: the only way in which people can regain the initiative, the only vertical social mobility, the only escape out of the system. A protest against social inequality Köbben calls it, and

Van Baal coins the term 'erring acculturation' explaining cargo cults as reaction to a thoroughly misunderstood cultural change. However, not all evaluations are negative; Balandier argues that this kind of movement really does give some 'reprise d'initiative,' Redfield sees it as a creative moment in culture (Redfield 1968) and Wallace uses the most positive term of all: cultural revitalisation. When the old structures have crumbled and the old culture is irrevocably lost, a prophetic movement can be a vigorous and positive factor in readjusting people to the new surroundings. Goodenough (1960) even advises development agents to ride the prophetic movement in their community development projects! Not all anthropologists would dare to go that far!

A recent development in these studies is the use of neo-marxist terminology. The main factors of change are conceived in terms of mode of production, productive forces, and the articulation of production. This materialistic approach is counter-balancing the recent trend in anthropology (see Oosten) towards cognitive studies, quite a dichotomy one might say! Materialism states that the societal superstructure reflects the clash of interests in the infrastructure and shields real conflicts from detection. Power structures are hidden by the ideological representation, thus preserving these very powers intact. Works by Werbner (1977), van Binsbergen (1979) and Schoffeleers (1982) exemplify this trend. In a way Burridge's (1969) treatment of millenarian activities fits in too. In his view religion primarily is a set of ideas about power, the ordering and distribution of it: where power structures break down, a millenarian prophet can construct new ways of dealing with power, creating a new power order.

Religion and the ecosystem

The second topic is just as materialistic. Religious rituals have other functions besides therapy, group cohesion, or catharsis; they have an ecosystemic function too. Ritual especially may serve as an ecological instrument. In several ways this can be shown. First ritual can be instrumental in shaping group consensus. Divination as a way of decision making is one example. Decision making is an important part of any production system: fields have to be sown, gardens cleared, trees cut down. What specific fields, trees, or gardens are to be treated is indicated by divination, the authority of the supernatural world guaranteeing a quick and easy consensus. In many instances the fact of deciding is more important than what decision is taken. If Sheridan's ass could have consulted a diviner, it would never have starved. Vogt (1952) draws attention to this aspect, to explain the persistence of the water witching practice in the USA. Scientific information on water availability is couched in probability terms, the—objectively—slightly less dependable water witching answers in clear terms, thus giving the farmer confidence in his labour intensive well digging. Divination can help in other ways too. Moore (1957) points at the problems of a Naskapi caribou hunter, who has no way of knowing the next caribou migration route as this changes every year. His safest means is, according to Moore, to randomise his hunting sprees in order to avoid over-hunting of an area and scaring the caribou away. Divination does just that. The Naskapi shoulder blade divination precludes patterning; human thinking always repeats itself, the cracks in the shoulder blade form a truly random indication.

In Harris's well known analyses (see Bibliography) ritual plays an even more crucial role. His goal is to disprove the independence of religion, by showing how it is tied in with the general ecology of the group. So he jumps into any case in which the people's life seems to be governed by religion. Starting with the *ahiṃsā* (non-violence) rule in India, Harris (1966) shows that the taboo on slaughter of cattle in India does not represent a classic case of protein waste in a poor community, but in fact is a needed protection of the cow, i.e., of agriculture. Cattle are so important for Indian agriculture that the no-slaughter rule is eminently feasible. Besides, cattle do not compete with humans for food; cows are scavengers in India, a useful niche anywhere. A 'naturally selected ecosystem' Harris calls this case, and the same could be said of the other instances in which the independent influence of religion on the economy has been reported. These range from pig-hating Middle Eastern cultures to pig-loving Melanesian tribes, from wife-beating Yanomamö to man-eating Aztec (Harris 1974). In all these cases the seemingly irrelevant taboos, the strange customs and curious practices stem from the ecology and on close inspection fit into the ecosystem. Of course a lively discussion resulted from Harris's somewhat simplistic all-encompassing theory building. Douglas (1973), of course, has a very different opinion on the origin of the pig taboo (see Jackson's paper); on the Indian case Harner gives at least a more balanced interpretation (1967). Whenever Harris draws heavily on one ethnographer, he usually is at odds with him, as with Rappaport (Melanesia, Tsembaga Maring, 1968) and Chagnon (Yanomamö, 1969). Harris's treatment of the classic Aztec material, is heavily disputed by Sahlins (1976). In Harris's view environmental depletion, lack of protein and population regulation are among the crucial factors influencing culture and religion, while the whole complex of warfare serves as an important cultural mechanism to cope with these problems. Sahlins (1976) argues that a culture is a symbolic system of meaning and should be understood in that way. Geertz, in a fascinating series of essays (1973), tries to bridge the two approaches. At the moment the discussions are in full swing. The dichotomy between cognitive and materialistic approaches centers on Harris and will not be resolved easily.

Bibliography

Baal, J. van (1947), *Over wegen en drijfveren der religie. Een godsdienstpsychologische studie*. Amsterdam: North-Holland.

— (1971), *Symbols for communication; religion in anthropological theory*. Assen: Van Gorcum.

— (1981), *Man's quest for partnership. The anthropological foundation of ethics and religion*. Assen: Van Gorcum.

Balandier, G, (1955), *Sociologie actuelle de l'Afrique noire. Dynamiques des changements sociaux en Afrique Centrale*. Paris: Presses Universitaires de France.

Beek, W.E.A. van (1978), *Bierbrouwers in de bergen. De Kapsiki en Higi van Noord Kameroen en Noord-Oost Nigeria*. Utrecht: Mededelingen Inst. voor Culturele Antropologie 12.

Beek, W.E.A. van (1979), 'Traditional religion as a locus of change,' in *Official and Popular religion; analysis of a thema for religious studies*: 514–543. eds. Vrijhof and Waardenburg. Den Haag: Mouton.

Binsbergen, W.M.J. van (1979), *Religious change in Zambia*. Dissertation Amsterdam
     University.
Binsbergen, W.M.J. van and Schoffeleers, J.W.M. (1981), *The social science of african
     religion: theoretical and methodological explorations*. (in press).
Burridge, K. (1969), *New heaven, new earth*. Oxford: Clarendon.

Castaneda, H.J.M. (1962), *The teachings of Don Juan: A Yaqui way of knowledge*. Los
     Angeles: University of California Press.
Chagnon, N. (1968), *The fierce people*. New York: Holt, Rinehart and Winston.
Cohen, Y. (1964), *The transition from childhood to adolescence. Cross-culture studies of initiation
     ceremonies, legal systems and incest taboos*. Chicago: Aldine.

Douglas, M. (1973), *Natural symbols; explorations in cosmology*. Harmondsworth: Penguin.
Du Bois, C. (1944), *The People of Alor*. Minneapolis: University of Minnesota Press.

Geertz, C. (1973), *The interpretation of cultures*. New York: Basic Books.
Gillin, J. (1948), 'Magical fright', *Psychiatry* 11: 387–400.
Gluckman, M. (1954), *Rituals of rebellion in South-East Africa*. Manchester: Manchester
     University Press.
Goodenough, W.H. (1966), *Cooperation in change*. New York: John Wiley and Sons.

Harner, R. (1969), 'Remarks on India's sacred cattle,' *Current Anthropology*, 222–245.
Harris, M. (1966), 'The cultural ecology of India's sacred cattle,' *Current Anthropology* 7:
     51–66.
— (1968), *The rise of anthropological theory*. London: Routledge and Kegan Paul.
— (1974), *Cows, pigs, wars and witches*. New York: Random House.
— (1978), *Cannibals and kings. The origins of culture*. New York: Random House.
— (1979), *Cultural Materialism. The struggle for a science of culture*. New York: Random
     House.

Kardiner, A. and Linton, R. (1945), *The psychological frontiers of society*. New York:
     Columbia University Press.
Kennedy, J.G. (1973), 'Cultural Psychiatry', in *Handbook of Social and Cultural
     Anthropology*. J.J. Honigmann (ed), 1119–1199. Chicago: Honigmann.
Köbben, A.J.D. (1959), '*Profetische bewegingen als uiting van sociaal protest.*' *Sociologisch
     jaarboek* 13: 5–88.
La Barre, W. (1972), *The ghost dance. Origins of religion*. London: Allen and Unwin.
Lambert, W.W., Minturn, L., Trandis, M. and Wolf, N. (1959), 'Some correlates of
     beliefs in the malevolence and benevolence of supernatural beings: a cross-cultural
     study', *Journal of Abnormal and Social Psychology* 58: 162–169.
Lévi-Strauss, C. (1958), *Anthropologie structurale*. Paris: Plon.

Mille, R. de (1980), *The Don Juan papers: further Castaneda controversies*. Californian Ross
     Erikson Publ.

Moore, O.K. (1957), 'Divination—a new perspective.' *American Anthropologist* 59: 69–74.

Murdock, G.P. (1969), *Ethnographic Atlas*. Pittsburgh: University of Pittsburgh press.

Norbeck, (1963), African rituals of conflict. *American Anthropologist* 65: 1254–1279.

Rappaport, R.A. (1967), *Pigs for the ancestors. Ritual in the ecology of a New Guinea people*. New Haven: Yale University Press.

Redfield, R. (1968), *The primitive world and its transformation*. Harmondsworth: Penguin.

Sahlins, M. (1976), *Culture and practical reason*. Chicago: University of Chicago Press.

Schoffeleers, M. and Meijers, D. (1978), *Nationalism and economic action. Critical questions on Durkheim and Weber*. Assen: Van Gorcum.

Silverman, D. (1967), 'Shamans and acute schizophrenia.' *American Anthropologist* 69: 21–31.

Spiro, M.E. (1952), 'Ghosts, Ifaluk, and teleological functionalism,' *American Anthropologist* 54: 497–503.

Spiro, M.E. (1966), 'Religion: problems of definition and explanation,' in: *Anthropological Approaches to the Study of Religion*. ed. M. Banton, ASA 3: 85–126. London: Tavistock.

Spiro, M.E. and d'Andrade, R.G. (1958), 'A cross-cultural study of some supernatural beliefs.' *American Anthropologist* 60: 456–466.

Swanson, G.E. (1960), *The birth of the gods: the origin of primitive beliefs*. Ann Arbor: University of Michigan Press.

Turner, V.W. (1969), *The ritual process, structure and anti-structure*. Chicago: Aldine.

Vogt, E.Z. (1952), 'Waterwitching: an interpretation of a ritual in a rural American community,' *Scientific Monthly* 75: 175–186.

Wallace, A.F.C. (1966), *Religion. An anthropological view*. New York: Random House.

Werbner, R.J. (1977), *Regional Cults*, ASA 26, London: Tavistock.

Whiting, J.W.M. & Child, I.L. (1953), *Child training and personality: a cross-cultural study*. New Haven: Yale University Press.

Wilson, B.R. (1973), *Magic and the millennium. A sociological study of religious movements of protest among tribal and third world peoples*. London: Heinemann.

Young, F.W. (1962), 'The function of male initiation ceremonies: a cross-cultural test of an alternative hypothesis,' *American Journal of Sociology* 67: 379–396.

— (1965), *A cross-cultural study of status dramatization*. Indianapolis: University of Indiana Press.

Index of Names of Scholars

Abe, Masao 22
Achard, A. 325
Adams, Charles 12
Adorno, T. W. 328, 337
Äkerberg, Hans 268, 287–8
Akishige, Y. 268
Albrecht, C. 264
Aletti, M. 268
Allen, D. 80, 123, 137
Allport, G. 257, 259, 260, 264, 268, 286
Amon, Jésus 268
d'Andrade, R. G. 389
Argyle, M. 256
Asmussen, J. P. 72
Attkisson, C. C. 297

Baal, J. van 391, 393
Baaren, T. P. van 80, 97, 106–8, 132–3, 161–2, 171–3, 352
Bahr, H. E. 336
Baird, R. D. 81, 85, 94–5, 128–9, 135, 138
Bakan, D. 283, 284
Balandier, G. 392
Barbour, I. G. 147
Barnhardt, J. E. 80, 136
Barth, K. 178, 180
Batson, C. D. 302
Bausani, A. 81, 102
Bediako, K. 17
Beek, Wouter van 385–97
Beirnaert, L. 266
Beit-Hallahmi, B. 256, 261
Bellah, R. N. 18, 333–5
Berger, P. 186, 340, 342–3, 360
Berguer, G. 267
Bianchi, U. 62, 72, 81, 95–6, 100, 102, 109

Biezais, H. 81, 109, 110
Bindl, M. F. 297
Binsbergen, W. van 393
Bird, Otto 236–7
Birnbaum, M. 333
Blank, T. 298
Bleeker, C. J. 42, 59, 61, 62, 64, 66, 69, 71, 77, 78, 81, 92, 94, 102, 104–8, 109, 110, 112
Bloch, E. 241
Boas, F. 366
Bock, D. C. 302
Bohr, N. 5, 239
Bolle, Kees 240, 241
Bolley, A. 264
Bonte, P. 234
Boos-Nünning, U. 264
Borhek, J. T. 335
Boring, E. G. 282
Bottero, J. 88
Boucouvalas, M. 257
Bovet, P. 267
Boyce, Mary 27, 38
Brandon, S. G. F. 61, 65
Braybrooke, M. 165
Brelich, A. 70, 86–8
Brennerman, W. L. 164
Brosse, Thérèse 267
Brown, D. P. 297
Brusselmans, C. 268
Buber, M. 16, 210–13, 222–5, 227–9, 234
Bultmann, R. 178
Burridge, K. 393
Butterfield, H. 238

Campbell, Joseph 256
Capps, D. 255, 256

Capps, W. H. 142
Carman, John 79
Carstairs, C. M. 256
Castellani, G. 72
Castenada, C. 388
Chagnon, N. 395
Chan, Wing-tsit 16, 192, 220–3, 224–9
Childe, I. L. 389, 390
Clavier, H. 92
Clostermann, G. 264
Coe, G. A. 306
Cohen, Y. 390
Colebrooke, T. 196
Coles, R. 291
Comte, Auguste 321, 322, 330
Condorcet, A. N. 322
Coomaraswamy, A. 16, 192, 197–201,
    203, 205, 213, 215, 222–5, 227–9, 234
Coupex, A. 297
Cousins, E. 38
Cronbach, L. J. 300
Culianu, I. P. 76
Curtis, R. F. 335

Dahremdorf, R. 332
Dammann, E. 75, 218
Daniel, Y. 325
Darley, J. M. 302
Davis, C. 149–151, 154
Davis, Kingsley 329–330
Deconchy, J. R. 267, 297, 302, 311
Desroche, H. 82
Dhavamony, M. 78, 100–1
Dilthey, W. 264
Dittes, J. E. 269, 275, 293
Döbert, Rainer 337, 338
Dostoievsky, F. 188
Douglas, M. 360, 376, 395
Dreger, R. M. 297
Drijvers, H. J. W. 80, 97, 98, 106,
    132–3, 142–3, 144
Du Bois, C. 389
Dudley, Guilford III 125, 146–7, 158

Dumezil, G. 25, 38, 376
Dumoulin, A. 267
Durkheim, E. 15, 20, 22, 23, 38, 80,
    303, 321–4, 330, 335, 340–1, 354

Edelheit, H. 299
Einstein, A. 5, 239
Eliade, M. 12, 20, 25, 38, 49–50, 65,
    72, 79–80, 82, 86, 89, 91, 122–6, 129,
    131, 135, 137, 146–8, 158, 163, 165,
    183, 187–8, 200, 232, 367, 378
Elkind, D. 290
Emerard, H. J. 325
Engels, F. 333
Engler, J. 267
Epstein, I. 210
Erikson, E. 258, 261
Evans-Pritchard, E. E. 218, 354

Festinger, L. 299, 300
Feuerbach, L. 354
Findeisen, M. 367
Fischer, G. H. 264
Flournoy, T. 277
Fontaine, J. de la 354
Forbes, G. B. 299
Foster, Durwood 22
Foucault, M. 196
Fowler, J. 258–9
Frazer, Sir J. 22, 88, 352
Frazier, A. M. 145
Freud, S. 15, 20, 22, 254, 256, 258–60,
    263, 266, 268, 272, 276, 296, 307, 354
Friedman, M. 212
Fromm, E. 257, 268
Fuchs, A. 264
Funderburk, J. 302

Gardavsky, V. 336
Geertz, C. 356, 360, 395
Gennep, van 379
Geyer, E. G. 336
Gibb, H. 195

Gillin, J. 387
Gins, K. 44
Girgensohn, K. 260, 263, 283, 292, 303
Glenny, M. 239
Gluckman, M. 392
Godin, Andre 260, 267–8
Godin, H. 325
Goldanger, K. 131
Goldman, Ronald 258, 290, 292, 297
Goldschmidt, D. 329
Gombrich, Richard 27
Goode, W. J. 329
Goodenough, E. R. 46, 85, 275
Goodenough, W. H. 393
Greeley, A. M. 295
Green, G. M. 277–9
Gromall, H. F. 299
Grønbaek, Villiam 260, 263, 306, 311
Gruehm, W. 260, 263
Guenon, R. 200
Guittard, L. 292
Guntrip, H. 261

Habermas, J. 336–8
Hajime, T. 208
Handler, L. 297
Hardin, Bert 321–349
Hare, R. M. 332
Harner, M. 395
Harris, M. 394
Havens, J. 275
Heelas, P. 149
Heidegger, M. 242
Heilbroner, R. L. 239
Heiler, F. 70, 77–8, 102–4, 151, 153, 264, 274
Heilmann, H. 265, 277
Heimbrock, H. G. 261, 278, 307
Heisenberg, W. 5, 239
Heisig, J. W. 262
Helfaer, P. M. 297
Helfer, J. S. 49, 126
Hellpack, W. 303

Henderson, J. 261
Hick, John 21, 38, 215
Hillman, James 262
Hiltner, S. 305
Hirai, T. 268
Hiroshi, S. 208
Hobbes, T. 322, 330, 386
Höffding, H. 306, 307
Holbach, P. H. T. 322
Holl, A. 264
Holm, N. G. 81
Homans, P. 256, 261, 307
Honko, L. 54, 62, 67–8, 108–12, 130–1, 139, 142, 144, 189
Hood, R. W. 302
Horton, R. F. 220
Hostie, R. 266
Hoult, T. F. 329
Hudson, L. 307
Huizinga, J. 380
Hultkrantz, A. 112–4, 119, 366
Hummel, G. 262, 307
Hunt, R. A. 270, 273, 293, 294, 295
Huntington, S. 5, 8, 37, 38
Husserl, E. 51, 86, 106, 107, 114, 182
Huxley, A. 200, 364

Idowu, E. B. 218
Illich, I. 239
Imoda, F. 267
Iqbal, M. 198
Isambert, F. A. 82, 114–5
Ivanov, V. 376

Jackson, A. 390, 395
Jahn, J. 217–8
James, W. 15, 208, 257, 259, 260, 265, 268, 272, 273, 282, 286
Jaspard, J. M. 267
Jensen, A. E. 380
Jésus-Marie, Bruno de 266
Jiyu, Ren 234
Joad, C. E. M. 202

Jones, Ernest 258
Jones, William 196
Jordan, L. H. 92
Jung, Karl G. 15, 187–8, 208, 241, 256, 260–3, 266, 268, 272, 276, 278, 303–4, 309, 387

Kagame, K. 218
Kakar, S. 261
Kant, I. 199
Kardiner, A. 388
Käsemann, E. 178
Katz, S. 128
Kehrer, G. 321–49
Kellner, E. 336
Kennedy, J. G. 388
Kennedy, Paul 37, 38
Kersevan, M. 234
King, M. B. 270, 273, 293, 294
King, N. Q. 73
King, Ursula 37, 38, 124, 224, 233, 240, 241
King, Winston 242
Kitagawa, J. 49, 82, 85, 94–5, 122, 127
Kitaro, N. 208
Klimkeit, H. F. 78
Klohr, Olaf 336
Klostermaier, K. 150
Klügl, J. 336
Kluckhohn, C. 357
Köbben, A. J. D. 392
Koepp, W. 302, 303
Kohlberg, L. 258
Kohut, H. 261
Kraemer, H. 129
Kretschmar, F. 367
Kristensen, B. 19, 38, 79, 182
Kroeber, A. 357
Kryvelev, I. A. 75
Külpe, O. 263
Küng, Hans 21, 38, 178
Kupar, Adam 354
Kuschel, K.-J. 38
Kvaerne, Per 134

La Barre, W. 391, 392
Laessae, J. 72
Laing, R. D. 241
Lambert, W. W. 389
Lanczkowski, G. 77, 81, 83, 164
Lange, A. 268
Lantis, M. 366
Larson, G. J. 156
Laszlo, E. 192–3
Latakos, I. 147
Le Bras, G. 325
Leeuw, G. van der 19, 39, 51, 53, 61, 78, 105, 110–111, 122, 182, 232, 303, 323, 352
Lehmann, E. 72
Leibniz, G. W. 138
Lenzer, G. 333
Lersch, P. 260
Leuba, J. H. 274
Lévi-Strauss, C. 23, 357, 360, 364, 367, 373, 376, 380
Lévy-Bruhl, L. 352
Lhermitte, J. 266
Lienhardt, G. 218
Lincoln, B. 376
Ling, T. 75
Linton, R. 388
Lipsey, R. 198
Lofland, J. 299
Lonergan, B. J. F. 150
Long, C. 120, 127
Lowe, W. M. 297
Lübbe, H. 340
Lubin, A. J. 299
Luckmann, T. 340–343
Ludwig, D. J. 298
Luhmann, Niklas 337, 338–340
Lundberg, G. A. 329

Macaulay, Lord 196
McDowell, V. H. 291
Maciejewski, Franz 337

Maduro, O. 234
Malinowski, B. 129, 321–323
Mallory, M. M. 293, 294
Mann, U. 81, 154, 278, 279
Marcuse, H. 241
Martin, David 340
Marx, K. 20, 321, 333, 354
Maslow, Abraham 257
Massignon, L. 195
Matthes, J. 329
Mauss, M. 380
Mbiti, John 16, 17, 192, 216–20, 223–5, 227–9, 234
Meerwin, F. 261
Mehanden, M. 131
Meissner, W. W. 255, 261
Mensching, G. 78, 81, 324
Meslin, M. 82, 140
Metz, J. B. 336
Meyers, D. 392
Milanesi, G. 268
Mille, R. de 388
Miller, J. F. 145–6
Minturn, L. 389
Mol, Hans 344
Moore, O. K. 394
Moore, P. 128
Moore, T. W. 263
Morgan, K. 230
Morgan, R. 81, 126–7
Müller, Max 11, 36
Müller-Pozzi, H. 261, 264, 277, 307
Mumford, L. 239
Munchhausen, Baron von 360
Murdock, G. P. 389
Murti, T. R. V. 203

Naravane, V. S. 198, 204
Nase, E. 261
Nasr, S. H. 16, 192, 213–17, 222–5, 227–9
Neusner, J. 234
Nietzsche, F. 199

Nketia, J. H. K. 218
Norbeck, Edward 392
Nottingham, E. K. 329, 331

Olson, A. M. 164
Oosten, J. 351–384, 393
Oppermann, R. 264
Otto, R. 20, 38, 72, 78, 88, 103, 131, 140, 183, 232, 260, 264, 274, 275, 324
Oxtoby, W. 52–3, 66, 135

Pahuke, W. N. 292, 301, 302
Panikkar, R. 17, 21, 39
Pannenberg, W. 150–1, 154
Pareto, Vilfredo 321, 322
Parratt, J. 220
Parrinder, G. 218
Parsons, Talcott 321, 323, 324, 326–32, 339
Pedersen, J. 72
Penner, H. 72, 115, 131, 141, 146
Pentikäinen, Juha 111, 163
Pettazzoni, R. 61, 72, 95, 107, 137
Pfennigsdorf, D. E. 274
Philp, H. L. 256
Piaget, J. 258, 290
Pohier, J. M. 266
Polanyi, M. 5
Pöll, W. 264, 281, 283, 284, 307
Poniatowski, Z. 145
Popper, K. 80
Pratt, J. B. 274, 290
Preuss, H. G. 261
Proust, Marcel 283
Pruyser, P. W. 277, 297
Puech, H. 69, 86
Pummer, R. 47, 83, 97, 138–9, 140
Pye, M. 81, 126, 127, 163

Radhakrishnan, S. 16, 104, 129, 192, 198, 201–6, 209–10, 213, 217, 222–5, 227–9, 234

Rahner, K. 336
Rajamanickam, M. 268
Rambo, L. 255
Randall, R. L. 261
Ransohoff, P. 255
Rapaport, D. 298
Rappaport, R. 395
Rasmussen, K. 366
Ratschow, C. H. 81
Redfield, R. 393
Reich, C. 241
Ricoeur, Paul 307
Ridick, J. 267
Riecken, H. W. 299
Ringgren, H. 75
Robertson-Smith, W. 354
Robinson, J. 178
Rochedieu, E. 267
Rogers, W. R. 305
Rokeach, M. 300
Rolland, R. 199, 272
Rouner, L. 205
Rousseau, J. J. 386
Rizzuto, A. M. 261, 297
Rudolph, K. 69, 72, 73, 76–8, 81, 104, 112, 119, 147
Rulla, L. M. 267
Rykwert, J. 198, 201

Sahlins, M. 395
Saichi, A. 208
Said, Edward 192, 194–7, 201–2, 209, 230, 232, 235
Saliba, J. A. 123
Sarma, V. S. 78
Sartre, J. P. 188
Saussaye, C. de la 51
Savramis, D. 322
Scharfenberg, J. 261
Schatz, Oskar 336
Schaub, E. L. 259
Scheler, M. 276
Schilpp, P. A. 204, 239

Schimmel, A. 61
Schmid, G. 39, 80, 130, 151–5
Schmid, L. 292
Schmitt, C. B. 200
Schoffeleers, M. 392–3
Scholem, G. 212
Schrader, R. R. 297
Schreuder, O. 329
Schröder, C. M. 69
Schüttler, G. 265, 292, 297, 299
Schumacher, E. F. 239
Scobie, G. E. W. 311
Segal, P. 6, 20–21, 39
Séguy, J. 82, 148–9
Shah of Iran 4–5
Shaku, S. 209
Shachter, S. 299
Sharpe, E. 36, 42, 51–2, 59–61, 63–7, 77, 79, 92, 135, 157
Shaw, M. E. 270
Shostrom, E. L. 295
Siebert, R. J. 164
Sierksma, F. 268, 307
Silverman, D. 387
Simmel, G. 321, 324
Simon, H. 61
Siwek, P. 266
Skinner, R. F. 274
Smart, N. 18, 19, 20, 34, 39, 66, 76, 82, 97, 100, 123, 126, 128, 140–1, 150, 163, 177–190, 220–1
Smith, Huston 6, 39
Smith, W. C. 17, 20, 21, 25, 65, 129, 134–6, 158, 230–252, 258, 259, 271, 284, 296
Smith, J. 49
Söderblom, N. 103, 268
Spencer, H. 321, 322, 323, 339
Spiegel, Y. 261
Spiro, M. E. 141, 144, 356, 388, 389
Spranger, E. 257, 264
Staal, F. 186
Stace, W. T. 186

Stählin, W. 282
Starbuck, E. 260, 272
Stephenson, G. 81
Stern, W. 279, 282–3
Stöhr, M. 336
Storey, C. 22, 39
Storey, J. 22, 39
Stratton, G. M. 272, 303, 304
Streng, F. 85, 91, 128–9
Ström, A. V. 75
Strommen, M. P. 255–6, 257
Sullivan, L. 165
Suzuki, D. T. 16, 192, 206–10, 212–3, 215, 217, 222–5, 227–9, 234
Swanson, G. E. 390

Tagore, R. 198, 202
Tamayo, A. 267
Tart, C. T. 257
Tauxe, N. C. 266
Taylor, J. V. 217–8
Tempels, P. 217–8
Terrin, N. 165
Te Vault, R. K. 299
Thrower, J. 58, 234
Thun, T. 264, 290, 291
Tillich, P. 26, 39, 178
Tingsten, H. 287–9
Toffler, A. 192
Tokarev, S. A. 75
Toporov, A. 376
Torataro, S. 208
Toulmin, S. 147
Tracy, D. 165
Trandis, M. 389
Traxel, W. 281
Trillhaas, W. 264, 278
Troeltsch, E. 151, 324
Turner, V. 380, 391–2
Tworuschka, U. 154
Tylor, E. B. 22, 188

Urban, G. R. 239

Van de Kemp, H. 259, 260
Venturi, P. T. 72
Vergote, A. 267
Veto, L. 264, 301
Vetter, G. B. 258, 287, 288, 289
Vogt, E. Z. 394
Voltaire, F. M. A. de 322

Waardenburg, J. 2, 11, 12, 37, 39, 42, 51, 53–6, 72, 76, 80, 87, 97, 100, 103, 106, 115–9, 131–36, 162–3
Wach, J. 79, 82, 122, 183, 324
Wallace, A. F. C. 286–8, 392, 393
Walther, G. 264
Warren, N. C. 302
Watson, J. B. 274
Watson, L. C. 292
Weber, Max 15, 185, 188, 211, 321, 322, 324–6, 332, 334, 335, 340–1, 361
Wehr, G. 307
Wei Ming-Tu 9
Weitbrecht, H. J. 265
Werblowsky, R. J. Zwi 61–5, 68, 71, 79, 110, 212
Whaling, F. 1–59, 124, 220–1, 191–251
White, Lynn 209
Whiting, J. W. 389, 390
Whitman, W. 199
Widengren, G. 61, 69, 71, 76–7, 90, 102–3, 182
Wiebe, D. 6, 20–1, 39, 145, 164
Wiese, Leopold von 324
Wilkins, C. 196
Wilson, B. R. 392
Wilson, H. H. 196
Winckel, van de 266
Wittgenstein, L. 355–6
Wobbermin, C. 277
Wolf, N. 389
Wood, W. W. 297
Wright, J. M. 270

Wulff, David   16, 253–320
Wundt, W.   303

Yarian, S. O.   164
Yinger, J. M.   144, 293, 332, 356

Yonan, E. A.   146
Young, F. W.   390
Young, K.   505

Zaehner, R. C.   186, 201
Zahrut, H.   261

General Index

Abstraction, Levels of 66
Acculturation of Religions 99
Actions, Religious 143–4, 152, 171
Adelaide 68
Administrations and Social Sciences 165–6
Aesthetic Criticism 52, 200
Aesthetics 35, 52, 200, 226
Africa 58–9, 158, 225, 232–3
African Christianity 216–20, 225–6, 228
African Independent Churches 24, 187
African Religion 3, 12, 102, 187, 216–20, 223
African Religious Studies 242
African Scholars 216–20, 225–6, 228
Agnosticism 186, 274, 322
Ahiṃsā 394
Ahistorical Approach 91
Akamba 217
Allah 29, 241, 355
Allgemeine Religionswissenschaft 85, 91, 92
Allport-Vernon-Lindsey Study of Values 295
Alor 389
Alus 388
Âme 373, 374
American Association for the Advancement of Atheism 287
American Government Policy 195
American Psychological Association 309
American Scholars 161, 232
American Society for the Study of Religion 46
American Theories in Religious Studies 34–9, 56

Amida Buddha 31
Amish 185
Amsterdam (IAHR) (1950) 60, 63
Amsterdam University 44
Analogy 96
Ancestors, Ancestor Worship 217, 226, 358, 263–4
Andhra University 201
Aṅgakkut 366
Anglo-Saxon Scholars 177, 232
Anima 387
Animal Psychology Research 274
Animal Tests 297
Animism 217
Aninga 378
Ankara 231
Anonymous Religion 152
Anthropologists 113, 131, 141, 144, 351–384, 385–397
Anthropology 23–4, 90, 112, 160, 187, 218, 228–9, 241, 255–6, 303, 306
Anthropology of Religion 33–4, 76, 108–9, 111–12, 191, 193, 203, 228, 232, 235, 346, 351–384, 385–397
Anti-Historical Approach 91, 123–4
Apologetics 202, 235, 254, 259
Aquinas, Thomas 31, 237
Archaeology 73, 89–90, 107
Archaic Religion (Religions of Antiquity) 79, 124–6, 160–1, 224–5, 342
Archetypes 187, 200, 229, 261–2, 305
Archetypal Psychology 262–3
Archiv für Religionspsychologie 263
A-Religiosity 117, 163
Aristotle 209, 237, 322
Art 198–9, 200–1, 215, 241, 286, 290, 357

Art (Is Religious Studies Art or Science?) 46
Asceticism 265, 357
Asia 158, 230, 232–3
Aspectual Studies of Religion 76, 140
Association internationale d'études medico-psychologiques et religieuses 309
Associationist Theory 259
Astonishment 152
Astronomy 237
Aśvaghoṣa 224
Athabascans 367
Atheism 117–8, 140, 256, 274, 276, 287–8
Ātman 29
Attitude Scales 270
Augustine, St. 237, 353
Aurobindo, Sri 198, 202
Australia 57, 59, 67
Austrian Scholars 227
Autobiography 286–9
Awe 281
Axial Age 28, 31
al-Azhar 240
Aztecs 26, 394–5

Baluba 217
Bangkok 68
Bankei 209
Bantu Philosophy 217, 219, 224
Barrington College (R. I.) 217
Behaviourism 280
Behaviour, Religious 143–4, 152, 228
Being 123
Belgian Theories in Religious Studies 260
Belgium 68
Belief(s) 123, 129, 135, 152, 180, 219, 270, 272, 293, 331, 355, 357, 358, 360, 365, 370, 372
Belief Systems 270, 328–9, 334–5, 342, 345, 355
Believer 134, 143, 180 (*see* Faith)

Bible 211, 370
Bible Stories 290, 304
Biblical Exegesis 120–1
Biblical Interpretation 52
Biblical Scholarship 178
Bibliography(ies) 42, 44, 69–84, 165–75, 245–51, 312–20, 382–4, 395–7
Biography, Religious 306
Birmingham University 217
Blake, William 199
Bòdhisattva 378
Body Symbolism 381
Bohr, Nils 5, 239
Bonaventura St. 31
Book, Religions of 369
Bosnia 4, 37
Bossey Ecumenical Institute 217, 225
Boston Museum of Fine Arts 198, 225
Brahman 29, 241
Brahmins 365, 370
Britain 59, 158, 225, 232
British Association of the History of Religions 68
British Empire 232 (*see* Imperialism)
British Scholars 57, 232
British Theories in Religious Studies 36, 38
Brussels 131
Brussels (1935) 61
Buddha 21, 27, 29, 35, 182, 199, 206, 262, 363
Buddhism (Buddhist Tradition) 3, 161, 179, 185, 198–9, 203, 206–10, 220–4, 358, 362, 363, 369, 371, 372
Buddhists 182, 199, 202, 210, 225, 230
Buddhist Scholars 161, 210, 225–7, 230, 233
Buddhist Studies 242
Buddhist Studies, International Association of 67
Buddhology 21, 179
Burial 28

Cairo 240
Calcutta University 201
Caitanya 31
Calligraphy 35
Calvinism 361
Cambodia 3
Cambridge University 217, 225
Canada 57, 68
Canadian Council of Religion 44
Canton 220
Cargo Cults 26, 393
Carmelites 46
Carnival 379
Caste System 353
Category Selection 275–6
Cathars 371
Catholic Psychology 254, 265–7
Catholics 325–6, 353, 370–1 (*see* Roman Catholics)
Causality Criterion 145
Causal Theories of Empathy 269
Cave Paintings 28
Celebration 152
Celibacy 557
Centres for the Study of Religion 231, 242–3
Ceylon (Sri Lanka) 198
Change, Religious 3–10, 22–4, 99, 162
Chatham College, Pittsburg 220, 225
Chechnya 4
Cherokee 367
Chicago School 57, 122, 231
China 68, 189, 197, 206, 211, 220–3, 225, 232, 240
Chinese Buddhists 199, 207
Chinese Language 45
Chinese Philosophy 220–3
Chinese Religion 217, 225, 363
Chinese Religious Studies 242
Chinese Scholars 196, 220–3
Ch'ing 221
Ching I 222
Christ 29, 199, 262, 291, 300, 358, 377

Christendom 8–10
Christianity (Christian Tradition) 102, 160–1, 177–9, 185, 190, 205, 210–12, 215, 224, 227–8, 258, 304, 323, 329, 340–1, 351–5, 358, 361, 362, 369, 371, 372
Christian Ethics 394
Christian Institutions 201
Christian Philosophy of Religion 149
Christian Studies 242
Christian Theology of Religious Studies 19–22, 177–190, 351–5
Christian Truth 178
Christmas 369, 371
Chuang Tzu 208
Chuckchee 367
Chu Hsi 31, 221–2
Church 291, 293, 353–5, 370, 372
Church History 177
Church of England 217
Church Offices 152
Church, Mission of 325, 351
Church, Nurture 325
Church/Sect Typology 324, 326, 345
Cicero 236
Ciel 373
Civil Religion 4, 18, 333–5
Claremont (1965) 61, 63, 65
Classical Approaches to the Study of Religion 1, 2, 11, 37–8
Classical Culture and Church 353
Classification (Systems) 51–2, 115–6, 188, 377
Classless State 331
Climates 238
Club of Rome 10, 238
Cognitive Function of Religion 143
Cold War (and its end) 5, 17–18
Colgate University 230
Collaboration of Religion Scholars 88, 243 (*see* Teamwork)
Colloquium 231
Colombo 197

Colonialism   3, 160, 183, 195, 230, 232
Commitment   78, 133, 178, 180, 203,
   205, 209–10, 219, 223, 228–9, 235
Communication of World Views   355,
   373, 382, 391
Communism   3–4, 8, 192, 234–5, 327,
   331
Communitas   391–2
Comparative Models   29, 34–5, 359
Comparative Hermeneutics   126–7
Comparative Mysticism   127–8, 207–8
Comparative Mythology   303
Comparative Religion   1, 54–5, 66, 72,
   78, 83, 85, 87, 100, 102, 105, 108, 110,
   137, 161, 177, 182–3, 193, 200–1, 214,
   226, 228, 231, 240–1, 303, 332, 390
Comparative Religion, Historical
   27–31, 95–8, 105, 133
Comparative Religion, Phenomenological
   119
Comparative Religion of History of Reli-
   gion   92, 177
Comparative Religion of Sociology   92
Comparative Symbolism   131
Comparative Typology   332, 390
Comparisons of Two Traditions   126–7
Complementary between Approaches
   33–5, 48, 65, 130, 193, 242–3
Complexity Concept   339–40
Comprehension   130, 153
Computers   5, 7, 15–16, 293
Concentric Circles of Religions   103
Concepts, Religious   112, 143, 188, 219
Conceptual Imperialism   195–7
Condolence Ceremony   392
Confession of Sins   102, 152
Conflict Situations and Theory   17–19,
   162, 332–4, 392–3
Confrontation of Religions   17–19, 118,
   355
Confucian Bloc   8–9
Confucian Centres   240
Confucianism (Confucian Tradition)
   220–3

Confucius   29, 221, 363
Conscience   291, 374
Consciousness   207
Consciousness, States of   257, 277
Consciousness, Stream of   282
Conservative Christian Theology   274
Constructive Dialogue   179
Constructive Traditionalism   178
Contemplation   200, 266
Contemporary Approaches to the Study
   of Religion   1–39
Contemporary Religions, Interest in
   1–39, 223–6, 229
Content Analysis   292, 301
Contingency Problem   339–40
Continuities in History of Religions
   27–32, 96, 99, 199
Contrastive Typologies   110
Conversion   210, 265
Converts West to East   210
Copenhagen University   73
Core Typologies   110
Correspondence Criterion   145
Cosmos of Nomos   343
Cow Slaughter   394
Creation   71
Creation Myths   367, 378
Creative Hermeneutics   126–7
Creed   308
Critique of Eliade and Lévi-Strauss
   125–6
Cross-Cultural Comparison   140, 144
Cultic Objects   152
Cults   71, 152, 342
Cultural Anthropology   1, 142–4, 351–
   384, 385–397
Cultural Role of Study of Religion   55
Cumulative Religious Tradition   134

Dalai Lama   7, 309
Danger and Taboo   351
Daniel   211
Danish Language   73

Dartmouth College 220, 225
Darwinism 136
Data of Religious Studies, Scope and
    Nature 22–4, 56, 171–2
Death 228–9, 291, 294, 337, 375, 379
Decay of Religion 99
Definition of Religion 22–3, 47, 55, 81,
    83, 86–7, 92, 96, 129–30, 140, 142,
    146, 153, 162–3, 269–70, 331–2,
    341–3, 355–7, 374
Definitions of Religion: Inclusive/Exclu-
    sive 14, 22–3, 331–2, 341–3
Definitions of Religion: Individual/
    Social 22–3
Definitions of Religion: Nominal/Real
    22–3
Deity, Conception of 82 (*see* God)
Delusion 254
Democracy 331
Demon Possession 304
Denominations, Religious 290, 308, 310
Depth Psychology and Religion 256
Depth Structures 144
Desacralisation 124
Description of Data 48–50, 65, 70, 86,
    95, 98, 100–1, 102, 105–6, 130, 148,
    153
Description *of* Normative 94–5, 119,
    122, 148, 163
Description *of* Explanation 254, 257,
    260–5, 275, 276
Destiny of Humanity 71, 229
Development of Religion 96, 99, 116
Devotion 73
Dharma 29, 374
Dhyāna 2–708
Dialectic 21, 237
Dialectical Materialism 234
Dialogue, Inter-Religious and Academic
    17, 21, 65, 134, 163, 179–80, 205, 212,
    219, 225–7, 231, 235
Diary 286
Differentiation and Identity in Religion
    262, 339–40, 344–5

Dimensional, Multi in Religion 148
Dinka 218
Directionality 145
Discipline, Religious Studies a Discipline
    or Field of Studies? 46, 55, 140, 142,
    162, 396–7, 232, 237, 241
Diversification of Data 11, 90, 99
Divine, Concepts of 304
Divine, Experience of 270
Divine Figure 123
Divine Reality 151
Divinity 351 (*see* Deity, God)
Divisional Studies of Religion 76
Doctrine 71, 178, 188
Dogma 353
Dogmatism 294
Dogs 367
Dorpat School 263–4, 300–1
Draw-a-Person Test 297
Dream Analysis 299
Dreams 283, 305
Drugs 283
Dutch Language 73
Dutch Scholars 52

East Germany 58, 234
East-West Symposium 63
Easter 369, 371
Eastern Europe 45
Eastern Religions 257, 268, 334
Eckhart 208
Ecological Crisis 5–10, 192–3, 215–6,
    236, 238
Ecological Models 368, 393–5
Ecology of Religion 108, 111, 241
Economic History 185
Economic Recession 158
Economies and Religion 4–10, 361,
    362, 368
Ecosystem and Religion 393–5
Ecstatic Religion 265, 304
Educational Models 236–43
EEG Recordings 286

Ego Psychology   261
Egyptian Religion   26, 358, 375
Eidetic Vision   51–2, 101, 106, 114
Einfühlung   17, 19, 32, 204, 230, 241,
   264, 269
Electronic Models   290
Emigration Worldwide   7–10
Empathy   51–2, 190, 221–2, 264, 269,
   357
Empires   3
Empirical Approach   100, 122, 148, 181
Empirical Essence   101
Empirical Positivism   146–7
Empirical Psychology   254
Empirical Research   380
Empirical Science   146–7
Empirical Study of Religion   86, 108,
   110, 146, 163, 181
Empirical Typology   110
Emptiness   208
Energy Problems   4–6, 192, 238
English Language   69–70, 123, 138,
   145, 177, 217–8, 232
Enlightenment   206, 322, 333
Entelecheia of Religious Phenomena
   106
Enthusiasm   152
Epistemology   141–2, 302
Epochē   17, 19, 32, 51–2, 101, 106, 114,
   133, 163, 202, 277, 278
Equanimity   289
Eranos Circle   208
Erscheinungen   52
Eschatology   71, 217, 337
Esprit   373
Essence   51, 53, 55, 63, 71–2, 78, 86,
   88, 93, 100–1, 106–8, 112, 116–7, 143,
   148, 163, 182, 215, 229
Essence of Religion   308
Essences   351
Essential Intuitive Reductionism   109,
   119, 148
Ethics   71, 162, 228, 302, 328–9, 371–2,
   376–7

Ethnic Nationalism   4
Ethnocentrism in Study of Religion
   351–5, 364, 375
Ethnography   73, 324, 395
Ethnology   75, 90, 112, 160
Ethnophilosophy   231
Études Carmélitaines   266
Europe (Continent)   59, 177, 206,
   232–3
European Scholars   25–6, 60, 210
Evangelical Christians   258
Evil   358
Evolution of Religion   55, 75, 87, 184,
   217
Evolutionary Models   329, 333–4,
   338–41, 345
Evolutionary Universals   329
Exclusion of Transcendent   277
Existence of God   78, 178
Existentialism   321, 333, 391
Existential Understanding   127, 212,
   222
Exorcism   304, 365
Exotic Religion   124, 161
Experimental Introspection   263, 267
Experimental Method   140, 146–7
Experimental Psychology   267, 300–2
Explanations of Religion   83, 97, 120,
   141, 143, 146, 187, 254, 354, 382
Expressive Culture, Religion as   67,
   143–4
Extrinsic/Intrinsic Religiousness   268

Factor Analysis   270, 293
Facts, Nature of   90–1, 102, 117
Faith   20, 75, 78, 109, 122, 129, 133–6,
   190, 205, 271, 275, 294, 296, 355, 359,
   363, 365
Faith, A.   53, 162, 179–80
Faith of Scholar   273–5
Faith, Scholarly Endeavour as   259
Faith, Stages of   258
Fall (into Profane History)   124

Fantasies 283, 305
Fascism 331
Father God 272, 305
Female in Religion 185
Ficino, M. 209
Field or Discipline, Religious Studies as
46, 55, 140, 142, 162, 188–9, 232, 237,
241
Field Work 66, 144
Finland (*see* Turku) 66, 68, 80, 189
Focal Point (View of Religious Studies
of Subject) 142
Folklore (Folktale) 102, 112
Folklorists 113, 144
Food 238
Food-Gathering 123
Founders, Religious 87
Francis, St 35
Frankfurt Jewish Institute 211
Frankfurt School 336–8
Free Association 281, 298
French Language 69–70, 79, 138, 145,
217–8
French Psychopathologists of Religion
265
French Religious Behaviour 325
French Scholars 49, 57
French Theories in Religious Studies
254, 265–6, 276
Freudian Notions of Religion 258,
265–7, 276, 307, 389
Freudian Psychology 256
Functional Definition of Religion 87,
128–9
Functionalism 329–32, 336, 338, 340
Function of Religion in Society 55,
107, 142, 144, 163
Functional Understanding 129
Future of Mankind 9–10, 162
Future of Religion 93
Future of Religious Studies 156–65,
233–43, 308–11
Future Reward 305
Future Time 220

Galileo, Galilei 353
Gandhi, M. K. 198, 202
Geisteswissenschaft 143
Genesis of Religion 96
Genetics 5, 192
Geneva University 267
Geographical Areas in Religious Studies
56–9, 233
Geographical Orient 75
Geography 237, 241
Germanic Areas 57
Germanic Religion 369
German Language 69–70, 72–3, 79,
119, 138, 144, 154, 217–8
German Scholars 52, 78
German Theories of Religious Studies
254, 260–5, 276, 324, 336
Germany 211
Gestalt Psychology 276
al-Ghazali 31
Ghosts 373
Gifford Lectures 214
Giotto 35
Global Context 2–10, 11, 59, 63, 125,
159, 164, 177, 191–251
Global Environment 135, 191–2,
232–3
Global History of Religion 27–32, 36
Global Problems 192–3, 203, 238–41
Global Theology 21–2, 36
Global Unity 64, 135, 204–6, 227–8,
232–3
Global Warming 7
Gnomes 365, 381
Gnosticism 26, 62, 73, 304
God 146, 180, 185–6, 193–4, 200, 215,
217, 219, 229, 237–9, 260, 262, 265,
267, 282, 291, 297, 339, 355, 360, 373
Gods 358, 360, 363, 364, 375, 377
Good Friday 301
Grace 289
Graeco-Roman Educational Model
193, 236–8

Grammar 237
Grant, C. 196
Great Tradition *of* Little Tradition 370
Greece 236
Greek Academies 240
Greek Culture 193
Greek Language 160
Greek Religion 26, 28, 324, 334, 361, 363, 369, 375
Groningen 80, 131, 142
Guilt 288
Guru 206, 210

Hagiography 73
Hamburg University 217
Han Confucianism 221
Handbooks in Religious Studies 69–84
Hands, Shaking and Symbolism 381
Han Yu 221
Harvard University 213, 220, 225, 231
Healing 364, 387
Heaven 229, 305
Hebrew Bible 211
Hebrew Language 210–3
Hebrew Texts 211
Hebrew University Jerusalem 211
Helicopter 386
Heresy 371
Hermeneutical Phenomenology 94, 100, 111, 115, 117 (*cf* Phenomenological Typology)
Hermeneutics 52, 54, 57, 80–1, 91, 98, 111, 120–37, 156, 163–4, 178, 181, 220, 224, 232, 235, 241, 293, 359, 374
Hermeneutics/Hermeneutic 121
Hermeneutics *of* Techniques 305–8
Hero 344
Heuristic Function 97–8
Hierophony 124–6
Hinduism (Hindu Tradition) 3, 73, 190, 198–9, 201–6, 296, 304, 371
Hindus 196, 225–6
Hindu Scholars 201–6, 226–8, 230, 233

Hindu Studies 242
Historical Criticism 58, 181
Historical Phenomenology 100, 107
Historical Positivism 97
Historical Typology 96, 109
Historical Universals 96
Histories of Religion/History of Religion 88
History 48, 179, 215, 237, 241
History and Phenomenology of Religion 41–176, 193, 259
History as Becoming 89
History as Knowledge 89
History as Unitary 86–7
History in the History of Religions 85–99
History of the History of Religions 71, 84, 157, 188
History of Religion(s) 1, 11, 27–9, 42, 57, 63–7, 72, 75, 85–99, 106, 111, 142, 156, 164, 183–5, 187, 190, 203, 205, 212–3, 228–9, 232, 235, 254, 255, 259, 280, 303, 311, 324, 329, 344
History of Religions in Wider Whole 97
History of Religions as Unitary 27–9, 89, 99, 124, 135, 183
History of Religions, Levels of Analysis 44, 46–56, 75–89
History of Religions *of* Phenomenology of Religion 50–1, 63–4, 69–70, 72, 76–7, 79–80, 85–6, 129
History of Religions *of* Systematic Approach 48, 53–4, 76–80, 85, 119, 129, 161
History of Religions *of* Theological Approach 64, 94
History of Religions, Views of it 85–99
History, Terror of 124
Holistic Studies of Religion 76, 118
Holland 57, 63, 115, 269
Holocaust 225
Holy 20, 264

Homo Academicus 229
Homo Religiosus 140, 158, 229
Hope 152, 205
Humane Sciences 64, 82, 145, 181–90, 241
Humanism 26, 122, 144, 187, 204, 222
Humanistic Psychology 257, 259
Humanitas 193–4, 226–8
Humanities *of* Natural Sciences 193–4, 238–43
Humanities *of* Theology 193–4, 238–43
Humanity (Humankind) 86, 124
Human Nature as unitary 87
Human Nature, Model of 257
Human Potential Movement 257
Human Relations Area Files 389
Hunter Gatherers 367
Hymns 304, 305, 375, 377

I-Thou 211–3, 227, 229
Ibadan 231
Iconography 39, 131
Idealism, Philosophical 202–6, 229
Identity, Concept of 344–5
Ideology/ies 17–19, 162, 331, 340, 342, 361–3
Idiographic *of* Nomothetic Methods 287, 292
Ifaluk 388
Images 131
Imagination 181
Imago Dei 337
Immanence 229
Immigration as a Religious Factor 7–10, 23
Imperialism 160, 183, 195, 230, 232 (*see* Empire)
Independent Nations, Religious Studies 56, 64, 192
Independence Movements and Religion 3, 23
Incas 26
India 57, 64, 67, 78, 198–9, 201, 206, 225

Indian Art 224
Indian Philosophy 196, 199–407
Indian Religion 8, 102, 161, 200–1, 223, 353, 358, 363, 374, 375, 395
Indian Scholars(hip) 201–6, 223, 268
Indian Renaissance 196, 203
Individual *of* Group 294–5
Individual Religiousness 385–95
Individuation 262
Indonesia 199
Induction *of* Deduction 238–9
Inductive Generalisation 98
Inductive Reasoning 146–7
Industrialisation 6–10, 325
Industrial Revolution 200
Industrial Sociology 325–6
Industrial West *of* Small-Scale Societies 321–4
Infant Psychology Research 274
Initiation 62, 379, 389, 390
Inspiration 265
Institutional Factors in Religious Studies 47, 118, 158, 184–5, 201
Institutionalised Religion 118, 342
Integration in Religious Studies 44, 47, 54, 57, 80, 117, 119, 122, 130, 137, 148–151, 158–9, 193–4, 235, 242–3
Intentionality 101, 115, 117, 130, 132, 142, 162, 241
Inter-disciplinary work 42–3, 47, 55, 66, 83, 139, 159–60, 234, 242–3
Inter-Faith Dialogue 17–19
International Association of the History of Religions 41–2, 44, 59–69, 81, 90, 104, 159, 165
International Association of the Study of the History of Religions 60
International Co-operation 42–3, 45, 56, 64, 164 (*see* Global Unity)
International Debate in History and Phenomenology of Religion 56–71
Internationale Gesellschaft für Religionspsychologie 309

Interpretation   49–50, 70, 76, 90, 102,
    111, 116, 120, 123, 126, 132, 155, 163,
    219, 224, 231
Interpretation of Reality (Religious
    Studies as)   163
Interpretative Phenomenology   100, 111
Inter-religious Rapprochement   104, 163
    (*see* Dialogue)
Interviews   290–2
Introspection   280–92
Introversion *cf* Extroversion   294
Intuitive *cf* Objective Approach   292
Intuition   51–2, 64, 109, 111, 116, 119,
    148, 199, 204
Inwardness   216
Ionian Philosophers   29
Iowa (1974)   138
Iqbal, Sir M.   198
Iran   4–5, 213
Iranian Scholars   213–16, 222
Iroquois   392
Irrational in Religion   116
Islam   3, 8, 102, 161, 196, 213–6, 219,
    223, 225, 352, 353, 355, 358, 369, 371,
    372
Israel   57, 59, 63
Israel (Ancient)   334
Italian Language   69, 72
Italian Scholars   57, 63, 196

Japan   3, 57, 59, 63, 67, 206, 210, 225,
    232, 268
Japanese Language   45
Japanese Religion   206–10
Japanese Scholars   161, 206–10, 223
Jehovah's Witnesses   26
Jen   221–2, 226
Jerusalem   211
Jerusalem (1968)   62
Jewish Bible   211–2
Jewish Literature   197
Jewish Scholars   196, 210–3, 225–8,
    233–4

Jewish Studies   242
Jews   268, 304, 352, 358, 361, 369
Job   360
John of the Cross, St   293
Jonestown   36
Journal for the Scientific Study of Reli-
    gion   256
Journal of Psychology and Theology
    258
Journals   68–9
Joy   289
Judaeo-Christian Tradition   304, 337
Judaism   178–9, 210–3, 223, 225
Judgements, Religious (*see also* Value
    Judgements)   101
Jungian Psychology   256, 261–3, 307

Kabīr   199, 207
Kapsiki   386
Kant, Immanuel   199
Karamazov   187
Karma   199, 374
Kenya   216
Kenyan Scholars   216–20, 223
Khomeini, Ayatullah   185
Kingdom of God   211
Kissing   381
Knowledge   229
Knowledge as Unitary   192–4, 239–43
Knowledge, Religion as   162
Korea   57

Laboratory Religion   302
Lancaster (1975)   61, 131, 189
Lancaster University   66, 126
Language, Nature and Role of   99, 120,
    237, 323–4, 372
Laos   3
Loa Tzu   199, 208
Latin Language   160, 209
Leaders, Religious   219
Lebensphilosophie   321
Leeds University   44

Legalism (China) 221
Leibniz, G. W. 138
Leicester University 61
Leiden University 61, 351–84
Leiden (1942) 61
Leipzig University 58, 112
Lenberg 211
Letters 286
Letters to God 297
Li 222
Li Ao 221
Liberation 37
Liberation of Man 125
Liberation Theology 219, 220
Life/Death 363, 377, 381
Life Sciences 145
Liminality 380
Limit Concept 136
Lingnan University 220
Linguistic Areas in Religious Studies
 233
Literary Criticism 52
Literature 121, 188, 241
Logos 106
London University 198
Loudun 304
Love 355
Lumen Vitae 266
Lund (1929) 61

McGill University 231
Maat 358
Machiavelli, N. 322
Madras Christian College 201
Madras University 201, 268
Magic 217, 329, 362, 364
Magic, Black/White 364–5
Mahāvīra 29
Mahāyāna Buddhism 206–10, 224
Maimonides 31
Major Religions *of* Primal Religions
 25–6
Makerere University College 216–7

Male/Female 377, 381
Man viz God 134, 164, 213, 263–43
Man *of* Nature 193–4, 213, 219, 236–43
Man, Concept of 71, 212
Man, Destiny of 61, 229
Man, Nature of 61, 219
Manchester College Oxford 201
Mandaism 73
Mandate of Heaven 18
Manichaean 26, 32
Manifestation 114
Mao, Chairman 4, 6, 189
Maoism 4, 6, 189
Marburg (1960) 61, 63–4, 92, 131, 138
Marriage 379
Marxism 75, 184, 187, 189, 192, 233–5
Marxist-Christian Dialogue 17–19, 336
Marxist Concepts of Religion 8, 17–19,
 335–6, 338, 393
Massachusetts Institute of Technology
 213
Master Race 331
Mathematics 237
Māyā 199, 205, 274
Mayas 26
Meaning 99, 101, 107–8, 111, 116–7,
 120, 122–3, 132–3, 162, 228, 376, 395
Media 7–8, 74
Medical Ethics 236
Meditation 257, 297, 302, 363
Melanesian Religion 394–5
Mental Illness 274
Merit/Demerit 375
Mesopotamian Religion 26
Messianism 361, 368
Messina (1966) 62
Metaphysics 198, 200, 214, 228
Metareligionswissenschaft 145
Methodenstreit 47
Method in Religious Studies 62–85, 92,
 102, 104, 109, 117, 137–56, 157–64,
 177–190, 234–5
Methodological Agnosticism 186

Methodological Atheism 186
Methods in Psychology of Religion
279–308
Mexico 67
Mexico (1995) 13
Microtechnology 192
Middle East 57
Milton Keynes 75
Millenarian Religious Groups 299, 393
Ming 221
Minor Religions 26
Miracles 222, 266
Mithraic Studies, Society of 67
Mithraism 13
Models of Religion 29, 34–5
Models in Sciences 125–6
Modern Reform Movements 192, 196,
203, 206, 209, 223, 225
Modernisation 4–10
Moerbeke, William of 209
Mokṣa 29, 374
Morphology 112
Monotheism/Polytheism 390
Moral Majority 8
Mormons 26
Mo Tzu 221
Mudras 35
Mughals 199
Muhammad 33
Multi-Methods in Religious Studies
83–4, 140, 142, 189–90, 234
Muntu 217
Museums of Religion 37
Music 35–6, 188
Muslims 226
Muslim Scholars 196, 213–6, 226–7,
228, 230, 233
Muslim Studies 242
Muslim Tradition 232 (*see* Islam)
Myōkōnin 208
Mysore University 201
Mystery in Religion 204
Mystery Religions 73

Mysticism 127–9, 131, 183, 186–7,
207–8, 210, 212–3, 223, 229
Mysticism, Church/Sect Type 264
Mysticism, Drugs 301, 387
Mysticism, Four Types 208
Mysticism, Spiritual 265, 266, 302
Mysticism, Transpersonal 257
Myth(s) 71, 102, 112, 123, 129, 133,
162, 211, 222, 235, 241, 261–2, 303–4,
308, 329, 358, 360, 367, 376–7
Mythology 295, 375
Myth/Ritual 378
Myths and Texts 67, 228

Nachman, Rabbi 211
Nālanda 240
Nānak, Guru 31
Naskapi Hunters 394
National Associations of History of Reli-
gions 42, 62–9
Nationalism 4, 18, 26, 189, 204, 331
Naturalistic Hypotheses 204
Naturalistic Observation 298–300
Natural Science 140, 144–6, 213, 226
Natural Sciences, Goals 287
Natural Sciences *of* Humanities 193–4,
238–43
Natural Sciences *of* Social Sciences 279,
306
Natural Sciences *of* Theology 193–4,
215–6, 238–43
Nature of Man 140, 181, 193–4, 212–3,
236–43
Nazism 225
Near East, Ancient 73
Neo-Confucianism 221–3, 225
Neo-Hindu Theology 179
Neolithic Religion 26, 28
Nepal 386
Neumann, Theresa of Konnersreuth
266
Neutrality in Approach 14, 112, 140,
147, 180, 204, 227

New Age 35
New Humanism 122
New Confucianism 9–10
New Narcissism 261
New Religions 6–10, 24, 26, 75, 118, 187
New Religious Movements in the West 6, 24, 325, 331, 337, 342, 345
New Religions in Japan 26
New Testament 217
New Year Festivals 378
New Zealand 59, 67
Nicaea, Council 377
Nietzsche, F. 199
Nigeria 67
Nihilism 288
Nirvāna 29
Nomos cf *Cosmos* 343
Nomothetic *cf* Idiographic Methods 287, 292
Non-literate Cultures *cf* Literate 334, 351, 353, 365–72
Non-Western Religious Studies 57–8, 63–4, 73, 160–1, 191–235
Normative/Non-Normative Approaches 54, 78, 94–5, 122, 123, 125, 127, 137, 147
Normative Understanding 129–30
North America 57, 59, 65, 100, 114, 121, 185, 191, 213, 230, 232–3
North Korea 3
Nuclear Power/Situation 5–10, 192, 236
Nuer 218
Nuliajuk 355
Numen 60, 66, 68, 81, 144
Numinous 89

Object-Relations Theory 261
Objectification 133, 153
Objective Events, Concept of 91, 116, 132
Objectivity 52, 65, 73, 90, 99, 101, 112, 143, 181, 229

Observation, Experimental 301–2
Observation, Naturalistic 298–300
Odin 375
Oedipus Complex 260–1, 389
Oil Crisis 192
Old Testament 67, 360
Old Testament Interpretation Society 67
Ontological System 130
Ontology 129, 140, 158, 218, 241
OPEC 3
Open University (UK) 74
Oral Tradition(s) 188, 362, 366
Organism, Religion as 206–7
Orient 195
Orientalism 192, 194–6, 230, 235
Origins, Religious 55, 99, 184, 303, 391
Otherworldly 144
Oxford (1908) 61, 92, 159
Oxford University 201, 217, 225
Ozone Layer 7

Padua 35
Paideia 237
Palaeolithic Religion 26, 28
Pali Text Society 198
Paradigms 149, 160
Parallelism of Religions 71
Paris (1900) 60, 92
Paris, École Pratique 49
Paris (C. N. R. S.) 44
Parsis 29
Participant Observation 291–2, 298, 299
Particular Religions *cf* General 87, 94, 103
Pastoral Care 254, 255, 277, 308, 310
Pathological Religiousness, Seven Criteria 278
Patiala Punjabi University 203–4, 231
Patristics 177
Patterns 100
Paulist Press 36

Peak Experiences 257
Peking Man 28
Pentecostals 297
Persia 199, 377 (*see* Iran)
Persona 387
Personal Association 291
Personal Documents 296–9
Personal Orientation Inventory 295
Personal Presuppositions 103, 118, 122, 136, 198, 200
Personal Stance of Social Scientist 308–9
Personal Understanding 129
Personalism 229, 231
Persons in Religious Studies 118, 122, 134, 153, 231
Petition 152
Phenomenological Interpretation of Research 116
Phenomenological Sociology of Religion 324–5
Phenomenological Typology 19–21, 33–4, 79, 106, 108, 110, 182–3, 186, 189
Phenomenological Understanding 129
Phenomenology in Social Sciences 51
Phenomenology of Religion 1, 11, 19–22, 32–3, 46–55, 57, 64, 67, 71, 74, 87, 92, 99–120, 138, 140, 142, 148, 150, 156, 164, 181–90, 204, 228, 232, 235, 241, 324–5
Phenomenology of Religion as Basic 108
Phenomenology of Religion as Part of Wider Whole 102, 106
Phenomenology of Religion, Criticisms of 115–120
Phenomenology, New Style 80, 83, 100
Phenomenology, Perspective viz Method in Religion 113–4, 119
Phenomenology with History of Religions 91, 92–4, 107–9, 113 (*see* History and Phenomenology of Religions)

Phenomenology *of* History of Religions 50–1, 85–6, 90, 93, 108
Phenomenology *of* Natural Sciences 140
Phenomenology *of* Typology of Religion 110
Philadelphia 213
Philology 48, 63, 77, 85, 89–90, 96, 98, 102, 107, 109, 198, 235
Philosophia Perennis 199–201, 205, 213–6, 225, 229, 234
Philosophical Anthropology 212–3
Philosophical Beliefs 363
Philosophical Phenomenology 51, 54, 182
Philosophical Speculation 49
Philosophical Theology 178
Philosophies of History 49
Philosophy 121, 131, 162, 181, 201–7, 211, 213, 215–6, 219, 222, 228–9, 235–7, 241, 265, 334, 354, 362, 363, 374
Philosophy of Religion 54, 76, 101, 109, 138, 143, 148–9, 154, 177, 181, 203, 228, 235
Philosophy of Science 5–6, 324
Physiological Indices 285
Physiological Psychology 268
Pictures 152 (*see* Aesthetics, Art)
Piety, Observation and Assessment of 270–1, 273, 277, 280–92, 294, 311
Piety Normal/Abnormal 254, 273, 277
Piety of Different Age Groups 264, 267, 306
Piety's Correlates 294–6, 308
Pig, Attitude to 394
Plato/Platonic Ideas 199, 209, 237
Plotinus 237
Pluralistic Religious Studies 140
Pluralistic Theology 178
Poland 58, 67, 145, 191, 211
Poland, Society for the Study of Religion 68

Political Alliances 57–58
Political Factors and Religion 36, 330–1, 353, 361–2
Pollution of Environment 192, 236, 238
Population Growth 192, 236, 238
Positionless Positions 22
Positivism in Religion 111, 116, 178, 239
Positivistic Science 147, 239
Possession 265, 304
Potlatch Rituals 379
Post-Modernism 6
Poverty 192, 236, 238
Practical Theology 254
Prajñā 207
Prayer 152, 208, 217, 264, 281, 291, 293, 301, 304, 364, 378, 381
Prayer Books 152
Prejudice 294
President of India 201
Primal Religions 22–3, 26, 33–4, 303, 321–4, 335, 343, 386
Profane *of* Sacred 124
Projection View of Religion 17, 147, 239, 268, 351, 389
Projective Techniques 296–8, 387
Prophecy 194, 304, 391, 393
Prophets 239
Propositions 134
Protestant Ethic 31, 335
Protestant Liberal Theology 53, 253–4, 257, 263, 267, 274, 324
Protestants 31, 268, 299–301, 325, 329
Protestant Seminarians 297
Psyche's Structure and Dynamics 261–2, 279, 284, 296
Psychiatry and Religion 255, 256, 265, 277
Psychoanalytic Approaches to the Study of Religion 139
Psychologism 259
Psychological Anthropology 385–95

Psychologies of Religion *cf* Psychology of Religion 277
Psychologists interested in Religious Issues 309
Psychology and Psychologists 131, 241
Psychology and Religion 255
Psychology *cf* Psychology of Religion 255–9, 354
Psychology of Personality 280
Psychology of Religion 1, 11, 76, 96, 109, 138–9, 142, 150, 154, 184, 187–8, 191, 193, 203, 208, 228–9, 232, 235, 253–320, 344, 356, 375
Psychopathology of Religion 254, 265, 266, 273, 277–8, 297, 300
Punjab 37, 203–4
Pure Land Buddhism 7, 207–8

Quality, Unique of Religious Phenomena 100, 116
Quantificatory Analyses 145, 241
Quantificatory Data in Religious Studies 16, 256, 265, 267, 268, 270
Quantificatory Research 270–2
Qur'ān 29, 33, 370
Quasi-Religions 118
Questionnaires, Open-Ended 256, 266, 286, 288, 289, 301

Radio 74
Rain Rituals 364, 365, 379
Rāma 21, 31
Ramakrishna 202
Rāmānuja 31
Rastafarians 26
Rating Scales 292
Rationalism 177, 204, 210, 226
Rationality in Religion 363
Realisation 152
Reality, Religious 116, 151, 152, 215
Reality of Religion 151–3
Reason 190
Rebellion 152

Rebellion Rituals 392
Rebirth 199
Redemption 62
Reductionism 21, 55, 109, 116, 141,
    146, 148, 158, 196, 258, 275, 354, 380
Reformation 31
Reference Works in Religious Studies
    69–76
Regional Conferences in History of Reli-
    gions 62–9
Reification 134, 198
Reincarnation 375, 390
Reinterpretation 206, 209, 225
Relatively Absolute 215
Religion and other Cultural Orders
    360–2, 382
Religion and Personality 387–8
Religion and Science 5–6
Religion and Social Cohesion 322,
    330–2, 385
Religion as Cultural Order 357–60
Religion as Generic Phenomenon 219
Religion as Organism 206–7
Religion of World 118
Religion, Mature and Immature 257
Religion, The Word 351–5, 231
Religions, Historical 7, 98, 122, 185
Religions, Major Living 25–6, 75, 122,
    224–5, 229, 231
Religions, Particular 71, 99, 183
Religions, Present 25–6, 71, 73, 75, 85,
    98–9, 102, 118, 122, 132, 160–1
Religions, Primal (*see also* Primal Reli-
    gions) 122, 124, 191, 225
Religionsgeschichte 92
Religionspsychologie 92
Religionswissenschaft 46, 54–5, 58, 76,
    82–3, 85, 88, 94, 98, 127, 137, 138,
    146, 162–3, 276
Religiosity, Measures of 256, 277,
    293–4, 296–7, 326
Religious Anthropology 101, 144
Religious Art 304

Religious Blocs 8–9
Religious Change 6–11, 340–1, 385
Religious Commitment 254, 258, 274,
    308, 322
Religious Concepts 297, 359, 372–7
Religious Conservatives *of* Liberals 297,
    299, 305
Religious Contents 272, 280, 303–5
Religious Developmental Psychology
    257, 266
Religious Education 24, 254, 255, 257,
    258, 266, 267, 308
Religious Experience 88, 103, 116,
    119–20, 127, 129, 148, 152–3, 186,
    207–8, 210, 213, 223, 229, 253, 257,
    263–6, 269–70, 273, 276, 281, 282,
    290–1, 293, 301, 306, 308, 354, 357
Religious Language 111, 130, 144
Religious Movements 304
Religious Orders 362
Religious Organisation 297, 359, 372–7
Religious Orgies 257
Religious Orientation Scale 257, 268
Religious Persons 272, 275, 280, 301,
    303–4
Religious Practice 253, 325, 341, 358–9,
    365, 372, 376–81
Religious Professionals 255, 335, 359,
    365, 370, 379
Religious Psychology 101, 208
Religious Revival 304, 345
Religious Sentiments 272
Religious Sociology 101
Religious States 283
Religious Studies *of* Studies of Religion
    63
Religious Traditions 303–5, 308, 370
Religious Truth 134
Religiousness re Cognition, Emotion,
    Action 269
Religiousness of Man 86
Remembrance 152
Renewals of Religions 192, 203, 206,
    209, 223, 225

Repentance 281
Representation, Nature of 195
Research Programmes, Methodology of 157
Revelation 53, 215
Review of Religious Research 256
Rhetoric 237
Right/Left 377
Risorgimento 353
Rites de Passage 185, 379
Ritual(s) 73, 112, 123, 129, 144, 219, 224, 262, 270, 272, 304, 329, 358, 360, 376–8, 380–1, 387, 393–5
Ṛta 358
Roman Catholics 34–5, 178
Roman Religion 26
Rome (1955) 60, 53, 67, 105, 107
Rome 324, 352, 361, 369
Rorschach Inkblot Test 297
Rosenzweig Picture-Frustration Study 297
Roy, Ram Mohan 198, 202
Rūmī, Jalālu-d-Dīn 199, 214
Russia 4, 20
Russian Language 145
Ruysbroeck 199
Rwanda 4

Sacred 86, 94, 123–4, 140, 215, 241
Sacred Cosmos Concept 343
Sacred Place 183, 378, 379
Sacred Time 183, 378, 379
Sacred Writings 272, 293, 303, 306, 365–6, 368
Sacrifice 102, 152, 183
Saichi, Asahara 208
Saints 371
Salvation, Path of 71, 78
Samādhi 302
Saṃvega 198
Śaṅkara 199, 204
Sāṅkhya 363
Sapiental Knowledge 215

Saraswati Dayananda 202
Sasa 218
Satan 306
Saturnalia 379
Scales of Belief 271
Scandinavia 59, 69, 72, 177
Scandinavian Scholars 49, 57, 79, 112, 269
Science, Natural *cf* Study of Religion 38, 53
Science in Science of Religion 66, 139–41
Science of Religion *cf* Art of Religion 121
Science of God 180, 186
Science of Religion, Scientific Study of Religion 2, 11, 45–6, 73, 82–3, 106, 112, 125, 137–57, 177–190, 193, 234
Science of the Ultimate (*see* Ultimology) 180
Scientific Empiricism 145
Scientific Method 238–9
Scientism 58, 73
Scientometrics 145
Scripture(s) 133, 152, 224
Second World War and Religious Studies 2–10
Sectarian Movements 331, 371, 372
Sects 185
Secular Culture (and Religion) 67, 152, 163
Secular Religion 6–10, 17–19, 26–7
Secularisation 4–10, 215, 226, 323, 325, 330–1, 340, 342, 343, 345
Selective Returns 289
Self Actualisation 262, 295
Self Observation 263, 280–5
Selly Oak Birmingham 217
Semiology 131
Semiotics 131
Sen, K. C. 202
Sensation in Religious Experience 266
Sentence Completion Test 297

Seqineq 378
Seventh Day Adventists 26
Sex 123
Shaku Soyen 209
Shamanism 185, 304, 355, 366–7,
    387–8
Sharī'ah 353
Shi'ite Islam 8, 31, 213–6
Shinto State 3
Sign-System 131
Signification 114
Sin 288
Śiva 199, 375
Social Anthropology/ists 1, 173
Social Dimension of Individual 88
Social Sciences 53, 82, 121, 126, 143–5,
    177, 184, 228, 241
Social Sciences *of* Natural Sciences and
    Humanities 15, 284
Socialist Countries 58–9, 67, 223, 225
Society for the Scientific Study of Reli-
    gion 256
Sociologie Religieuse 324–6, 340
Sociology/Sociologists 241
Sociology and Sociology of Religion
    346
Sociology of Knowledge 298
Sociology of Religion 1, 11, 58, 67, 74,
    76, 106, 109, 138–9, 142, 144, 150,
    159, 180–1, 226, 235–8, 240, 243,
    321–49, 356
Socrates 237
Solipsism 117
Songs 152
Soul and Body 273–5
South Africa 68
South America 58
South Asia 59
South East Asia 57
Soviet Academy of Science 58
Soviet Bloc 4, 20, 59, 232, 233
Soviet History of Religions 75
Spalding Trust 201

Spanish Scholarship 268
Speaking in Tongues 265, 304
Specialisation 49, 93, 160, 193–4, 226,
    235–8, 240, 245
Specialisation in Religious Studies 11
Spirit 373
Spiritual Aim of Religious Studies 93,
    125, 136, 158
Spirituality 6, 35, 228
Sri Lanka 37, 66, 197–8, 223, 225
Statistical Analysis 270, 273, 292, 307
Statistics 111, 145, 186
Statistics of Religious Communities
    266, 267, 270
Stigmata 265, 266
Stockholm (1970) 42, 61, 65–6, 90, 92
Strassburg (1964) 62
Structural Anthropology 367, 375
Structural Functionalism 326–32,
    338–9, 345
Structuralism 187, 196
Structured Empathy 182–7
Structure of Religious Phenomena 86,
    100, 102, 106–7, 112, 115–6, 139, 162
Study of Values 257
Subjective Meanings 132
Subjectivity⁻ 52–3, 90, 99, 108, 143
Substantive Function of Religion 143
Sudan 37
Suffering 328–9, 336–7, 339, 358, 360,
    389
Sūfī 213–6, 222–4, 226
Sui Generis Religion 161
Sumerian Religion 73
Sung China 221
Sunni Islam 8
Supernatural, Concepts of 331, 343,
    389
Supernatural *of* Natural Order 327–9,
    331, 389
Superstitions 352, 359, 362, 364–5, 370
Supreme Gods 229
Swahili 218

Swedenborgians 26
Swedish Scholars 57, 77, 268
Switzerland 67, 217
Sydney 68
Symbolism/Symbolisation 144, 162, 187
Symbols 111, 123, 125, 130–1, 144, 152, 185, 187, 198, 208, 261–3, 304, 391
Syncretistic Sects 187
Systematic Theology 150, 154, 177
Systematische Religionswissenschaft 119, 154
Systems Theory 337, 338–41
Szondi Test 297

Tagore, R. 198, 202
Taiping Movement 189
Talmud 211
Tao 189, 211–2, 372
Taoism 29, 208, 212, 220–3, 372
Tauler, J. 199, 207
al-Tawhīd 214
Teaching, Religious 152
Teamwork 88, 243
Techniques *of* Hermeneutics 305–8
Technology, Growth 192–3, 202, 213, 226, 238
Television 74
Temples 152
Temple University 213, 225
Tenach 211
Test, Religious 178
Texts 85, 105, 139, 180, 185, 188, 209, 212, 224, 228–9, 232, 235
Thailand 57, 68
Thematic Aperception Test 297
Theodicy 328–9
Theologia 193–4
Theological Assumptions 53–4, 77–8
Theological Exclusivism 183
Theological Positivism 179
Theological Science of Religion 149–50

Theological Treatises 152
Theology 19–22, 49, 53, 65, 75, 101, 140, 142, 148, 162, 179–80, 215, 224, 232–3, 234–5, 237, 323, 334, 337, 340, 346, 353, 354, 361, 374, 377
Theology and Psychology 255, 261
Theology and Religious Studies 21–22
Theology of Religion 149–56
Theology, Christian 103, 133, 160, 177, 205, 216, 224, 227
Theology Faculties 159, 177
Theology/Religious Studies Demarkation 21–22, 81, 133–4, 140, 149–56, 180–87
Theoria 106
Theoretical Science 146
Theory in Religious Studies 80, 97–9, 104, 111–2, 121, 127, 137–56, 157–64, 177–90, 234–5
Theravāda Buddhism 207
Thorr 375
Tibetan Religion 7, 73, 199
Tibetan Oracle Priests 265, 297, 299
Time, Views of 218–9
Tirutani 201
Tokugawa Religion 333
Tolerance 202
Tokyo (1958) 61, 63–4, 104
Tokyo 231
Torah 29
Total Hermeneutics 124
Totem and Taboo 389, 394
Transcendence 241
Transcendence, Different Views of 241
Transcendent as Experienced 186–7
Transcendent Categories 148, 229, 235
Transcendent Elements in Religion 19–21, 277, 295, 341
Transcendent Experience 257, 263, 271, 277
Transcendent Focus 148
Transcendent Reality 19–21, 53, 241, 263, 295

Transcendent Unity of Religions   214
Transcendental Meditation   258
Transference   298
Transgressions and Taboo   358–9
Translation   199, 206, 209, 211, 220–1,
    224, 228
Translation of Religious Worldviews
    277, 295, 341
Transpersonal Psychology   257
Transplantation of Religions   99, 163
Tribal Beliefs   102
Truth   53, 65, 123, 164, 178, 179, 215,
    229, 237
Truth Claims, Kinds and Levels   14,
    19–22, 266, 276–9
Truth Notions in Social Sciences
    276–9, 354, 359
Truth, Degrees of   129
Truth, Monolithic   123
Truth, Pluralistic   123
Tübingen   76
Tulsī Dās   31
Turin   72
Turku (1973)   62–3, 66, 80, 108–11,
    130–1, 138–9, 144, 189
Types and Typologies of Religion   92,
    102, 109–10, 112, 141, 185
Types, Three Concepts   110
Typology, Static   141
Typology of Natural Sciences   144

Uganda   7, 216–7
Ulamās   370
Ultimacy   95, 129, 329, 339
Ultimate   178, 180, 185–6, 204, 235
Ultimate Concern   94
Ultimate Sense of Life   133
Ultimology   22
Unbelief   117
Unborn, The   209
Unconscious, Personal   261–2
Unconscious, Universal   261–2, 376

Understanding   52–3, 55, 82–3, 99, 108,
    112, 115, 120–7, 141, 146, 154, 182,
    200
Understanding Religion   264, 287, 307,
    354
Understanding of Science of Religion
    141
UNESCO   63–4, 66
Unification Church   26
United States   57, 206, 209–10, 220,
    225, 230
Universal History   124
Universality of Religion   329, 339
Universities and Colleges, Religious
    Studies in   158, 178, 201, 203, 230
University, Notion of   195, 236–43
Upaniṣads   29, 199, 202
Urbanisation   6–7, 238, 325
USSR   45, 58, 69
Utrecht University   385–97

Vaishnavite Theism   202
Value-Free Approach   99, 112, 181–90,
    354
Value Judgments   179–81
Value(s) of Religion   92, 143, 198, 224
Veda(s)   196, 199, 370
Vedānta   196, 204, 208, 211–4, 226
Vedic Period   199
Vergleichende Religionsgeschichte   112, 119
Verification   146–7, 181, 230, 238,
    283–4
Verstehen   52, 264, 307–8
Verstehen Philosophie   52
Vidyā   207
Vienna   211
Vienna University   211
Vietnam   3, 7
Virgin Mary   358
Visions and Values, Constraints of   193,
    202
Visions   358
Viṣṇu   375

Vital Force 218
Vivekananda 179, 198, 202
Voluntarism in Sociology 321, 323, 324
Vyānjanā 198

Waco 36
Wang Yang-Ming 221–2
Warsaw (1979) 62–3, 67
Warsaw 68, 145
Waterloo 61
Water Witching 394
Werewolves 365
Wesen 52
Wesenschau 114
Western Culture, Concern for 214–6,
    225, 227, 229
Western Ethnocentricity 351–5, 386
Western Europe 56, 69, 115
Western Materialism 203–4, 229
Western Nature of Religious Studies
    19–21, 45, 73, 187, 191–243
Western Religion, Stress on 17–18
Wheaton College Massachusetts 253–
    320
Wilkins, C. 196

Winnipeg (1980) 61, 66, 68
Wisdom 377
Wissenschaft 138
Witchcraft 329, 364–5, 381, 389, 390,
    392
Women in Religion 37
Womens' Movement 185
Word Association 297
Work 123
World Rejection 334–5
Worship 71, 152, 183
Wu-wei 212

Yahweh 29, 241
Yanomano Tribe 394, 395
Yin Yang 221
Yoga 208, 267, 302

Zamani 218
Zarathustra 27, 29
Zen Buddhism 207–10, 212, 215,
    222–4, 226, 292, 302
Zen Masters 265
Zionist Movement 211

DATE DUE

			Printed in USA